FREE AND FAITHFUL IN CHRIST

"You are light to the world . . . salt for the earth" (Mt 5:13-14)

BERNARD HÄRING

Free and Faithful in Christ

Moral Theology for Clergy and Laity

VOLUME 3
Light to the World

CROSSROAD • NEW YORK

1981
The Crossroad Publishing Company
18 East 41st Street, New York, NY 10017

Printed in the United States of America

LIBRARY OF CONGRESS CATALOGING IN PUBLICATION DATA
Häring, Bernard, 1912–
Free and faithful in Christ.
Includes bibliographical references and index.
CONTENTS: v. 1. General moral theology.
—v. 2. The truth will set you free.—v. 3. Light to the world.
1. Christian ethics—Catholic authors. I. Title.
BX1758.2.H27   1978   241'.04'2   78-12253
ISBN 0-8164-0398-8(v. 1)   ISBN 0-8164-0205-1(v. 2)
ISBN 0-8245-0009-1(v. 3)

CONTENTS

PART TWO: HEALING OF PUBLIC LIFE

Chapter Four

RESPONSIBILITY IN AND FOR THE WORLD

Chapter Five

ECOLOGY AND ETHICS

Chapter Six

CULTURE AND ETHICS

Chapter Seven

THE ETHICS OF SOCIO-ECONOMIC LIFE

Chapter Eight

THE ETHICS OF POLITICS

Chapter Nine

PEACE ON EARTH

ACKNOWLEDGMENTS

My gratitude to God for the strength to complete this work flows over to all who helped to prepare it for publication.

I am especially grateful to Mrs Josephine Ryan who during the past four years has taken part in this work, generously and competently giving the text the best English expression. Wherever it is clear and readable the merit is hers; wherever it is difficult, the fault is mine.

Again I am greatly indebted to Sr Gabrielle Jean who has helped me so much in the past and has transcribed many of the tapes for this volume. I received also the generous help of Mrs Alice Paroby and Mrs Virginia Malachowski in transcription of tapes, and of Miss Marian McCracken for the no less difficult transcription of my handwriting in the last chapters.

Fr Charles Curran graciously offered pertinent suggestions concerning the American socio-economic scene.

And finally, very special thanks go to Sr Mary Gallagher for her competent and patient work on the index.

B.H.

Introduction

You are the light to the world

The whole Redemption is a work of healing; therefore the whole of theology, but particularly moral theology, has an essential therapeutic dimension. Christ the Saviour is also the Healer. He came to heal the individual person in his or her relationships, but he also proclaimed the all-embracing kingdom and therefore a healthful world to live in. Christians are, in Christ, healers. They have a mission to heal themselves, to heal each other and to join hands to create a healthier world.

While pointing out that this third and last volume treats of social ethics, I want to remind readers that in the other volumes, too, the social dimension always had to be present, for Christ's calling is essentially a rallying call, a call to live the covenant reality. However, this third volume treats explicitly and systematically the social dimensions and the social mission of human and Christian life.

PART I treats of the problems of bioethics: the responsibility for all human life, our life and that of others (Chapter One); the meaning of health and illness, our common responsibility for our health and that of others, and the particular vocation of the healing profession (Chapter Two); death and dying: our own responsibility and, again, that of the healing profession (Chapter Three).

PART II treats of the vocation of all Christians to be a light to the world, to bear fruit in justice and love for the life of all: covenant morality and our responsibility for the world we live in (Chapter Four); the ethics of ecology (Chapter Five); ethics and culture (Chapter Six); the ethics of social-economic life (Chapter Seven); the ethics of politics (Chapter Eight); the peace mission of Christians (Chapter Nine).

1

PART ONE

Bioethics

The unfolding of life and its protection, health and healing, death and dying, are all decisive focal points of social responsibility. Bioethics cannot be separated from the broader task of Christians to join hands for the building up of a healthier world.[1] The perception of meaning and the effective promotion of life and health depend on religious interpretation and, at the same time on the socio-economic development, the cultural strength and the structure of authority. What, then, does co-responsibility, creative liberty and creative fidelity mean in this fundamental field of morality?

Truly human life can unfold only with the unfolding of creative liberty and fidelity. As believers, we realize that our life in Christ Jesus is a life consecrated to the fullness of life for all people. Fidelity to Christ implies fidelity to the promotion of life, of health, and the right interpretation of death and dying. It is not only a matter of decision-making but, first of all, a question of vision, of value and meaning.

Our main concern and perspectives will be the promotion of healthy relationships and of co-responsibility in creative liberty and fidelity. From this we will also gain important criteria for basic decisions about our own life and that of others, about health and healing, and facing the reality of death.

Chapter One

Responsibility for human life and its transmission

I. MEANING AND VALUE OF HUMAN LIFE

Human life, as a lofty gift of God, is sacred. The human person is called in this bodily life to realize himself or herself as an image and likeness of God. Life is a key concept in the gospel of John. Not only is human life the most marvellous creation of the word of God; its dignity appears, above all, in the Word of God becoming flesh, a live body (Jn 1:14).

In his bodily life, Jesus glorifies the Father especially by giving up his life as a supreme sign of his love for his friends (Jn 15:13). The mystery of redemption is completed in this same bodily life. The foundation of the life and prayer of Jesus, according to the letter to the Hebrews, is "Thou hast fashioned me a body. Behold I have come, O God, to do thy will" (Heb 10:5-7).

The bodily life is the most precious gift of the Father to Jesus. Glorifying the Father in all his life, he is glorified by the Father in his risen body. And if his disciples join him in honouring God in their body (1 Cor 6:20), their earthly life will be the beginning and foundation of everlasting glory.

The believer does not cling to his physical life at any cost. People who are concerned solely with conserving their physical life lose their true self. The authentic meaning of life eludes them if, through selfishness, they refuse to share in God's life-giving love (cf, Mt 10:39; Mk 8:35; Jn 12:25).

Jesus is the Bread of Life, a source of life for others. He reveals himself as the bearer of true life by laying down his bodily life as the Good Shepherd (Jn 10:11). He gives his life so that his friends may have life in abundance. The disciple of Christ knows, therefore, that he attains the authentic value of his life in the service of God and fellowman. "No one of us lives and equally no one of us dies for himself alone. If we live, we live for the Lord; and if we die, we die for the Lord" (Rom 14:7-8).

Just as we cannot discover the true dignity of our conscience without respect and responsibility for the conscience of others, so it is with our human life. We find the truth of our life by respecting everyone's life and caring for each other. In this we find the supreme meaning and value of our bodily life.

Life is entrusted to man's freedom and co-responsibility. He is not an independent lord of his life but a steward under the sovereignty of God. To accept responsibility for one's own life and that of others is a prime expression of covenant morality. Caring for each other's life, transmitting life responsibly and promoting its quality are signs of true monotheism, of our awareness that, under God, we are one family.

II. THE BEGINNING OF HUMAN LIFE

The origin of human life is a great mystery. It is the common conviction of today's scientific world that human life is the crowning of a stupendous process of evolution. Life developed from its most primitive forms into greater complexity and ever new forms of unity. To us who are believers, it seems that matter and life respond to the presence of the Creator by a wonderful self-transcendence. Perhaps we can say that all of matter and life points to the transcendent God by this innate dynamism towards self-transcendence into ever higher forms of life.

Because God's work is a word, a message, we can see the unfolding of life as a kind of unfolding of his revelation. The life of the plant is essentially more than that of mere matter. Its subsequent phase of development is more than the previous form. There is always something more, something new unto the appearance of the human being, a person who can admire, adore, consciously remember, smile and love. Growth and development are the most striking signs of the creative presence of God and of his marvellous design in creation.

Man's appearance on earth is the highest and most real symbol of the world's transcendence responding to its Creator, reaching out to him by explicit adoration and love, but at the same time also reaching out to ever higher and newer forms of development and greater fullness of life.

The development of the individual human being is not just a repetition of the process of hominization. Rather, in a wonderful way it participates in this same dynamic of self-transcendence, growth and unfolding.[2] Each phase contains the potentialities of the next, and yet the next phase is something more than the previous one. There is no more tangible sign of God's creative presence on earth than this wonderful beginning and growth of human life.

The ovule which ripens at the rate of one each month in the woman's ovary, and the hundreds of millions of sperms produced each month are not yet human life; however, they are bearers of rich informations. Their fusion or union at the moment of procreation produces something new and marks the beginning of a new human life. It is truly human life and shares in that dynamic of self-transcendence that is the most distinguished mark of humanness.

Past philosophy and theology spoke about the beginning of the individual human life in terms of "ensoulment". To some trends of thought, it seems that the soul would come from without, of course from above. Ensoulment seems to mark the moment of God's intervention in which he calls this unique individual by name and for communion with him.

St Albert the Great was one of the first who thought about ensoulment at the very moment of conception, although the biological fact of the fusion of the two gametes (sperm and ovule) was not yet known. His disciple, Thomas Aquinas, however, stayed with the previous tradition that there is a successive ensoulment whereby a human life goes through the phases of vegetative life with a vegetative soul, animal life with a merely animal soul, until a decisive phase of ensoulment with a human, immortal soul. Like Aristotle, he thought this would happen for the male fetus around the fortieth day and for the female fetus around the eightieth day: an opinion that has no basis whatsoever in scientific data but came from the superstitious opinion that woman is somehow more marked by animalism than the male.

The positive aspect of Thomas Aquinas' position was that the whole of this being is developing through various stages of self-transcendence in a unique synthesis between the bodily reality and its life principle.

The opinion of successive ensoulment had strong support among both biologists and theologians. But when E. Von Baer in 1827, discovered the ovum and the full process of fertilization, philosophers and theologians favoured the opinion of simultaneous ensoulment at the moment of fertilization. This is surely the beginning of a human being, as such.

Is it already endowed with an immortal soul?

The more accurate knowledge about embryonic development led biologists, many philosophers and theologians to acknowledge uncertainty about the moment or phase in which we can speak surely about the givenness of a human person endowed with an immortal soul and therefore endowed with all the rights of a person.

We cannot rule out completely the suspicion that the general trend of the last decades towards approval of abortion might have exercised some influence on new opinions. But there are also scientific data that force even defenders of all human life not to assert more than can be proved scientifically.

1. The origin of the genotype

With the fertilization of the ovum, the genotype has been determined. There is a new human life distinct from that of father and mother, with a unique, never-to-be-repeated genetic code (DNA), although its own RNA is not yet immediately active.

The morula or blastocyst develops gradually its own dynamics of life. After five to seven days of cell division, the zygote finds its way to the uterus and takes on its own great tasks of implantation and further embryonic development. Before its implantation its own communication network is already sending hormonal information into the maternal host organism, inviting it to prepare for the forthcoming solidaric life during nine months. Thus, on this level, there is already a dialogical principle expressed in an increasingly miraculous communication between mother and embryo.

Can we say that there is already given an immortal, distinctly human soul? Have we to suppose its givenness in order to explain the entelechy, the miraculous dynamics towards development of a fully human life? Or is this entelechy just a sign of God's creative presence and of his design to bring forth the fully human life if unfavourable conditions do not block it?

2. The moment of diversification

The cell divisions during the first fourteen days or so bring only replications of all the new cells having an identical character. This explains the possibility of the phenomenon of identical twins. Each of, for instance, thirty-two cells after cell division could be teased away and, under favourable conditions, could develop into an individual. This fact strongly poses the question of whether the blastocyst, during the fourteen days after fertilization, can truly be called a human person, since only individuals can have the status of person. "Individual" means not being divisible, being unique also by excluding replication.[3]

Franz Boeckle surely speaks for many others when he asserts: "The individuality or independent subsistence of a spiritual being presupposes absolutely that this being is to be unique and, by its very nature, indivisible."[4] But Boeckle is rightly careful in warning against dangerous conclusions made in view of this statement: "The being that just develops is, from the very beginning, worthy to be protected. On this point there should be no discussion. However, we have to discuss what kind of value has to be given to it in the hard case in which the conflicting goods would have to be valued against each other."[5]

Even at the time that replication or twinning is still possible, we are faced with truly human life with a wonderful programme of relatively autonomous development that draws our attention directly to the presence of the divine Creator and his design. We have to distinguish three different questions: (1) Is it morally certain that we are not faced with a human person as such? (2) Or are we morally certain that what is self-transcendence into what we call a human person has happened? (3) Or is there a doubt in the strict sense?

For the time being, we can only say that all three opinions have followers among honest and intelligent people. If one has a strong and sincere conviction that there is surely not given the level of human life that entitles us to speak of a human person, an interruption of this miraculous life process is still a weighty moral problem; however, it cannot be called abortion in the same ethical sense as when faced with the moral certainty of taking the life of a human person or at least of a human being that, according to a strict doubt, might be a human person.

3. The cerebral cortex and hominization

The newer insights about "brain death" as the termination of a human life-history introduce another theory of the beginning of personhood or the beginning of the immortal principle of human life. Is the development of the typically human cerebral cortex the decisive phenomenon in the ontogenesis of the human person?[6]

The basic structure of the human cerebral cortex is outlined between the fifteenth and twenty-fifth day or at least after the fortieth day of normal development. When diversification begins around the fourteenth day after fertilization, there is developing almost immediately or very soon the cell that has the potentiality to develop into the cerebral cortex. By eight weeks after fertilization, electric brain activity is detectable. By the twelfth week the brain structure is more or less complete.

May we assert that after the fifteenth or the twenty-fifth, or at least after the fortieth day, there is no further qualitative leap but only a quantitative development of the already given structure of the cerebral cortex?

It seems to me that the following opinion has high probability. If, around the fifteenth day or some days later, unfavourable conditions block the development of the cerebral cortex, resulting in an anencephalic embryo or fetus, then this is tantamount to brain death (in the sense of death of the higher brain). Normally the mother organism spontaneously rejects such an embryo.

The qualitative leap that happens when, after the fourteenth day, the embryo develops the outline of the cerebral cortex, cannot be simply compared with the phylogenesis. The phylogenesis is an extraordinary and indeed unexpected leap from animal history into the human history, a leap that is prepared by a long process of evolution and, of course, guided by God. In the ontogenesis of the embryo or fetus, with the development of the typically human cerebral cortex, there is no doubt a stupendous self-transcendence, an admirable leap; but each blastocyst encapsulates this innate tendency which is always successful if there are not specifically unfavourable conditions, such as a maternal environment poisoned by smoking or drugs.

Even if we are fully aware of the great difference between phylogenesis and ontogenesis as described above, it remains always true that human consciousness — which distinguishes humanity from animality — has an indispensable substratum in the cerebral cortex. Without it, no manifestation of specifically human personal attributes is conceivable.[7]

In spite of the great dissimilitude between phylogenesis and ontogenesis, the following theory, although very cautiously, can possibly be ventured: "that the spiritual soul comes into existence only in a later phase of embryonic development. This means that between fertilization of the ovum and the development of the organism with a spiritual life principle, there are certain biological phases which cannot yet be called man."[8] However, I would not dare to affirm the following statement by the same author: "Then we might really say that such an ontogenesis does correspond to the human phylogenesis; in both cases an organism that is not yet human is tending towards that complexification and condition in which the existence of the spiritual soul finds its biological substratum."[9]

It seems to me that in the case of ontogenesis, even before the development of the cerebral cortex, we have to say that it is a human organism, although one would then go on to say that while being human, it might not yet be called the biological substratum of the spiritual life principle.

I want to state my tentative opinion on this point, as follows: the theory of hominization as essentially dependent on the development of the cerebral cortex does not give me a moral certainty that we are not yet faced with a human person; at least it does not provide any ground for depriving the embryo of the basic human right to life and the right to be protected.

4. Distinction between "human life" and "humanized life"

A group of French scientists and Catholic and Protestant theologians have suggested that the fetus, as long as it is not accepted by the mother, is biologically "human life" but not yet "humanized life", and consequently is lacking the quality of right of a human person.[10]

While I consider the non-acceptance or refusal of a human life as a most devastating and de-humanizing act for all concerned, I would not at all agree that the very act of dehumanizing deprives the human life of its dignity and its quality as human person. These authors pretend that abortion has not the malice of "homicide", since rejection or non-acceptance of the fetus precedes abortion. They argue with an "I-Thou personalism". But to my mind, it is thoroughly unacceptable. The human life that is called into being by God is called "Thou" by the divine "I". And if I refuse to recognize this being who is called by God by a unique name, I practically refuse the divine "Thou" who gives us all the quality of "We", "Thou", "I".

The beginning of human life is a mystery. And all the scientific knowledge we have available does not diminish its character as mystery that calls our direct attention to God. The covenant of God with humankind calls for mutual acceptance and co-responsibility.

III. THE TRANSMISSION OF LIFE

One of the most wonderful ways of celebrating gratitude for the gift of life is by generous and responsible transmission of life and the loving acceptance of this life.

Generativity characterizes the highly developed life of persons who have found their identity, their maturity and the capacity for intimacy. This does not mean that every human person has the vocation physically to transmit life; however, it implies that we all share, according to our particular charisms, in the solidaric task of caring for the future generations. We all can make that investment of love and justice, of creative liberty and fidelity, that creates a human milieu in which responsible parenthood is possible.

The transmission of human life was always one of the most noble, most arduous and, at the same time, most rewarding tasks calling for fundamental moral responsibilities. In today's world, however, it presents new dimensions and problems.

The basic questions of responsible parenthood in the light of conjugal love and covenant fidelity are treated in Volume 2.[11] We can review the basic truths as follows: Healthy and fully human generativity expresses itself in the transmission of life in the context of covenant fidelity. The conjugal act itself is not on the fully human and responsible level if the spouses exclude arbitrarily the transmission of life. Yet responsibility and genuine conjugal love can motivate spouses to express their full conjugal union while not seeking to transmit life. The methods, however, must always respect the health and personal dignity of the partners in healthy mutual relationships.

Here we address ourselves to some problems that more directly concern medical and all social ethics.

1. Transmission of healthy life

The rapid development of genetic knowledge poses new problems of moral responsibility in the transmission of life.[12] The subject of eugenics was brought into disrepute by Hitler who, on the basis of very imperfect knowledge and the most arbitrary criteria, curtailed the freedom of spouses to transmit life. We have to distinguish between the eugenic question as it applies to the race or the human species and, on the other hand, the genetic problem that concerns primarily the happiness of the family, namely, the health transmitted to the children.

Our main emphasis is on the parents' responsible transmission of life and the care not to limit freedom unnecessarily in this most intimate sphere of life. But the growing burden caused by defective genes is a matter that concerns both individuals and the whole human society.

The genetic knowledge that is now available and constantly expanding should be part and parcel of the education of the young generation and of all those within the generative age. The genetic situation is a dimension that should be seriously considered in the choice of a spouse, and later in the decision to transmit or not to transmit life within marriage.

Genetic studies recognize today about 800 inherited diseases from which heterozygotes are suffering. (Heterozygotes are individuals who carry a pair of different genes formed by the union of different gametes, only one of which is affected by unfavourable genetic information. Homozygotes are those with zygotes formed by the union of gametes having the same unfavourable genetic information). Individuals may be homozygous for one gene pair and heterozygous for another.

One of the most frequent and most devastating forms of heterozygoty is Huntington's chorea. If transmitted, this kind of disease is always dominant, never recessive. It makes no difference whom the bearer of this genetic disease marries. The transmission can be avoided only by renouncing marriage or by renouncing procreation within the marriage and having recourse to the adoption of children - which is praiseworthy - or to a questionable artificial insemination with the sperm of a healthy donor (when the husband is the bearer).

The situation is different where the genetic disease is recessive in the heterozygotes while active only in homozygotes. Today, genetic science knows about six to seven hundred diseases having autosomal recessive presence. ("Autosomal" means concerning one of the 22 chromosomes not related to sex determination). Transmission of life with the direct risk of active suffering occurs only when the parent is either a homozygote or is heterozygote who happens to have a partner who is also heterozygous in the same respect. The heterozygote of this kind has no reason to renounce marriage or the transmission of life if he or she chooses a spouse who is not a carrier at all of the same autosomal recessive genetic misinformation.

Human genetics have verified about 120 genetic diseases affecting the sex chromosome. In almost all the cases it is attached to the X chromosome. Since the female has two chromsomes in the form of X, and usually only one is affected, she is only a carrier of the recessive genetic misinformation, although with a 50 percent risk of having sons affected by a dominant form of genetic disease. In these cases again, the problem cannot be resolved by the choice of the spouse.

According to various estimates, the average person is the carrier of about five to eight unfavourable genes. In most cases they will not affect their children in the form of genetic disease unless the spouse is a carrier of the same unfavourable genes. Furthermore, the greatest number of the now known genetic defects do not cause unbearable burdens for the persons affected.

Both in the choice of the spouse and in the concrete decision to transmit or not to transmit life, the genetic aspect is only one among many others. Spouses with considerable genetic risk but of high human qualities and outstanding pedagogical capacities may act more responsibly in transmitting life than others who have no genetic problem but are less qualified to offer their children a dignifying human environment and experience of genuine love.

Society discharges its duty first of all by providing balanced genetic information and by consciousness-raising. One of its main responsibilities, however, is to care for the environment and conditions of living that reduce the danger of new mutations.[13] It seems that under today's conditions there are almost as many people affected by new genetic mutations as by parents who are carriers of either a recessive or a dominant form of genetic disease.

2. Responsibility for the health of the fetus and child

Church and society have an important duty to educate people to a deep sense of responsibility for the health of the fetus. Often it is gravely threatened by the mother's abuse of alcohol, drugs or smoking. Small children, too, can suffer all their life from constant exposure to smokers. Conduct that is irresponsible towards the pregnant mother and to parents in general will also affect negatively the mental and even the physical health of the children.

3. Population problems

The population problems of today's world are among the burning issues of social ethics.[14] They can deeply affect all human relationships. There is not just one population problem; there are a number of them. On the one hand there is a disproportionate population growth, with the danger of over-population in some areas of the world. On the other hand, there is a drastic population decrease in, for instance, both East and West Germany and other European countries, and perhaps in a short time in North America.

A rapid decrease within one generation may bring with it a gigantic immigration, an input of guest workers (migrants, immigrants) with great danger of unrootedness for themselves and their families.

A too rapid population increase causes not only difficulties for education and nutrition but, above all, the danger of unemployment, for it is not easy to create millions of new jobs in a short time. Absolute overpopulation in a certain area can cause not only enormous risks for the ecosphere but also hazardous social tensions and conflicts and even the danger of war. There are problems also, of course, about air and water pollution and even shortages of drinking water.

With A. J. Dyck, I want to make a preliminary statement: "Neither ethical nor social scientific expertise is sufficient by itself for ascertaining the best course to follow in population policy."[15]

Population problems and family planning have to do with each other. The population trend, however, transcends the individual family's responsibility. It should be realized that responsible transmission of life and responsible education on the family level would avoid many aspects of population problems. Parents who educate their children well as persons and as citizens of human society are not causing severe problems, for the major difficulties are caused not so much by the number of people as by the number of irresponsible and socially immature people. If, by procreation and education, the good and wise people "fill the earth", there will be enough wisdom to resolve most of the problems. However, a social ethics has to be realistic. The decisions about the transmission of life are not only rational and ethical; they depend on many social and cultural conditions.

In many areas of the world today, there is need of both population-influencing policies and population-responsive policies. The first try to influence the growth or decrease of population, while the latter respond to the social necessities caused by the actual population trend.

The various approaches to the problem of rapid population growth and eventual over-population reveal quite different value systems that can have a long-lasting impact on the whole social fabric of humankind.

The *crisis environmentalists* tend to dramatize the food crisis, the exhaustion of the earth's basic resources, depletion, pollution, environmental degradation. Convinced that the population growth, if it continues unabated, is a matter of humanity's survival or death, they consider even the most drastic means of manipulation and coercion to be allowable and even unavoidable. Their writings contain enormous exaggerations and unproved presuppositions, for instance about the food crisis.[16] It seems that, for many of them, the mere biological survival of humanity, even of all species of animals, and space for wildlife, are more important than the survival of human dignity and freedom. Meanwhile, it has been proven that their predictions about the drastic food crisis are without scientific foundation. There are scientists who believe it would be technically possible to feed as many as ten times the present population.[17] But it cannot be denied that an unlimited population growth can produce the most serious ecological crises (cf. Chapter Five of this volume).

At the present time, it is not so much the population increase as the tremendous wastefulness of our western affluent society that causes serious problems for health, for the environment and the conservation of the indispensable and non-renewable resources of our planet. That this wastefulness can and must continue seems to be a basic presupposition of many environmentalists. At least they seem unable to conceive the idea of a radical cultural change rather than coercion.

The *family planners* of various North American and western Planned Parenthood associations think that the chief means, if not the only means, of resolving the problem of disproportionate population growth should be the distribution of contraceptives, information about their use, and access to abortion which they consider a "normal" means of population control. They emphasize one-sidedly an individualistic vision of freedom, especially the freedom for unlimited consumption. Abortion and intrusion into the intimacy of family life seem to them a lesser evil than any constraint on consumer attitudes. Furthermore, they do not see how human fertility is related to all social conditions, including basic value systems and religious convictions.

A third group can be called *developmental distributivists.* Among them are Roman Catholic authorities and equally Marxists and many others. They are convinced that certain kinds of improvement in socio-economic conditions may lead to a lower birth rate. The World Plan of Action, accepted by the Population Conference held at Bucharest in 1974, follows this theory. The main perspectives and recommendations are: promotion of literacy and nutritional education, especially for women, good health services available to all, including unbiased instruction on controlling conception, equality for women in education and job opportunities, labour-intensive development especially in the agricultural field, social security for the elderly, and a more equal distribution of income. The interests of individuals and families on the one hand and, on the other, the needs of societies can be harmonized only when there is a reasonable degree of social justice, general education and conditions favourable for the growth of co-responsibility.

4. Sterilization

Sterility is the incapacity to transmit life. Infertility does not necessarily exclude the capacity to conceive but does include the incapacity to give birth. Sterilization leads to sterility but it can have a diversity of meanings according to the different situations and purposes.[18] The task of moral theology here is to offer proper criteria for discernment.

Medically, sterilization can be carried out by vasectomy, which is a minor intervention with almost no risk, or tubal ligation, which requires hospitalization and can carry some risk. Hysterectomy is not to be considered as a proper medical procedure for sterilization, but if performed for other reasons, it does, of course, lead to sterility. Although in the case of vasectomy and tubal ligation, interrupted organs can be reconnected, in most cases the person will remain practically sterile. Of itself, sterilization has no negative influence on sexual relationships or on the person; but enforced sterilization followed by anxieties, frustrations, distress, will have a strong negative influence on the expression of one's sexuality and can impair mental health.

Sterilization is quite different from castration. Castration deprives the body of important sexual hormones. If performed before or during puberty, it will greatly impair personal maturation. Castration of adult women (ovarectomy) will lead to an early menopause. Castration deeply alters a person's sexual endowment, especially the male's.

In Italy, the castration of young boys to preserve their voices for choir singing was practised for centuries with approval of church authority, although it was constantly challenged by some moral theologians whose critique finally brought a change of attitude, and official doctrine. Still discussed among moralists is the question of the state's right to impose castration as a penalty for sex criminals, especially to protect others and to help the criminal to overcome his dangerous tendencies.

The question of sterilization is an urgent issue in today's medical and social ethics. A discussion needs careful distinction.

a) Direct and indirect sterilization

In the recent history of moral theology, the distinction between direct and indirect sterilization played a major role. Here we can see a clash between two mentalities and two world-views.

For those mainly concerned with easy control, only an action that deals directly with a sick sexual organ is considered to be an indirect and licit sterilization. Any medical intervention for therapeutic or other purpose is considered a direct sterilization even if the sterility is not the direct intention or inner purpose of the action.[19] However, for most of today's moral theologians, what counts for the moral evaluation is the direct intention and the inner meaning of the action as such. The main question is: is it an arbitrary destruction of fertility where sterility is directly sought? If so, the intervention is morally unacceptable. It is not only the personal intention that counts but also the purpose of the action as such. The traditional distinction between direct and indirect is not sufficient for a thorough-going discernment.

b) Anti-baby attitude

There are people who seek sterilization because they radically refuse their parental vocation. For them, material success, a comfortable life or a costly dog is more important than children. They have sterilized themselves spiritually and psychologically before they seek sterilization. The evil in this case is not so much sterilization itself as the basic attitude of the persons concerned. It would be worthless to discuss with them the moral evil of direct sterilization. But the counsellor or physician whom they choose might warn them that one day they might change their value system and be converted to the great gift of life; then they would regret their physical sterilization. But the physician may well judge that implementing the anti-baby attitude by sterilization is a much lesser evil than abortion.

c) Sterilization for the sake of intemperance

In North America one can find males who wear, as a symbol of a performed vasectomy, a broken ring. It is a message that says to women: "With me, without risk!" These males are making a public statement that they are sex consumers and nothing more.

This kind of sterilization is truly a moral evil. But the underlying disorder of people who do not want to transcend the consumer level, and have reduced sexual relationships to this low level, is the source of many other evils besides arbitrary sterilization. A doctor should not be willing to cooperate in such cases. It has nothing at all to do with therapy. Rather, it is an action that symbolizes the degradation of human life.

d) Sterilization and responsible parenthood[20]

To seek sterilization as a radical means of contraception is an irresponsible decision by a spouse or a couple who, on insufficient and wrong grounds, do not want any more children. If the decision to want no more children is the result of basic selfishness or other wrong attitudes, then all means of birth control, including total or partial abstinence, are contaminated by the moral disorder in the fundamental decision not to want any more children. Normally, spouses should not decide once and forever how many children they want. They should, rather, always be open to a new consideration before God, according to the circumstances of life. A sterilization, since it is more or less irreversible, makes this new consideration almost impossible.

It may be, however, that spouses have convincing reasons not to have more children, and have made the decision with a sincere conscience. Yet even in this case, the decision to be sterilized may be morally wrong. It can be the expression of that widespread attitude that takes for granted that technological solutions are always the best. It can be a lack of effort to resolve their problems by less drastic means.

But let us think also of spouses who have resolved properly the basic question of the responsible transmission of life, and have come to a clear conviction that, in their situation, a new pregnancy must be excluded now and forever. Think of spouses who know quite well that love is the answer, and accept periodical and even total abstinence whenever love itself requests it. The health of the marriage, healthy relationships between the spouses, the harmony in the family so much needed for the proper education of the children already living, the liberation of the spouses, especially of the woman, from dangerous anguish, the risks implied in other methods of carrying out the convinced decision not to have more children: all this has to be taken into account when it is a matter of assisting the spouses to discern the moral meaning of a sterilization.

e) Therapeutic sterilizations

We have already seen that the reduction of the whole problem to a simple distinction between direct and indirect sterilization does not lead us anywhere and does not make us credible to today's world. We should look into the meaning of therapeutic sterilization in its various dimensions. And here we are faced with two concepts of man and medicine.

For some, sterilization is "therapeutic" only if it is therapy concerning solely a sick sexual organ. In spite of the reality of psychotherapy as an important asset in today's medical world, these people would confine healing to organs alone. This not only leads to wrong and narrow-minded solutions in the case of sterilization, but is more dangerous because it betrays a wrong image of man and God. God does not care only for the health of discrete organs; he cares for the healthy person and for healthy relationships.

The problem can be illustrated by a not-infrequent case. A woman who has had pregnancy psychosis during one or more pregnancies is unable to relate to her husband in daily life and, being constantly obsessed by the fear of another pregnancy, is especially unable to relate in a normal way in marital intercourse. The psychotherapist is convinced that normal relationships in this marriage can be restored by psychotherapy after a sterilization, and that this wife can again act as educator of her children and live a normal marital life with her husband. Any effort to condemn this kind of action by quoting church documents not only shows a lack of discernment but can also effectively discredit the magisterium of the church.

In a holistic vision of the human person and of health and healing, there can be scarcely any doubt about the positive evaluation of such a healing intervention. But to another view it appears that normal moral principles cannot be applied here, since the sexual organs belong not to the individual but to the species. This is ridiculous mystification! We are not faced with an abstract species but with the human family which is more concerned with healthy people than with preserving physical fertility where transmission of life would be absolutely irresponsible. Where the spouses' need of infertility is clear, and where sterilization has a therapeutic meaning according to a holistic vision of the human person and of health and healing, there is a clear medical indication.[21]

f) Against enforced eugenic and genetic sterilization[22]

Roman Catholic church authorities protested vigorously against the attempts of Hitler and of other governments to enforce sterilization on eugenic grounds of "the healthy race". It was a necessary and urgent protest against a thoroughly wrong concept of health that contradicts healthy relationships and basic freedoms. People with the most precious human qualities and the ability to transmit them to their children by good education were sterilized because of nearsightedness and other relatively minor physical defects in their genetic codes. There is still a strong tendency, especially in the United States, to advocate enforced sterilization of retarded people. But the retardation and intelligence quotients are measured by the standards of a success-orientated society[23] and not by the truly human standards of the capacity to love and be loved.

The absolutely free decision to seek sterilization because of a genetic heritage that, in the spouses' sincere conscience, forbids them to transmit life, is a thoroughly different moral question. Whoever knows the anguish of parents who already have a severely handicapped child and are fully aware of the high risk situation in the case of future offspring, will agree that sterilization can be in many cases a truly therapeutic intervention. It can set the spouses free from disturbing anguish and for a peaceful and trustful conjugal life.

But nobody should try to drive loving spouses into an anguished decision if it is a matter of a moderate retardation.[24] They might well be able to conduct a healthy conjugal life and to raise their children in a loving way. And parents should not agree to have their daughters sterilized because of a relatively low I.Q. On the contrary, everything should be done to help these people to reach a higher level of truly human maturity.

g) Sterilization for population control

Several over-populated nations have already begun to induce spouses to let themselves be sterilized after the second or third childbirth. This persuasion can occur in the form of psychological manipulation with positive and negative reinforcements or even coercion. Although we may have a profound understanding of the complexities and gravity of the situation, we can never approve this approach that deprives people of their freedom in the most intimate sphere of their life. It is also damaging to society, for society itself needs freedom, and needs also the children of families who can raise and educate even several children for a high level of creative co-responsibility.

Of course protest alone or a moral judgment on these laws and practices does not fulfil our Christian duty. As Christians we must participate actively and creatively in resolving population problems, and offer more than just prohibitions. While many of us might not be able to agree with freely chosen sterilization to alleviate an extreme situation of over-population, nevertheless we must clearly discern between the free and conscientious decision of people who are convinced that they may accept sterilization and, on the other hand, the great injustice of enforced sterilization. The precious cause of freedom and integrity is surely not served by fostering guilt complexes among those who yield to pressure and coercion.

h) Cooperation with sterilization in Catholic hospitals

Some Catholics think that, in view of the dangerous trend

towards immoral sterilization, Catholic hospitals should refuse any form of sterilization except in cases of a diseased sex organ, just as they refuse any form of direct abortion. I think that we would give the world a more convincing witness by judicious discernment between morally acceptable and morally unacceptable forms of sterilization. But as long as there is no agreement yet, on an official level, on the concept of therapeutic sterilization other than treatment of a diseased organ, Catholic hospitals can follow a policy based on discernment between morally acceptable and unacceptable forms of cooperation in cases of sterilization that may not be approved according to the narrow concept of therapy.

Of course there should be no cooperation with evidently immoral trends of sterilization. A Catholic hospital cannot cooperate with the principle of sterilization on request. There can be, however, and in my opinion there should be, an allowance for material cooperation by the administration of Catholic hospitals in those forms of sterilizations that, in the eyes of many Catholic moral theologians and almost all Protestant ethicists, are therapeutic in the broader, holistic sense of the word.

There is no similarity between cooperation with abortion and cooperation with sterilization. "Because the goods and evils at stake are different, in my judgment cooperation with sterilization can be permitted but abortion must be resolutely rejected."[25] A discerning cooperation in cases of sterilization that are disputed within the Christian community can be a sign of tolerance, even a necessary one in areas where there is only a Catholic hospital to serve the needs of the whole community.

5. Artificial intervention in human reproduction

A technocratic age coined the expression, "human reproduction". The same spirit can mislead humankind into allowing artificial intervention in the process of transmitting life, in such a way that human life and human relationships are degraded. Not the artificial, as such, is opposed to life, but the technocratic spirit that disregards basic values.

The human being can be thoroughly manipulated in his ontogenesis from fertilization to birth. Various forms of engineering are thinkable or even already possible: artificial insemination and egg grafts, fertilization *in vitro* (in the test tube), the growth of early embryos in the laboratory, the exchange of the nucleus in the ovum, development of unfertilized ovules (parthenogenesis).[26]

a) Homologous insemination and sperm-shopping

In 1949, Pius XII declared morally illicit the artificial insemination either with the husband's sperm (AIH) or with the sperm of an anonymous donor (AID). However, he left open an unspecified kind of "assisted insemination".[27] After three decades of discussion, George Lobo can be assured of finding vast assent when he writes, "It seems that in the present state of the question, a couple eagerly desiring a child and sincerely finding the procedure of assisted insemination unsatisfactory, would not be doing wrong by having recourse to AIH.".[28]

Very different is sperm-shopping through a sperm bank for artificial insemination by the sperm of an unknown salesman. Even a militant proponent of this procedure admits that "AID has limited social acceptance and is useful only for rare disorders."[29] It is a morally unacceptable procedure not only because of the anonymous parentage and the danger of in-breeding, but also because it separates thoroughly the unitive and procreative purposes of sexuality.

AID carries with it serious dangers of disturbance in basic relationships on various levels. How will the teenager react if she or he learns that the biological father is a sperm salesman who may have sold his sperm to father many children for whom he will never take responsibility and never give a name? In many cases, the woman who resorts to this procedure manipulates her husband to gain his consent. There is considerable risk, too, that the mother, realizing that her husband is a stranger to the new being, will develop a possessive attitude towards "her" child. In most of the cases where I happened to be consulted, I found already disturbed relationships between the spouses, or an attitude on the part of the woman that disallowed real hopes for a good outcome. Yet in one instance it was a very loving husband who had finally suggested AID for his wife; but when she was pregnant she developed a serious guilt complex that could not easily be dissipated.

There are additional risks if women are inseminated with frozen semen. They "should be told that the risks are far from being fully and clearly elucidated."[30]

b) Fertilization *in vitro:* moral implications

The moral meaning of fertilization *in vitro* can be very different if it is done in one case simply for research, with the intention of disposing of the embryo or fetus at a certain stage of experimentation, and in another case, if it is done to assist spouses who want children, and with the intention to implant the fertilized ovule as soon as possible in the mother's womb.

According to Overhage, Russian researchers have been able to keep about 250 fetuses alive for as long as two months. One was kept alive for about six months until it weighed a pound.[31] By reasoning that great advantages can be hoped for fetology and therefore in favour of human life, the scientists may try to justify these experiments that result in an enormous waste of human life. However, it is my conviction that the damage done to respect for human life cannot be outweighed by some hopes of effective therapy.

Fertilization *in vitro* with the intention to implant the blastocyst in the mother's uterus, can be evaluated on the same principle as artificial insemination with the husband's sperm, as against insemination with the seed of a sperm salesman. Yet, especially in the initial phase of experimentation, there are additional reasons for a reserved evaluation. The chances that the fertilized egg will survive and reach normal development are still very slim and up to now the success rate is very low. For the time being, I would not dare to approve the numerous hazards imposed on the child-to-be.[32]

c) Gene therapy

Gene therapy is a modest part of the field of new biological engineering. It differs from traditional eugenics where various methods of treatment have been developed for genetically caused disorders, for instance, treating PKU (phenylketonuria) by a special diet for the newborn. Gene therapy intends a direct attack surgically, by chemical means or radiation, on the dangerous genes in order to reverse a mutation or eliminate erroneous informations in the DNA. The chances and the prospective techniques of gene therapy differ according to the chief forms of genetic disorders.

In principle, there is nothing to be said against gene therapy. It can be a blessing for many generations. The risk involved has to be judged, as in general medicine, according to the hoped-for good and the proportionate risk of damage.[33]

d) Genetic engineering: improving or changing the human species?

The stupendous progress in genetics allows dreams or even some realistic plans to so mould the genetic code as to improve some dimensions of the human being, such as memory or the resistance to some illnesses. As long as it is an improvement that remains within the human species and does not jeopardize the higher human qualities, new efforts have to be judged according to the proportion between the hoped-for advantages and the risks. However, the individual must never be a mere means of experimentation for the betterment of the species.

The moral evaluation is quite different if the intention is to change the human species and to produce some new combinations between the human genetic code and others. Here are hierarchical boundaries that never should be transgressed.

e) Asexual reproduction

At a time when he had not yet completely rid himself of his Manichean past, Augustine ventured to say that it would be an ineffable joy if spouses could have children without sexual cohabitation.[34] He surely could not foresee that the technical man of the future might try to "reproduce" a human being in an asexual way.[35]

In some animals, as in frogs, rabbits and turkeys, monogenesis (called also parthenogenesis or gynogenesis) can happen naturally. The famous scientist Pincus succeeded in obtaining, some time ago, well developed and fertile rabbits by various manoeuvres of stimulation of the egg.

A different procedure is called "cloning". It involves the infusion of a nucleus with diploid genome into the ovule. The nucleus of an unfertilized egg is removed and replaced by the nucleus of an asexual cell taken from a male or female organism. This is technically possible with frogs and may one day be possible with humans.

I hope that this kind of asexual reproduction of human beings will never be done. Besides the evident risks implied on the biological level, it would do great injustice to the child-to-be. A human being has a God-given right to be rooted, to be a part of the human history in which life is transmitted along with parental love. Children may not become just carbon copies of a possessive parent. A fatherless or motherless society would not at all have the rich humanness and the diversity which the Creator intended to give to humankind.

IV ABORTION[36]

The moral problem of abortion has existed throughout history and among almost all peoples. However, public morality and legislation has strongly protected unborn life. In àll of Christian tradition the prohibition of abortion was considered an essential part of the commandment, "Thou shalt not kill".

Today we find ourselves in a new situation. Not only have abortion techniques developed to such a degree that public control becomes ever more difficult, but public opinion has also greatly changed. Almost all the Marxist countries authorize abortion for the first three months of pregnancy. So-called free countries go even further and withdraw almost all protection from the unborn life, and even use common taxes to cover the expenses for abortion.

1. A moral and a social-legal question

In spite of all the efforts of pro-abortionists to declare abortion a private choice, it becomes ever more evident that it belongs as much to social as to individual ethics. Sexuality and human life cannot be privatized. A normal conscience tells the individual that it is not enough to abstain personally from abortion; he has also the responsibility to protect all human life and to remove, as much as he can, the causes that lead to abortion. It is also a matter of being or not being for the good of society and state.

What meaning can a state have that declares abortion to be a private matter or even a right of its citizens? Is not the first function of a state and society to protect every human being in the basic right to live and to develop, and above all, to protect those who are the weakest?

An individual decision to have an abortion in a complex and distressing situation is a tragic event; but to make abortion a part of one's own ground plan and a guaranteed right of the citizens, even supported by the medical profession and by public taxes, changes all human relationships.

The first thing to be seen is that the relationships between men and women will change: the woman will become much more an object of sexual exploitation. A marriage in which abortion is a part of the calculation from the very beginning can surely not be a sacrament of salvation. All the sexual expressions between the husband and wife, and even all their mutuality, will be deeply marked by their planning to "resolve" an unplanned pregnancy by abortion. And what will adolescents think if they learn that in their family, too, abortion is a means of avoiding births? Will they not, in their hearts or even with explicit words, sometimes ask their parents, "Why did you not abort me?" If unwanted children are aborted, then is there not also aborted, in the heart and in the conduct of the parents, the deepest meaning of the life of their children?

Further, our relationship with the medical profession - or a sub-species of the medical profession that is as ready to earn money by abortion as by other "treatment" - will be totally changed. We would at least claim the right to know which doctor belongs to the aborting or non-aborting profession. And finally, our relationship with a state that refuses to protect unborn life and even requests our taxes to finance the "right" to abortion can only be one of deep distrust.

Abortion is never a merely private choice.[37] There are always at least two persons concerned besides the fetus: the two who have transmitted life and decide, alone or together, to do away with this life. And to deny that such a decision has a social dimension is tantamount to denying that the human person has a social dimension at all. When sexuality and the denial of responsibility for its use become a private choice, the whole of sexual life will be disordered. Whoever is willing to do away with one human life as a commodity, considers all of human life as a mere commodity.

If a state declares abortion on demand to be a right of its citizens, it also declares irresponsible sexual relations and irresponsible transmission of life as a right. It practically approves sex consumerism as a social standard.

All that has been said so far, however, must not lead to a one-sided interest in legal sanctions. Nobody has a right to call for punitive sanctions against women who have aborted unless he conducts himself responsibly in his relations with the other sex and is willing to do all that he can to protect life, born and unborn. Moreover, it can be rightfully doubted that a state has any right at all to decide and apply legal sanctions if it does not fulfil the minimum requirements of social measures in favour of the pregnant woman and the child to be born. I am in favour of legal sanctions, above all, against those who make money by abortion unless it is the intervention of a doctor in a strictly therapeutic situation.

However, much more has to be done. Positive measures to remove the main causes of abortion are the first and most urgent duties of society: more help and more human openness towards unwed mothers, better housing for mothers without husbands, easily accessible consultations for those in need, the guarantee of wages appropriate to the size of the family as in most European countries, a more just distribution of taxes according to the expenses of raising and educating children, avoiding double taxation for parents who do not want to expose their children to state schools where religion and ethics are taboo, a better sex education, and many other things.[38]

It is, further, a duty of society to inform people that besides the psychological and moral damage it inflicts on many people interruption of pregnancy can have serious complications. The increase in abortion causes higher risks of early delivery and various other complications in later births.[39]

2. Spontaneous and not so spontaneous abortion

Many women suffer greatly because of undesired loss of the fetus. Fetology still has much to do to find the major causes of spontaneous abortion, especially in early pregnancy, and young couples should be properly informed about the causes that are already known or suspected.

One cause of spontaneous abortion can be the woman's own carelessness. Her negligence can arise from a more or less unconscious desire to be rid of an unplanned pregnancy, perhaps under the impact of a hostile environment. Interruptions of pregnancy can be caused by mistreatment on the part of the husband or others.

Pro-life activity should care, above all, to diminish undue stress for the pregnant woman and to guarantee ample time free from work before and after childbirth. State legislation and the sensitivity of all citizens could be much improved in this area.

3. Selective abortion

For some of our contemporaries, a reflective attitude towards transmission of life has resulted in responsible parenthood marked by a spirit of maturity. For others, however, it has led to utilitarian calculation not only about the number of children desired but even what kind of child alone would be fitting for them, and as a consequence, "resolving" an undesired situation by selective abortion.

Adolf Hitler destroyed hundreds of thousands of individuals as "unfitting". It is a shocking development that the same spirit is loudly advertised as a prerogative of parents to select the "fitting" children and to do away with those not desirable. The expression, "selective abortion" is frequently used and publicized by genetic counsellors who themselves are products of a utilitarian non-culture.

Amniocentesis and the stupendous progress in genetic medicine allow a diagnosis of whether or not the fetus is affected by genetic disease and what the probability of risk will be. The purpose of interuterine biochemical diagnosis can be very positive, allowing for appropriate treatment as soon after delivery as possible. It also assures a less emotionally charged pregnancy if the absence of disease is diagnosed. This can liberate some parents from the temptation to ask for an abortion on the basis of an unknown degree of risk.

But in many cases, genetic counsellors are primarily concerned "to allow for termination of the pregnancy if so desired by the parents".[40] Some authors and practitioners of genetic counselling would present abortion as a solution if the amniocentesis shows, for instance, that the fetus is a male and, in the given situation, at some risk of being affected by hemophilia. Some suggest abortion even if the risk is of maple wine disease, the results of which can be minimized by dietary restrictions.[41]

Genetic counsellors tend to be non-directive or to give the impression of being so, but frequently they act in the firm conviction that, in the case of any risk, abortion is a proper solution and poses no moral problem. L. E. Karp reveals his absolute ethical relativism: "Morality systems are totally subjective, arbitrary and changeable according to the consensus in different locations and different times."[42] It is no wonder, then, that he can say, "I would wholeheartedly support the prerogative of parents to abort diseased fetuses."[43]. But at the same time he makes sharp moralistic judgments against physicians who do not encourage the pregnant woman to use amniocentesis for the information necessary for a selective abortion.[44] Karp suggests that health insurance should give a reduced insurance premium to those parents who promise to accept abortion as a solution if indicated by a pre-natal diagnosis.[45]

It seems to me evident that this dangerous trend calls for a strong commitment to reverse the cultural trends and to do all that is possible to promote respect for all human life and to overcome a naked utilitarian way of life and thinking.

All these problems cannot be resolved by mere penal law; there must be, rather, a healing approach. Spouses who are aware of a considerable risk of having a genetically diseased child need assistance and proper information about the various ways to regulate conception.

We cannot expect that all mothers who wanted an abortion and were refused it can wholeheartedly accept the child if the whole environment is permeated by a utilitarian outlook. A study concerning 120 children, whose mothers had desired an abortion but were refused it, indicates a higher than average criminality rate. This does not at all prove, however, that abortion would have been the proper solution. The fact that the mothers wanted the abortion is a sign that the seeds of maladjustment were already sown. The mothers were contaminated by their utilitarian environment and therefore did not succeed in fully accepting their children and educating them well. The criminality rate, too, has probably very much to do with the children's environment.[46]

4. Abortion as birth regulation

One of the most shocking signs of our times is the lack of discernment that offers abortion as a means of birth regulation side-by-side with non-abortive contraceptive means. A part of the accountability for this falls on those moralists who did not make a sharp distinction between contraception, meant to regulate conception, and on the other hand, abortion. There is an absolute and enormous qualitative difference between the two. However, the various means offered as contraceptive must be thoroughly studied as to whether they are unintentionally or intentionally abortive. The doubts about the IUD (inter-uterine-device) are not yet resolved.[47]

Under foreign pressure, post-war Japan introduced and publicized abortion as a means of population regulation. Since then, almost 30 million abortions have been registered. This is a holocaust no less deplorable and abominable than the holocaust caused by Hitler. Newer statistics show that in Japan, where there is proper information about the various means of regulating conception, the frequency of abortion is greatly reduced. Those moralists who object to the accessibility of such information about contraception should feel responsible before God for the frequency of abortion. The fact that they consider all artificial contraception as immoral does not excuse them, for traditional moral theology teaches clearly that there are cases where we have to choose the minor evil in order to avoid the greater one. And here there is a tremendous difference.

5. Life-saving interruption of pregnancy

Prominent representatives of traditional moral theology, Alphonsus de Liguori among them,[48] have justified or at least considered as probably justifiable the life-saving interruption of pregnancy that is called "indirect abortion". This means that saving the mother's life is not only the direct intention of the agents but also the direct meaning of the overall *action*. If, in a life-saving interruption of pregnancy, there were also the intention of avoiding having children at all, then there would be the full malice of abortion.

Thanks to the progress of medicine, the conflict situation is not very frequent today, at least in well-equipped hospitals. But it still can happen. In this situation it is not proper to say that the life of the mother is preferred to the life of the unborn child, for there are no cases in which the life of the fetus can be saved by taking the life of the mother. Rather, we are faced here with cases where the sole choice is to let both die or to save the life of the mother. In such an intervention, the child is already deprived of any chance to be kept alive, and its unconscious life is shortened by only a brief period.

Franz Boeckle has well phrased what seems today to be the almost common opinion among Catholic moral theologians and the common conviction of doctors of all world views: "It is not a matter of preferring either the mother to the child or the child to the mother, but a choice between the life that can be saved and that cannot be saved. As in all practical judgments of this kind, there is not more requested than a moral certainty. In this evaluation of the goods we see the moral justification of an interruption of pregnancy medically indicated in a vital conflict. Beyond this case I do not see any plausible reasons that could morally justify an interruption of pregnancy."[49]

Some moralists would object to life-saving interruption of a pregnancy, saying, "It is better to let two lives die than to kill one life, even if it is a matter of shortening that life by only a few minutes." The decisive question is whether we see the action as a whole or as split into parts. Moralists of the latter view condemned the kidney transplant from mother to daughter or son which twenty years ago was the only way to save the person's life. They considered the taking out of the kidney as "mutilation" and condemned it as intrinsically and absolutely immoral. Our way of looking at an action is different. The whole of the action gives the meaning to its parts.

6. Therapeutic abortion in the broader sense

Doctors distinguish clearly between the life-saving interruption, where nothing less than the life of the mother is at stake, and therapeutic abortion in the broader sense where only the health of the mother is endangered. Many Protestant theologians and most of the humanist ethicists would justify an interruption of pregnancy, at least in the earlier stages, where otherwise the health of the mother would be permanently and greatly impaired.

I do not consider their reasons convincing. However, we should not oppose legislation of the pluralistic state that leaves freedom in these cases to the physicians and the mothers to decide according to their consciences. We should remember that for centuries, Catholic theologians and doctors had the same convictions, based on the opinion that in the early stages of pregnancy we are not yet faced with a human person in the full sense. As well-grounded as our convictions may be, we should not be intolerant to the point of causing overall reactions against our Catholic positions.

Therapeutic abortion is quite different from the so-called genetic indication. In that case the fetus, and not the mother, is the patient. Killing the patient is no therapy whatsoever.

I consider probable the opinion of those who justify the removal of a fetus that surely cannot survive, when the action is taken in order to prevent grave damage to the mother. For instance, an unencephalic fetus not only cannot develop into a conscious human life but cannot even survive. To remove it in order to spare great damage to the mother is truly therapeutic, while no injustice is done to the life of this fetus already doomed to death. Traditional moral theology would have called this intervention an "indirect abortion".

V. SINS AGAINST HUMAN LIFE

The most frequent sin against human life is surely abortion, but it is by no means the only one. Our defence of life must be integral. Therefore we treat here the most frequent and the gravest sins against human life.

1. Letting die

By not caring, the priest and the levite in the parable of the merciful samaritan were gravely sinning against human solidarity. They would have let the man die who had fallen into the hands of the robbers. This sin happens all over the earth day by day. The wealthy neighbours and the wealthy countries let millions of children and adults die of starvation because they are not willing to care and to share a part of their superfluous wealth.

A society that spends billions of dollars on the abuse of alcohol and nicotine, and does not provide health care for the poor, is accountable for many deaths and many impaired lives. And it is not only the sin of the legislators but the sin of all the citizens who do nothing to change the situation.

Especially lamentable is the case of the handicapped child who is let die by refusal of a life-saving intervention. This is nothing less than a death sentence on an undesired child. Typical is the case of a strong, healthy child born with Down's Syndrome. Letting the child die by starvation in a painful and long-lasting process is surely no less cruel than a direct killing. From a moral point of view, the decision to refuse the minor intervention in order to get rid of the undesired child has the ·malice of a direct killing. Quite different, however, is withholding treatment from a child who is doomed to death, if the treatment would not be at all beneficial to the child.

2. Causing death by negligence

Ethics and legislation distinguish carefully between (intentional) murder and (unintentional) manslaughter. Many miners and other workers would not have been killed in accidents if all the necessary security measures had been taken. In West Germany in 1976, 14,500 persons died in traffic accidents and 48,000 were seriously injured.[50] The record in other countries is not much different. Reckless driving, or driving after drinking too much alcohol is a sin against one's own life and that of others even if no accident actually happens. The sin is not caused by the actual happening but by the irresponsible conduct.

3. Suicide

Man is not the sovereign of his own life but is expected to be a faithful steward, to conserve and promote the fullness of his life while serving others and promoting the fullness of their lives. The most shocking infidelity of the steward of life is to throw it away as worthless.

Suicide can be the last and final sign of despair and distrust in God. It can be plain rebellion, the ultimate expression of a destructive autonomy in the face of God. But in the reality of life, suicide is seldom this deliberate malice. If we hear of the suicide of a friend whom we have known as a loving and good person, we can be almost sure that it was a psychological short circuit and not a morally accountable act.

In many cases of suicide the blame falls on society or a particular environment, for despair often reflects the failure of those who should have shown justice and tender care for the distressed person. All too many old and crippled people are treated in such a way that they are practically invited to disappear from the theatre of life. And an attempted suicide is often a last desperate effort to call for proper attention and help.

Faced with a neighbour who attempts suicide, we will do all we can to save his life. In doing so, we are not attempting to diminish his freedom; rather, we can presume that his attempt at suicide is not an expression of his freedom but of the temporary absence of freedom.

I do not intend to justify objectively the suicide of people involved in a non-violent and courageous resistance to cruel dictators. To take one's own life is, in my eyes, a violent action. But those who do it might well intend to tell the dictators, "We are not the kind of people to take other people's lives but are willing to sacrifice our own life in order to appeal to your humanity." These men and women, of whom we have read in the past years, wanted to tell the world, "It is better to die than to surrender to dictators and to sell our liberty."

I do not dare to accuse of the sin of suicide persons who sacrifice their life by their own hands when faced with a situation of being brainwashed and thus forced to betray the lives of many other people. This action may have the material aspect of suicide, but in its formal meaning it is not at all what we mean by "suicide" in its moral malice.[51]

4. Murder and participation in mass murder

Murder is the sin of intentional homicide. If the defence of one's own life or that of others, or other human good, causes the death of the unjust aggressor, this has not at all the malice of murder and does not fall under the biblical commandment, "Thou shalt not kill." But if unjust rulers, dictators and tyrants are attacked by those who suffer great injustice, they have no right to react with violence. And if, in the course of the violent reaction, they kill those who make just claims, they are murderers. And all who participate in this violence against people who are seeking nothing more or less than their liberty and basic human rights are accountable for the same sin of mass murder.

There is discussion among ethicists about whether oppressed and exploited people in extreme situations can claim their rights by violent revolution. My conviction is that we should do more to make known the power of non-violent action; and only if all these means are exhausted have we a right to discuss whether the good that can be reasonably hoped for from violent revolution is proportionate to the evil it may cause. But the moral evil of killing in a battle for a just cause, such as basic freedom and human rights, is not at all the same as killing in favour of one's own unjust privileges and unjust power and abuse of power.

Terrorists and hijackers who use innocent people as a means for their political goals, even if they seem to be justified, are by intention murderers, and are indeed murderers if they kill the innocent people. By using these means, they reveal themselves as no better and perhaps worse than their oppressors. Should such people come to power later, they will continue to use people as tools, as "means".

The greatest sin and crime against the biblical prohibition, "Thou shalt not kill", is killing in unjust wars. And all those who have disseminated the hatred, the imperialism or the ideological fanaticism that leads to war are participating in this sin. Rulers who decide for war and use citizens to carry out their intention are the first who will have to answer before God for all the killing and hatred they have unleashed. The less justifiable the war and the greater the injustice of the evils they are aiming at, the greater is their sin. Authorities of a state that requires unconditional surrender in war, thus making a truce and peace impossible, are accountable for all the killing that continues on both sides.

5. The death penalty[52]

According to the tradition of probabilism, I would say that at the present time there are two probable opinions within Christianity and within the Catholic church. There are those who think that the death penalty can and should be inflicted on dangerous criminals, in order to protect innocent people. This opinion finds favour especially in view of those skilled terrorists who, time and again, escape and cause new slaughter.

Personally I incline to the opinion that the abolition of the death penalty is the better course. We have to look at the overall consequences, and we need careful reflection on experiences and probable consequences of the course of action.

There are many texts in the Old Testament that do justify the death penalty. However, we should not overlook the gradual revelation throughout the Old Testament that led steadily to a diminution of violence. In the light of the New Testament it seems to me that the abolition of the death penalty corresponds more closely to Jesus' non-violent message and to his own gentle spirit, as well as to the witness of his disciples. Surely dangerous criminals must be kept where they cannot continue to harm others; but our main task is to heal those who have fallen into a mind-set of violence.

One of my main arguments in favour of the abolition of the death penalty is the fact that in the past most states have participated in mass murder through war or violent oppression of those who were claiming justice. And military and civil tribunals have all too often and too lightly condemned people to death without sufficient proof of the crime and/or with no proportion to the fault committed.

It is my conviction that a state has no right to uphold the death penalty unless it has done all in its power to give better education and to care for a more just and humane environment.

A supreme court that practically forces parents to send their children into an educational system where the teaching of religion and an ethics based on faith is forbidden should not be entitled to endorse the death penalty, for many crimes flow from that very system of education.

NOTES

[1] General bibliography: Cf. B. Häring, *Medical Ethics*, Slough/England and Notre Dame/Ind., 1974³ (pp. 219-235: bibliography); B. Häring, *Manipulation. Ethical Boundaries of Medical, Behavioural and Genetic Manipulation*, Slough/England and New York, 1975; U. Eibach, *Recht auf Leben und Recht auf Sterben. Anthropologische Grundlegung einer medizinischen Ethik*, Wuppertal, 1974; Id., *Medizin und Meschenwürde, Ethische Probleme in der Medizin aus christlicher Sicht*, Wuppertal, 1976; H. Pompey, *Fortschritt der Medizin und christliche Humanität. Der Dienst der praktischen Theologie an einer Medizin im Umbruch*, Würzburg, 1974; J.B. Nelson, *Human Medicine. Ethical Perspectives on New Medical Issues*, Minneapolis, 1974; P. Krauss, *Medizinischer Fortschritt und ärztliche Ethik*, München, 1974; M. von Rad (ed.), *Anthropologie als Thema psychsomatischer Medizin*, Stuttgart, 1974; G.V. Lobo, SJ, *Current Problems in Medical Ethics*, Allhabat, 1974; A.V. Campbell, *Moral Dilemmas in Medicine*, Edinburgh, London, New York, 1975²; J.M. Gustafson, *The Contribution of Theology to Medical Ethics*, Marquette, 1975; J.F. Dedek, *Contemporary Medical Ethics*, Kansas City, 1975; P. Sporken, *Menschlich pflegen. Grundzüge einer Berufsethik für Pflegeberufe*, Düsseldorf, 1975; Id., *Die Sorge um den kranken Menschen. Grundzüge einer neuen medizinischen Ethik* , Düsseldorf, 1977; N. Andersen, *Issues of Life and Death*, London, 1976; A.S. Duncan, R. Dunstan (eds.), *Dictionary of Medical Ethics*, London, 1977; J. Chiari, *Reflections on Life and Death*, London, 1977; Cl. Bruaire, *Une éthique pour la médicine*, Paris, 1978; W. Reich (ed.), *Encyclopedia of Bioethics*, 4 vols., New York and London, 1978 (with abundant bibliography); M. Reidy, *Foundations for a Medical Ethic*, Dublin, 1979; R. Munson, *Intervention and Reflection: Basic Issues in Medical Ethics*, Belmont, 1979; L. Walter (ed.), *Bibliography of Bioethics*, Washington, D.C., 1975, 1977.

[2] Cf. P. Krauss, *Medizinischer Fortschritt und ärztliche Ethik*, München, 1974, 20; K. Rahner, "Die Hominisation als theologische Frage" in K. Rahner and P. Overhage, *Das Problem der Hominisation*, Freiburg, 1968³, 74ff.

[3] Regarding twinning cf. B. Häring, "New Dimensions of Responsible Parenthood", in *Theological Studies* 37 (1976), 120-132; G. Altner,"Human-genetische Aspekte", in *Handbuch der christlichen Ethik*, Freiburg, 1978, 17-36; F. Böckle, "Medizinisch-ethische Aspekte", in *Handbuch der christlichen Ethik*, II, 36-59.

[4] F. Böckle, l.c., 43.

[5] l.c., 44

[6] Cf. W. Ruff, SJ, "Individualität und Personalität im embryonalen Werden" in *Theologie und Philosophie* 45 (1970), 24-59.

[7] Cf. P. Teilhard de Chardin, SJ, *The Phenomenon of Man*, New York, 1965, 163-190.

[8] K. Rahner and P. Overhage, l.c., 79.

[9] l.c., 79,

[10] "Dossier sur l'avortement", in *Etudes* 388 (1973), 55-84, 511-534; 389 (1973), 262-282; B. Häring, "Reflexión sobre el 'Dossier sur l'avortement' ", in *Pentecostes* 11 (1973), 263-270.

[11] Cf. *Free and Faithful in Christ* II, 516-530.

[12] G. Altner, l.c., 17-36; B. Häring, "Genetics and Responsible Parenthood", in *The Kennedy Institute Quarterly Report*, Winter 1975, 6-9.

[13] Cf. "Genetik - Qualität des Lebens. Ein ökumenischer Bericht", in *Zeitschrift für evangelische Ethik*, 1975, 182.

[14] Cf. A.J. Dyck, *On Human Care*, Nashville, 1978², 32-51; R.M. Veatch (ed.),

Population Policy and Ethics: The American Tradition, New York, 1977; A.J. Dyck, M.S. Teitelbaum, W. Peterson, J.J. Spengler, P.G. Brown, R.B. Potter, "Population Ethics", in *Enc. of Bioethics* III, 1215-1316; *Gaudium et Spes*, Patstoral Constitution on the Church in the Modern World, n. 87.

[15] A.J. Dyck, *On Human Care*, 32.

[16] P. Ehrlich and A. Ehrlich, *Population and Environment: Issues in Human Ecology*, San Francisco, 1970.

[17] R. Ravelle, "Food and Population", in *Scientific America*, Sept. 1974, 231.

[18] E.S.E. Hafez and T. N. Evans (eds.), *Human Reproduction, Conception and Contraception*, New York, 1973; L. Lader (ed.), *Foolproof Birth Control. Male and Female Sterilization*, Boston, 1973; R.A. McCormick, "Sterilisation und theologische Methode", in *Theol. d. Gegenwart* 20 (1977), 110-114; *Theological Studies* 37 (1976), 471-477; L.H. Hellman, K. Lebacqz, J.M. Friedman, "Sterilization", in *Enc. of Bioethics* IV, 1606-1618.

[19] Typical of a certain kind of argumentation that, if made in the name of the church, can best turn people away from her, is the article of T.J. O'Donnell, SJ, "Sterilization", in *The New Catholic Encyclopedia* 13 (1967), 704-705. For instance, in the case of pregnancy psychosis which cannot be healed without sterilization, O'Donnell has a response: "Directly contraceptive sterilization is always immoral, whether its purpose is medical, eugenic, punitive, for the generative organs are clearly designed . . . for the preservation of the species". Can such an argument have any sense in the case in which the transmission of life would be irresponsible as much in view of the species as in view of the individual and the couple?

[20] Cf. J.F. Hulka and J.E. Davis, in Hafez and Evans, l.c., 427-446 (with bibliography). The common Synod of the Swiss Dioceses appealed to the ecclesiastical authorities to reconsider the problem of sterilization where there are strong reasons against the risk of a new pregnancy.

[21] F. Böckle, l.c., II, 49.

[22] Cf. N. Kittrie, *The Right to be Different*, Baltimore, 1971, 297-339; I.D. Joyce, *Who should have Children? An Environmental and Genetic Approach*, Indianapolis, 1973; J. Robitscher (ed.), *Eugenic Sterilization*, Springfield, 1973; A. Milunsky (ed.), *The Prevention of Genetic Disease and Mental Retardation*, Philadelphia, London, Toronto, 1975; P. Overhage, *Die biologische Zukunft der Menschheit*, Frankfurt, 1977; I. Gottesman, E.B. Hook, J.C. Loehlin, A.L. Caplan, "Genetic Aspects of Human Behaviour", in *Enc. of Bioethics* I, 527-578.

[23] Typical is the suggestion of V.M. Riccardo: "Legal action is necessary to have retarded or otherwise handicapped persons sterilized" (*The Genetic Approach to Human Diseases*, New York, 1977, 251).

[24] A.E.H. Emery (ed.), *Antenatal Diagnosis of Genetic Diseases*, Edinburgh, 1973; D. Bergsma (ed.), *Medical Genetics Today*, Baltimore, 1974; R.M. Veatch and others, "Population Policy Proposals", in *Enc. of Bioethics* III, 1273-1316.

[25] J.P. Boyle, *The Sterilization Controversy. A New Crisis for the Catholic Hospital?*, New York, 1971, 91; cf. I.N. Trainin, F. Rosner, B. Häring, T.S. Derr, "Religious Directives in Medical Ethics", in *Enc. of Bioethics* IV, 1428-1439.

[26] Cf. B. Häring, *Manipulation*, op. cit., 192-206 (with bibliography).

[27] Pius XII, Address to Catholic Doctors, September 29, 1949, AAS 41 (1949), 560. Fr. F. Hürth, the main adviser of Pius XII in moral matters, suggested that natural law would be respected when through natural intercourse with a somehow perforated condom part of the sperm would be deposited in the vagina while what remained could be used for "assisted insemination". This method is far less convincing than plain artificial insemination with the sperm of the husband.

[28] G.V. Lobo, SJ, *Current Problems in Medical Ethics*, 132.

[29] V.M. Riccardo, l.c., 219. The author adds: "It is not entirely clear why there is such a wide aversion to this technique as genetic alternative".

[30] L.E. Karp, *Genetic Engineering: Threat or Promise?*, Chicago, 1976, 143.

[31] P. Overhage, "Die Evolution zum Menschen hin", in J. Hasenbügel, *Gott, Mensch, Universum*, Graz/Köln, 1974, 403.

[32] Cf. Leon Kass, "New Beginnings in Human Life", in M.P. Hamilton (ed.), *The New Genetics and the Future of Man*, Grand Rapids, 1972, 27.

[33] Cf. B. Häring, *Manipulation*, 173-179; a good description of the now possible or thinkable form of Gen-therapy in W. Klingmüller, *Gen-Manipulation und Gen-Therapie*, Berlin and New York, 1976, 331ff.

[34] Augustine, *Sermo* 51, c. 15 PL 38, 346.

[35] Cf. B. Häring, *Manipulation*, 202-206 (on cloning and partenogenesis).

[36] Cf. B. Häring, *Medical Ethics*, 94-119 and bibliography, 225-229; W. Siebel, *Soziologie der Abtreibung. Empirirische Forschung-theoretische Analyse*, Stuttgart, 1971; D. Hoffmann (ed.), *Schwangerschaftsunterbrechung. Aktuelle Überlegungen sur Reform des § 218*, Frankfurt, 1974; J. Connery, SJ, *Abortion: The Development of the Roman Catholic Perspective*, Chicago, 1977; R.L. Ganz (ed.), *Thou shalt not Kill: The Christian Case against Abortion*, New Rochelle N.Y., 1978; A.E. Hellegers, D.M. Felman, J.R. Connery, J.B. Nelson, Ch.E. Curran, J.M. Finnis, "Abortion" in *Enc. of Bioethics* I, 1-32; J.T. Noonan, *A Private Choice: Abortion in America in the Seventies*, San Francisco, 1979.

[37] Cf. J.T. Noonan, op. cit.

[38] Cf. P. Krauss, *Medizinischer Fortschritt und ärztliche Ethik*, München, 1974, 47-57.

[39] l.c., 66.

[40] V.M. Riccardo, l.c., 163.

[41] l.c., 83, 110 and especially 209, where the author suggests that a 3 percent risk may justify a "selective abortion".

[42] S.E. Karp, l.c., p. xiii, cf. 45.

[43] l.c., 81.

[44] l.c., 43ff.

[45] l.c., 123; cf. Riccardo, l.c., 265.

[46] P. Krauss, l.c., 37.

[47] Cf. B. Häring, "New Dimensions of Parenthood" in *Theological Studies* 37 (1976), 120-132 (with bibliography).

[48] Alphonsus de Liguori, *Theologia moralis* lib. III, n. 394 (ed. Gaudé 1905) p. 644, p. 646.

[49] F. Böckle, l.c., II, 58.

[50] *Herderkorrespondenz* 1977, 141.

[51] Cf. A Eser (ed.), *Suizid und Euthanasie als human- und socialwissenschaftliches Problem*, Stuttgart, 1976 (bibliography); D.H. Smith and S. Perlin, "Suicide" in *Enc. of Bioethics* IV, 1618-1627; S. Perlin (ed.), A Handbook for the Study of Suicide, New York, 1975.

[52] Cf. G. Godwin, *Die Geschichte der Abschaffung der Todesstrafe in der BRD*, Schwenningen, 1952; P. Althaus, *Die Todesstrafe als Problem der christlichen Ethik*, München, 1955; A Koestler, *Reflections on Hanging*, London, 1956; E.O. Tuttle, *The Crusade Against Capital Punishment in Great Britain*, London, 1961; United Nations (ed.), *Capital Punishment*, New York, 1963; G. Gloege, *Die Todesstrafe als theologisches Problem*, Köln and Obladen, 1966; B Schöpf, *Das Tötungsrecht bei den früchristlichen Schriftstellern*, Regensburg, 1968; E. Regan, "The Problem of Capital Punishment" in *Studia Moralia* 14 (1976) 209-237.

Chapter Two

On Health and Healing

I. MEANING AND VALUE OF HUMAN HEALTH AND HEALING[1]

1. Christ the "Saviour and the Healer"

A Christian theology, and especially a theology on health and healing, is possible only in view of Christ. To know him as the Saviour and the divine and human Physician tells us much about salvation and healing, and how they relate to each other.

For Christ, healing the sick is more urgent than literal observance of the sabbath. Healing is an essential part of his gospel message and of his active life. The healing power of Christ and the mission of the faithful to be a sign of healing in the world constitute an essential dimension of a therapeutic theology.[2] From the beginning, the church Fathers could not imagine speaking of Christ the Saviour without honouring him at the same time as the divine Physician: "One is the physician, who is body and spirit, even in his death true life, born from Mary and born from God; for a time able to suffer with us, but then liberated from all suffering: our Lord Jesus Christ."[3]

For Christ, the divine and human physician, nothing is worse than to see people in their suffering and to "pass by" without wanting to help.

It is dangerous reductionism in theology to treat Christ's healing activity only insofar as the miracles can be used for apologetic goals. Healing is a part of Redemption. A theology that dealt with healing-through-Christ only in apologetics practically reduced redemption and salvation to souls concerned chiefly or

42

only with the soul and life after death. Salvation, as Christ preached it by his deeds and his words, includes above all, healthy relationships with God and with one's fellows. At the centre of his message is God's concern for all people in all their dimensions and situations.

A biblically grounded theology is therapeutic, healing, in all its perspectives. It implies a diagnosis of man's sickness, his sinfulness and alienation, his suffering because of an alienated world, unhealthy authority structures, socio-economic conditions and relationships, and so on. But sin and sickness are treated only in the context of conversion and healing.

The biblical message on healing through Christ and his disciples is related to the global vision of salvation. It proclaims the power of Christ's love and his trust in the Father, and is a manifestation of his continuous presence through his disciples. It is always related to faith. It is not the miraculous event alone that strengthens faith; it is more the experience of the power of Christ's love as revelation of the loving care of. the heavenly Father.[4] Christ awakens faith by his message of salvation that is always united with his solicitude for people and the healing power of his love and trust. His healing is related also to the people's own faith, their openness and their recognition that everything, including health, is an undeserved gift of God.

The whole message and faith of the church, including the truly Christian character of theology, are an expression of faith in Christ the Saviour, who came not only to save souls but to heal people, to restore healthy relationships, and to bring the message, the mission and the ongoing action of saving justice and reconciliation.

Christians do not become credible to today's world by proving apologetically that Jesus performed miracles of healing. They can hope much more to be listened to and to win faith if they are clearly dedicated to their mission to heal, while they proclaim the good news by words and love that lead to healing. Today's people are less interested in arguments than in whether the Christians and their message can help them in the sicknesses and alienations of their lives. If the whole of the church, her theology and apostolate, become a manifestation of "the convincing power of the Spirit" (1 Cor 2:4), then we can hope that more people will come to faith in Christ the Saviour and Healer.[5]

The church would not be fully faithful to her mission if she were unable to communicate to today's world that Jesus is the Saviour and that, in him, is the promise not only of an other-worldly salvation but also of the restoration of health and healthier relationships in a healthier world.[6]

2. Faith healing, prayer and healing

In view of one of the worst sicknesses in today's world, a sickening utilitarianism, it has to be said plainly that for people who look to God only as a servant for their selfish goals, faith and prayer are not useful; they will not heal in a world of selfish consumers. But faith in the true sense has a great healing power that radiates from persons, through personal relations with others, unto the construction of a healthier world.

We speak here on faith as a gratuitous gift of God, received gratefully, joyously, humbly, in total surrender to him and in total trust. This faith is expressed by prayer in its own right. Faith and prayer that honour God as God, and render thanks, make people more thoroughly aware that everything comes from God and can lead back to him only if they share his gifts and share responsibility for health and healthy relationships in the sight of God.

At the heart of prayer as expression of faith are praise and thanksgiving. This prayer that honours God as God is unthinkable without an ever increasing appreciation of others, and gratitude for all that they are and do for us. The very expression of faith creates a healthier relationship with God and with the others. The unreconciled person sees in God a threat, and this attitude incites anxiety, discouragement, mistrust before God and about others.

The reconciled person has an absolute trust in God, and an overall attitude of trust in others which, however, does not exclude a discerning distrust subordinated to the overall trust. When Christ met people who turned to him in faith and trust, he increased their trust by helping them to discover anew their dignity and their inner strengths. He made them new people with new hearts, new healthy relationships.

Faith that honours God as God, and experiences reconciliation with God, enables persons to accept themselves with all their limitations and shades. Then they will always discover first the inner resources, all the good, and will help each other in this ongoing process of discovery. Reconciled through faith, and in constant realization that all this is grace, an undeserved gift of God, they come to a genuine reciprocity of consciences, a mutuality in sharing and trusting. And from these wholesome relationships flows a new power of mutual healing and of solidarity in the common effort to create healthier conditions of human life.

All this is a psychological and social reality as well as a religious one, and always points to transcendence. It is God's gift which, gratefully received, helps people to transcend themselves in genuine mutuality, and thus find the direction of their transcendence towards God-with-us.

This healing faith comes to its greatest strength in a community of believers who join in the praise of God and in mutual love.

The reality of faith and ongoing thanksgiving, celebrated in mutual gratitude and recognition, creates healthy memories and heals hurt ones. It overcomes many ailments caused by unhealthy memories of people who have been hurt and refused to forgive, and therefore constantly hurt others by blaming them and refreshing the painful experiences. A life of faith that has its centre in the Eucharist, in the ongoing thanksgiving, can overcome many of these lifelong sicknesses.

From faith and prayer in its own right arise mutual relationships of reverence and respect.[7] Although reverence is an attitude of mutuality of persons, it extends also to the whole of creation as a gift of the common Father, to be respected as a gift for all people. Today's world needs a more reverential attitude towards the whole of creation, towards plants and animals and the environment given to us as an abode in which to live healthily.

3. Sense and nonsense of sickness and suffering

The liturgy praises God for having redeemed us from death, but in reality we are not liberated from physical death. Yet we are set free from senseless death. We are not liberated from all suffering and all sickness, but sickness and suffering are redeemed. And if we fully accept redemption, then many sources and causes of sickness and suffering will be removed.

My own experience, and even more the experience others have shared with me, is one of profound gratitude in difficult moments for the gift of faith that illumines us about the redeeming power of suffering. It also awakens a profound compassion for those who have to suffer as much or even more without reaching an ultimate meaning of life or coming to any understanding of suffering and sickness.

The experience of sickness reveals the frailty of human existence. Man has illnesses, and to some extent it can be said that he creates his ailments; but in any case he gives them meaning or fails to discover meaning. In its various forms and degrees, illness has its personal character that indicates the experiences of life, the way of confronting them, and especially the relations with fellowmen and the surrounding world. "Illness belongs to human existence". It can force us "to assess again the perils that beset us and to recognize again our human destiny and vocation."[8]

The capacity to endure illness and frustration depends mostly on the ability to find and to give meaning to the whole of life and therefore to these experiences that befall everyone. "It has to do with the capacity of dialogue and sharing, that is, the experience of co-humanity."[9]

Through faith and communication of the experience of suffering, much of it can be transfigured and enter into the history of liberty and liberation. While in prison, Dietrich Bonhoeffer found the opportunity to share this experience. "Not only action but also suffering is a way of liberty. The liberating experience is given in the capacity to put our cause into the hands of God. In this sense death is the crowning event of human liberty. The question whether man's action is a matter of faith or not will be decided by this. Then man will understand his suffering as continuation of his action and as the summit of freedom. I find this very comforting."[10]

Illness can be a temptation. The patient can withdraw into self-pity. But he can also frankly confront his situation, use his time for contemplation and self-examination, and affirm his basic freedom to know and to mould the deterministic events. He can face freely what cannot be changed and heal and change whatever can be moulded.

The failure to find and accept the challenge and meaning of sickness can be a sin. However, this failure can be caused by an inadequate, purely biochemical explanation of illness. "Disease has formed itself upon us as a critique of human life and human relationships. We can no longer avoid confronting it as a touchstone of human conduct and behaviour."[11]

This does not at all allow us a moralistic judgment on people who are sick. It is not only the sick person who has to ask himself whether he has properly resolved the erotic or moral crises of his life. Those who live with him and those who, like the priest in the gospel, have "passed by on the other side" must ask themselves whether they have caused unhealthy situations or relationships that unfavourably influenced the condition of the sick. "Illness cannot automatically be brought into relation with personal sin, since human nature is extremely vulnerable to the environment. There are diseases which man causes (the illness of the anthropological school of medicine) and there are others to which man is subjected (the illness of the classical school of medicine)."[12]

4. What is human health?

The understanding of human health depends on the basic understanding of man's being and vocation, on the type of society and its ideas, and on the particular purpose of a definition of health. It will be quite different if the definition is inspired by a vision of wisdom and holiness on the one hand and, on the other, by a consideration of success in professional life, sport, or other fields.

The biblical vision of creation and salvation history does not permit a narrow concept of health. It tells us that God has not created us just for bodily fitness or for any purpose other than to be his faithful stewards and to become for each other a true image and likeness of his love and justice. Therefore the holistic vision of health takes into account the bodily, psychic, spiritual and religious dimensions of man. "The newer results of the behavioural sciences favour this understanding of human health that arose from historical experiences, although they would deny that it depends exclusively on Christian faith."[13]

If it is a matter of defining rights for health delivery, then by necessity the definition will be narrower and include only a minimum requirement. A casuistry, or ecclesiastical norms that focus on control of professional practice cannot grasp the breadth and depth of the holistic concept which, by its very nature, is expression of knowledge of salvation and wholeness.

The definition used by the World Health Organization expresses a maximum of health as a right, but it does not mean a right to health delivery but a right in view of the overall responsibility of each individual and the society. "Health is the state of perfect bodily, spiritual and social well-being, and not only the absence of illness. The highest possible situation of health is one of the most basic rights of man."[14]

The social dimension of health is important. Health is an endowment of the individual and the group, and attests to cooperation and interdependence of people in the fields of nourishment, housing, prenatal and child care, education, and care of society's dependent members. But while this vision enters into the description of health, it is clear that social evils cannot be healed by medical intervention. This is to be said especially in view of the tendency to justify abortion by "social indications".

A comprehensive understanding of human health includes the greatest possible harmony of all of man's forces and energies, the highest possible spiritualization of man's bodily reality, and the best possible embodiment of the spiritual. True human health is revealed in the self-actualization of persons who have attained the freedom that marshals all their talents and energies for the fulfilment of their total human vocation.

5. Personal and social responsibility for health

In modern states the cost of health delivery is soaring and may soon reach the limits of possibility. The progress in technology and the organization of social medicine have led all too many people to expect their health from health delivery and advances in science. They forget their own responsibility. Everyone needs to be reminded that "health is a decisive dimension of our existence and therefore has to be promoted from within."[15]

Health is, first of all, our personal responsibility. It requests a certain style of life that fosters health and refrains from all that would damage it. We cannot ignore the old health rules such as the proper rhythm between work and leisure, fasting and prayer, and thus learning about the mutual conditioning and oneness of body and soul. People should not be offended and should not accuse a doctor of moralism if he tells them sincerely that they have to change their style of life and rely more on their own inner powers.

No less important is the social responsibility of all citizens and the decisive organs of society. The greatest progress in health comes from a better popular understanding and consequent improvement of those environmental conditions that influence human health at large, such as better housing and nutrition, clean drinking water, avoidance of water and air pollution, enforcement of speed limit laws, and so on.

New insights and new dangers make indispensable a carefully elaborated ethics of environment. Man has to be a more careful and loving steward of the creation entrusted to him. For both the present and future generations, one of the most urgent tasks of society is to protect and improve the biosphere. The educational system has to awaken a sense of common responsibility for societal and economic structures that foster a healthy environment, healthy relationships, and the ordering of life for the benefit of all the people. Especially the churches have a particularly urgent responsibility in this respect.

A word must be said, too, about the relatively new responsibility in today's society to warn and protect people against over-medication induced by some doctors and attendants, and especially seduced by the powerful advertisements of the drug industry.

II. THE HEALING PROFESSION

We are all wounded by the overall sickness of a disordered world. But we all have inner resources and healing powers, and it is part of our total vocation to heal our own and others' wounds and to work faithfully for a healthier world and more healing relationships. Throughout history humanity has realized, however, that there is need for special healers. Since ancient times, priests were also healers, doctors, or the healers somehow gained a priestly dimension. The healing action points to God and his healing compassion and powers. The sick person seeks a human doctor to discover the physician within himself, so that his inner powers may receive new energy. Both the doctor, who himself is a "wounded healer", and the inner resources draw attention to Him who alone is the source of all health and healing.[16]

1. The ethos of the physician

The healing profession, along with the priest, was the earliest professional group to develop a special ethos, a strong tradition and solidarity. Not without good reason has this profession held, from the most ancient times up to the present, one of the highest social positions insofar as honour and trust are concerned.

It is essential to the ethos of the healing profession that physicians should promote the conviction of the sacredness of human life and the responsibility for one's own health and that of others. A doctor would contradict the very essence of his vocation if he were to wish many people to be sick in order to have enough customers. His wish is to see people as healthy as possible; and for this purpose he will never stop learning in order to exercise his profession better and to acquire a widely humane formation. In its best tradition, the healing profession has a unique awareness of the need for a broad and deep vision of wholeness. A saying in ancient Greece called the physician a "friend of wisdom", a philosopher.

The good physician is entitled to enjoy social honour and that special trust that is, in itself, a healing factor. He is equally entitled to enjoy that degree of material security that allows him a total dedication to his professional task without neglect of his family. But earning his living can be only a secondary motive for his vocational choice.

For those in the healing profession to retain their professional ethos, today's situation requires their unfailing attention and a spirit of cooperation. Frequently they are employees of huge organizations with great socio-economic powers that follow their own inherent laws guided by the principle of profit and loss. As a consequence, members of the profession as well as their patients may readily become objects of profitable calculations. It is therefore the task, not only of the healing profession and the administrators of health organizations (hospitals, etc) but also of the whole of society, to watch out for the rights of those who are especially in need, the poor, the handicapped and the retarded. It is more than a matter of charitable action by the individual doctor or nurse; the very ethos of the physician requires a joint action to bring forth those changes that allow total dedication to the health of all, and a general trustful doctor-patient relationship.

Technical and scientific progress requires specialization and a tremendous armamentarium. The hospitalized patient is subjected to test after test, led from one technologist to another. He might well have the impression that the equipment is controlling the specialists rather than the specialists controlling the equipment. This new situation requires a complex bureaucracy. All this may lead to a feeling of estrangement. Care must be taken that the patient finds someone with whom he can establish a personal relationship, a particular doctor or nurse to guarantee that he will not be lost.

2. The ethical code

Since antiquity, the medical profession has expressed by an ethical code its ethos and its effort to guarantee a high moral standard.[17] The code is an expression of solidarity within the healing profession but also a sign of solidarity with the patients. The public at large and each individual patient should thereby be assured of professional standards and ethical conduct by the members of the profession.

By the ethical code and control of its observance, the healing profession exercises an important role of responsibility in society. It also avoids unnecessary interference and legislation by the state. The legislator should observe the principle of subsidiarity and not legislate or interfere by controls in areas where the medical community, with the general approval of the community, properly fulfils its function. Yet modern health care is such an important social and political issue that not all the decisions can be left to the medical profession alone. Wherever the common good really requires it, there must be legislation. This, however, should not come about without broad participation by the public at large and especially by the healing profession.

The profession's ethical code and state legislation can guarantee, however, only a minimum of ethical and professional standards. Beyond that, and in order to keep legislation and the ethical code up to date, there is a special need for a professional medical ethics (today frequently called "bioethics") that covers a broad field of questions concerning medicine and the progress of biology. The ethics require a constant dialogue between the ethicist and the members of the healing profession. Special attention must be given to those physicians who are, in an outstanding way, creative and dedicated to their vocation.

The Catholic doctor will not ignore or disregard the moral teaching of his church. However, the teaching of the magisterium on matters concerning the medical profession needs a careful hermeneutics and requires ongoing cooperation between church authorities, the community of moral theologians and ethicists, and the members of the healing profession. It is not and should not be a one-way street. As moral theologians and doctors accept guidance by those in authority, so those in authority need the constant influx of reflection and suggestions from practitioners who work in this field. Here the church, as in so many other things, is a pilgrim church, and those in authority cannot expect to have always ready-made responses or to find in their archives relevant answers to totally new questions.

3. The doctor-patient relationship

The relation between members of the healing profession and their patients is a covenant reality; it goes far beyond a contractual or commercial relationship.

What we said earlier about reciprocity of consciences applies in a very particular and urgent way here.[18] Each of the partners has his or her conscience that must never be betrayed; however, it is a mature conscience only by its openness to and respect for the partner's conscience. By this reciprocity of consciences the two will come closer to the truth and to truthful solutions in each new situation. The doctor will see his patient as a unique person with an inviolable dignity, personal rights and expectations.[19] Hence he will constantly take into account the patient's relationships with God, with family, friends and the community.

Their reciprocity of consciences entails a shared responsibility towards society. The doctor is obliged to alert, when necessary, the conscience of his patient about his responsibility towards family and society, for instance, in the case of contagious disease or when the patient is a carrier of genetic disease.

Mutual trust, so important for a healing relationship, requires truthful information about the prospects and risks of the various treatments. The patient and members of his family must never be cheated or deceived. They should be allowed to participate in the decision-making process as much as they are able and willing. Today's physician should avoid any kind of paternalism unless he is dealing with people who, because of their cultural background and level of development, desire a paternalistic attitude and way of action by the doctor.

The covenant of trust must be thoroughly observed in all matters of confidentiality. Professional secrecy was always considered an essential part of the medical ethos. The oath of Hippocrates says, "If it be what should not be noised abroad, I will keep silence thereon." The American Medical Association code says, "Confidence . . . should never be revealed unless the law requires it or it is necessary to protect the welfare of individuals or communities." I would like to qualify this by insisting that confidence can be revealed only where *just* laws require it.

If the patient refuses or is unable to reveal what should be revealed where the common good or the good and right of others is at stake, then in keeping with the principle of subsidiarity, the doctor may give the necessary information.[20]

Any unjust conduct, such as filing unjust lawsuits against doctors, harms not only an individual person but undermines the general atmosphere of trust between patients and doctors.

III. HEALTH DELIVERY AND HEALTH POLICY

In a society in which people see themselves mainly as consumers, it is no wonder that they consider health as something that can be delivered to them, possibly at the expense of the state or society at large. Today, all too many consider it a "right" that has to be administered and delivered. They forget the more basic truth that health is one of the most binding human duties, a matter of joint responsibility.[21]

There is a powerful "health industry", considered as a very

important part of the modern market. The tremendous progress in
biochemistry, and especially in medical technology in the last
decades, tend to make doctors and nurses the servants of the
expensive tools of this market. In this situation it seems an
important task of the church, and especially of moral theology, to
challenge the present system.

1. The classical model of health delivery

We have almost forgotten the long history of health care
during which doctors, paramedics and nurses saw their main task
as visiting the sick and assisting families in the care of the sick at
home. The now classical model is health delivery in huge
hospitals. Most people die there or go there for regular check-ups,
which is good; but they also spend most of the time of their
sickness there, not seldom in an environment of estrangement.

The church, too, in western countries and in the third world,
has disproportionately concentrated on building hospitals that
most generously serve the people's needs but also are more or less
forced to operate according to the now classical model. Enormous
amounts of money and of generous action by devout people are
spent in and for the hospitals. Church hospitals are willingly and
unwillingly a part of today's health industry.

This system requires ever greater expenditure by the sick, but
even more by the taxpayers. The moment can be foreseen when
these expenses will no longer be bearable. Therefore we see a need
for a creative challenge to this present model.

2. New creative approaches

Almost everywhere in the world there are people who think that
the present model can and must be creatively transformed.[22] The
role of the healing profession can be seen in a way that is new
and at the same time more effective. Could it not be the most
noble and most urgent task of the profession to help people to
prevent sickness and ailments, to discover the meaning of
sickness, and to accept it in such a way that what can be healed
will be healed, and what cannot be healed can be integrated into
the growth of the whole person?[23] Could not the professionals
instruct a great number of volunteers who are willing and able to

promote the right attitudes towards health and ailments? They should influence the whole of society not to allow technology and the drug industry to become the masters of doctors and nurses or to expand their markets through over-medication and dangerous advertising.

A study has shown that in Great Britain 43 percent of the total expense for health care goes to pharmaceutic services.[24] Not without good reason has Ivan Illich spoken and written on medical nemesis.[25]

There could and should be a profound shift in the training of doctors, medics and nurses. The most urgent task is to promote a holistic vision of persons, of health, of sickness and therapy. There are promising beginnings. For instance, the Society for Health and Human Values, which publishes the Journal of Medicine and Philosophy, has greatly contributed by introducing into many medical schools programmes on human and spiritual values and on neuroses and bioethics.[26]

The first thing for us, of course, has to be a change in the programme and activity of the church, including the mission churches. There should be a radical challenge to those Catholic moralists who, concerned with dominion and control, are opposing the holistic vision of health, healing and sickness, and confining their analyses to partial acts and actions whereby therapy is rejected where it concerns the whole person, while attention is focused only on organs that are diseased.

We do believe in the possibility of more creative ways of serving, of medical practice, and of promoting health as a part of human co-responsibility in the common effort for a healthier life in a more just society.[27]

Would it not be well for the church to diminish the number of hospitals owned and subsidized by her, and do more creative work in conscience-raising and health education?

3. Health policy[28]

The problem of a more constructive and helpful health policy is gigantic. Not only the medical profession and the church, but all citizens, should actively participate in seeking better solutions. There is, of course, a special obligation on governments and legislators. Actually, world health organizations and state legislatures have already done much for preventive health care. Indeed, general health depends more on these preventive measures than on the most expensive techniques of modern medical industry.

Although the cost of health delivery and care is rapidly increasing, my suggestion is not to reduce the cost for health but rather to restructure spending. Much more can be done for general health education, for a more healthful environment, better housing, and for more emphasis on spending that improves the health situation of the whole population, more care and education for adjustment of the handicapped and retarded, and more spending on health care for the poorest and less on those techniques that serve mainly to prolong the process of dying.

Could there not be specific taxes on alcohol and nicotine in favour of new methods and institutions to heal the addicts of these and other drugs? Personally I think there is a need also for a special tax on things that cause noise pollution. Unnecessary noise, for instance by motorcycles, cause considerable damage to the total health environment.

IV. PATHOLOGY AND PSYCHOTHERAPY

1. Psychosomatic illness and neurosis

The anthropological school of medicine and the development of psychoanalysis and other forms of psychotherapy have brought a sharper distinction between the various types of pathologies.[29] The endogenous illnesses - those arising from within the body - are properly treated by biochemical means or by surgery. However, their development and the inner energies of the healing process have always a psychosomatic dimension. Hence the word of Paracelsus applies even here: "The best medicine is loving respect." For love never disregards whatever means can be used to heal the body.

The psychogenic illnesses, of mental origin, are distinguished from the somatogenic, of organic etiology. The physician is obliged to acquire competence in diagnosing differentially the somatic and the psychogenic ailments. He needs sufficient psychological knowledge to recognize when he should refer his patient to a competent psychotherapist. No less should the psychotherapist know the limits of his own discipline and its methods, and not try to treat psychopathologies without taking into account the possibility of somatic disturbances influencing the psychic life.

Newer psychotherapy speaks also of "noogenic pathology", existential in origin, related to various types of failure in the quest for ultimate meaning.[30]

Pastoral counsellors and confessors should be informed about these various dimensions in order to avoid the danger of moralizing where the various forms of medical help are required.[31]

Moreover, everyone should be aware that the origin and type of diseases, diagnoses, and the forms of healing have much to do with the prevailing culture.[32]

2. Neurosis and Psychosis

The discovery of neurosis[33] and the development of the various forms of its therapy have revolutionized the concept of healing, broadened the scope, and greatly influenced modern pastoral care.

"A neurosis affects a person who is in a state of unresolved conflict and yet is unconsciously pressured towards a healing change. It appears that, under the given circumstances, it is better to be affected by a neurosis than to be beaten and flung about as the plaything of uncontrolled forces in subhuman inarticulateness. Of course, a neurotic resolves an existential problem on a level lower than the one on which it is situated."[34] The neurosis plays its game from within the unconscious. It arises from the repression of unresolved experiences of stress which, at least partially, are shelved in the subconscious. If a man does not fulfil his potentialities as a person, he becomes to that extent constricted and ill. "This is the essence of neurosis - the person's unused potentialities, blocked by hostile conditions in the environment (past or present) and by his own internalized conflicts, turn inward and cause morbidity."[35]

Man has an inner striving for health, wholeness, integrity. The neurosis is a sign that his inner yearning for wholeness is not totally silenced. Psychology warns against a judgmental attitude towards neurotics; it would be a great mistake and a harmful injustice to them. Among morally obtuse persons with a totally undeveloped or destroyed sensitivity, neurosis does not readily occur. The seemingly robust "health" eliminates the need for repression although it is a sign of a shocking unhealthiness on the level of wholeness and true humanity.

Neurosis is never simply or generally reducible to sin or to personal guilt. It can, however, be the continuation of the outcry of conscience that calls for inner healing and conversion. The moral conscience faces consciously a dreadful disintegration in the innermost depths of the person; but due to a failure to search consciously for the healing of conscience's wound, the longing for wholeness is locked in the unconscious. The neurosis remains on the subconscious plane but manifests itself in discernible symptoms.

In many cases of neurosis there may be no personal guilt or very little. The incapacity to face life's conflicts may well arise from a thoroughly hostile environment. "There is less reason to be puzzled by the fact that there are so many neurotic people than by the phenomenon that most people are relatively healthy in spite of the many adverse influences they are exposed to."[36]

3. Psychotherapy

a) Various schools of psychotherapy

The father of psychoanalysis is Sigmund Freud. He sees the human being as driven by the unconscious, the *id* and the *superego*. "Caught in the middle and helpless to mediate was the individual ego."[37] Freud's daughter, Anna Freud, ascribes to the ego a more important function as a modifier and genuine agent for the impulses that come from the unconscious. "This led to the understanding of the autonomy of the ego and the view that the individual was not simply acted upon by the *id* and *superego* but rather had some conscious degree of choice and power of his own to mediate and reconcile these forces in a variety of ways."[38] Erik Erikson, following this trend of development, gives to the creative capacities of ego-strength their proper role.

While Freud overemphasizes the sexual factor and the self-destructive impulses, Alfred Adler seeks the source of all neuroses in feelings of inferiority. The goal of the therapist is to re-educate the patient so that he sets realistic goals and gives up his struggle for power beyond his ability. Adler appeals more to the conscious mind.

Carl Gustav Jung gives great attention to the *collective unconscious* which represents the wisdom of generations and self-knowledge at the deepest level. A growing awareness of it fosters mental health. His therapy, emphasizing especially the integration of the feminine part of man (*anima*) in the masculine mindset, and the masculine part of woman (*animus*) in the feminine character, helps to promote healthier relationships. Jung introduces a concept similar to but not identical with Freud's superego. He speaks of *"persona"*, a kind of social façade worn by every individual for inner protection. Therapy should give this mask its proper place without blocking the individuation, the true identity.

Jung gives attention also to the therapist-patient relationship insofar as the subconscious and unconscious are concerned, and consequently to the process of transference.[39] The analyst recognizes his own wounds and vulnerability and, together with his patient, strives towards greater self-realization and healthy relationships on the conscious and unconscious levels. As a wounded healer, the therapist bears the burden of the other.[40]

E. Fromm, P. Horney and H. S. Sullivan consider the cultural as much as the instinctual origin of neurosis. Their personalism excludes self-centredness. Persons are to be healed in their relationships and in their vulnerability to the physical and social environment. Childhood experiences are given less importance than the patient's background.

The various schools are not necessarily exclusive. The therapist may well combine the different approaches and choose the particular emphases that accord with his patient's needs and his own capacities. "Everyone who treats patients adds his own unique character to the therapy he conducts, and his honesty to self is probably the most important ingredient for the accomplishment of useful treatment. Integrity and spontaneous emotional interaction that is personal in every sense of the word are essential to good therapy."[41] The choice of one's therapist is an important decision. Therapy needs a high degree of mutual trust, yet this trust must not be undiscerning.

The most mature approach to neurosis therapy seems to me that of Viktor Frankl[42] and his school of logotherapy. It is not his intention to replace psychoanalysis by logotherapy. Rather, his concern is for a sharper diagnostic distinction that would rule out the somatogenic pseudo-neuroses which call for biochemical treatment, and focus on the endogenous psychopathologies that require the expertise of psychiatry and clinical psychology. Frankl gives particular attention to the noogenic neurosis which he considers the "neurosis of the future", the sickness of an age of aimlessness, boredom, lack of ultimate meaning and purpose.

Frankl gives to transference its full personalistic direction. He considers it a vehicle of existential encounter in which the patient finds the realization of his dialogical, reponsorial existence. Through this encounter the person becomes better able to recognize the essential importance of genuine love. The therapist does not try to impose his world view, his religion or ethical convictions on his patients, but helps them to discover their own inner resources and to gain freedom in the search for ultimate meaning. The therapist "can assist the patient to achieve a value system and outlook that can blanket or absorb the troublesome factor."[43]

Frankl's school has discovered the healing power of a sense of humour, and its significance as a sign or factor of progressing health. It implies genuine self-acceptance in the experience of being accepted.

b) Therapeutic modes

One of the decisive questions of high ethical relevance is whether the therapy tends to be directive or more non-directive. The directive gives the initiative one-sidely to the therapist. He selects the area to be covered and the pathway towards health in accordance with his own insights or assumptions about the causes of the illness.

Non-directive therapy is based on the conviction that the patient has precious inner resources and can be helped to discover these resources through genuine friendship and understanding. The non-directive therapy is most careful to awaken in the patient a spirit of self-respect and trust in his own freedom without, however, dimming his awareness that he is in need of help for better self-understanding.

The non-directive method is more than a method; it presupposes for its proper functioning a non-domineering therapist. "The primary point of importance here is the attitude held by the counselor toward the worth and significance of the individual. . . Do we see each person as having worth and significance in his own right? Do we respect his capacity and his right to self-direction? Or do we basically believe that his life would be best guided by us? To what extent do we have a need and a desire to dominate others?"[44]

Non-directive therapy does not at all mean non-involvement or mere passivity. The client must feel that he is fully accepted and respected. The impression must never be given of a lack of interest in his life. However, the therapist has to re-examine himself constantly about whether his basic trust in the worth of his partner is an abiding attitude and a consistent, organic application of genuine convictions. Is it absolute respect for the freedom and autonomous responsibility of the client in a relationship of co-responsibility? "Client-centered counseling, if it is to be effective, cannot be a trick or a tool. It is not a subtle way of guiding the client while pretending to let him guide himself. To be effective, it must be genuine."[45]

This non-directive mode of therapy can best help the patient to discern the field of his freedom, and to amplify it while at the same time gaining distance from his obsessions (hangups). "The experience which in the church is called 'repentance' could, together with the experience of psychoanalysis, instruct us that healing is not possible if we accept our psychic obsessions and blockages as our being, but only if we distinguish ourselves from them as obsessions and accept that guilt which is truly ours."[46]

c) The main issue: freedom

Psychotherapy and logotherapy are to be judged by the service they render to the increase of creative liberty and fidelity. Both therapist and patient are to be faithful to their conscience and are to help each other to discern thoroughly what is a genuine conviction of conscience and what is a psychic obsession. The freedom of each is best served when both make themselves and each other conscious of their world view, their basic convictions, and commit themselves to respect each other's conscience. They should meet each other as persons who seek freedom through the pursuit of truth and meaning, and do so consciously as autonomous persons.

Psychoanalysis frequently tends to assert its independence from all value systems, yet the method and goals of the therapist may imply a definite world view, a concrete concept about the meaning of life, of health and sickness. If the therapist does not bring forth all this to his own and the patient's consciousness, there is great danger that he is operating under a most insidious repression, namely, a denial in consciousness of his own outlook and direction. The carefully veiled and smoothed quest for the meaning of health breaks through unhealthily, like any other kind of repression, and plays its concealed games.

The transference which, in a long-lasting process of therapy, is unavoidable and can well be very beneficial, may also turn into a harmful manipulation of the patient. It is all too human for the therapist to enjoy his influence in moulding the psychic life of his patient. The criterion for the proper use of the transference is whether it enables the patient "to find freedom from re-enacting the infantile dependencies and distortions of attitude to the analyst as parent . . . Obviously a lot of medical practices do not permit this goal, that is, freeing the individual from his infantile dependence on an all-giving or withholding parent."[47]

Another danger in some psychoanalytic models is that, consciously or not, they revolve around an individualistic concept of self-fulfilment. Best humanistic psychology has shown that many neuroses have their roots in a navel-gazing type of introspection, a one-sided attention to one's own self-fulfilment. Healing is possible if both therapist and patient together learn ever more surely that the human person's self-actualization is possible only in genuine self-transcendence, in dedication to the others and to the common cause.

4. Behaviour modification

In the past decades a great many American and European psychologists gave up classical psychotherapy in favour of behaviour modification, using the recipes of behaviourism whose most influential representative is now B. F. Skinner.[48] Skinner's behaviourism denies the reality of conscience and human freedom. He believes that throughout all history man has been conditioned and practically manipulated by his environment through various positive and negative reinforcements. He concludes that it is better to have the manipulation done consciously and systematically by those most competent.

The point of departure for behaviourism is the findings of I. P.

Pavlov on the phenomenon of "substitute stimulus" or "conditioned reflex", and his whole psychology is built on the conditioned reflex.[49] He composed for Stalin the textbook on brainwashing.

Skinner experimented with rats and the higher primates, and focuses on what man and animal have in common. I think he has proved that people, whose motives are no higher than to avoid pain and to be remunerated for whatever they do, can be thoroughly manipulated by a combination of "adversive" (punitive) and "non-adversive" (rewarding) reinforcements. His practical system is underlined by a utilitarian concept of happiness.

Others, however, without sharing Skinner's philosophy, feel that they can accept, at least partially, his techniques.[50] He deserves credit for showing us splendidly that we will all become manipulated manipulators if our motivation does not transcend mere fear of punishment and hope for reward. A greater awareness of his findings and of the threats they imply for our freedom could, for instance, induce the Catholic church to change its system of promotions, titles and honours. But what is more basic is that we propose a positive solution of genuine therapy that respects conscience and freedom and calls for responsibility. By watching over our motives we can change our conduct more radically and permanently. And for a Christian, the basic motive is grateful love for God, and a burning zeal for his kingdom of love, justice, peace and freedom.

Skinner does tell us, however, something constructive about the importance of actively and wisely shaping our environment if we do not want to be shaped unfavourably by a distorted and dehumanized social environment.

5. Therapy for alcoholics and drug addicts[51]

Alcoholism and drug addiction constitute one of the major causes of suffering, disruption of families and widespread criminality, not to speak of the enormous costs and the loss of working capacities that affect the whole of society. Today the problem has reached proportions that compel the medical profession and all parts of society, especially legislators and governments, to research the manifold interwoven causes of this social evil, and to trace a holistic course for prevention and healing.

Not only do drug addiction and alcoholism require a multidimensional therapy; they also are worldwide social problems that call for profound changes in culture and in the whole of society's way of thinking. During the last years, almost all governments and great numbers of reponsible citizens everywhere have come to realize that heavy smoking, too, has devastating consequences not only for smokers themselves but also for those who have to live with them. The illnesses caused or worsened by these abuses cost society more than is brought in by taxes on the products.

To poison one's body and mind by the abuse of alcohol, drugs and nicotine is a grave moral disorder. However, moralistic, judgmental attitudes must be excluded. The major part of responsibility often falls on society itself or on those who have failed to provide an education properly directed towards a truly human community and favourable social conditions.

These evils have to be seen in the context of a consumer society and a culture in which possessing and consuming count for more than being and loving, a culture in which a selfish seeking for only one's own self-fulfilment is consciously or unconsciously the main leitmotif.

The problem begins when children are not truly accepted as a gift of God, when parents and educators who do not give them genuine love, compensate by giving them more and more things. Often children have no chance to learn and appreciate a simple lifestyle and to rejoice in healthy, loving relationships. Their education is based on rewards and punishment, and they are not motivated to give up superfluous things in order to be free for others and free to respond to their higher inner needs.

Chronic alcoholics and narcotic addicts are generally described as immature and excessively dependent individuals, usually with a history of disturbed interpersonal relationships. They tend to overcompensate for their personal deficiencies and the distress caused by environmental factors by escaping into a make-believe world.[52] The fact that they seek this form of escape cannot be explained without the social context of people with socially approved habits of drinking, using drugs and smoking.

One of the main causes of today's widespread drug addiction is the constant and powerful advertising of psychotropic drugs as a remedy for all human problems. This might also be true, though to a lesser extent, of addiction to smoking and drinking, since television commercials and the heroes and heroines of so many movies and television shows are constantly exhibiting these habits.

Addicts are sick people, and they are in need of healing within a sick society that needs radical renewal in its way of thinking and in its structures.

Penal laws should hit the drug dealers rather than the addicts themselves, who are already suffering people. A society that wants to resolve these heavy plagues by penal methods aimed at the addicts is indulging just as much in escapism as the addicts are.

What is needed first is proper education, and information that will influence the whole of society, especially those who are most exposed to the dangers of addiction. The second most needed action is to make available the best possible services for healing the addicts. These plagues could probably be drastically reduced by a gradual and heavy increase in taxes on drugs, alcohol and tobacco, but this measure can be effective only if it is part of the broader approach of re-education of the whole of society for appropriate motivation and constructive action.

To renounce a judgmental moralistic attitude, however, does not at all mean to exclude personal responsibility. Whatever therapy is initiated has to appeal to the addict's still existing though limited freedom. While the vocation of the doctor and of all of us is to heal and not to sit in judgment of others, the very dignity of our suffering brothers and sisters requires that we appeal to their own freedom and conscience. This is possible without moralistic overtones if we are aware of the complexity of the situation.

In many cases the therapy has to extend to the family. Frequently, group therapy is indicated. The experience of Alcoholics Anonymous is very illuminating. Their success is based on a kind of in-group therapy. Those wounded and in the process of healing are often the most effective healers, having learned compassion by experience, and having reached a new insight in solidarity. There are healing communities organized by rehabilitated drug addicts and alcoholics.[53]

For persons who are thoroughly addicted to nicotine or alcohol, healing becomes possible only if the patient accepts total abstinence. An occasional lapse into the old habit reactivates it. This holds true even more in cases of narcomania; the craving for the drug remains after the body has been detoxified, especially if psychotherapy has failed to lift the psychological dependency.

Particularly desirable would be the offer of continued education for addicted patients, especially if long periods of hospitalization are necessary. A part of this ongoing education could be informative discussion about the main causes of such social evils as alcoholism and drug addiction.

A general education for responsibility and co-responsibility would probably eliminate or at least reduce many of the conditionings and causes. If people were motivated by a spirit of responsibility and co-responsibility, they would realize, for instance, how much harm the misuse of alcohol, drugs and nicotine does to others, and could therefore more easily withstand temptations and break incipient habits in time. A word by the author of this book is relevant here. When analysis proved the existence of throat cancer, the doctor's first question was, "Are you a smoker?" When I assured him that I do not smoke, his second question was whether I had to live and to lecture in rooms where others smoked. If parents were informed that children whose own parents are smokers have serious breathing problems more frequently than others, they would, as loving parents, easily be able to change their habits.

6. *Therapy of sexual deviances*[54]

Sex therapy has become a new discipline in recent years. Many people feel that they are sexually inadequate, and explain their troubles in marriage and in other relational situations by this type of inadequacy. A number of ethical problems arise about different forms of sex therapy.

Masters, a pioneer in this field, touches three delicate matters. Of the first he writes, "Dr. Redlich develops a compelling position against therapeutic-patient sex by pointing out the exploitation implicit in this situation of particular vulnerability, as well as the breakdown of trust that invariably accompanies termination of such a relationship."[55] This is not at all a preconceived moral norm but the result of experience and shared reflection in the light of human growth and dignity.

On the second problem, Masters notes that he himself and the institute founded by him have "discontinued our use of surrogates", while other institutions have initiated programmes in which the surrogate functions as a teacher or therapist. His third observation is also very pertinent: "The sex therapist who demands observation of sexual activity as a part of treatment is more likely to be doing so for reasons of personal titillation than of professional concern."[56] These notations manifest good common sense.

Sex therapy requires a holistic vision, and that implies a general therapy that aims at healthier relationships, fuller self-acceptance and acceptance of others as others. Mere external sexual functioning alone is not healthy sexuality. Fully human and healthy sexual relationships require growth in love and respect, and the capacity to love and to be faithful.

There are sexual deviations like sadism and masochism, fetishism and bestiality that affect and wound the whole person and lead to deeply disturbed relationships with others and within oneself. The sadist finds sexual gratification in acts of cruelty to others, while the masochist is sexually aroused by acceptance of cruel treatment by another, usually a prostitute or some such person. The sexual fetishist (different from the magical fetishist) displaces his sexual and erotic arousal onto inanimate objects such as an article of clothing or the hair of another person. These are grave pathologies. Those affected are in urgent need of a thorough-going therapy and the most compassionate human help to develop better self-understanding and self-acceptance. This has to go hand in hand with education for true love.

Bestiality is sexual gratification by a kind of intercourse with animals. This aberration reveals that the unfortunate person has not reached a full understanding and realization of his or her specific human dignity at all. One of the causes, among many others, can be a long-lasting self-indulgence and a sexual orientation that is totally severed from growth in human love.

In all these situations, healing is not possible through judgmental approaches; there are psychic troubles. The victims are suffering and need acceptance. But the process of healing may well require an appeal to these patients to use every bit of their available freedom to grow in maturity and towards a truly human understanding of sexuality and its integration in the totality of their relationships with God, with themselves and with their fellowmen.

One of the commonest sexual aberrations is homosexuality (lesbianism in the case of women).[57] Whether it is widespread or confined to exceptional cases depends greatly on the given culture. In a culture where sex is an added article of consumption and uncontrolled experimentation with sex is a widespread trend, a high percentage of recurrence of homosexuality is to be expected.

Doctors and counsellors have to distinguish carefully between a deeply ingrained homosexual trend and an occasional homosexual experience. Furthermore, there are homosexual prostitutes without homosexual conditioning. In certain circles and subcultures there is a widespread phobic anxiety among people who fear that they are homosexual. The misgiving is often triggered by an imprudent remark by a friend or relative.[58] The phobia can actually lead to a mental collapse or a pseudo-homosexuality.

Persons who have a strong or exclusive trend to erotic attraction to their own sex but do not indulge in homosexual or lesbian activity should not call themselves or be labelled by others as homosexuals; it is better to speak of "homophilia". It is a great achievement if these erotic tendencies are kept on the level of genuine friendship, free from indecent behaviour.

Those who are ambivalent in their erotic attraction, that is, are attracted by people of the other but also of the same sex, can more easily develop a clear heterosexual pattern. A happy marriage will then remedy the situation.

Not infrequently, homosexual tendencies are combined with or linked to other psychopathologies. In these cases, therapy must be oriented to the deeper causes. Personal growth can then lead to a new balance within the dynamic components of the personality, including the sexual dimension.

It cannot be excluded that in some cases the homosexual mindset is based on the hereditary character. In this case it would be irreversible.[59] Most studies, however, agree that the majority of homosexual problems are either caused or at least aggravated by erratic behaviour patterns in the familial or immediate social environment. If a child goes through the painful experience of seeing father and mother as a threat to each other, and besides is constantly warned about the other sex as threat or danger, it is no wonder if a homosexual tendency develops as an unconscious posture of self-defence.

Today there are many homosexuals and lesbians who want to be what they are, and confirm each other in this position. Many will later regret it if they see themselves deprived of marriage and family and of abiding friendships.

It is the conviction of many therapists, as well as my own, that in most cases relatively young homosexuals (before their thirties) can be healed if they find a competent therapist and are strongly motivated. Greater efforts and successes in sex therapy can be hoped for. Much more should be done on the level of individual therapy, and even more in terms of prophylaxis dealing with the socio-pathological causes and implications.

V. EXPERIMENTATION WITH HUMAN BEINGS[60]

1. Man, the explorer and experimenter

In a certain sense, man is a self-creator although always as a steward under God. Man's experimentation has its prehistory in the long process of evolution, with its groping in the material and biological world. Without that groping and without a continuous gathering of experience, our existence in the present order of creation would not be conceivable. "We can never forget that the distinctiveness of man lies in creativity and freedom, even if they are limited."[61] The newness of the situation today is the systematic approach to experimentation. Man has invented the art of scientific experimentation and invention.

The great questions in bioethics deal with how far man can shape his *bios*, his biological endowment. The fact that he constantly does shape and reshape his psychological endowment cannot escape our attention. This question arises in the new context of awareness of how greatly human progress depends on scientific experimentation, the ongoing assessment of experience and systematic experimentation.

Man has to be careful when experimenting with highly explosive and dangerous material as, for instance, atomic energy. He has to be no less careful when experimentation extends to his biological and psychological endowments. Scientific experimentation has entered areas that are most sensitive and loaded with particular risks. We think, for instance, of brain research[62] and genetics, especially in cutting and recombining DNA. These fields of research promise great advantages for the whole of human life, but the risk cannot yet be fully assessed.

In this context the question arises of how much authority society delegates to the researchers.[63] There can be no doubt that in modern life experts enjoy high professional prestige and authority. However, where health, freedom and the life of countless people are at stake, society as a whole cannot simply delegate its authority to a professional group. Hence new problems arise, leading finally to the one question: "Who controls the controllers?"[64] Everyone should participate, according to his capacity, in the process of forming sound public opinion and influencing the decisions to be made on the levels of both the professional group and the state.

A number of ethical codes on experimentation with human beings try to set limits that, on the one hand, protect the dignity and freedom of each human being and, on the other hand, leave enough leeway for the progress of medicine and biology, to the advantage of the present and future generations. Well known is the Nuremberg code on "permissible medical experiments" that served as a guideline for trials against criminal experiments but was also intended to prevent similar crimes in the future. The most mature codification is the declaration of Helsinki: recommendations guiding doctors in clinical research, a resolution adopted at the 18th World Medical Assembly in June of 1964, by the World Medical Association.[65] Most of the modern states where a great deal of research is going on have added particular legislation for new fields like that of recombinant DNA technology.

2. Therapeutic experimentation

The covenant relationship between doctor and patient, and the climate of trust and respect so indispensable for therapy, disallow the use of a patient as a mere experimental subject. The doctor has to use the safest and most certain methods. However, he must be free to use a new therapeutic measure if, in his competent judgment, it offers hope of saving life, re-establishing health or alleviating suffering (Code of Helsinki II, 1).

Where the chances that traditional and approved methods will be less effective, the daring new ways will be more easily justifiable, but only in the hands of a truly competent doctor. The decisive criterion is the proportion between the hoped-for result and the risk of eventual harmful results for the patient. As far as possible, the doctor has to inform the patient or the family about the chances and the risks, and can act only with free consent. The hope must be assessed in view of the good for this individual patient and not in view of humankind as such. Non-therapeutic experiments with patients must be absolutely excluded. Permission must not even be asked for them.

3. Non-therapeutic clinical research

Non-therapeutic experimentation should be conducted only by highly qualified teams. The proportion between risk and the hoped-for progress must be carefully assessed, not by the team alone but also by other competent people. The programme must be most carefully planned, and during the process of experimentation there should be an ongoing evaluation of the projected research by competent non-participants as well as by the team.

In the history of medical progress, self-experimentation by doctors and researchers has played an important role. A medical author writes: "Whenever meaningful and possible, the self-experiment of the researcher should precede the test with others."[66] And if he finally asks others to participate, he should first ask himself most seriously if he would like his own wife or children or best friends to be participants. This thought would prevent disproportionate risks.

Informed consent by the volunteers is absolutely indispensable. They must be informed about the purpose, the meaning of the research, and about all foreseeable inconveniences and hazards reasonably to be expected. The consent should never be accepted before the volunteer has sought advice from others. It is most desirable to have persons outside the research group cooperate in the informing process and the continuing moral evaluation concerning whether or not, for a certain person, the experiment should be carried further or stopped.

The mentally retarded, who cannot give a proper informed consent, must never be invited to participate.

Prisoners of war and political prisoners must never be the object of non-therapeutic research. Their freedom and dignity should be guaranteed by law; but even where there is no written law, the moral imperative is self-evident.

In today's non-therapeutic experiments, prisoners in correctional systems are the main participants. Many ethicists feel that they should not be invited or admitted because of the total situation that might prevent truly free consent. In my opinion they should not be excluded if they truly want to participate, and if all guarantees are given that they are properly informed and in no way manipulated. However, I would thoroughly exclude behaviour-modification experiments with delinquents if Skinnerian methods are applied that disregard the dignity and freedom of the person. This does not exclude a genuine behaviour therapy for delinquents if they themselves desire it.[67]

Some ethicists veto any kind of non-therapeutic experimentation with children.[68] In my opinion, experimentation is acceptable if parents and tutors give an informed consent, and under the conditions that there is no discernible risk and the research is highly relevant for children. The reason for this opinion is that research, with all this caution, will better serve all children than the two alternatives of either giving up all new medications and treatments for children or using medications tested only for adults.

NOTES

[1]   Cf. Th. Bovet, *Die Ganzheit der Person in der ärztlichen Praxis*, Zürich, 1940; G. Sigmund, *Der kranke Mensch. Medizinische Anthropologie*, Fulda, 1951; H. Weicker, M. Eder, A. Jores and others, *Möglichkeiten und Grenzen der Medizin*, München, 1969[2]; B.P. Bliss and A.G. Johnson, *Aims and Motives in Clinical Medicine. A Practical Approach to Medical Ethics*, Pitman Medical, 1975; J. Zander (ed.), *Arzt und Patient. Erwartungen und Wirklichkeit*, Düsseldorf, 1976; G. Davanzo, *Etica sanitaria*, Milano, 1976; J. Wunderli and K. Weisshaupt (eds,), *Medizin im Widerspruch*, Olten/Freiburg, 1977; M.H.

Logan and E.E. Hunt (eds.), *Health and Human Condition: Perspectives on Medical Anthropology*, Boston, 1978.

2   E. Bieser, "Das Heil als Heilung. Aspekte einer therapeutischen Theologie", in J. Sudbrack (ed.), *Heilkraft des Heiligen*, Freiburg, 1975, 102-139.

3   Ignatius of Antioch, *Letter to the Ephesians* 7, 2.

4   G. Siegmund, "Die Deutung von Wunderheilungen", in *Arzt und Christ* 22 (1976), 87-97 (with bibliography).

5   E. Bieser, l.c., 139

6   Deutsches Institut für ärztliche Mission (ed.), *Auf der Suche nach Gesundheit*, Tübingen, 1979, 16f.

7   Cf. G.H. Schwabe, "Ehrfurcht als Lebensbedingung", in Sudbrack, l.c., 140-176.

8   V. von Weizsäcker, *Diesseits und jenseits der Medizin*, Stuttgart, 1953, 199.

9   R. Leuenberger, "Probleme um das Lebensende", in *Handbuch der christlichen Ethik*, Freiburg, 1978, II, 105; cf. H. Tews, *Soziologie des Alterns*, Heidelberg, 1971; L. Hayflick, B.L. Neugarten, D. Christiansen, E.W.D. Young, "Aging and the Aged", in *Enc. of Bioethics* I, 48-68; Arzt und Christ 20 (1974), N. 3/4: Probleme des Alterns (with bibliography).

10 D. Bonhoeffer, *Widerstand und Ergebung, Briefe und Aufzeichungen aus der Haft*, new edition, München, 1970, 407; A. Altenähr, "D. Bonhoeffers Gedicht 'Stationen der Freiheit' ", in *Studia Moralia* 15 (1977), 283-309; J. Mohana, *Soffrire e amare, Psicologia e teologia della sofferenza*, Brescia, 1975.

11 V. von Weizsäcker, l.c., 104.

12 R. Kautzky, "Die Bedeutung der Person des Menschen in der modernen medizinischen Wissenschaft", in *Arzt und Christ* 10 (1964), 172.

13 H.D. Engelhardt, in *Handbuch der christlichen Ethik* II, 61.

14 Cf. P. Krauss, *Medizinischer Fortschritt und ärztliche Ethik*, München, 1974, 65.

15 R. Degkwitz, "Was können wir unsere Gesundheit kosten lassen?" in *Handbuch der christlichen Ethik* II, 78.

16 Cf. C.J. Groesbeck, "Der Archetyp des verwundeten Arztes", in J. Sudbrack (ed.), *Heilkraft des Heiligen*, Freiburg, 1975, 177-208.

17 Codes of Medical Ethics, in *Enc. of Bioethics* I, 162-180.

18 Cf. *Free and Faithful in Christ* I, Chapter Six.

19 Cf. P. Ramsey, *The Patient as Person*, New Haven, 1970.

20 Cf. H.A. Davidson, "Professional Secrecy", in E.F. Torrey (ed.), *Ethical Issues in Medicine*, Boston, 1968, 193; W.J. Winslade, "Confidentiality", in *Enc. of Bioethics* I, 194-200.

21 Cf. J.C. McGilvray, "Auftrag und Dienst der Kirche bei Krankheit und bei der Frage der Förderung der Gesundheit", in *Auf der Suche nach Gesundheit*, Tübingen, 1979, 9-14.

22 Cf. R.W. McNeur, "Ein Versuch, das medizinische Modell zu verändern", in *Auf der Suche nach Gesundheit*, 20-28.

23 Cf. J.C. McGilvray, "Ungereimte und verworrene Vorstellungen über Gesundheit", in *Auf der Suche nach Gesundheit*, 19.

24 Cf. T. Heller, *Restructuring the Health Service*, London, 1978.

25 Cf. I. Illich, *Medical Nemesis. The Expropriation of Health*, London, 1975; Id., *Limits to Medicine*, London, 1977; H. von Nussbaum, *Die verordnete Krankheit*, Frankfurt, 1977.

26 *Auf der Suche nach Gesundheit*, Tübingen, 1979, 24.

27 l.c., 13.

28 Cf. V.R. Fuchs, *Who Shall Live? Health, Economics, and Social Choice*, New York, 1974; R. Tancredi (ed.), *Ethics and Health Care*, National Academy of

Sciences, Washington, D.C., 1974; R,M, Veatch and R. Branson, *Ethics and Health Policy*, Cambridge/Mass., 1976; E. Ginzberg, *The Limits to Health Reform. The Search for Realism*, New York, 1977; B.M. Ashley and K.D. O'Rourke, *Health Care Ethics: A Theological Analysis*, St. Louis, 1978; E.F. Oatman (ed.), *Medical Care in the United States*, New York, 1978; "Health Care, Health Policy", in *Enc. of Bioethics* II, 610-654.

29 Cf. K. Seybold and U. Müller, *Krankheit und Heilung*, Stuttgart, 1978.

30 Cf. V. Frankl, *The Doctor of the Soul*, London, 1969.

31 Cf. D.L. Farnworth and F.J. Braceland (eds.), *Psychiatry, the Clergy and Pastoral Counseling*, Collegeville, 1969²; E. Nase and J. Schafenberg, *Psychoanalyse und Religion*, Darmstadt, 1977; H. Burckhardt, *Der unverstandene Mensch. Psychologie oder Heilslehre?*, Freiburg, 1977.

32 Cf. D. Landy (ed.), *Culture, Disease, and Healing. Studies in Medical Anthropology*, New York, 1977.

33 Cf. A.J. Koemeda, *Überfordertes Dasein. Entstehung und Erscheinungsformen von Neurosen*, Freiburg, 1977.

34 V. von Weizsäcker, l.c., 64.

35 R. May, *Man's Search for Meaning*, New York, 1953, 95.

36 E. Fromm, *Man for Himself*, Greenwich, 1969, viii.

37 G.B. Blaine Jr., "Schools of Psychotherapy", in *Psychology and Pastoral Counseling*, Collegeville, 1969², 324 (323-330).

38 l.c., 324f.; A. Freud, *The Ego and the Mechanisms of Defense*, New York, 1964; cf. K. Horney, *New Ways in Psychoanalysis*, New York, 1966⁶.

39 C.G. Jung, *Analytic Psychology. Its Theory and Practice*, New York, 1968; Id., *Psychologie der Übertragung, Gesammelte Werke*, vol. 16, Zürich, 1958.

40 Cf. C.J. Groesbeck, l.c., especially 192-196.

41 G.B. Blaine, l.c., 328.

42 V. Frankl, *The Unconscious God: Psychotherapy and Theology*, New York, 1975; E. Fizzotti, *La logoterapia di Frankl*, Milano, 1974.

43 W.G. Allport, *Personality and Social Encounter*, Boston, 1960, 173.

44 C.R. Rogers, *Client-centred Therapy. Its Current Practice and Theory*, London, 1973³, 20; cf. Id., *On Becoming a Person*, Boston, 1961; G. Giordani, *La relazione di aiuto secondo l'indirizzo di Carl R. Rogers*, Brescia, 1977.

45 C.R. Rogers, *Client-centred Therapy*, 30.

46 C.F. von Weizsäcker, *Der Garten des Menschlichen. Beiträge zur geschichtlichen Anthropologie*, München, 1978², 592.

47 L.H. Beecher, in Cl.A. Frazier (ed.), *Faith Healing*, New York/Nachville, 1973, 59.

48 On behaviour modification see my book *Manipulation*, 109-136, 151-158; cf. R.M. Restak, *The Brain. The Last Frontier*, Garden City, 1979; R. Neville, "Behavior Control", in *Enc. of Bioethics* I, 85-93; M.E. Lloyd, "Behavioral Therapy", l.c., I, 101-107.

49 Cf. I.P. Pavlov, *Conditioning Reflexes and Psychiatry*, New York, 1941.

50 Cf. B.F. Skinner, *Beyond Freedom and Dignity*, New York, 1971; Id., *About Behaviorism*, New York, 1974, 149.

51 G.W. Schimmelpenning, "Das Sucht- und Drogenproblem", in *Handbuch der christlichen Ethik* II, 80-88; M. Keller, "Use of Alcohol", in *Enc. of Bioethics* I, 69-75 (with bibliography); R. Neville, "Drug Use, Abuse, and Dependence", in *Enc. of Bioethics* I, 326-334; cf. B. Häring, "The Therapy of Drug Addiction and Alcoholism", in *Medical Ethics*, 189-192; A. Legnaro, *Drogen und soziokultureller Wandel*, Köln, 1975.

52 G. Claridge, *Drugs and Human Behaviour*, London, 1970, 229-230; W. Feuerlein, *Alkoholismus – Missbrauch und Abhängigkeit*, Stuttgart, 1975; H. Haisch, *Hilfe für Alkoholiker und andere Drogenabhängige*, Mainz, 1977².

[53] Cf. J. Durand-Dassier, *Psychothérapies sans psychothérapeutes. Communauté de drogués et psychopatiques*, Paris, 1970.

[54] For bibliography on sex deviances see *Free and Faithful in Christ* II, 571, fn 165; W.H. Masters, V.E. Johnson, R.C. Kolodny (eds.), *Ethical Issues in Sex Therapy and Research*, Boston, 1977.

[55] W.H. Masters, l.c., 215.

[56] l.c., 216

[57] Cf. B. Häring, "Omosessualità", in *Dizionario enc. di teologia morale*, Roma, 1976⁴, 682-689; R. Gallagher, "Understanding the Homosexual", in *The Furrow* 30 (1979), 555-569.

[58] A. Massone, *Cause e terapia dell'omosessualità*, Varese, 1970, 83.

[59] l.c., 112ff., 117ff.

[60] Cf. J. Katz, *Experimentation with Human Beings*, New York, 1972 (with a most comprehensive bibliography); P. Krauss, *Medizinischer Fortschritt und ärztliche Ethik*, München, 1974, 79-101; B. Freedman, "A Moral Theory of Informed Consent" in *Hastings Center Report*, Vol. 5, N. 4 (Aug. 1975), 32-39; B.H. Bray, *Human Subjects in Medical Experimentation: A Sociological Study of the Conduct and Regulation of Clinical Research*, New York, 1975; V. Jackson (ed.), *Genetic Engineering: The Recombinant DNA Research Controversy*, Birmingham, Al., 1977; J. Wojcik, *Muted Consent: a Casebook in Medical Ethics*, West Lafayett, 1978.

[61] Ch.E. Curran, *Politics, Medicine and Christian Ethics*, Philadelphia, 1973, 203.

[62] Cf. B. Häring, *Manipulation*, 132-158.

[63] Cf. J. Katz, l.c., 376-513.

[64] Cf. B. Häring, *Manipulation*, 82-84, 207-211.

[65] Full text to be found in B. Häring, *Medical Ethics*, 209-212.

[66] P. Krauss, l.c., 90.

[67] Cf. J.S. Stumpfhauser (ed.), *Behavior Therapy with Delinquents*, Springfield/ Ill., 1973.

[68] Cf. P. Ramsey, *The Patient as Person*, 20ff.

Chapter Three

Death and Dying

The search for a holistic vision of human life and health, and especially our own experiences of sickness and suffering, confront us constantly with the question of death - our death. Human life in the body is a life towards death. In the midst of our life, death is our neighbour. How we face death, our own and that of others, is revealing for the life of the individual and for the quality of our society and culture. It is a basic criterion of how we face truth, which includes the truth that our life is destined to death. This of itself makes it necessary for moral theology to give special attention to the subject of death and dying.[1] But over and above that, the progress of modern medicine and the mentality of our culture also pose ever new problems that demand our attention and a fresh approach.

I. DISCOVERING THE MEANING OF DEATH

1. A question of "to be" or "not to be".

Whether one can face the reality of death, and the way one faces it are questions about being or not being fully human. Heidegger's focus on the subject of death is ontological, in that he claims that one's awareness of death raises the fundamental question of what it means for anything to *be*. The chief feature of his work is a theory on the meaning of death, which shows that "facing one's own personal death concretely offers life a purposefulness and urgency that would otherwise be lacking."[2] It is not just a matter of thinking about death but of facing the reality of my own mortality and how all of my life relates to my death.

In Rainer M. Rilke's thought, confronting one's death becomes spontaneously a prayer: "Lord, give to everyone his death, the death that arises from his life, in which he found love, meaning and distress." The conscious experience of human fragility striving for one's personal identity within the human family makes the experience of pain, sickness and the prospect of death an integral part of one's life. Ivan Illich considers as basic for truly human health the capacity to integrate these experiences autonomously.[3] Not an abstract thought about death but a penetrating self-examination about "what will be my death?" is decisive for the discovery of the whole truth about one's life.[4]

To face the merciless fact of living constantly in the shadow of death is particularly important for the healing profession. The relationship with patients, and especially with the moribund patient, will depend greatly on how the health professionals have integrated in their own life the reality of their mortality.[5] The existential attitude of the doctor or nurse to death will determine not only all of his or her relationships but also the very understanding of the healing profession.

The decision to face one's mortality and to confront life with the meaning of one's death is a part of our fundamental option. The fundamental option for the good can easily be aborted if we refuse the truth about our death.

2. Natural mortality

By his very nature, man is mortal. He has only one life history on earth. Death belongs to his historical reality as much as birth.

The story of the Fall in Genesis does not speak of mortality as such, but of a life of distress and pain as a consequence of sin. It does not contradict the generally prevailing vision of the Old Testament that "on the one hand the death of an individual man can occur through divine punishment, but on the other hand, that mortality of the human race belongs to the divine order of creation."[6]

If we say that death belongs to the very nature of man, this does not mean that he experiences death as something quite natural. "It is in the face of death that the riddle of human existence becomes most acute. Not only is man tormented by pain and by the advancing deterioration of his body, but even more by a dread of perpetual extinction. . . Man rebels against death because he bears in himself an eternal seed which cannot be reduced to sheer matter."[7]

The "fear and trembling" with which man approaches death, the anguish which the riddle of death causes for many people, is not only an expression of the natural desire for immortality; it also has to do with the historical situation of fallen humankind. And that very situation manifests itself iń the fear and trembling with which Jesus took death upon himself, though he knew it to be a redeeming death.

In the language of the New Testament and the Christian liturgy, death entered into human history because of sin. But this does not necessarily mean that, in the original design, man would not have died at all. New Testament writings and the liturgy state simply that we are "set free from death." Salvation language does not mean the mere physical fact of death but its overall meaning. So we can say that death, as we have to face it, is both natural and unnatural. The Second Vatican Council says: "that bodily death from which man would have been immune had he not sinned will be vanquished, according to the Christian faith, when man who was ruined by his own doing is restored to wholeness by an almighty and merciful Saviour."[8]

Death, in its total meaning, must be seen in the perspective of creation, the Fall and Redemption. Physical death receives its meaning from one's fundamental option of faith in the death and resurrection of Christ, or from the refusal of salvation.

3. Is our death a curse?

"As sin established its reign by way of death, so God's grace might establish its reign in righteousness, and issue in eternal life through Jesus Christ our Lord" (Rom 5:21). The apostle Paul speaks of the "perishable being" of the "first man" (1 Cor 15:47-

54). This does not necessarily mean that mortality, in itself, is a curse. What makes death and dying horrifying is the fact that unredeemed man cannot integrate death into his life, and the sinner refuses to accept it in the new dimension that Christ gave it.[9]

The question of whether death is still judgment and curse cannot be answered in the abstract. Each of us has to ask existentially, "Do I accept death in conformity with Christ and in the hope of resurrection, or do I choose the old curse in sin solidarity?"

We treat here particularly natural death as distinguished from unnatural death, premature death caused by a hostile environment or individual and collective irresponsibility. By "natural" death we mean the death of a person who has fully lived his or her life, which then comes to an end through old age. We have to live our life responsibly so as not to be guilty of an early and, in this sense, "unnatural" death. But the more important task is not just to reach this natural death but rather a redeemed dying as the crowning of a redeemed life, whether in old age or in earlier years.

By the divine promise of the Redeemer, the death of the faithful is no longer a curse. Christ is the Victor over death, and by faith we participate in his victory, praising our liberation: "The life-giving law of the Spirit has set you free from the law of sin and death" (Rom 8:2). Yet we are constantly tempted by our own selfish self and enticed by collective selfishness. "Those who live on the level of our lower nature (our selfish self) have their outlook formed by it, and that spells death; but those who live on the level of the Spirit have the spiritual outlook, and that is life and peace" (Rom 8:5-6). Our lower, selfish nature has no claim upon us. But we live in a world that is "made the victim of frustration" (Rom 8:20); hence, even those "to whom the Spirit is given as first fruit of the harvest to come, are groaning inwardly" (Rom 8:23).

Despite his or her faith, the dying Christian can suffer estrangement in an alienated environment. One's outlook on death can be perturbed by a pessimistic teaching in the religious community and by the failure of the society in which one lives to reach the truth about a redeemed death. The readiness to open oneself to the dire aspect of death and to its redeemed horizons is also affected - helped or hindered - by the conduct of those nearest to the dying person, and by the total quality of the culture.

4. From denial to acceptance

Although the Christian does not see death as the final catastrophe, he has to take responsible care of his life; and this very love of life as a God-given gift and task precludes an untimely death. To live until one's lifetime has reached its fulfilment in the love of God and neighbour is a just desire. It is natural to resist death before our time is fulfilled.

When the sick or wounded person realizes that death is more or less irreversibly approaching, a process begins that can become either a creative detachment or a frustrating refusal. E. Kübler-Ross notes that in this period the dying person normally goes through the following stages: (1) denial and isolation; (2) anger and resentment; (3) bargaining and attempt to postpone; (4) depression and sense of loss; (5) acceptance.[10] The process is in no way automatic. An unfavourable environment, lack of assistance, efforts to deceive the dying person can block the development of this creative detachment.

The description of the stages given by Kübler-Ross "is a useful framework for those who work with terminal patients."[11] The quality of the creative detachment and the death itself depend greatly on personal relationships and on the meaning the person has discovered or given to his or her life. Frequently it is observed that healthy personal relationships allow a longer life than the diagnosis supposes.

The useful typology must not, however, induce anyone to forget the uniqueness of each person and of the personal death. A strong believer can reach a quite different positive acceptance of death than another person whose faith is not so deep and who was not totally dedicated throughout life to the will of God. Yet, from my own experience in assisting dying persons, I must add that, not infrequently, I was surprised by the serenity and trust that persons could finally attain - persons who, during their life, were less than successful in combating sin.

5. Summit of freedom?

Man the maker, if he has never come to a deep and grateful perception of his dependence on God, the giver of life, will experience death as loss, as final destruction of his freedom. But man the adorer, having lived his life in gratitude and as a co-worker with God, the giver of all that is good, can reach the summit of human freedom in facing death.

Dietrich Bonhoeffer, who gave his life in the cause of freedom for all, wrote most meaningfully about freedom in accepting death, once he had become aware that he would probably be executed. "Not only the action but also the suffering is a way of freedom. Liberation occurs in suffering when a man can detach himself from his cause and entrust it into the hands of God. In this sense, death is the crowning of human freedom. Whether the human action is a matter of faith or not will be decided by whether he understands suffering as the continuation of his action, as completion of his freedom, or not. I find this very important and very consoling."[12] His acceptance of death allowed him to say, "On the road to freedom, death is the highest feast."[13] And his poem on the stages of freedom explains this: "Only for a moment you blissfully touched freedom, then you handed it over to God, that he might blissfully perfect it."[14]

This does not mean that one disposes of the highest level of freedom at the immediate moment of death. The question is whether, while still enjoying consciousness and freedom, one has accepted one's life, all that is good and beautiful, in view of death, trusting that it is the door to final freedom in God. "We die not just at the end but throughout life."[15]

Christian faith celebrates the victory of Christ on the cross; and when we proclaim the death of the Lord until he comes, we understand and accept our death both in the light of his painful death and of his glorious coming.

Christians do not need flight from death. Christian faith forbids us "to seek analgesics in a way that we would not be able to drink freely with Christ the chalice of death."[16] We can humanize death in the sight of the cross and resurrection of Christ by preparing ourselves throughout our whole life. Nevertheless, if we perceive the truth of approaching death, we might well have the special grace and unique opportunity to gain the summit of our freedom, entrusting ourselves into the hands of God in the deepest knowledge and sharing of the death and resurrection of Christ that we could possibly reach in a lifetime.

With death, the earthly history of human freedom comes to an end, and it should be an end that honours freedom. This is a central criterion for medical ethics dealing with the edges of life. What good is it for the dying person if the death process is prolonged at the cost of loss of consciousness and freedom? Yet prolonging a life irreversibly doomed to death can be meaningful if it allows the patient to reach out for the highest possible freedom in accepting death, and in his or her relationships honouring these decisive moments of life.

Death cannot be experienced as summit and feast of responsible liberty by those who irresponsibly cause their early death. In the western world, four causes of death are rapidly increasing: first, heart infarction; second, lung cancer and bronchitis; third, cirrhosis of the liver; fourth, traffic accidents. Heart infarction is frequently the result of overeating and/or psychological stress; lung cancer and bronchitis are often the consequence of cigarette smoking and, to some extent, of air pollution; cirrhosis of the liver is almost always a consequence of irresponsible use of alcohol; and the countless deaths by traffic accidents are caused by senseless haste, often combined with alcohol or drug abuse. The government of West Germany reports that about 140,000 citizens die an early death each year because of smoking, while another 100,000 smokers are made invalids before their due time.[17] Such deaths cannot be for anyone the crowning and feast of liberty without a rebirth through repentance.

II. ABORTING THE MEANING OF DEATH AND LIFE

Aborting the meaning of one's own death or that of others is surely a great sin. However, we speak of sin only in the context of our positive vocation to help each other to discover the meaning of life and of death, and to realize it in freedom. It is a question of co-responsibility, of creative liberty and fidelity.

1. Repressing the prospect of death

Our western consumer society does not help to make death an event of freedom; it does all it can to repress the thought of death. Our whole social system, even the new family structure, avoids the thought or appearance of ageing and death. Most people die in hospitals and nursing homes where their existence is hidden as much as possible from the public eye. The atmosphere in highly technical modern hospitals, especially in the intensive care units, surely does not humanize death. And in the outside world, the normal exposure to consumer products and their advertisements fosters a mentality described by the prophet Isaiah: "Let us eat and drink; for tomorrow we die" (Is 22:13).

In preparing for a meaningful, freely accepted death, the best help is the experience of people who, dying, give us this witness. But today, many people seldom if ever have the opportunity for such an experience. The fact that so many people are practically set aside before their physical death is an enormous challenge to every Christian and the whole church and, of course, to a civilized society. How can those who inflict or accept for others a kind of social and psychological death make their own death a summit of freedom? Depriving others of vital relationships, denying them practically the right to participate in the moulding of the life around them, is nothing less than inflicting on them social death.

We shall later address ourselves to the grave problem of the enormous efforts spent by a segment of the medical profession to prolong the death process, thereby diminishing or making impossible that loving care that would allow death to be an event of freedom.[18] People can so suffer from the loss of all vital relationships that it may seem that they are already buried while still alive.

2. Denial of death in medical practice

The purpose of medicine is to restore health and diminish suffering, especially when the course towards death is irreversible. But frequently the medical profession is thoroughly imbued with the ideology that their overall purpose is to fight death and prolong life as long as it is technically possible. The consequence often is that suffering is not only senselessly prolonged but the thought of death is repressed also. Practically no help is given to the dying to die their own death, to prepare themselves for the highest possible awareness and freedom, and to live the last days and hours of their life in the most meaningful human relationships.

To free the healing profession from this ideology is perhaps one of the most urgent tasks of medical ethics. Members of the profession have to be dedicated, above all, to freedom, and especially to that freedom that allows creative detachment and final acceptance of death.

3. Suicide and euthanasia

Entrusting one's life into the hands of God at the proper time, and giving one's life to the service of others even if this should lead to an earlier death, are totally different from throwing one's life away as worthless.

One of the most frequent causes of death today is suicide. It is all too easy to explain the cause of suicide as "mental disturbance". In many cases it is the result of social death, of being deprived of the most basic and vital communications. Suicide then means, "You have already deprived me of those relationships that give meaning to life; now you have my dead body to bury." An attempt at suicide is sometimes the last resort, "a communication, a cry for help to persons important to the attempter."[19]

The word "suicide" covers quite different phenomena. There can be an egoistic suicide: a person who does not want to be for others or to live with others cuts all the bonds by the act of suicide. Or it can be an act of plain despair about the meaning of one's life under concrete circumstances, or even despair about any meaning to life. Again, it can be the rare case of altruistic suicide, the heroic sacrifice of one's life in order to save others from great evils.

The meaning and frequency of suicide are "influenced by historical, cultural, social and personal relationships, and no single psychological, social or medical theory suffices for its understanding and prevention."[20] Historically, suicide was not infrequently a "form of euthanasia", a way of escaping mistreatment and a humiliating death at the hands of the enemy. This is so in the case of Saul (1 Sam 31:3-5) and of Samson

(Judges 16:22-31). The author of the book of *Judges* seems to consider Samson's action somehow meritorious, a part of his ongoing fight against the enemies, besides seeking a more honourable death than at their hands.   The euthanasia which we address here enters into the realm of suicide and cooperation with it. It is a kind of manslaughter, not to say murder. I expressly exclude from this text on euthanasia the quite different decision not to prolong life where this decision is in no way a refusal of treatment that would be helpful.

I am aware that the word "euthanasia" historically had a quite different meaning. It could mean: (1) affectionate and competent assistance to give the dying person the experience of loving care and caring love, and thus to make his death the best possible; (2) a kind of treatment which, by its nature and by the agent's intention, alleviates the pain of the dying process but has a foreseeable side-effect of shortening the life; (3) what moralists and doctors sometimes called "passive euthanasia", which meant giving up technically possible means of prolonging life. I shall treat this question separately in order to avoid confusion; (4) what Hitler's national socialism called "euthanasia" and "mercy killing", whereby his agents mercilessly and systematically killed people considered undesirable or useless for their purposes. The word "euthanasia", intending the best possible death, is clearly out of place here; (5) vastly different meanings, where an agent inflicts death upon himself or another, by commission or omission, and with or without the consent of the person who is to disappear from the theatre of life.[21]

What we are directly treating of here is: (1) shortening life consciously and directly by withholding helpful treatment to which the patient is entitled (negative euthanasia) or (2) directly taking measures to bring that life to an end or to shorten it (positive euthanasia). In both cases there is a positive decision against the life of the other, against the commandment "not to kill". Surely, there is a great difference between the robber who beat the man who came from Jerusalem and the priest who passed over to the other side. But for a doctor, the case is much more serious, since the patient is entrusted to the doctor by a covenant which obliges him or her to do no harm, to commit no sin against the patient's life by the very profession he or she exercises.

Promoters of the right to euthanasia use mainly two arguments:

first, compassion in view of the suffering, and second, the quality-of-life argument. The motivation from unbearable suffering becomes less and less convincing since, in almost all cases, modern medicine has new and very effective means of combating great pain, means that do not deprive patients of consciousness.[22]

The quality-of-life argument in favour of euthanasia, because of its unavoidable consequences, is the most harmful for life in society. It is based on the presumption that there are people who have the right to judge whether or not other persons' lives are still worthwhile and valuable for their living together. Their judgment can not only be contemptuous, but it represents a death sentence. Although some would confine this argument to cases in which consciousness is lost or the death process seems to be irreversible, in principle it would entitle others to pass judgment on our life and to execute us on the basis of their evaluation. Such an attitude would never be confined to the narrow limits that some would originally assign to it.

The ideological basis of many promoters of euthanasia is a dangerous application of Darwin's theory of the survival of the fittest, which he himself did not apply to the present history of civilized people.[23] The main cause of freely accepted or desired euthanasia - the desire to be killed either by neglect of treatment or by direct measures - is the feeling of "social death", the feeling that, for others, they are already dead and buried because they are refused the most basic social communications.[24]

Some argue that in the case of idiocy, these persons are, by that very fact, socially dead, since fully human communication is not possible. But communication is not limited to lofty ideas; there is a communication of love, and this is still possible. Bonhoeffer's response was simply that here, too, we are faced with human life. There is always a divine communication and a response required from us: "The question whether, in the case of innate idiocy, there is human life at all is so naïve that it scarcely demands a response. It is life born from people, sick life that can be nothing other than human life although a most unfortunate one."[25]

Most promoters of euthanasia make the consent or the request of the suffering person an absolute condition. To assist by direct cooperation in the desire of the person is then not considered as murder. The presupposition remains, nonetheless, that the suffering person has the right to decide about his or her death, a right to suicide and, as a consequence, a right to be assisted in it. However, this presupposition is wrong. The argument of Thomas Aquinas, it seems to me, is still valid: "Because life is God's gift to man, whoever takes his own life sins against God even as he who kills another man's slave sins against that slave's master."[26] According to Karl Barth, suicide is an "act of ingratitude, a failure to recognize that God is the 'owner' of human life."[27]

4. Duty to prevent suicide

There is much discussion about the duty to prevent suicide or to save the life of another against his own will.[28] Frequently the argument for the duty to prevent suicide is that a person tries to commit suicide only in a moment of mental disturbance, and therefore must be helped. Under this presupposition, the help does not contradict respect for the liberty of the other. But this argument is not generally valid, because a person might try to commit suicide in full consciousness.

A strong argument in favour of the duty to prevent suicide and to deny a request for euthanasia (mercy killing) is the well-established fact that attempts at suicide and requests for euthanasia are, in most cases, a last desperate cry for more attention and love, for more effective help.[29] If this is true, the best prevention is not just to interfere in the attempt or to impose constant control, but to give loving attention and competent help. Thielicke tells the story of a man completely and hopelessly crippled who, crying out for euthanasia, found much sympathy and effective efforts at rehabilitation. The happy result was a renewed will to live and an astonishing improvement in health.[30]

Preventing suicide is a duty of much broader dimensions than is normally seen.[31] The deeper causes have to be discovered and, as much as possible, removed. "If suicide prevention is not to be merely palliative, it must involve an attack on more general forms of malaise within society."[32]

The fact that the attitude towards suicide and euthanasia and the frequency of these phenomena depend greatly on a given culture[33] is a great challenge to all who have accepted their Christian mission to be "salt for the earth and light to the world". The moral principles must not simply be adjusted to cultures, but cultures must be reformed and renewed in view of the highest and abiding values. If we could change the weather, we would not be content to offer umbrellas to people. The casuistry relating to euthanasia and techniques to deter individual cases become meaningful only within a strategy of shared reflection and action to change the world. On this point, Christian individualists had to be shaken by Karl Marx.[34]

5. Against legalization of euthanasia

Suicide and euthanasia cannot be treated solely within the realm of individual ethics; they are also problems of social ethics in that they concern all basic human relationships.[35] The protection of life and the problems raised by suicide and euthanasia impose great responsibility on legislators. I am thoroughly against any form of legalization of euthanasia. A state that legalizes it would undermine the ethos of the healing profession and the trust of patients in the members of this profession.

The state has to promote and protect the solidarity of the family. Legalization of euthanasia would all too easily tempt weak families to suggest to their burdensome members that they choose euthanasia and thus leave the theatre of life. If it were to become a legal right even under limited circumstances, it would turn into an explicit or implicit public appeal to the sick and the aged to consider whether the hour had come to request the "service" of euthanasia. This would strengthen all the dangerous trends that inflict a kind of social death on the aged and suffering. The state would then no longer be in the service of the weak, the suffering and the elderly.

The legalization of euthanasia would also strengthen the trend towards suicide by those who, explicitly or without so many words, are told that they are a burden to others and to society.

And further, if euthanasia were to become a legal right for patients and doctors, it might split the medical profession into those who absolutely respect life and those who are willing to kill on request.

If a doctor, in a very extraordinary situation, feels entitled or obliged to act against the law as a kind of conscientious objector, then he should be willing to give a public account in view of a law that fulfils an indispensable function in a civilized society. It is not simply a question of law sanctioning moral principles but a basic question of the common good and the fulfilment of an important function of the legislature.

III. THE MOMENT OF DEATH AND THE PROCESS OF DYING

1. Cortical death versus cardiac arrest

On the occasion of the first heart transplant, the public became aware of a new concept of death: brain death. However, the concentration on brain death has brought new uncertainties.

Brain death means that death is determined on the basis of neurological criteria, thus distinct from cardiac death determined by cardiological criteria. But the question of how the neurological criteria should be used has not yet been decided. Some speak more specifically of "cortical death".[36] These argue for a new concept of death determined solely by the cessation of the higher faculties of the brain, the cerebral cortex, upon which cognition and personality depend, thus contradicting the "whole-brain-oriented" concept of death.[37] The fact is that after the complete and irreversible cessation of the higher brain (cortex), the primitive brain or brain stem can continue to enable respiration. This means that after cortical death, respiration is still possible.

The movement of the heart can be even more independent of nervous system control. Neurologists speak of the "apallic syndrome" when the organism continues to "live" at the metabolic level only - respiration and heartbeat - while those parts of the brain controlling consciousness, cognition and other distinctively human expressions are irrevocably dead.[38]

Thielicke expresses the opinion of many when he asserts that with irreversible cessation of those parts of the brain without which there can be no communication and consciousness, "human existence ceases."[39] But this opinion does not stand uncontradicted. J. Wunderli thinks that "babies born without a distinctively human brain, and dying persons with the apallic syndrome are 'living human beings' who may lack what is distinctively human but, as living human beings, have the right to

a maximum of care."[40] Robert Reichardt would disallow a direct
action to bring this remnant of human life to an end, but would
require only minimal care.[41] It might be argued that after the
cortical death there might still be processes in the brain stem
comparable to dreams.[42] Here it becomes evident that the
problems of declaring death and of allowing someone to die are
quite distinct.[43]

2. Artificial reanimation

The redefinition of death draws a line between what is called
"brain death", where irreversible changes have taken place that
destroy the functioning of the central nervous system, and what
has been called "metabolic death" where the functions of the
heartbeat and respirations have ceased. Through artificial means,
resuscitation is still possible after cortical death. Through life-
support systems, the organism can continue to "live" at the
metabolic level while the person, as agent, is dead.[44]

The possibility of reanimation or resuscitation in intensive care
units is an ambiguous advance in the medical field. About one in
thirty resuscitated persons never awakens to consciousness but
continues to function as an organism with the apallic syndrome.[45]
For others, the results of resuscitation may be a few more days or
hours of "dying life".[46] There is frequently a great risk of
impaired psychic life. The problem is that decisions must be made
quickly, and when the doctors consider their main purpose to be
"preserving life", sometimes more harm than good is done to the
patient and his or her family. Resuscitation should never be
undertaken if there is considerable risk that the cerebral cortex is
already essentially damaged.

3. The irreversible coma

With the progress in diagnostic means, doctors can often
identify with absolute or moral certainty the irreversible coma
that predicts death without return to consciousness, but does not
indicate when the death process will end. The person in
irreversible coma must still be treated as being alive. Organs for
transplant cannot be taken until the fact of death has been
definitely determined. If artificial support is successful enough to
be continued even for a long period of time, but holds no

significancee for recovery, this kind of prolongation of the death process serves no one.

"The complete destruction of the brain, including loss of spontaneous respiration, may occur while the cardiovascular system continues to function autonomously. Apnea (the absence of spontaneous respiration) has been considered by most medical authors to be a cardinal sign of total brain destruction."[47] In a significant number of moribunds deep in coma from trauma or from deterioration, "artificial support is successful enough to be continued indefinitely with no prospect that the patient will ever recover, but also with no point in sight at which bodily functions will cease so long as medical care continues."[48]

4. Organ transplant

Organ transplantation poses a number of problems regarding human relationships, personal and social responsibility, and foreseeable psychic and other consequences. One of the problems in transplanting a living organ from a dead person is how to determine the death that authorizes removal of the organ before there is any danger of decomposition. In principle, there is no ethical problem if, after the death is proved, blood circulation (perfusion) is continued in order to preserve the organ that is considered for transplantation. It is, in fact, only a matter of removing organs from an unburied corpse.[49]

However, a problem centres around cortical death in apallic syndrome cases. Ulrich Eibach holds, against Pompey and others, that the removal of an organ is not at all allowed in cases of the appalic syndrome but only after total brain death.[50]

Many think that modern medicine has given disproportionate effort and expense to organ transplantation. Heart transplants have not had lasting success. However, they did contribute to the development of new forms of open heart surgery.

The kidney is the most frequently transplanted organ. Heart, liver, lung, pancreas, and especially corneal and bone marrow transplants are also performed clinically. The discovery of immunosuppressive agents and of tissue-typing and blood-typing have made modern transplants possible and successful.[51] A person with blood-type O can get an organ transplant only from a donor of the same blood-type; an AB type can get one from any donor, and so forth.

At the beginning, only kidney transplants from twins were successful, then transplants from relatives, due to the similarity of tissue antigens. Today, except where the donor is related, the results from kidneys of live donors are no better than those from kidneys of cadavers. This is especially true in the United States, where many states allow death to be declared when there is no evidence of brain function. "The heart can still be beating and the patient can be on a respirator. Consequently, the internal organs are usually functioning normally."[52] In most European countries, however, a person is declared dead only when the vital functions of heartbeat and breathing have ceased. According to recent statistics, patient survival for recipients of cadaver allografts are comparable to those treated by dialysis. Dialysis is not only much more expensive but also causes much more distress and discomfort. But "most physicians would agree that some patients do better with chronic dialysis and others with kidney transplants."[53]

The subject of kidney transplant from a living donor brought about a long-lasting and passionate discussion within the Catholic community. With many theologians, I emphasized from the very beginning the high moral value of a free gift. But a number of moral theologians considered it to be absolutely immoral. The negative group evaluated the "mutilation" or "self-mutilation" as an act in itself instead of evaluating the total meaning of the removal of an organ and giving it in a life-saving action. Their main argument was a concrete understanding of the principle of totality explained by Pope Pius XII: "Outside the organism, the organ has not, by its very nature, any sense, any finality. It is wholly absorbed by the totality of the organism to which it is attached."[54]

Augustine Regan distinguished the main concern of the Pope's utterances as defending the individual against a totalitarian concept of society that would allow infringement on the integrity of one's bodily life. But while the organ has its direct meaning within the whole organism, it is as much a part of the whole person in his/her sublime vocation of fraternal charity. Thus the well-ordered gift of an organ is the fulfilment of man's highest vocation. This does not mean, however, that a search for self-perfection would justify this application of the principle of totality. "In theological perspective, it is precisely a departure from self that guarantees a satisfying return to self, even if that return is not the primary or dominant motive of departure in self-giving."[55]

The criterion is the due proportion of benefit to the recipient and the loss or risk to the donor. Informed consent is an absolute condition for its admissibility and the inner value. No pressure of any kind must be exercised. This free gift creates a new bond of friendship between the donor and the recipient. The relationship is healthy only to the extent of the freedom of the gift and the gratitude of the recipient.[56]

Organ donation on the part of persons incapable of informed consent is morally unacceptable except in the case where the future of the donor greatly depends on the survival of the recipient. Normally, the gift of a kidney from a living person should not be requested or accepted if a fitting cadaver organ is available.

5. Legal regulation of transplant from a cadaver

Many lives could be saved by the transplant of a kidney taken from a cadaver, and many blind persons could have their sight restored by a cornea taken also from a cadaver. The possibility depends on the generosity of people and on the legal regulations surrounding the determination of death and the removal of organs from cadavers.

In the United States, an average of 2500 kidney transplants from cadavers are performed, while about 60,000 patients die annually from renal failure. There would be a sufficient supply of transplant centres if enough organs were available.[57] The situation is even less favourable in West Germany. In 1976, only 246 kidney transplants were performed, and some of the kidneys came from neighbouring countries. As a consequence, there is general recognition of the need for legal regulations favouring life-saving transplants.[58]

There are basically two possibilities: (1) the routine taking of needed organs if no objection is registered; (2) the premortem donation of organs by individuals. Paul Ramsey and others favour the premortem donation because it better promotes a consensual community and expresses freedom and generosity.[59] Ulrich Eibach favours the first solution with a good argument. The point of departure would be that we honour people by the presumption that generally, if properly informed, they would realize the high moral value of allowing doctors, after one's death, to remove an organ in view of saving another's life or restoring sight, and so on. Giving the possibility to every citizen and to his or her family to register objections would be enough to guarantee freedom.

A further important argument is that, psychologically, it is not easy to approach the family in the terrible moment of shock, asking for permission, and precious time is being lost.[60]

However, because it touches a most sensitive area of life, the legislator has to take into account the attitudes of the average citizen. The first step is not a law but the forming of a sound public opinion.

IV. THE HEALING PROFESSION AND THE MORIBUND PATIENT

1. Favouring consciousness, freedom and communication

The healing profession tends to concentrate one-sidedly on healing, as such, or on the prolongation of life. Facing the moribund patient in an irreversible process towards death is, however, one of the highest challenges for the medical profession.

The primary task is loving attention and solidarity, an attitude and conduct that communicates to the dying patient that he is not an object but a most valuable companion. Everything has to be done to help the patient to reach the summit of his or her freedom and faithfulness. "Moribund and dying patients need, unto their end, special sympathy and personal attention. They expect human nearness and care. They should be spared estrangement through local or psychic isolation."[61]

Except in rare cases, any medical treatment of the moribund person that aims at prolonging life to the detriment of consciousness, the capacity to communicate and the identity of the person, is radically irresponsible.[62] This principle is not easily safeguarded in highly modern intensive care stations where the whole surrounding armature directs attention to the functioning of discrete organs more than to the dying patient who frequently seems to be at loss, forgotten as a person.

2. The moribund patient's right to truth

A truthful and trustworthy relationship between doctor and patient is a condition for healing in a holistic sense. When it is a question of communicating the truth about one's terminal illness, there must exist a healthy mutual relationship of trust and loving concern.

In a more paternalistic age when doctors thought that they alone could and must make the proper decisions, they were easily induced to withhold all information that could disturb the patient's feelings. They did not credit enough their patients' desire to know the truth and their ability, in most cases, to integrate it.

A good number of studies have shown that, for most moribund patients, open awareness is an optimum setting. Studies have also proved that people, while in good health but also in bad, express their desire to be properly informed. They want their nurse and their doctor to advise them not only on vital decisions such as surgery, but also on matters of personal concern, like family problems before their departure. But above all, they want to live the truth of their situation. Any consoling words by doctors who, on principle, are not willing to tell the truth are no consolation at all but a degrading experience.

Several studies in the western world show, however, that there is an enormous difference between the thinking and attitudes of the doctors on the one hand and, on the other, the great majority of lay people.[63] This is especially true with regard to the question of whether doctors should, when possible, inform the patients about their terminal illness. A considerable number of doctors acknowledge that they seldom speak openly with their moribund patients about their death. "With amazing consistency, however, individuals indicate themselves as capable of desiring the necessary information to understand their prognosis, while being less certain that others are similarly desiring."[64]

Recent inquiries seem to indicate a change of attitude in at least a considerable minority of doctors who have freed themselves from a paternalistic concept and want their patients to be truly their partners. However, the fact that the majority of the health professionals have not changed might be partially explained, as Robert Veatch suggests, by uncertainty about diagnosis and prognosis, but even more because physicians tend to have a uniquely high fear of death. "If an individual has high or low fear of death, and then asks himself what the impact would be on another of disclosure of terminal illness, he may systematically misjudge the impact by appealing to his own high or low death fear."[65]

Bowers states the problem even more forcefully. "Truth at the bed of the sick is less the problem of those who should be informed than rather of those who have to communicate truth".[66] Thielicke points in the same direction, asking the basic question about whether the physician himself is "in the truth", whether he has discovered the truth about his own relationship to life and death, for instance, by knowing the Lord over life and death. "Has he reached clarity about the basic truths about life and death, and has he confronted himself with them, then he will be able to find the word of truth."[67] Without this existential condition, there is no solution to the problem of how to communicate the nearness of death.

The Christian knows that the truth exists only in love. A truth that requires and enables a fruitful and final decision can be communicated only with a great sensitivity and great compassion. For while it is true that genuine love requires truthfulness, this truthfulness, as a requirement of a harvest of love, will be patient and wait for a favourable moment.[68] Life is an unfolding of truth and love, and the communication of such an existential fact as the approaching messengers of death needs a sense of graduality. Temporary silence or momentary emphasis on the still remaining hopes in view of uncertainties of diagnosis can be plain lies if they arise from an unwillingness to speak truth; yet they are a communication of love in truth and truth in love if they are aiming at the best possible communication.[69]

Unfortunately, the modern doctor frequently has not time to sit down with the sick and to pursue patiently the full process of communication.[70] And in modern education, not enough is done for this great art of truthfulness and discretion in communication.

3. Cooperation

In today's hospital, "the team" takes care of the sick. The task of informing the moribund patient does not fall only on one physician. It is a co-responsibility, and therefore a shared spirit of solidarity with the sick must become operative. The most negative expression of the team is a conspiracy of silence or even of deception up to the last moment. The ideal is a conscious cooperation of all the members of the healing profession, including the chaplain, with the family and friends of the dying person.

Some hospitals have a specialized chaplain who is psychologically prepared to deal with moribund patients and to assist the nurses and visitors by instruction and advice on how to act responsibly and to radiate peace in truth. Eventually, the chaplain can also coordinate the difficult gradual process of helping the dying patient to understand his or her situation and to accept it.

In various parts of the world, precious efforts have been made by nurses, nuns and others who dedicate themselves almost exclusively to assisting the lonely, aged and dying people in their private homes or in hospitals. They pray with the patient and establish that personal friendship that allows them to communicate the truth of the Lord's coming for his final visit and his final invitation to stay always with Him.

The desire of the dying patient to die at home in the midst of his or her beloved should not easily be refused, especially if the family also wants it.

4. After death

After the death of a patient, the role of the hospital chaplain, the doctors and nurses, has not ceased. They have an important task to assist the members of the dead person's family in these crucial moments and hours.

In the Middle Ages, some theologians considered the funeral as a kind of sacrament, a visible and consoling sign of our Christian hope of the resurrection, a shared experience of the communion of saints. The honour we give to the body of the dead is meaningful when we realize that those who have gone to their rest are with us and, being with God, are even nearer to us than before their death.

V. ADDING LIFE TO THEIR DAYS OR PROLONGING THE DEATH PROCESS?

1. The newness of the problem

Regarding the edges of life, the progress of medicine is sometimes ambivalent. Regarding the beginning of life, we have seen the ambiguities surrounding amniocentesis and selective abortion. In the case of approaching death, there are today enormous possibilities for prolonging life in a way that nobody is helped, neither the sick person nor the family. Frequently this is not so much adding true life to the patient's days as it is adding burdensome days to the process of death.

a) Important distinctions

The question of whether to prolong life by all kinds of means or by some means has different answers if (1) there is some hope to restore health or at least to give back to the patient a tolerable life; (2) we are faced certainly with a sickness that irreversibly leads to death; (3) we are faced with imminent and irreversible death, that is, with the process of death. These are three different situations that require different approaches by the healing profession.

The new situation makes it necessary to take a new look at the traditional distinction between "ordinary" and "extraordinary" means; for what are already ordinary means in one area are still extraordinary in another, and what earlier were extraordinary means and generally not helpful can be helpful today, or can be ordinary means for some situations and in no way helpful in others.

b) Who shall live?

The main question in this section is, rather: who should be allowed to die? This question arises sometimes in conflict situations where we are faced with the other question: who shall live?

It can happen frequently that the best qualified personnel and the most modern techniques are used to prolong the death process of some patients while these techniques are not available for those whose life could be saved. Besides, there is the question of the allocation of funds. Are there not enormous means allocated and practically used only for prolonging unconscious life of people doomed to death? Yet there are surely not enough means allocated for those who could be healed and rehabilitated.

As a medic in World War II, I was frequently faced with the crucial question: who among these dangerously wounded people should receive my first help? The decision had to be made in one moment.

In the highly modern hospitals with well-equipped intensive care stations, two quite different problems can arise. First, because personnel and equipment are available, people are delivered and treated in these stations who would better be allowed to die in more desirable conditions than in the midst of all this machinery and disturbance. The second and most frequent problem is: who should be given first treatment, for instance, access to the dializer? Should the order of the waiting list decide, or are there other more important criteria?

Generally, the following criteria are used: (1) whoever is most urgently in need and still can be saved should be given the first place; (2) those who have the better chance to be restored to health, in comparison with those whose illness irreversibly will lead to death; (3) a decisive criterion is the hope or lack of hope to restore the person to a conscious life and normal communication; (4) last but not least, there must be considered the sick or injured person who is irreplaceable by other persons, for instance, a parent of children or even of handicapped children, who still need education or personal care.[71]

2. Ordinary versus extraordinary means

Traditional moral theology relied greatly on the distinction between ordinary and extraordinary means, sometimes without distinguishing whether the case was one of prolonging life in an irreversible and deadly sickness or one where health could be restored. Catholic and non-Catholic ethicists and even court decisions quote the Pius XII Discourse of November 24, 1957:

"Normally one is held to use only ordinary means - according to circumstances of persons, places, times and culture - that is to say, means that do not involve any grave burden for oneself and others."[72]

Today "ordinary" means are equated with standard treatment, and "extraordinary" with unusual means. To profit from the wisdom of the past tradition, we have to explore what was really meant by the distinction between ordinary and extraordinary.

The extraordinary was considered a treatment where the risk and pain was out of proportion with the hoped-for benefit to the patient. It is the disproportionate risk and suffering that make the means extraordinary. But traditionally, when the family alone had to bear the whole burden, attention was also given to the proportion between the family's financial burden - or the grievance caused thereby to the patient - in comparison with a dubious result.

Since many countries today have medical programmes that promise standard treatment for all, it might be better to evaluate the proportion of the hoped-for medical help by comparing the expenses for armaments with the total allocation of funds for medical care. In wealthy nations, the expense should be the last point to be evaluated, but still there must be some proportion between expense and the hoped-for health.

The concrete decision also has to take into consideration the personal judgment of the patient if, for instance, he or she has a great desire to die in the midst of the beloved at home rather than to endure the prolongation of terminal illness in estrangement in the hospital.

In the evaluation, no difference should be made between people useful for the process of production and handicapped or retarded people. Wherever there are beneficial means available, decisions to treat or not to treat should be the same for the normal and abnormal alike. "If an operation to remove a bowel obstruction is indicated to save the life of a normal infant, it is also an indicated treatment of a mongoloid infant."[73]

3. A *new vocabulary*

In view of the new situation, many ethicists and doctors propose abandoning the traditional vocabulary "ordinary" versus "extraordinary" in favour of "beneficial" (or "helpful") versus "nonbeneficial".[74]

Thielicke puts it this way: "unto what boundary does helping still really help?"[75] The discussions on this important question centre round the traditional principle of medical ethics: "to do no harm". Man is not obliged to fight against death under all circumstances. "To preserve or to prolong life at the price of losing the capacity to create, to believe and to love is theologically and ethically not to be approved. To renounce such treatments is no arbitrary disposal about the meaning and value of life determined by God, and not a decision against the person and his or her life, and does no harm to his or her dignity."[76]

It is not easy to determine what is beneficial in general, and it is even less easy to determine in the case of an individual person. But there are at least approximate criteria. The principle, "first of all to do no harm" allows, according to traditional medical ethics, the infliction of suffering and loss only in order to remove a greater evil and to obtain a proportionately greater benefit.[77]

According to W. K. Frankena, the principle of beneficence says at least the following four things: first, one ought not to inflict evil or harm (what is bad); second, one ought to prevent evil or harm; third, one ought to remove evil; fourth, one ought to do or promote good. The last (fourth) is not a duty in the strict sense but in the sense that one feels that the first takes precedence over the second, the second over the third, and the third over the fourth.[78] Where it is decided that it is right to inflict injury on patients, it is on the grounds that life and health will be better served by causing the injury - for example, surgery - and that, if not in the short run, certainly in the long run, pain and suffering will be diminished by this intervention.[79]

"Beneficial means" is not necessarily the same as "standard treatment". Of course one should not reject standard treatment for his patient unless he is sure that the application is not at all beneficial. Sissella Bok dares to deal with a concrete and delicate problem: "Take the case of the person dying of cancer, in great pain, close to death, who develops pneumonia. Certainly antibiotics are now the standard arsenal of medicine; yet many would consider it cruel and extraordinary to use them to prolong such a patient's care."[80]

A grave question is whether the evaluation of "beneficial"

versus "non-beneficial" may take into consideration convictions about the quality of life. The problem does not centre around dying terminal patients but around non-dying terminal patients or others who, at the price of painful and detrimental interventions, can survive.

Paul Ramsey warns against "the entrance of a quality of expected life policy into medical practice."[81] Of course a judgment on "quality of life" can never justify mercy-killing. The question is whether a doctor, before he uses all the modern means of treatment, may or must take into consideration what kind of life would result. Ulrich Eibach speaks on an "enormous number of defect-healings of which many are much more signs of failure and ambivalence of modern medical progress than those which, without these means resulted in death."[82]

Most experts in medical ethics would, certainly, allow the patient to refuse an intervention that probably might be life-saving but reduce his life to extreme misery. "Both the dying and the incurable, if conscious and competent, have a right to refuse treatment, or better said, to participate in the choice of their treatment (including the choice of no further expected cures)."[83]

The question must be asked whether the doctors should not, in solidarity with the patient's family, come to the conclusion to give up possible life-saving treatment that once was extraordinary but today is standard treatment, if there is a high probability that medical "success" would make life miserable beyond the true proportion. We cannot avoid taking into consideration the quality of life. However, as Christians we do this in the light of the Paschal Mystery, the suffering, death and resurrection of Christ, in view of the capacity to suffer and to love in the midst of suffering, and always in view of the great commandment of love for God and neighbour, which includes the willingness to sacrifice in the care of the sick.

4. The right to die with dignity

From all corners comes the accusation against members of the healing profession that they use the highly developed modern methods in an inhuman way, to prolong the dying process at any cost.[84]

In 1977, the Swiss Academy of Medical Sciences and the

German Society of Surgeons issued guidelines for physicians, claiming for them wide discretion. They favour permitting doctors not only to initiate but also to discontinue medication as well as technical measures such as respirators, blood transfusions, chemodialysis, intravenous nourishment, if the dying person's basic condition has taken an irreversible course and the use of these measures would mean unreasonable prolongation of sufferings.[85] This has nothing to do, however, with euthanasia or with direct killing or denying any beneficial means.

If the dying patient is still conscious and competent, he or she must absolutely be a partner in any important decisions regarding his or her death. But the doctor should honestly inform the patient if he is certain that all the life-saving means can do nothing more than prolong the death process and increase the suffering beyond acceptable limits.[86]

When there is no longer reasonable hope of saving the life of the patient or prolonging it in a beneficial way, either the patient or those closest to him should participate in the choice of action after receiving the necessary information. However, if the patient is in coma and the death process is irreversible, the physician should normally not burden the family members with the hard decision to remove life-supporting means. Where the physician does not take this decision, Pius XII spoke in an approving tone about families who bring pressure to bear on the physician "to remove the respirator so as to allow the patient, already virtually dead, to depart in peace."[87]

In all these discussions about "death with dignity", as Christians "we try to reconcile the conflicts between the needs of the individuals, their families, the requirements of society and the tradition of good professional medical ethics."[88]

Reanimation should not be initiated whenever there is a disproportionate risk that the patient may be impaired beyond what is tolerable for him and his beloved. In West Germany there are about 50,000 reanimations each year, and at least each thirtieth will "live" with the apallic syndrome, which means with cortical death but with the primitive brain stem somehow alive.[89] And many others would never have allowed reanimation if they would have known the sad results.

In cases where withdrawing the life-support systems leads most probably to immediate death, the external appearance might be

that this is actually causing the death; and direct killing can never
be allowed. However, the meaning of this cessation of a no longer
beneficial treatment is not killing, but removing an artificial
obstacle that impedes the natural process of death. It is not even
a question of indirect killing. The very meaning of the action itself
as well as the intention of the attending physician is not to kill or
to bring the life to an end, but only to remove meaningless
obstacles in a senseless fight against the imminent death. The
action can also be justified by the traditional arguments about an
action with double effect.[90]

The fear that doctors may not allow the patient to die with
dignity but might, instead, impose treatment, the overall effect of
which would be considered hurtful, has induced many people to
participate in that decision while they are still in good health. The
"living will" is a communication undertaken by a person when
fully competent. It is called "the right to death with dignity". In
Germany it is usually called "a letter of the patient". One
communicates one's will and conviction about the kind of
treatment one considers beneficial or not beneficial even if it is a
question of death and life. This makes clear the person's intention
as participant with the doctors in the ultimate decision.[91] Of
course the physician is not bound by such a "living will". Good
medical ethos, however, will move the doctor to give special
consideration to this will if it is still in effect at the time of
decision and is not unreasonable.

5. From healing to caring

The decision to give up non-beneficial treatment - treatment
that would only prolong the death process and cause
disproportionate suffering - does not mean that the doctor
retreats from the patient absolutely. Health professionals have not
only the duty to save life and prolong it, but equally as well the
duty to care for those whose life cannot be saved.

Dyck speaks of "benemortasia", which includes at least the
following care for patients whose death is considered imminent:
to relieve pain and suffering, to give loving attention and
nearness, to respect the patient's right to refuse treatment, to
make the patient as comfortable as possible, and to do all this
regardless of the patient's ability to pay.[92]

If the Christian doctor has established a relationship of mutual trust with the patient, the latter, if he or she is a believer, will greatly appreciate the doctor's offer to join together sometimes in prayer. This last phase of life requires, above all, the loving presence of the chaplain, whose role also includes sustaining the family and friends of the dying person, and helping them to make their visits a real comfort to the sick.

Feeding the patient is an important way of communication, and should therefore be done with special care and cheer. If the patient is conscious but cannot take food in the normal way, artifical feeding should be offered as long as the patient wishes it. Withholding food is not the same as withholding non-beneficial treatment. It would be more like withholding communication. If, however, the patient is irretrievably unconscious, artificial feeding may be stopped if it becomes too difficult.

The present situation of estrangement of the dying patient in the modern hospital, and especially in the intensive care unit, has led to a constructive initiative pioneered twenty-five years ago by Dr Cicely Saunders at St Joseph's Hospice in London. In Great Britain, and now lately in the United States, there are a number of these hospices. There is no effort to prolong the death process by means that are not really helpful, but intensive assistance is offered by a multi-disciplinary team of physicians, nurse clinicians, social workers, members of the clergy and volunteers who provide competent care for the dying patients and their families, either at home or in special health facilities or in a special section of a hospital. There is absolute honesty and truthfulness about our mortality, and a loving effort to confront the situation of death and dying. Everything is done to make the patients feel comfortable and "at home", and to let them experience that they are loved and fully respected in their particular situation.[93]

NOTES

[1] General bibliography on Death and Dying: K. Rahner, *On The Theology of Death*, New York, 1961; Id., "Das Sterben vom Tod her gesehen", in *Mysterium Salutis* V, Zürich and Einsiedeln, 1976, 473-493; *Archives of the Foundation of Thanatology*, New York, 1969, 1970, 1971 and so on (with abundant bibliography); W. Shibles, *Death. An Interdisciplinary Analysis*, Whitewater/Wisc., 1974; D.P. Brooks, *Dealing with Death - A Christian*

Perspective, Nashville, 1974; F. Cutter, *Coming to Terms with Death. Facing the Inevitable with Wisdom and Dignity,* Chicago, 1974; J. Caruso, *Die Trennung der Liebenden. Eine Phänomenologie des Todes,* Bern and Stuttgart, 1975; E. Jüngel, *Death: The Riddle and the Mystery,* Philadelphia, 1975; O. Thibault, *La maîtrise de la mort,* Paris, 1975; G. Heuse, *Guide de la mort,* Paris, 1975; J. Ziegler, *Les vivants et la mort. Essai de sociologie,* Paris, 1975; E.-H.W. Kluge, *The Practice of Death,* New Haven and London, 1975; P. Steinfels and R.M. Veath, *Death Inside Out: Hastings Center Report,* New York, 1975; J. Ch. Hampe, *Sterben ist doch ganz anders,* Stuttgart and Berlin, 1976; M. D. Heifetz, Ch Mangel, *Das Recht zu sterben,* Frankfurt, 1976; Ph.A. Ariès, *Studien zur Geschichte des Todes im Abendland,* München, 1976; St. Baum, *Der verborgene Tod - Auskünfte über ein Tabu,* Frankfurt, 1976; G.H. Poteet, *Death and Dying. A Bibliography (1950-1974),* Troy/N.Y., 1976; P. Sporken, *Umgang mit Sterbenden. Medizinische, pflegerische, pastoral-ethische Aspekte der Sterbehilfe,* Düsseldorf, 1978[4]; R.M. Veatch, *Death, Dying and the Biological Revolution: Our Quest for Responsibility,* New Haven, 1976; J. Feiner, "Die Krankheit und das Sakrament des Salbungs-gebetes", in *Mysterium Salutis* V (1976), 494-550; L.-V. Thomas, *Anthropologie de la mort,* Paris, 1976; U. Eibach, *Medizin und Menschenwürde. Ethische Probleme in der Medizin aus christlicher Sicht,* Wuppertal, 1976 (with abundant bibliography); H.Ch. Piper, *Gespräch mit Sterbenden,* Göttingen, 1977; W. Hofer (ed.), *Leben müssen - sterben dürfen. Die letzten Dinge, die letzte Stunde,* Bergisch Gladbach, 1977; D. Landy and others, "Death", in *Enc. of Bioethics* I, New York, 1978, 221-307 (with abundant bibliography); E. Kübler-Ross, *Leben bis wir Abschied nehmen,* Stuttgart, 1979; Id., *On Death and Dying,* New York, 1968; J. Glover, *Causing Death and Saving Life,* London, 1979[2]; H. Thielicke, *Wer darf sterben?,* Freiburg, 1979.

[2] D.M. High, "Death. Definition and Determination", in *Enc. of Bioethics* I, 304; cf. M. Heidegger, *Sein und Zeit,* Gesamtausgabe Bd. 2, Freiburg 1977, 319, 349, 353.

[3] Cf. I. Illich, *Die Enteignung der Gesundheit - Medical Nemesis,* Hamburg, 1975, 180.

[4] Cf. R. May, *Man's Quest for Himself,* 65.

[5] Cf. U. Eibach, l.c., 145.

[6] L. Wächter, *Der Tod im AT,* Stuttgart, 1967, 203.

[7] *Gaudium, et spes,* 18; Commentary by J. Ratzinger, *Das Zweite Vatikanischen Konzil* III, Freiburg, 1968, 333-335.

[8] *Gaudium et spes,* 18c.

[9] Cf. E. Jüngel, *Tod,* Stuttgart, 1971, 98ff.; H. Gollwitzer, *Krummes Holz und aufrechter Gang. Die Frage nach dem Sinn des Lebens,* Düsseldorf, 1971, 109.

[10] Cf. Kübler-Ross, *Death and Dying,* New York, 1968.

[11] R.A. Kalish, "Attitudes Toward Death", in *Enc. of Bioethics* I, 287.

[12] D. Bonhoeffer, *Widerstand und Ergebung, neue Ausgabe,* München, 1970, 407, cf. 308.

[13] l.c., 408.

[14] l.c., 403.

[15] K. Rahner, *Grundkurs,* 390.

[16] l.c., 390.

[17] U. Eibach, l.c., 535f.

[18] Cf. U. Eibach, l.c., 309; K. Jörns, *Nicht leben und nicht sterben können, Suizidgefährdung und Suche nach dem Leben,* Göttingen, 1979, 136.

[19] D.H. Smith and S. Perlin, "Suicide" in *Enc. of Bioethics* IV, 1618.

[20] l.c., IV, 1620.

21 Cf. J. Wunderli, "Möglichkeiten und Grenzen ärztlicher Lebenserhaltungs pflicht", in J. Wunderli (ed.), *Medizin im Widerspruch*, Olten and Freiburg, 1977, 199ff.; general literature on euthanasia: P. Mohr, *Die Freiheit zum Tod*, Hamburg, 1973 (one of the first German writers after Hitler who favours active euthanasia); D.C. Maguire, *Death by Choice*, Garden City/N.J., 1974; K. Menninger, *Selbstzerstörung, Psychoanalyse des Selbstmordes*, 1974; J. Wunderli, *Euthansie oder Über die Würde des Sterbens*, Stuttgart, 1974; H.-D. Hiersche (ed.), *Euthansie. Probleme der Sterbehilfe. Eine interdisziplinäre Stellungnahme*, München and Zürich, 1975; J.A. Robertson, "Involuntary Euthanasia of Defective Newborns: A Legal Analysis", in *Standford Law Review* 27 (Jan. 1975), 213-267; J.A. Behnke and S. Bock (eds.), *The Dilemma of Euthanasia*, Garden City/N.Y., 1975; Th. Lohmann, *Euthanasie in der Diskussion. Zu Beiträgen aus Medizin und Theologie seit 1945*, Dusseldorf, 1975; V. Eid (ed.), *Euthanasie oder Soll man auf Verlangen töten?*, Mainz, 1975; J. Toulat, *Faut-il tuer par amour?*, Paris, 1976; A. Eser (ed.), *Suizid und Euthanasie als human- und sozialwissenschaftliches Problem*, Stuttgart, 1976; Sacra Congregatio pro Doctrina Fidei, "Declaratio de Euthanasia", in *AAS* 72 (1980) 542-552 gives a very clear and detailed response to this problem. My definition of "euthanasia" is exactly the same as that of this important document.

22 Cf. A. Mayrhofer and P. Porges, "Möglichkeiten und Grenzen der Schmerz-ausschaltung mittels Nervenblockade", in A. Eser (ed.), l.c., 121-124.

23 Cf. U. Eibach, l.c., 280.

24 Cf. K. Jörns, l.c., 17f.

25 D. Bonhoeffer, *Ethik*, München, 1964[7]; cf. U. Eibach, l.c., 287, 295ff.

26 S.Th. II/II, 64, 5.

27 K. Barth, *Church Dogmatics*, vol. III, Edinburgh, 1961, pt. 4, 402.

28 Cf. D.H. Smith and S. Perlin, "Suicide", in *Enc. of Bioethics* IV, 1618-1627 (with abundant bibliography).

29 l.c., 1624f.; cf. U. Eibach, l.c., 232; P. Sporken, "Euthanasie im Rahmen der Lebens- und Sterbehilfe", in A. Eser (ed.), l.c., 278ff.

30 H. Thielicke, l.c., 27.

31 H. Pohlmeier (ed.), *Selbstmordverhütung. Anmassung oder Verpflichtung?* Bonn, 1978; K.P. Jörns, *Nicht leben und nicht sterben. Suizidgefährdung und Suche nach dem Leben*, Göttingen and Freiburg, 1979.

32 D.H. Smith and S. Perlin, l.c., 223ff.

33 Cf. D. Landy, "Death: Anthropological Perspective", in *Enc. of Bioethics* I, 223ff.

34 H. Thielicke, l.c., 55.

35 Cf. B. Häring, "Moraltheologische Überlegungen zu Suizid und Euthansie", in A. Eser (ed.), l.c., 261-270; Id., "Eutanasia e teologia morale", in P. Beretta (ed.), l.c., 221-232.

36 G.F. Molinari, "Criteria for Death", in *Enc. of Bioethics* I, 292-296; A.M. Capron, "Death: Legal Aspects", in *Enc. of Bioethics* I, 296-301; W. Kösl and E. Scherzer (eds.), *Die Bestimmung des Todeszeitpunktes*, Wien, 1973.

37 Cf. R.M. Veatch, "The Whole Brain-Oriented Concept of Death: An Out-moded Philosophical Formulation", in *Journal of Thanatology* 3, N. 1 (1975) 13-30.

38 H. Goerke and others, *Der Grenzbereich zwischen Leben und Tod*, Göttingen, 1976, 102-108.

39 H. Thielicke, l.c., 63.

40 J. Wunderli, *Euthanasie oder Über die Würde des Sterbens*, Stuttgart, 1974, 108.

[41] R. Reichhardt, "Ethische und soziologische Probleme im Grenzbereich zwischen Tod und Leben", in H. Goerke, l.c., 45-67.

[42] l.c., 50.

[43] A.M. Capron, l.c., I, 298ff.

[44] T. Parsons, "Death in the Western World", in *Enc. of Bioethics* I, 259.

[45] Cf. U. Eibach, l.c., 299, 403.

[46] A.R. Jonsen and G. Lister, "Life-supporting Systems", in *Enc. of Bioethics* II, 845.

[47] G.F. Molinari, l.c., 293.

[48] A.M. Capron, l.c., 396.

[49] H. Thielicke, l.c., 50.

[50] U. Eibach, l.c., 313f.; W. Ruff, SJ, *Organverpflanzung. Ethische Probleme aus katolischer Sicht*, München, 1971; H. Pompey, *Fortschritt der Medizin und christliche Humanität. Der Dienst der praktischen Theologie an einer Medizin im Umbruch*, Würzburg, 1974; Id., "Gehirntod und totaler Tod. Moraltheologische Erwägungen zur Herztransplantation", in *Münchener med. Zeitschrift* 111 (1969), 736ff; R.V. Calme, "Transplantation", in *Journal of Medical Ethics* I, N. 2 (1975), 59-60; T. Dalyell, "Tissue for Transplantation", l.c., 61-62; J. Mahoney, "Ethical Aspects of Donor Consent in Transplantation", l.c., 67-70; M. Honecker, "Ethische Überlegungen zur Dialyse und Transplantation", in *Zeitschrift für Evangelische Ethik* 19 (1975), 129-147; J.G. Ziegler (ed.), *Organverpflanzung*, Düsseldorf, 1977; A.L. Jameton, "Organ Donation", in *Enc. of Bioethics* III, 1152-1160; R.J. Howard, J.S. Najarian, R.C. Fox, R.A. McCormick, "Organ Transplantation", in *Enc. of Bioethics* III, 1160-1173.

[51] R.J. Howard and J.S. Najarian, l.c., 1160.

[52] l.c., 1161.

[53] l.c., 1160.

[54] Pius XII, AAS 44 (1952), 779-789, quote pp. 786-787; cf. AAS 48 (1956), pp. 461-462.

[55] R.A. McCormick, "Organ Transplantation: Ethical Principles", in *Enc. of Bioethics* III, 1171; A. Regan, "The Basic Morality of Organ Transplantation between Living Humans", in *Studia moralia* 5 (1968), 320-361.

[56] Cf. R.C. Fox, "Organ Transplantation: Sociological Aspects", in *Enc. of Bioethics* III, 1166-1169.

[57] *Enc. of Bioethics* III, 1164.

[58] Cf. Die rechtliche Regelung der Organtransplantation, *Protokolldienst der Evangelischen Akademie Bad Boll* 6/1979 (with abundant bibliography).

[59] P. Ramsey, *The Patient as Person*, New Haven, 1970, 212-214.

[60] U. Eibach, l.c., 496-497.

[61] Resolution of the German Society of Surgeons, 1979, N. V.

[62] U. Eibach, l.c., 169, 391; K. Rahner, "Die Freiheit des Kranken in theologischer Sicht", in *St. d. Zeit* 100 (1975), 31-40.

[63] For the USA see R.M. Veatch, "Truth Telling: Attitudes", in *Enc. of Bioethics* IV, 1677-1682; A. Pustet, *Die Wahrheit am Krankenbett*, München, 1969²; H. Gödan, *Die sogenannte Wahrheit am Krankenbett*, Darmstadt, 1972; E. Ansohn, *Die Wahrheit am Krankenbett. Grundfragen einer ärztlichen Sterbehilfe*, Hamburg, 1975; P. Bolech, J. Huber, "Die Kommunikation der Wahrheit am Krankenbett", in *Arzt und Christ* 22 (1976), 97-102; P. Sporken, *Umgang Mit Sterbenden*, Düsseldorf, 1978⁴.

[64] R. Kalish, Attitudes Toward Death", in *Enc. of Bioethics* I, 290.

[65] R.M. Veatch, l.c., 1681, referring to R. Schulz and D. Ademan, "How the Medical Staff Copes with Dying Patients: A Critical Review", in *Omega* 7 (1976), 11-21.

[66] M.K. Bowers (ed.), *Wie können wir Sterbenden beistehen?*, München, 1971, 100.

[67] H. Thielicke, l.c., 71.

[68] R. Leuenberger, *Handbuch der christlichen Ethik* II, 112.

[69] Cf. *Free and Faithful in Christ* II, 39-54 ("Truthfulness and Discretion in Communication"); cf. H. Thielicke, l.c., 74.

[70] Cf. S. Bok, "Truth Telling: Ethical Aspects", in *Enc. of Bioethics* IV, 1683.

[71] Cf. U. Eibach, l.c., 468ff., 181.

[72] Pius XII, quote in *The Pope Speaks* 4 (1958), 393-398; cf. H. Thielicke, l.c., 30; S. Bok, "Euthanasia", in *Enc. of Bioethics* I, 270.

[73] P. Ramsey, *Ethics at the Edges of Life. Medical and Ethical Intersections*, New Haven, 1978, 192, cf. 206.

[74] Cf. P. Ramsey, l.c., 177.

[75] H. Thielicke, l.c., 13.

[76] U. Eibach, l.c., 343; cf. 345, 254ff.

[77] Cf. A.J. Dyck, *On Human Care*, Nashville, 1978², 73.

[78] W.K. Frankena, *Ethics*, Englewood Cliffs, N.J., 1973², 47.

[79] A.J. Dyck, l.c., 88-89.

[80] S. Bok, "Death and Dying: Ethical Views", in *Enc. of Bioethics* I, 271.

[81] P. Ramsey, l.c., 182, where he expresses himself polemically against R.A. McCormick's article, "To Save Life or to Let Die: The Dilemma of Modern Medicine", in *America*, July 13, 1974, 6-10; Oct. 5, 1974, 169-173.

[82] U. Eibach, l.c., 504.

[83] P. Ramsey, l.c., 182.

[84] I. Illich, *Die Enteignung der Gesundheit - Medical Nemesis*, Hamburg, 1975, 9f., 53ff., 115ff.; U. Eibach, l.c., 525ff.; H. Thielicke, l.c., 34ff.

[85] Cf. V. Eid, R. Frey (eds.), *Sterbehilfe oder Wie weit reicht die ärztliche Beistandspflicht?*, Mainz, 1978, 23.

[86] R.M. Veatch, *Enc. of Bioethics* I, 279; cf. Resolution of the German Society of Surgeons, in *FAZ*, April 26, 1979, N. 79; Text of the Swiss Academy of Medical Science in V. Eid, l.c., 56-59.

[87] Pius XII, Discourse to Doctors, November 24, 1957, AAS 49 (1957), 1029.

[88] Cf. M. McGatch, "Death and Dying: Post-biblical Christian Thought", in *Enc. of Bioethics* I, 235.

[89] U. Eibach, l.c., 433.

[90] Cf. R.A. McCormick, *Ambiguity of Moral Choice*, Milwaukee, 1973, 1-112.

[91] Cf. R.M. Veatch, "Euthanasia and Sustaining Life", in *Enc. of Bioethics* I, 280-282; W. Uhlenbrink, "Der Patientenbrief - die privatautonome Gestaltung des Rechtes auf einen menschenwürdigen Tod", in NJW, 1978 N. 12, 566-570.

[92] A.J. Dyck, *On Human Care*, Nashville, 1978², 83ff; cf. Resolution of the German Society of Surgeons, loc. cit.

[93] Good information and reflections on the Hospice Alternative in *Hospital Progress*, March 1979, 37-76.

PART TWO

Healing of Public Life

In all of his mission, Christ the Redeemer, the Saviour, is also the Healer. With St Irenaeus and our best tradition, I see redemption and the whole history of salvation as therapeutic intervention coming from God through Jesus Christ by the power of the Holy Spirit. Therefore, just as Christians cannot privatize their faith and hope, so also must they manifest their participation in the healing presence and coming of Christ. My health and yours, our healthy relationships, and our self-actualization in ongoing conversion and healing stand in absolute interdependence with the therapy offered by Christ to a world sick and estranged by lack of gratitude, by arrogance and all forms of selfishness.

I have treated medical ethics as a part of social ethics, a part of our co-responsibility in and for the world. Healing and health are not matters just for the "healing profession". We all are inducing our illnesses and their dangerous course by not caring for a healthy style of life, for healthy relationships and a healthy environment. And we all can aim at true human health only by taking our share of responsibility for the health of those around us and, indeed today, for the health of the millions of people suffering starvation because of a chaotic economic and political situation in the world.

We express our faith in Christ, the Saviour of the world, in true orthodoxy and orthopraxis by joining actively in the fight against the evil and alienating powers in the world. We do this by committing ourselves to restore fully human conditions, not only where our I-Thou relationships are concerned, but equally and simultaneously in public life, by working for more humane structures in the cultural, social, economic and political spheres, for peace among all people and against the threat and evil of war and armaments, the greed of consumerism and the abuses of power.

We are not indulging in unrealistic dreams about a paradise on earth. We harmonize our faith in redemption already wrought, with the essential dimension of our hope, which has its pledges but is *not yet* reaching the final goal.

The vision in this last part of my comprehensive moral theology is that of "healing the public life"[1], a process which, like that of the healing profession, never comes to an end until the final coming of Christ.

Looking back on the first part of this volume, I want to state, with D. Roessler, that "the structures of health care activities are as good and as bad as the society under consideration".[2] But human health is not total absence of disturbances and crises. Rather, it is the capacity to live with them, mastering them to a certain point, and being able to integrate the rest into the whole of life. The same is true of our efforts to bring forth a healthier world. We do not indulge in superficial optimism or in an ideology of absolute progress, but we believe that in the midst of crises there is a place for creative fidelity and freedom.

As believers, we shall never accept foul compromises with injustice, falsehood, an arms race and all those attitudes and situations that lead to terrorism and war. Faith in the death and resurrection of Christ, and trust in the Holy Spirit will prevent us from despair and non-involvement as much as from ideologies of easy progess. The saving truth is that we are reconciled and can act as reconcilers, that we can be more radically converted and work more faithfully for a healthier, more humane world. Letting Christ shine upon us (Eph 5:14), we receive the gospel consolation and mandate, "You are light to the world" (Mt 5:14-16).

NOTES

1 The expression, "Healing of Public Life" expresses the programme of one of the earliest pioneers of Catholic social thought and action, Franz Josef Ritter von Buss, in his three volume work, "System der gesamten Armenpflege" (1843-1846); cf. H. Schipperges, "Zum System der Armen und Krankenpflege des Ritter von Buss" in *Renovatio* (Regessburg) 32 (1976), 2-9.

2 D. Roessler, "Ethos des Arztes der Zukunft", in *Renovatio* 32 (1976), 103.

Chapter Four

Responsibility in and for the world

Creative liberty and fidelity in Christ, genuine self-actualization in self-transcending love and justice, imply world-wide openness, a sense of mission to manifest by one's whole life the dimensions of God's covenant with humanity and with the world. The very faith-relationship in Christ, the adoration of God in spirit and truth engender responsibility in and for the world.[1]

The Second Vatican Council focuses our "attention on the world of men and women, with the sum of those realities in the midst of which that human family lives. It gazes upon the world which is the theatre of man's history, and carries the marks of his energies, his tragedies and his triumphs; that world which the Christian sees as created and sustained by its Maker's love, fallen indeed into the bondage of sin, yet emancipated by Christ."[2]

Since I consider the whole social ethic in the light of the Lord's word, "You are light to the world" (Mt 5:14), it is necessary to clarify our understanding of what we mean by world. This meaning is succinctly expressed by the Council text quoted above, and must be deepened in the light of the whole Pastoral Constitution on the Church in the Modern World. However, this and the following chapters concern not only the relationship between church and world but the whole realm of human and Christian responsibility in and for the world.

The English word "world" and the German "welt" come from the old-germanic root "weralt", which originally meant the

114

"community of men", but also the ambiance in which people live and which they, in turn, shape. The Greeks saw in the world a "kosmos", the well-ordered and somehow divine realm, of which man considered himself very much a part, and to which he had to submit. The biblical view, however, and even more the modern outlook sees the world in total interdependence with human history: a world entrusted to creative human freedom, to be shaped and re-shaped, a world not only to be contemplated but also to be transformed.

Our theme here is on responsibility in a Christian perspective, addressed above all to Christians, but not in an integralistic sense, as if the world were just the task or even the monopoly of Christians. The emphasis, as in the Second Vatican Council, is on the solidarity of all human beings, and on the world as a common abode and a common task.

It is the faith experience of the one God and Father of all that makes this our world, one world, and this human history one history. "The joys and hopes, the griefs and anxieties of the men and women of this age, especially those who are poor and in any way afflicted, these, too, are the joys and hopes, the griefs and anxieties of the followers of Christ".[3] My intention is to show that a world-view arising from faith in Christ gives a specific understanding of this common responsibility and the special mission of Christians to be "salt for the earth" and "yeast in the dough".

Of utmost importance for our approach to public morality and the "healing of public life" is a clear understanding of the scene and, at the same time, a sharp awareness of different visions within the faith-community.

I. IN THE WORLD, YET NOT OF "THIS WORLD"

Faith in the fellowship of Christians makes us aware of being called, like Abraham, out of a certain kind of world, called to become free from the various bondages that characterize "that world", those historical conditions of our world. This rallying call in Christ, the experience of a new form of fellowship and the beginning of "freedom in Christ" are the most radical kinds of experience of mission and commitment to the liberation and salvation of all people.

In the high-priestly prayer of Jesus (Jn 17), we hear about a "world" that is impermeable even to Jesus' prayer, to the salvation he offers. The astonishing fact is, however, that this world is especially the situation of a priestly class which, in absolute self-centredness and self-glorification, and with a thoroughly disintegrated "knowledge of dominion", makes religion itself the final bondage for themselves in order to keep the others in the same bondage.

But in the same prayer, Jesus beholds the "world" to which he is sent by his Father and into which he sends his disciples, a world of people called to faith and salvation if only the disciples offer it the witnessing word of unity and love. This world is the soil into which the good seed of the gospel should be sown.

1. The complexity of the biblical concept of "world"

The Bible speaks of "world" and of "men" in view of salvation offered by God. The complexity of the discourse arises from the complexity of man's response to God's offer.[4] In all this is reflected the divine mystery of justice and mercy.

An absolute dualism between world and salvation is unknown to the Bible. Salvation does not occur outside the real world but in the midst of it. Scripture is not interested in a neutral world of things. The whole universe is created by the Word of God (Jn 1; Gn 1). It is a message, a gift-revelation of God's glory, a gift for man to admire and to appreciate as sign of God's greatness and goodness. All of creation, represented and climaxed by man, stands before God, can adore him in truth and find repose (sabbath) in him or - this is the paradox - can reject him and thus obscure and contaminate the world, with all the consequences of this decision.

The world is always the world for man and of man. His relationship with the world is decisive for his relationship with God, and vice-versa.[5] For man, the world is the blessed gift if he recognizes it as God's creation, gift and message.

Humankind, rebelling against the Creator, condemns itself and draws the world - the earth entrusted to the whole of the human race - into misery and darkness. Yet God's saving will is greater. "The light shines in the dark, and the darkness cannot quench it" (Jn 1:5).

The great truth about the world that sheds light on everything else is that "God so loved the world as to send his only begotten Son (Jn 3:16). The God-Man, Jesus Christ, is the One who reveals the right understanding of world and man. He unmasks the world's sinfulness in the work of redemption. The paradox is that he, who revealed God's love to the world, is refused by that world; it resists his human and divine love. The "victory of the world" in the crucifixion of Jesus, who is the utmost manifestation of co-humanity, becomes the victory of God's love over the world. The last word, therefore, to the world and of the world is not rejection; it is God's acceptance of the world, God assuring the world and man that he, in his love, is greater than the misery of the sinful world.

The life of the authentic disciples of Christ is a life in "this world" (cf. Jn 13:1; 17:11; 1 Cor 5:10), in this paradox of a world created by God, fallen, and yet the object of his abiding love, a world confused and ungrateful. The disciples are not "from this sinful world" (cf. Jn 15:18f; 17:14, 18). They can be a shining light in the world, not of themselves or by any earthly wisdom, but by the power that comes from above. They are able to reflect God's love in their co-humanity, able to love even their enemies, able to love those who, in the eyes of the selfish and arrogant world, do not count.

A common feature in all parts of the Bible is the dynamic vision of the world: the world is history, has a history; it is the ongoing event and process of decision before the Lord of world and history, who was, who comes and will come.[6] Through the divine promises and the promptings of the Spirit, the "world to come" is already somehow present.[7]

The different usages of the word "world", pointing to such disparate realities as God's good creation, solidarity of perdition in a fallen world, solidarity of salvation through faith in Christ, are inter-related in one difficult synthesis by the fact that this world of men and women is history still happening.

2. The complexity of the world in which we live and act

The complexity of today's world is studied by people of various disciplines. Philosophy and theology can fulfil their respective tasks only if they are fully aware of these complexities.[8] The

Second Vatican Council, intending to enter into a fruitful dialogue with all people of our times, has scrutinized the most characterisitc signs of this world of today.

The Pastoral Constitution on the Church in the Modern World describes in an Introductory Statement "The Situation of Men in the Modern World".[9] "Though mankind today is struck with wonder at its own discoveries and its power, it often raises anxious questions about the current trend of the world."[10] It is typical of the spirit of this Pastoral Council that, like its initiator John XXIII, it gives first attention always to the good, and thus becomes more able to face the evils. It does not ascribe all difficulties to sinfulness, but rather sees the situation as "crisis of growth". As happens in any crisis of growth, the transformation has brought serious difficulties in its wake.[11] But the reality of sinfulness is not minimized: "Indeed, as a weak and sinful being, he often does what he would not, and fails to do what he would. Hence he suffers from internal divisions, and from these flow so many and so great discords in society."[12]

This vision of the world is heightened by the note of history as the time of decisions: "Since all these things are so, the modern world shows itself at once powerful and weak, capable of the noblest deeds or the foulest. Before it lies the path to freedom or to slavery, to progress or retreat, to brotherhood or hatred. Moreover, man is becoming aware that it is his responsibility to guide aright the forces which he has unleashed and which can enslave him or minister to him".[13]

Modern man does experience this, his world, in a new sense as his history, a world that can be planned and manipulated to an extent unthinkable until now.[14] There is, however, a danger that he may use these new powers to manipulate his fellowmen and end up as a manipulated manipulator.[15]

Many people of this modern world are shockingly aware that the growth in wisdom does not at all equal the growth in technical skills and in "knowledge of control". The progress in natural sciences and technology makes it possible to feed at the end of this century, the more than six billion people, but humankind is unable to distribute and administer the resources of the earth and the fruit of its skill in a just and reasonable way. The consequences are not only starvation and illness but also extremely dangerous tensions between the wealthy and the poor nations, between the northern and southern hemispheres, and so on. Mankind, having refused the orientation of the beatitudes, experiences the curse of avarice and the lust for power.[16]   Many people also realize the prime importance of being and becoming authentically a person in healthy I-Thou-We relationships, and the priority of being over that of having. But at the same time we experience the shaping power of unhealthy social, economic and political structures, the "they" and "it" relationships. Martin Heidegger analyzes this new experience as "being-in-the-world". "World" is the language, time and space of meaning, of "Being" revealing itself to man and inviting him to build an abode for it and thus for himself. He becomes more and more aware that he cannot actualize and find himself as person without taking full responsibility for his world. There is no possibility of flight to an I-Thou island. There is no escape from the world shaped by modern mathematics, technology and the new consciousness raised by the behavioural sciences. But mankind must ask the urgent question of ultimate meaning, of radical responsibility in the use of all the modern possibilities.

Prechristian thought, especially Greek thought, submitted Man radically to the kosmos, a pre-existent, immanent order of the world of being and things.[17] A magic world-view bowed before many taboos. Modern man, who desacralized the world as kosmos or as expression of divine immanence, must ask himself whether he has not surrendered himself to technocracy, to the idols of value-free empirical sciences. Has he really found the authentic secular world, free from ideologies, or has he so secularized himself and his world that he has enslaved himself in more superficial myths and ideologies?

Christian and human responsibility can be meaningfully exercised only in full recognition of the world in which we live, with its triumphs and failures, its chances and dangers. Karl Rahner invites us to discover our share in Christ's cross in the fact that we have to "endure the sober dourness of an unromantic, planned, technical world, with all the dire consequences that this world has for Christianity".[18]

But such acceptance of the real situation has nothing to do with fatalism. Realism is only the first step in taking up our responsibility. It is characteristic of humanity's most foresighted and creative members that they realize the possibility and duty to change themselves and the world around them at the same time. In the name of the Lord we cannot accept anything that is dehumanizing. "The very God who creates man in his image and likeness creates the 'earth and all that is in it for the use of all men and all nations, in such a way that created goods can reach all in a more just manner' (G.S. 69) and gives them power to transform and perfect the world in solidarity. The uniqueness of the Christian message does not so much consist in the affirmation of the necessity for structural change as it does in the insistence on the conversion of men which, in turn, will bring about this change. We will not have a new continent without new reformed structures but, first of all, there will be no new continent without new men who know how to be truly free and responsible according to the light of the Gospel".[19]

Faced with enormous problems, modern man, and especially modern Christians, have to free themselves from a static concept of nature that would sacrifice the good of persons and of humankind to so-called "natural laws". "By nature, man is a cultural being, which means that his very nature imposes on him the absolute responsibility to actualize himself and his world".[20]

3. Two opposed mentalities and options

a) Flight from the world

In the great world religions, in philosophies and ideologies, we find two contradictory attitudes towards the world.

Manicheism and gnosticism regard the visible, material world as evil, as a threat to salvation. In side-streams of monasticism, Buddhist and even Christian, there is a biased scepticism about the world. The emphasis is not on the magnificence of God's work nor on the redemption of the world, but one-sidedly on the world's fallenness.

This tendency occurs, more or less unconsciously, in those manuals of moral theology which speak of the world, our human environment, the mass media, the arduous vocations and so on, only under the heading, "occasions of sin".

Contemplative monastic life is not, however, necessarily inspired or contaminated by this attitude of flight. It can be a desert-experience, the exodus in full solidarity with those who, in the midst of the world, try to make it more human, more just, more beautiful. Contemplative communities can embody the synthesis between love of God and love of neighbour, the synthesis between the message that "the whole frame of this world is passing away" (1 Cor 7:31) and the promise of a new way of living together and living for the others. Whatever may be said of the opportunities and risks of this particular vocation, Christians cannot choose flight from responsibility in and for the world.

J. Moltmann rightly warns that the "flight of the beautiful soul" into an otherworldliness, away from the hard reality, "means exactly the option to abandon the social and political reality to senseless and inhumane powers."[21] Gerald and Patricia Mische say it even more pointedly. "When persons withdraw from society, rejecting the 'evils of this world' as dissociated from themselves, fixing the source of evil to external devils - human or otherwise - and seeking only their personal salvation and exemption from guilt, they feign an innocence and powerlessness that contribute to the perpetuation of those evils, and are perhaps as dangerous as the more overt destructive decision-making and behaviour they reject."[22]

D. Bonhoeffer, who went the whole way of the exodus and the desert, and surely did it for the world of people and for a more humane order of things, says: "The isolation from the world of things is idealistic and not Christian. Christ does not detach the person from the world of things but from the world of sin; there is a great difference."[23]

Irresponsible flight belongs as much to the "world of sin" as an irresponsible way of acting in the world of things and persons. "Abnegation of the world and affirmation of the world have in the gospel an accent quite different from modern thinking and language use."[24] By faith, the human person entrusts himself or herself to God with mind and will, and by doing so, overcomes the "sinful world" of ungrateful independence and arrogance in thinking and acting. This creative detachment proves fruitful for the world of fellowmen.

In a biblical vision, self-denial and detachment from the world are expressions of faith. They allow us a critical distance from an idolatrous and confused world, giving us freedom in discernment and in action for the betterment of the world. We are able to put ourselves and the reality around us into the right place, facing God and his kingdom. But nowhere does the New Testament allow simple flight from the world and from responsibility for the world. The thought that "the whole frame of this world passes away" serves our freedom for Christ, and that implies essentially freedom for others.[25]

It is true, however, that the New Testament does not offer a programme for changing the innerworldly structures of economic, cultural and political life. The reason is not only the expectation of the nearness of Christ's return but also the situation of the "small flock" of Christians.

The temporary exodus-experience is necessary for Christians not only because of the sinfulness of the world "out there" but even more because we are aware "that our concrete attitude towards the world in faith is still 'concupiscent'."[26] The apostle's warning, "conform yourself no longer to the pattern of this present world" (Rom 12:2) does not overlook the Christians' solidarity with the world of their brethren. It is a call to that inner transformation that allows us to be present in the world as discerning and wise persons: "But let your mind be remade and your whole nature be thus transformed, then you will be able to discern the will of God, and to know what is good, acceptable and perfect" (Rom 12:2).

It is in this way that asceticism belongs to a theology of the world. It implies not flight, but fight against every form of individual and collective selfishness. It conforms the disciples to the "kenosis" of Jesus, so that they may authentically participate in the work of the Redeemer of the world.

A modern scientist and philosopher, Carl Friedrich von Weizsäcker, tells us of the relevance of the genuine religious asceticism that disallows any form of flight from responsibilities. Through its convincing testimony it can radiate on the world and make people freer in the use of power and of earthly things.[27]

b) Responsible participation

Vatican II has classically expressed the relationship of Christian hope and attitude towards earthly realities: "The expectation of a new earth must not weaken but rather stimulate our concern for cultivating this one. For here grows the body of a new human family, a body which even now is able to give some kind of foreshadowing of the new age. . . For after we have obeyed the Lord, and in his Spirit nurtured on earth the values of human dignity, brotherhood and freedom, and indeed all the good fruits of our nature and enterprise, we will find them again, but freed of stain, burnished and transfigured."[28]

The commitment to the cause of brotherhood and justice in the world is a sign of the total conversion to God's kingdom: "Whoever, in obedience to Christ, seeks first the kingdom of God, will as a consequence receive a stronger and purer love for helping all his brothers and sisters, and for perfecting the work of justice under the inspiration of charity."[29]

Through his bodily reality, man is connected with the "history" of evolution and with the whole of the material and living world. But he alone is a free and creative agent in a unique history that concerns the world around him, the biosphere and all of humankind.

Since Galileo, there has come to the foreground a new concept of science, a science for the transformation of the world. Man discovers the possibilities hidden in the created world. The danger is, however, that he can invest his energies so one-sidedly in shaping the world around himself that he fails to actualize his humanness and co-humanity. The consequence then, in the final analysis, is that his dominion over the world will not be beneficial to the individual or to the world at large.

A new impetus for changing the world comes from Karl Marx. In his eleventh thesis on Feuerbach he states: "The philosophers have only offered different interpretations of the world; what counts is to change the world." The goal of the Marxist analysis is to pave the way for the intelligence of the inner dynamics of world, history and society, with the conviction that the working out of these dynamics will offer the chance for freedom: the freedom for man, the worker, the maker, to be subject and not mere object in future history.[30]

It cannot be denied that an aggressive interpretation of the whole of history and of societal processes, with the firm intention to impose it on all people in order to change the world, bears enormous dangers in itself. For Christians, this is a vital challenge to direct the change of the world for the better by giving great attention to right interpretation, sincere conviction and careful, non-violent application, and by refusing to indulge in any ideology of rapid or superficial change dissociated from the profound change of one's own heart, mind and will.

This does not mean, however, that Christians should care only for personal conversion. Karl Marx is not wrong when he asserts that "morals is a frivolous science if it does not pay attention to politics and legislation."[31] Our morality and our freedom remain dreams if they have no impact on socio-economic and political life.

Throughout history, man has created thought-patterns, structures of life and institutions which, in turn, influence even his interiority. "The social dimension is not something that is added to our person-identity, it is a dimension of this very identity."[32] However, there is frequently the dangerous tendency to sacralize the given social order or the underlying presuppositions, which lead people to accept inhumane situations as if they were a fate or "natural laws". On the other hand, no less dangerous is it "to take a stand outside the given historical action and thought of man."

This, our world, has God's promises. But within this realm of God's initiative, of his constant coming, his people have a decisive role and shared responsibility. It is offered to them as the realm of creative liberty and fidelity. The world is created for Man, and for Man's salvation the Word of God took flesh. These basic truths disallow any individualistic interpretation. They are grace, promise, and call to togetherness and co-responsibility. "Thus the believer acts not only 'within' the world, but he changes it, he transforms it himself within the framework of this divine promise, which was given and is present to him as an individual only in the solidarity of the covenant."[33]

D. Bonhoeffer writes: "Ethics as formation means the bold endeavour to speak about the way in which the form of Jesus Christ takes form in the world. Concrete judgments and decisions will have to be ventured".[34] The word of God is addressed to us in Jesus Christ, in whom and for whom all things are made and who fully entered the reality of our world. "Since this word is addressed to our entire life, the response, too, can only be an entire one".[35]

In this context, Bonhoeffer is polemic against any interpretation of Luther's theory of the two reigns and realms that would allow salvation and responsibility in the secular world to be dissociated. However difficult it may be to harmonize the vision and dynamics of faith with rational interpretation of historical action, the Christian knows that his action in and for our world has to be faithful to his faith and to the promises and the calling coming from God. A. Köberle, as well as Bonhoeffer, makes the point that a life in faith requires also a constant effort to come to a vision of the world inspired by faith. "A worldview arising from faith" has, however, nothing to do with a static, self-satisfied approach.[36]

4. In the light of the mysteries of salvation

Theology cannot offer ready-made recipes for moulding the world, but it can give decisive perspectives and criteria reflecting on the mysteries of salvation.

Knowledge of God, knowledge of self and of the world, coincide in the knowledge of Christ. We must open ourselves to the full reality of Christ, without any arbitrary selection (heresy). Neither Incarnation alone nor his cross and death alone, nor the eschatological expectation alone suffice. The relationship of God to the world and of the world to God is revealed in the whole mystery of Christ: incarnation, his life as the servant of God and Man, his passion and death, his resurrection and ascension, the mission of the Holy Spirit and the promise of his final coming.

"By becoming flesh, the Word has become also history, indeed in a very distinctive way, namely in that special history that belongs intimately to the history of Jesus Christ, the covenant history of Israel, since the steps God takes with his people belong, in their historical reality, to the content of history."[37] Hence, we have to try to understand what the Old Testament tells us about God's relationship to the world and the world's relationship to God.[38] But only in Christ has God fully revealed his relationship to the world; and Christ embodies the new form of relationship of the world to God. "As Jesus is the eschatological event of God in the world - towards the world - so he is also the eschatological event of the world and of Man in the world on the road to God."[39]

The world is creature. Its creatureliness forbids any kind of divinization of the world. But God loves the work of his hands. The gospel of John speaks on the incarnation of the Word of the Father already as a sign of God's saving, loving relationship to the world that, through sin, had been estranged. "God loved the world so much that he gave his only Son, that everyone who has faith in him may not die but have eternal life. It was not to judge the world that God sent his Son into the world, but that through him the world might be saved" (Jn 3:16-17).

God reveals himself as "Emmanuel", God-with-us, as loving presence, "the God of an historical hour. Transcendence itself becomes an event".[40] In the "Son of Man", God has become "one-of-us", for each of us and for the world, in an abiding covenant. Indeed, Christ *is* the Covenant, the sacrament of God's fidelity to his creation.

The world's relationship to God, however, manifests itself in the most shocking way. In Christ's crucifixion, the "godless world", represented in the power of the priests and of the Roman empire, rejects the Emmanuel. But at the same time, Jesus Christ, "one-of-us" gives to God in the name of all creation, the response of loving trust, total obedience. By his co-humanity, which goes so far as to pray even for those who crucify him, Jesus is the adorer in spirit and truth. In him, God's power of love becomes manifest as power in a human being, power of the new world to love the fellowmen as God does. Indeed, in Jesus, this redeeming human love is at the same time God's love.

The world's history stands in a dual way under the sign of the cross: (1) it is still, in so many and horrible ways, protesting and rebelling against God; but (2) in the midst of all this, there is a new creation, the absolute victory of divine and human love, of saving justice. Whoever is a disciple of Christ has to make a radical option against that rebellious attitude, against arrogance and lovelessness, against the horrifying abuse of law and power that led to the crucifixion of Jesus.

"God forbid that I should boast of anything but the cross of our Lord Jesus Christ through which the world is crucified to me and I to the world" (Gal 6:14). But just as that rebellious attitude of the world that was manifested in Christ's crucifixion must itself be "crucified", put to death in us, so does the very cross of the Redeemer direct us to love the world with him: that is, to love all mankind and all creation, even those who would crucify us.

Hence, with J. B. Metz, we can say that the cross is at the centre of our faith and also of our interpretation of the world. "Christ entered into the flesh of sin, he became open to suffering; his 'integrity' (the power to give the *whole* of his being to the obedient love of God) is simultaneously his openness to suffering . . . The 'integrity' of Christ does not preserve him from the abyss of human suffering and human paradox, but is precisely the most acute possibility of undergoing it more radically, fully, and without compromise than we 'concupiscent' men".[41]

Christ's life and death is the final sign of God's acceptance of the world and, at the same time, the sign of "One-of-us" who responds utterly. He does so as the *Servant*, thus offering to the world the remedy that heals arrogance and lust for power. It is the road of absolute poverty in the service of God and of mankind, to make us all rich in that love with which God has accepted the world and the *Son of Man* has responded in order to pave the way for us. By the same power of the Holy Spirit with which Christ has manifested God's descent into the world, the believer can live the fruitful tension of being crucified to the (arrogant) world, while accepting the world and its burden with a redeeming, healing love.

Here once more we turn our attention to the therapeutic vision of redemption. The salvific action of Christ means not only that he takes away the enormous guilt of all our sins, but even more that he liberates us and the world from the power of sin and sin-solidarity.[42] God reconciles us and reconciles the world (cf. 2 Cor 5:1-19).

Redemption is liberation and healing through God's saving justice, by faith in Christ who died for us and is risen. "All are justified by God's free gift of grace alone, through his act of liberation in the person of Christ Jesus. For God designed him to be the means of expiating sin by his sacrifical death, effective through faith. God meant by this to demonstrate his saving justice" (Rom 3:24-25).

"For Paul, worldwide reconciliation becomes the *telos* (purpose) of the earthly mandate, and by this mandate's reaching us, it becomes visible that the glorified Lord has begun to reign."[43] The reconciling power of the death and resurrection of Christ becomes particularly visible in his disciples when they show reconciling love to those who hate them, and accept the poor and downtrodden who impose their needs on them. Thus they are crucified to the old world, but crucified in order to live with Christ. "In Christ's cross, God's love becomes manifest to human abandonment because in this love men are accepted in their misery."[44]

We speak of the crucified Lord and his redemptive death always with faith in his resurrection. By raising Jesus from the dead, God has assured the world forever that he is a healing and reconciling Father. So we finally interpret God's relationship to the world in the light of the integral Paschal Mystery; for, relying only on empirical experience, the unbeliever argues that the crucifixion and death of Jesus is proof that God has abandoned him and that therefore he was not sent by God.[45]

Furthermore, our relationship to the world and to God has to be seen and lived in the light of the eschatological promises. Our participation in the on-going reconciliation is as urgent for us today as for those early Christians who expected an early parousia of Christ. So that "men may be not only spectators but active participants in the harvest which follows the seed",[46] God leaves time and space to the creatures who, reconciled in Christ, are partners in this work. Karl Barth warns the believer, "The resurrection as truth is not grasped through theories but only in the practice of the combat."[47]

II. THE RELATIONSHIP BETWEEN THE CHURCH AND THE WORLD

Theological discussion centred for a long time around the relationship between church and state, between "sacerdotium et imperium". There was the famous and dangerous problem about whether the church had direct or "only" indirect power over the temporal sphere. The church was practically equated with its central government, exercised through a monarchal papacy and, under him, monarchal bishops.

Then, for a long time, the church-state relationship was studied under the presupposition that both church and state are "societas perfecta" - that is, practically a self-sufficient society - although with different purposes and competences. This was a quite "worldly" way of reasoning, since the point of departure and experience was the nation-state whose powers frequently were held by individuals who, like Louis XIV of France would say, "L'état, c'est moi"!

The Second Vatican Council has brought to the fore the best of biblical and ecclesiastical tradition with a renewed self-understanding of the church. For this, a wholly new reflection was necessary, going beyond the church-state relationship (this will be considered in Chapter Eight on political ethics). The focal point is, rather, the relationship of church and world: on the one hand, the church as messianic people of God, as God's household with a hierarchical structure with divine and human traditions and, on the other hand not only the rest of humanity but all that is "world" in its various biblical and modern meanings.

1. Abiding mission and changeable structures

There are, no doubt, abiding and always binding perspectives and attitudes regarding the relationship between church and world. The norm and criterion is God's own relationship with the world, revealed in Jesus Christ. He comes as the Redeemer and offers the remedy as a servant. And although glorified by the Father, he wants the church, founded by him to continue his mission and quasi-sacramental presence to the world, to be a church that follows him radically as a servant.

The world is not for the church; rather, the church is for the world. An outstanding orthodox theologian expresses this well: "Ecclesiology, unless it is given its true cosmic perspective ('for the life of the world'), unless it is understood as the Christian form of 'cosmology', is always ecclesiolatry: the church considered as 'being in itself' and not (as it should be) the new relation of God and man and world."[48]

By divine calling and grace, the church is "holy", but she is "world", too, in the various biblical meanings[49]: she is that privileged part of the world where the divine acceptance should become clearly visible and effective. Office holders and structures of the church can manifest a rejection of Christ the Servant and thus of God's way of accepting the world. There is plentiful redemption for and in the church, but there can also be marks of sin-solidarity. She is not always and everywhere simply "civitas Dei", God's city; but as far as God is concerned, she is always called out (ekklesia) of the sinful world to holiness. Yet this very call and grace make the sin in the church more sinful.

The church of the Word Incarnate does legitimately integrate some of the thought patterns and structures of a concrete culture and society. There is much that she can rightly receive from the world. After the reflections on what help the church can offer to individuals, society and human activities, the Second Vatican Council speaks explicitly on "the help which the church receives from the modern world".[50] She has not a monopoly of all that is true, good and beautiful. She realizes ever more how much her history is interwoven with that of the whole world.

To become visible and effective, the church needs institutional structures. These structures can change according to the changing historical and social conditions, but they can also somehow make themselves independent of their original purpose. The institutional elements can become overloaded at the expense of the mission, and so on. In times of persecution, and in a different way in times of spiritual strength, the institutional structures can be reduced to a minimum, while the life of faith and the witness of the members of the church can be outstanding.

But the church is always a "socialis compago"[51], a visible social entity. "Whether the church wants it or not, as a social entity she is a reality of some impact in the social and political realm, a Sociologicum, a Politicum, even an Oeconomicum of considerable weight. This weight does not belong to the essence of the church; the Christianity of the first times did not have it; but today it exists in a worldwide way, although with various forms and degrees in the various parts of the world. In all these realms the church cannot avoid, even if she would like to, the fact that both her activity and her omissions exercise a weighty influence. From this fact a number of responsibilities arise. They include the whole realm of interaction between church and world."[52]

The great expert on social ethics, Oswald von Nell-Breuning, expresses here a fact to which the so-called "political theology" has strongly pointed; but he cannot grasp the full depth of a sound political theology because of his too narrow understanding of the mission of the church. In practice, he gives the church an enormous mission for society and the world at large, but he limits her specific mission to the liberation of individuals from the bondage of sin. "It is only sin that oppresses and burdens humankind, and only this can be taken away through the redeeming action of Jesus. All other forms of oppresion are intrahuman, that is, they arise from men who oppress others; and the moral evil is not the passive oppression, namely, that others suffer under it and long to be liberated. Only the active oppression which men inflict on others is sinful". Of course the famous author calls for compassion and is happy when, as a *result* of the sinners' liberation from their sins, the terrible situation is removed from the oppressed and alienated people. But he concludes: "Liberation from exploitation, from oppression and any kind of temporal evil is not the task of the church. Otherwise she would lose her characteristic notes that distinguish her from secular societies."[53]

I agree with Nell-Breuning that all men and women, Christians and non-Christians, have the task to fight together against these temporal evils. However, as a Christian I see in these evils the incarnate expression of sin-solidarity, of institutionalized temptations. Christ, the Redeemer of the world, wants the church to be in the forefront of liberation from those realities that are engendered and perpetuated by the sins of the many, and which provoke ever new sins. It is not only an act of meritorious compassion if we all, and the church through her leaders, call prophetically and act in solidarity for the removal of these stains from a sinful world.

Nell-Breuning's thought has nothing to do, however, with an older theology that gave the official church "indirect power over the temporal sphere *ratione peccati*", which means active power and earthly competence to tell state and society to forbid and to punish whatever the church declares to be sin. What he is concerned with is the limit of both the direct and the indirect competence of the church. At the same time, he cares for all the practical, historical possibilities of the church, as institution and as people of God, to act for the best for all the world, in solidarity with all people of good will.

2. From the beginnings to the Constantinian era

The Acts of the Apostles indicate the ideal presence of the small community of disciples of Christ: "They enjoyed the favour of the whole people; they were all held in high esteem" (Acts 2:47; 4:33). They were a model community where the praise of

God was reflected in mutual love and generous solidarity. Around the year 200, the letter to Diognetus indicates beautifully how the powerless Christians of that time understood their role in the midst of persecution. They intended to be "to the world, what the soul is to the body".[54] They trusted in the power of prayer and the convincing witness of life as their service to the world.

While it was normal that the prophets and exemplary communities in Old Israel would make a great impact on the whole life of the people, fledgling Christianity could not hope to be listened to by the powerful Roman empire.

Then came the momentous historical turn under Constantine the Great, who realized that the Christian church could be of great importance for his political goals, especially for the unification of his empire. He brought with him, as the pagan heritage, the amalgamation of emperor and high-priest (Pontifex Maximus). By this time, bishops had gained great prestige among the faithful because, in the time of persecution, they were the ones who had suffered and risked more than all the others. Hence, Constantine and his successors lavished on them all kinds of privileges and earthly riches and powers, under the condition that they would use the church's influence for the established order and for the emperor chosen by God to protect religion. The emperors built magnificent temples to their own glory and "also to the glory of God".

Many Christians realized the depth of these changes and the grave risks they presented. The great movement of monasticism in the fourth and following centuries was a non-violent but strong protest against the trend of a church becoming too worldly, too much a part of the worldly powers. The communities of monks wanted to embody the model of the pre-constantinian church.

Within the given situation, Augustine, in his famous work "De Civitate Dei", proposed the best possible model of mutual relationship between church and world. He described the duality of two reigns, two choices, the City of God and the city of men.

The official church (usually identifying "church" with "higher clergy") made numerous meritorious contributions to culture and order, frequently humanizing the situation and sometimes protecting the independence of the church in her spiritual realm. However, there arose ever new temptations inherent in power, especially in the combination of spiritual power with earthly power.

How could the church exercise her prophetic role while she was politically and economically interwoven with an overdeveloped system of honours and privileges, and thus practically a part of the earthly powers? One example may illustrate the dangers. Over a period of three centuries, the Spanish crown sent from Spain all of the priests and bishops for the Philippines, paying them salaries and giving them high honours on the condition that, besides preaching the gospel and celebrating the sacraments, they would educate the people of the Philippines to absolute allegiance to the "crown". Not seldom it happened that some priests or bishops took sides with the exploited or oppressed and were as a consequence, punished as disloyal.

The situation in Latin America was not much different. And when the empire broke down, there were new rich and powerful élites to take over the role of the defunct régime. I think Gremillion is not too harsh when he writes: "In general the Christian churches clung to their Augustinian categories of the two empires and the two swords, juridically joined and constantly crossing. They fought rearguard skirmishes to retain a direct role, legally inherited and ethically supported by faith, in temporal affairs . . . The Catholic church, perhaps because it has the longest and richest memory, was foremost in these pretensions a century or so after secularization was on its definitive way."[55]

3. Martin Luther's "two reigns and regiments"[56]

Martin Luther's idea on the "two reigns and regiments" is one of the most interesting and influential models for an understanding not only of the relationship between church and secular world, but also and particularly of how the individual Christian and the Christian community belong at the same time to the realm of faith proclaimed and celebrated by the church and to the realm of the secular profession and citizenship.

It holds that God has chosen two realms and modalities to establish his reign over believers and sinful men. Both realms point, although in quite different ways, to one kingdom of God on earth. In the spiritual realm there is the presence of Christ, the Father's revelation, through the proclamation of the gospel, the celebration of the sacraments, the justifying power of faith. This is the direct realm of the on-going action of the Holy Spirit, the realm "at the right hand of God". But because man is a sinner, and even those who are justified by faith and grace are at the same time "sinners and justified", there is the "realm at the left hand of God" where, due to man's sinfulness and the world's rebelliousness, men are not directly and properly under the saving reign of God.

This second regiment is that of politics and economics, the secular vocations (professions). It seems that the church - insofar, and only insofar, as it is institution and shaped by human traditions - belongs also somehow to the realm at the left hand of God, in which there is no direct guidance by "gospel and law" but rather by human experience and reason. For Luther, the church, even in preaching law and gospel, has no competence or jurisdiction over this realm.

Is it too much to say that we see here a first theological outline of secularity? But it is surely not at all secularism, because it is always *God's government*. It is God's will that man should draw profit from experience and rationality; and it is also God's will that sinful man should somehow be checked by law enforcement and punishment.

This theory contradicts the ideologies of the power of the church over the temporal sphere. In this matter we understand Luther's doctrine to be that the secular realm, family, economics (professional life) and politics do not bring salvation. Salvation comes only through faith as an undeserved gift of God. And since, in the secular regiment, there is not the realm of salvation (works do not bring salvation), there is also no competence of the church. This last Lutheran thought was pursued most radically by Friedrich Gogarten, and gives rise to his particular understanding of secularity.[57]

Luther's doctrine on the two reigns and regiments found very different and sometimes contradictory interpretations, especially within the Lutheran church. One of its abiding truths is that we may distinguish *two dimensions* of man. In one, the decisive thing is a radical and grateful acknowledgement of man's dependence and of the undeserved gift, an acknowledgement and a receptivity that saves the God-given freedom from ideologies and enslavements. The second dimension calls for creative activity, rational and conscious participation in the world.[58]

But all too frequently the two realms were dissociated, so that the Christian lived a kind of dichotomy. And unfortunately, some pitfalls in Luther's theology or experience led to a rather unprophetic and uncreative "presence" of believers in the "realm at the left hand of God". The historical fact that Luther's reformation chanced to come under the influence of the "Christian princes" made the doctrine of the earthly realm and regiment more and more anti-prophetic. Luther even took an un-nuanced stand against the farmers who were longing for liberation from serfdom; he called for absolute submission and obedience to earthly authorities.[59]

Almost the same thing happened with the Catholic doctrine on natural law. For many reasons, including the existent political and religious circumstances, it became frequently confused with the existent unjust order. Lutheran theologians, refusing natural law theories as a reason for protesting against civil laws, spoke on "orders of creation", thus backing, in different forms and degrees, both the existing conditions and the abuse of authority.

Luther praised the secular professions. He saw faithfulness and orderliness in professional life, and saw the state of life in which one was born as primordial over and against the traditional priestly and monastic vocations. But because of the way salvation was confined to the spiritual realm, it easily happened that religion withdrew into "pure interiority" or confined itself to the private sphere of life.

Although Luther and Lutheran theologians knew that a profound faith option would shape the believer's character and thus influence his life in the professional and political realm, in the anti-prophetic church establishment the prophetic incentives and challenges for a creative presence in civic and political life could not easily arise.

That Lutherans generally were much less dynamic in the economic life than the Calvinists might be judged today much more positively, especially in view of the ecological crisis and all the dangers inherent in the progress and growth ideology in socio-economic life. But it cannot easily be denied and not enough deplored that neither Lutherans nor Catholics - for different but sometimes for similar theological reasons - were not moved by the strength of Christian discernment to make themselves critically present to the temporal world.

A one-sided interpretation of Luther's doctrine led several Lutheran theologians of the nineteenth century to assert that not only natural sciences and mathematics but the whole realm of economy, art and even politics are to be studied in a "value-free" manner: they are so governed by their own laws and determinisms that Christians should not interfere with ethical or religious statements. Thus, from different premises they came practically to the same conclusions as Adam Smith and other representatives of modern liberalism.[60]

Luther's doctrine reacted against the abuse by Church authority especially the tendency to overstep the competence of the office as well as of insight, experience and rationality. But in the wake of the development and interpretation of his doctrine, Lutherans did as little as Catholic manualists to deal with the massive sin of the abuse of authority and power.[61]

While Lutheran and Catholic authors repeatedly enforced obedience to political and socio-economic authorities and structures (invoking Romans 13), they rarely gave proper attention to the apostle's warning: "Adapt yourselves no longer to the pattern of this present world" (Rom 12:2) or to the instruction on discernment immediately following in the letter, or to what Paul says in so many contexts on his experience and vision about the power of the gospel in combating the powers of this era and this world.[62]

Ulrich Duchrow offers a typology of the various interpretations of Luther's doctrine on the two reigns and realms[63] which, to my mind applies also to various theories of Catholic authors and even more to the practice of many Christians: (1) the undifferentiated integrated adaptation to the given structures; (2) a dualistic differentiated adaptation to the power structures; (in neither case is there any real discernment in the light of the gospel and the prophetic tradition); (3) the discerning and integrated participation in the godly combat against the evil powers, in view of transforming the secular world in the service of the common good and the legitimate freedom of all. The Lutheran author concludes these reflections with an appeal for an ecumenical effort in this direction.[64]

4. Powerless and prophetic presence

The church becomes ever more aware that she can help the world only to the extent that she is deeply united with God, trusts in the power of his love and wisdom, and therefore renounces all earthly pretension to power.[65] The prophetic experience is an experience of one's own powerlessness in the experience of the power of God; and there is always the experience of God's holiness and mercy in a total solidarity with the suffering, the downtrodden, the poor.

The renewal initiated by the Second Vatican Council goes in this direction. The Synod of bishops in 1974 declared emphatically that the church should be present to the world in this way: "Faithful to her evangelizing mission, the church as a truly poor, praying and fraternal community can do much to bring about the integral salvation or the full liberation of men. She can draw from the gospel the most profound reasons and ever new incentives to promote generous dedication to the service of all men - the poor especially, the weak and the oppressed - and to eliminate the social consequences of sin which are translated into social and political structures."[66]

The church knows that she can fight as a prophetic voice against these investments of sin if she is a praying community without any pretension to power and is close to the people. Preaching the good news that conversion is possible and urgent, she can never separate personal conversion from social renewal. "The demons of today are not only power inherent in human freedom but also sins embodied in social structures, customs, and false systems of values and ideas, like social exploitation, inequality, casteism . . . A church that does not fight against these 'demons' is nothing less than an institutionalized betrayal of Jesus."[67]

Probably the church's most forceful official document along this line is the encyclical *Redemptor Hominis* by John Paul II, following the concern and the vision of "Peace on Earth" by Pope John XXIII, "The Progress of People" by Paul VI, and especially the Second Vatican Council's Pastoral Constitution on the Church in the Modern World. With Christ, the church reaches out to everybody. "Man is the way for the church . . ., the real, concrete, historical Man" who, with great anguish, experiences 'alienation'. "The dignity of the redeemed - of every person - must be respected in the whole ordering of the world."[68]

The church as a whole (the "people of God") is meant to be a prophetic presence, for the Spirit of Pentecost is given to all. "Yes, I will endue even my slaves, both men and women, with a portion of my spirit, and they shall prophesy" (Acts 2:18).

In order to speak effectively and convincingly to the world there must reign that openness to the Spirit that brings together the religious and the human experience, all the best knowledge of modern man. The office as such, even the highest, has a chance to be listened to only if the office holders also are ready to listen and thus to acquire true competence, including competence in communication with modern men and women.

In today's world the behavioural sciences - all the sciences dedicated to the knowledge of Man - are considered indispensable. They have acquired a certain autonomy. Those who speak to the world in the name of the church will be better heard if they have brought into the forum all the available competence.[69] The encyclical *Redemptor Hominis* shows a particular awareness that the great world religions (an important part of our world) are bearers of profound human experience, wisdom and spiritual treasure. We cannot speak of the modern world and to it without uniting ourselves with its people in the search for God and for the full meaning of human dignity. However, the adherents of all religions have to ask themselves what the presence of organized atheism means for them.[70]

The official church and official ecumenical bodies surely have to address themselves to the world. But when it is a matter of discernment in concrete situations, they need the competent help of the lay people, the men and women who are experiencing the situation. Frequently the modern world is addressed by churchmen who practically have never listened to representatives of 53 percent of this world - the women whom God gave to man explicitly as "partner" (Gen 2:18).

Gremillion asks pointedly: "Why is there no adequate structures for fuller lay voice and service 'from top to bottom, from periphery to centre' within the Church of Rome? It cannot become truly the loving, serving church unless all God's people are at least invited to participate realistically in community and ministry."[71]

No less outspoken is a leading Protestant layman, R. von Thadden: "In the exercise of their claim to be called to the service of the world, they (the church leaders) are frequently all too quick to consider themselves as competent. And thus they incur the bondage of the spirit of the era (Zeitgeist) which they would confront better by limiting their claim of competence."[72]

In many situations and on many occasions, Christians and others know what is right. There, it is easy to sound a strong call to action if we ourselves are willing to act unitedly. But there are other more complex situations and problems where the first step is to acknowledge the limits of our competence and the need for common efforts. "An emphasis on certainty may be merely a way of escaping anxiety of uncertainty and the necessity of genuine listening to people who disagree with us. But on the other hand, an emphasis on uncertainty may be used as a pretext to allow people to avoid responsibility."[73] This challenge concerns us all, but in a special manner those who have great public responsibilities.

The prophetic, powerless, unpretentious presence to the world is the absolute condition for fulfilment of the church's divine mission to be "the salt for the earth and light to the world" (Mt 5:13-14). The service to the kingdom of God on earth, a kingdom of peace and justice, can be fulfilled only by "undertaking the narrow way of the cross".[74] An essential part of this cross is the necessity for the church to re-examine constantly her whole life, structures, use of authority, her effort, or lack of effort to listen to disagreeable prophets and to allow people as much active sharing and participation as possible.

The 1971 document of the Synod of Bishops on Justice is an outstanding example of this courage of self-examination: "We must undertake an examination of the modes of acting and of the possessions and life style found within the church herself. . . We also urge that women should have their own share of responsibility and participation in the community life of society and likewise of the church. . . The church recognizes the right to suitable freedom of expression and thought. This includes the right of everyone to be heard in a spirit of dialogue which preserves a legitimate diversity within the church. The form of judicial procedure should give the accused the right to know his accusers and also the right to a proper defence."[75]

Only One is *the* Prophet, Jesus Christ, true God and true man, absolutely holy. Confronting the injustice of the world, he gave the example of radical poverty and of the readiness to suffer in the exercise of his mission.

While all who share in Christ's prophetic ministry must be ready to suffer as he did, they must also realize that they have to learn and to grow in the process of exercising their ministry. This is true for all, office holders and others. All have to ask themselves constantly whether they are ready to accept the prophetic challenge that comes from within or outside of their own community.

The prophetic presence to the powerful, the oppressors, the violent, is authentic only to the extent of our poverty and our complete solidarity with the powerless and oppressed.[76] There is need for a spirit of non-violence, together with the consciousness that we ourselves are in need of penance and constant conversion to that powerlessness of non-violent action that points to the power of God's love and saving justice. The presence of Christians to the world is that of an exodus-community, following the *kenosis* of *the* Prophet, Christ.[77]

Dietrich Bonhoeffer expresses this truth with deepest feeling when it becomes clear that cause for liberation has failed for him and his associates: "Man is called to participate in the suffering of God with the godless world . . . , allowing oneself to be caught up in the way of Christ, into the Messianic event". A few days later he continues his meditation: "This is what I mean by worldliness - taking life in one's stride, with all its duties and problems, its successes and failures, its experiences and helplessness. In such a life we throw ourselves utterly in the arms of God. Then we no longer give importance to our own sufferings but to the sufferings of God in the world, and watch with Christ in Gethsemane. That is faith, that is *metanoia*, and that is what makes a man, a Christian. How can success make us arrogant and failure lead us astray, when we participate in the sufferings of God living in this world? I am grateful that I was allowed to learn it, and I know that I could have done so only along the road I have travelled."[78]

The prophetic ministry has to watch for the *kairos*, the appropriate time to speak or to wait. "There are always forerunners in a dialectic tension between structures and persons. Some ideas fall into a vacuum because they are not communicated with the appropriate means; this is true for the social and religious reform ideas as well as with scientific discoveries."[79] However, an initial failure can be the first decisive step to prepare the future harvest.

The most urgent problem seems to be the education of Christians for discernment and prophetic courage, for creative liberty and fidelity. Then we can hope that believers will be clearsighted for what the world needs. Carl Friedrich von Weizsäcker feels that the Christians of the so-called Third World know this better than we of the Western world, since the former are less enslaved than we are to rationalistic abstract schemes.[80]

The church is learning the hard way that the world is not to be changed by the imposition of laws. If she is to fulfil her healing presence to the world, she has first to form her members, to convince them of their mission, and then to give them space for freedom to act as responsible members of church and society. Participation in the process of forming healthy public opinion is fundamental.[81] Lay people are to take up their own responsibilities. Not everything has to be done in the name of the official church.

In order to be church for the whole world, the separated parts of Christianity have to go through an ecumenical learning process on how to be church for the world, how to speak of, and to, the world, how to work together in order to make the whole inhabited world (the *oikumene*) truly inhabitable, a home for all people.[82] All these dimensions will be jeopardized, however, if the cause of Christian unity is severed from the common effort to understand what Christ intends for his church in her relationship to the world and for the common service to the world.

III. THE WORLD AND THE SIGNS OF THE TIMES

Christian humanism and Christian love are concrete, related to the historical situation of our neighbour. Our relationship with neighbour and world requires a constant scrutiny of the signs of the times. We cannot change the world and ourselves in the proper direction without knowing the present opportunities, needs and risks.

Among the most tangible and urgent signs of the times are: (1)

the ways in which the world of today is becoming *one* world; (2) with, however, a new perception of plurality[83] and a new perception of the secularity of the world[84], the chances of an authentic secularity and the threat of a spurious secularism; (3) the new chances but also enormous risks for the dignity of each person; and (4) the dynamism and ambiguities of our technical world and culture.

1. *One world and one history*

Examining the signs of the times, the Second Vatican Council makes this basic statement: "The destiny of the human community has become all of one piece, where once the various groups of men had a kind of private history of their own."[85] History becomes now an important object of Christian life. It implies a new vision of creation and evolution of the *one* world entrusted to the whole of humankind. The fundamental truth of revealed morality, the *covenant* of God with humankind, its meaning of history and of a life in faith, the decision for that *solidarity* which Christ has revealed to us, all appear in a new actuality and urgency. The crises of population, of ecology, of energy, or worldwide economics, make humanity experience in a shocking way that we are all in the same boat, and that a restless humanity, polarized and torn into opposed camps by group egotism and ideologies, may well sink the boat altogether.[86]

This world that, by the whole development of technology and communication is irrevocably one, lives still in a kind of moral tribalism with caste systems and antiquated institutions that remain on the level of provincialism.[87] Moral questions of vital importance to all of humanity are treated even in Christian churches with a mentality of individualism, and with speculations on the "whatness" of a human nature conceived by individualism and abstract theorizing.

The foreseeable consequences of narrow individualistic theories and "laws" applied to the whole of history and humankind are not yet taken realistically into account. Most political action, economic planning or failure to plan, development of technology and so on are still determined within the straitjacket of each nation's or group's security complex. These basic approaches cannot be overcome without a totally new thinking and new forms of worldwide organs and structures. In view of the growing consciousness of interdependence, Christians, with all people of good will, should be able to free themselves from "the old, restrictive paradigms" and create a new framework for confronting the new situation "liberated for new initiatives".[88]

Conversion has to be preached to Christians, too, and first of all to them, with a renewed covenant vision, a call to a morality of worldwide responsibility. How can we accept the abyss between the Christians of the Western world and those of the developing nations of the Southern hemisphere, while the newly developed "élites" of those nations, educated by Christian churches, frequently imitate the life style of their Western brethren?[89] In this historical moment, our faith in one God is tested by our freedom to act in solidarity for this one world. In this light we shall later face the mission of believers for peace and justice.[90]

2. Authentic secularity and a spurious secularism

The recent experience of religious fanaticism that contradicts all rules of rationality[91] cannot undo the process of secularization. It is, no doubt, an extremely complex phenomenon and process. The interpretation is therefore not at all easy.

In secularity we find the ambivalence of a world that is God's good creation, fallen into the bondage of sin, and yet redeemed. Such theologians as Karl Rahner and Johann Baptist Metz see the most profound reality of the secular world in the light of redemption (whereby creation, too, is understood as part of the salvific action of God). A decisive fact is, then, that "the world is set free into its own secularity".[92]

True progress of salvation history, genuine fidelity of Christ's disciples and especially of the official church, will ever more manifest this divine design. It is disturbed by concupiscence, by the sinfulness of humankind and the actual sins, and especially by all attitudes and actions of representatives of religious bodies who intend to domineer over the world. So if we speak positively on the event of secularization and on secularity, we recognize that religious leaders are more and more liberated from transgressing the bounds of their competence, and from everything that unjustly limits the realm of creative liberty and fidelity in authentic secularity.

But probably the heart of the matter is the transformation of the whole interpretation and self-understanding of the world at large, "the transition from a divinized to a humanized world".[93] Through growth of consciousness, fostered also by the Judeo-Christian vision of history, humankind at large is set free from a magic world-view and from that kind of pantheism that almost identified God with nature. Typical of this view is Spinoza's expression, *"Deus sive natura"* (God and/or nature).

Perhaps no modern church document adheres to this kind of thought and language more clearly than the encyclical *Casti Connubii* of Pius XI. It frequently follows, probably unconsciously, the vocabulary of Spinoza, for instance: "natura Deoque jubente" (singular) thus "nature and God" are one undivided subject who "gives the precept"[94]; or "Deo Creatore ipsaque naturae lege jubentibus" (plural: "whereby the imperative comes from God and from the law of nature itself"), "quae a Deo et natura auctoribus instituta sunt"[95] ("that by God and nature itself as authors, was instituted").

The language that frequently recurs throughout the encyclical[96] gives the impression that there are two authorities or legislators, God and nature; not only as if God speaks directly through the nature of the world and of things, but even as if physical nature were an intangible hypostasis simply found and approved by divine wisdom. Nature, considered here as unchangeable, is a kind of *causa formalis* ("Urgrund"), a final source and formal cause that stands side by side with God and/or before God when he creates and thus promulgates unchangeable laws.[97]

With this kind of thinking, the encyclical gave a higher imperative to the mere functioning of organs than to the exigencies of the natural male-female attraction and need, blessed by God in the Old Testament and affirmed by Christ in the New Testament.

Equally typical of the mentality before secularization is the unproblematic attitude that asserts that the church knows all these natural laws once and forever, and has no need to recur to common search, experience, reflection or dialogue with the world.

In faith and through faith, freedom from the world - that is from all tendency to divinize, from lust of power, from fatalism - becomes ever more manifest as *freedom for the real world*, the world created and redeemed and, in spite of its ambiguity, accepted by God; a world, however, "waiting with eager expectation for God's sons and daughters to be revealed . . . groaning in all its parts as if in pangs of childbirth" (Rom 8:19-22).

Friedrich Gogarten, the Protestant theologian who, for forty years, concentrated his studies on the phenomenon of secularization, writes: "The church offers the world a double service; she helps it to recognize that it is only world; but thus she uncovers to the world also the other knowledge, namely, that it is a creation of God".[98] In the same line we can say that a church which, by her relationship with the world honours God as God and renounces all domineering attitudes, can announce God's universal reign and denounce the world whenever it is a rebellious world, and at the same time remind it that it is accepted (redeemed) by God.

For J. B. Metz, the full recognition of the world's secularity is acknowledgement of God's transcendence and absolutely free descent into the world. God "dwells in unapproachable light" (1 Tm 6:16). "For the Greeks, the world had always had a numinous side; there was always the dark beginning of God himself; all their horizons merged into a twilight of the gods. This view never allowed the world to become wholly secular because it never let God become wholly divine."[99]

Secularity means then, for Metz, the reflection of God's freedom in the created world. God so creates and, as liberator, so accepts the world that the world gradually can discover authentic freedom, insofar as it accepts this "being accepted". "Let us think of two people in friendship. The more deeply one is 'accepted' by the other and taken into his own existence, the more he discovers himself, the more radically he is made free for his own possibilities. 'Being accepted' and 'autonomy' are not here opposed but correspond to one another."[100]

While we fully recognize the world's development towards secularity, we realistically ask ourselves if it is simply secularity that our world of today lives. On the one hand there are still the old images of a divinized world with its taboos and spurious raptures. On the other hand there are new myths such as that of constant progress through technical development or of improvement through violence, and many others. And there is the distorted secularity of a world opposed not only to clericalism but rebellious against God or totally uninterested in the God question. The latter is a main cause of our world's susceptibility to all the disorders of these secularist myths.

Only by considering authentic secularity and recognizing it existentially in faith, in the full light of the Christ event, can we unmask the distortions of authentic secularity and denounce a veiled cult of a humiliating profanity.[101] The manifold ways in which sinfulness has inscribed itself in the world create violent antagonisms against authentic secularity.

Karl Rahner gives some very valuable indications of how Christians can, in faith, live a "spirituality" that points the way to authentic secularity. "An absolutely honest life in the world is already part of a 'pious' life, because God himself loves the world, reconciles it and is never in competition with it . . . Whatever is meaningful and creatively alive in man is already reached by Christ's gracious calling, before it is explicitly 'baptized'; indeed it does not always and everywhere need this explicit 'baptism', if only the Christian does not lock his heart against God."[102]

In the same framework he approaches the problem of how Christians accept the pluralism which is an essential characteristic of secularity. "The life of the Christian is characterized by an unbiased acceptance of the pluralism of human existence. Some might think that the Christian is someone who wants to construct everything starting from God and from a religious concept that gives everything directly its meaning. Of course it is true that he knows that all his earthly existence, an existence in spirit and nature, in life and death, is embraced by the One, the Incomprehensible whom we call God and whom we confess as the Father of *the* Eternal Love, the Father of our Lord Jesus Christ . . . But God cannot become a part of our calculations. . . If we confess that God can be so much God that he creates what is different from him and sets it free into a pluralism that absolutely disallows simple calculations, then, for the Christian it follows that he can expose himself to this pluralism without being embarrassed."[103]

Faith in the Creator of the world and the God of history does not allow religious integralism, and forbids the straitjacket of a deductive system that represses everything that does not fit into it. The Christian should distinguish himself by the art of listening, searching together with others, allowing reality to speak to him. Discernment has its noble place within this worldwide openness.

3. Adoration in Spirit and truth as the guarantor of authentic secularity

There are many Christians who, theoretically, are not ready to recognize the secularity of the world, yet their religiosity is thoroughly severed from their professional, political and cultural activities. And this leads to an unholy worldliness. Since authentic secularity is made possible by God's action in accepting the world and setting it free, only those who accept their freedom and their activity in the world as a gift and a mandate from God can reach a true understanding of secularity and the attitudes and actions that correspond with it.

"Basically, only Christians can take secularity in full seriousness by accepting it as what it is itself, without infiltrating it or throwing an ideology over it, thus destroying its sober, objective, almost sightless factuality." Metz draws a radical conclusion from this thought: "The truly non-believing non-Christian will always ultimately give an ideological falsification to this heightened secularity - either in utopianism or in a naïve belief in progress, of a paradise on earth or a tragic nihilism and resigned scepticism about the world."[104] Using Karl Rahner's concept, Metz sees an "anonymous Christian" in those non-Christians who truly face this world openly, without myths and ideologies.

Yves Congar discovers, in the historical processes tending towards an authentic secularity, the presence of the Spirit of God.[105] The Second Vatican Council's evaluation of the overall human endeavour as a creative value arises, at least partially, from this activity of the Spirit within world and history even outside the church. "All this holds true not only for Christians but for all men of good will in whose hearts grace works in an unseen way."[106] "God's Spirit, who with a marvellous providence directs the unfolding of time and renews the face of the earth, is not absent from this development."[107]

True secularity is not at all served by a merely theoretical belief that there is a God, but only by that authentic orthodoxy that honours the one God as God in all of one's life, by direct adoration and a life coherent with adoration, in solidarity with all people and in respect for each person's dignity. For unbelievers there are, as Paul tells us, "many 'gods' and many 'lords', yet for us there is one God, the Father, from whom all being comes, towards whom we move; and there is one Lord, Jesus Christ, through whom all things came to be, and we through him" (1 Cor 8:5-6). If we live this truth not only in our inner conviction and our private life but also in all our activities in the world, then we are adorers "in spirit and truth", and are set free from an idolatrous and self-righteous world, set free for true secularity.

According to our faith, the world is held by God and his affirmation of the world. "He alone, in the free mystery of his love, is the place of all true convergence between faith and world."[108] The meaning and purpose of creation and redemption and of all history of the world is "that God may be all in all" (1 Cor 15:28). By a life marked by "adoration in spirit and truth", the believer adheres to the divine design. Those who are on this road will help to set the world free from the shackles of magic, of myth, of violence and lust for power. They will be given the gift of discernment. Their life and their word will be the best "social criticism". In the midst of true adorers of God, there will be no lack of prophetic vision and interpretation.

For true believers and adorers of God, the best gateway to faith experience today is the experience of creative liberty and firm commitment to the dignity and liberty of all. The test of true faith and adoration is faithfulness to the shared task of "a deeper humanization of human life."[109]

4. Autonomous morality within the horizon of faith

It seems to me that here is the theological locus for the much discussed problem of autonomous ethics in the Christian's responsibility in and for the world.

First of all, it is to be emphasized that most of the Catholic moral theologians, who were in the avantgarde in insisting on an autonomous ethics in the sphere of the world,[110] have never denied or minimized the importance of faith as the horizon of understanding and of fundamental option that opens to the liberating grace and light coming from Christ. Their main concern has been the credibility and rationality of our moral norms and imperatives, dialogue with the modern world and cooperation with all people of good will, the affirmation of the oneness of the order of salvation for all, and liberation from nonrational traditionalism and legalism.

We should not forget here that the social encyclicals from Leo XIII to Paul VI use mainly rational arguments (natural law concepts) which, in the eyes of these pontiffs, should be accessible to all people. The Second Vatican Council has made far-reaching statements on the autonomy of the various spheres. They speak to our point. The destination "that in all things Christ may take the first place" (Col 1:18) "not only does not deprive the temporal order of its independence, its proper goals, laws, resources, and significance for human welfare, but perfects the temporal order in its own intrinsic strength and excellence, and raises it to the level of man's total vocation on earth." As a practical consequence of this vision, the decree on the Lay Apostolate reminds the laity that "the temporal order must be renewed in such a way that, without the slightest detriment to its own proper laws, it can be brought into conformity with the higher principles of Christian life and adapted to the shifting circumstances of time, place and person."[111]

The Pastoral Constitution on the Church in the Modern World speaks on the concept of the autonomy of earthly things, in view of the fear of many of our contemporaries who consider religion as an enemy of their independence and moral autonomy. "If by the autonomy of earthly affairs we mean that created things and societies themselves enjoy their own laws and values which must be gradually deciphered, put to use, and regulated by men, then it is entirely right to demand that autonomy."[112]

Here, all forms of integralism are disallowed. The emphasis is on the need gradually to decipher the values and on "methodological investigation within every branch of learning. . . to penetrate the secrets of reality with a humble and steady mind." In this context, a footnote of Article 36 points to the case of Galileo Galilei and to "habits that cannot be but deplored".

However, it should not be overlooked that the Council speaks to Christians whom it invites, as does John Paul II in his encyclical *Redemptor Hominis*, to let Christ enter fully into their hearts to illumine and move them.[113]

We are reminded here that Luther, who so forcefully denounced proud rationalism as a "whore", believed that rationality is the road also for Christians in the civil order, provided they dedicate themselves by faith to Christ. "Fallen humanity is not only evil but also stupid."[114]

Faith, not just as an acceptance of a catalogue of doctrines but as a total conversion to Christ and docility to his Spirit, does liberate the believer not only from evil ways but also from any estrangement of his intelligence. But faith, by itself, does not automatically resolve problems in the social, economic, cultural and political realms. Rather, it impels believers to search in solidarity and to share experience and reflection with all people of good will.

All too often in the past, solutions were offered in the name of God when shared learning and awareness of the limits of one's competence (not only of office but also of knowledge) would have allowed freedom for better ways of thinking and acting. Karl Rahner feels that the church's growth in self-understanding and awareness of her identity sets man free for a common effort in the earthly sphere. This implies greater humility in the official church when teaching moral norms, especially in fields in which others enjoy greater experience and competence.[115]

The more Christians respect the relative autonomy of the various realms of life, and particularly when they work out and propose ethical norms, the more will they be able to fulfil their prophetic role. That role is to integrate carefully all that is good, true, beautiful and noble, to eliminate everything that contradicts faith, and to purify whatever is in need of purification and allows it.[116]

We do well to be critical of modern rationality that has lost the vision of wholeness and follows only a disintegrated knowledge of dominion.[117] C. F. von Weizsäcker suggests that this critical help is best offered to the scientific community in the form of pertinent questions, for instance, on the idea of value-free technology and science that allowed the construction of atom bombs, the destruction of the human environment and so on. Neither science nor technology, as such, needs our norms; rather, a dangerous trend to absolutize scientific or technical progress without concern for ultimate meaning[118] calls for our critical and creative presence.

IV. VOCATION AND SANCTITY IN THE WORLD

Understanding our responsibility in and for the world implies also a renewed vision of vocation and profession.[119] Social ethics cannot give too much attention to the various professional ethics. The prophetic concept of "sanctity in the world" has to take flesh and blood in the concrete stuff of our existence. Responsible action in one's profession is part and parcel of a "holy worldliness".

1. On the history of a theology of vocation

Some professions such as those of priest, physician, king appeared in almost all cultures in a numinous light. They were seen as participating directly in the realm of sacredness, bearers of divine powers. In the constantinian era, especially throughout the middle ages, and as much in the Roman-Germanic as in the East Roman empire, theology gave great attention to the divine mission of emperors and kings, not only in the pejorative sense of "the king's priests" but also frequently in a constructive way. It treated of the exigencies emanating from the divine investment in kingly powers.

In a world order considered as sacred, kings and nobility were pillars. Because their place in society was understood to be directly sanctioned by God, it required a high vocational ethos. In the sixth and following centuries, numerous treatises entitled "Fürstenspiegel" (a mirror for self-examination for princes and kings) were written and widely read.[120] They made clear that privileges and rank, as gifts of God, must be responded to by faithful service rendered to the church and the emperor, but above all, to the people. Christian members of the nobility considered their duties not just as job plus privileges but as a vocation given them by birth and to be honoured by a high ethos.

In Thomas Aquinas, we find some fundamental ideas for the ethos of all social states of life. Each person could conceive his place in the order of society as willed by God, honourable, and somehow sacred. Thomas quotes Pseudo-Dionysius: "More divine than everything else is to become God's cooperator".[121] "Thomas sees all professional activity in essential connection with God's action which creates and conserves the world order. This is its *finis operis*."[122] Professional activity in the state of life willed by God is part of his divine design to create man in his image and likeness.

But one aspect which today we consider essential for the concept of vocation was absent in the medieval reflection - free choice. Even for entrance into the monastic or priestly state of life, freedom was frequently an acceptance of what other people or the circumstances had determined more than a personal choice. But theologians gave special honour also to these "vocations" because a special providence and "free response to the calling" were taken into account.

While today's concept of profession and presence in the world implies, above all, a mission to shape the world, to "create" a human environment, the medieval concept was to accept one's place in a *given* world, a *given* social order.

2. Luther's concept of vocation

Luther not only accepted but sharpened the emphasis on the *given* place in the social order, while Calvin made some remarkable openings for possible eventual change of one's place, although only in view of the theocratic Calvinist community.

The revolutionary aspect (within the very conservative view of the states of life) was Luther's anti-monastic passion. For him, the monastic life did not fit into the vision of divine calling (Berufung), since God did not call anyone to acquire salvation by works that serve nobody on earth. Vocation-profession was not a question of meritorious acts but of taking one's place in faith-obedience. This obedience deserved special honour because the social states of life, the professional activities honoured God's regiment in the world and served others. "Omnes status huc tendunt ut aliis serviant" (Each profession has its meaning in the service to others).[123]

Luther gave particular attention to the state of "household", which includes husband and wife, children and servants, as the basic state of life and vocation that keeps the world. He had no regrets for the serfdom of the German farmers; they should content themselves with the place divine providence had assigned to them. He also had no worries about the vocation to military life. The good soldier should think that it is God himself who, through him, "beats, stabs and chokes".[124]

Luther, no doubt, made a constructive contribution to appreciation of life in the world, doing God's will there in the given order and rank, being honest and reliable, and sanctifying one's life in the worldly reality. But his conservatism[125] made the Lutherans subservient subjects to the Calvinist kings-emperors of Prussia, with pernicious consequences even up to the time of Hitler.

On the other hand the Catholic position, which frequently tended to reserve the honour of vocation to priests and religious, failed to integrate activity in the world - professional life, family and politics - into the fundamental "calling", the calling to cooperate with God's activity in the world, with his loving intention to perfect all men and women in his image and likeness.

3. Sanctity in marriage and family

Society arises from marriage and family. There, life has its intensity. When the church teaches that marriage is a sacrament, this says that religion is in life, and life in its most vital experience is a way of salvation. Unfortunately, the theological interpretation of the sacrament of marriage, given by canonists and even by official documents for a long time, has obscured this important truth of Catholic doctrine. The sacrament was identified with the "contract" validly performed in a "church ceremony". The content of the contract was the right to "acts fitting for procreation", while love was declared a "secondary" end! Augustinian tradition stressed the "friendship of souls", while the conjugal act needed always to be excused by its procreative intention.

The Second Vatican Council has made gigantic strides in bringing the very heart of marriage and family into a sacramental vision.[126] The spouses are called to be, for each other and their children, a true image of God's love, fidelity, reconciling compassion and patience. Marriage is not just for procreation but for that kind of responsible and loving parenthood that points to the parenthood of God.

There is still much to be done to teach all Christians that

marriage should be considered truly a vocation based on the fundamental calling of each Christian to holiness, a vocation for the building up of the Mystical Body and for the good of society. This vision requires an appropriate preparation and spirituality.

4. The crisis of the priestly vocation

The development of the self-understanding of the church, expressed in the Pastoral Constitution on the Church in the Modern World, might well be the best key for discernment of the present crisis of the ministerial priesthood.[127] Priests who were formed in minor and major seminaries were somewhat separated from the reality of the world. They were not prepared to fulfil their role in a church which understands herself in service to the world and accepts the basic reality of secularity of the world in the sense explained above. Surely the priest must be, above all, a man of prayer, but he must also be outstanding in knowledge of man and the world, able to guide by discernment, and to form discerning Christians.

Today there are enormous resources for good priestly vocations within the group of men who, around the sixtieth year of life, retire from their main profession and feel completely free to serve the cause of the kingdom of God. Frequently they bring better qualifications to the ministry of the church as she understands herself in the Second Vatican Council, than most of the young men who have had no opportunity to learn by experience about people in their real conditions. The church today needs more diverse types of priests, able to cooperate with the laity, accepting them as partners.

5. Vocation, profession and the "job"

There are two different ways to construct a theology of vocation and profession. According to Alfons Auer, Karl Barth offers such a theology "from above". The point of departure and constant reference is Christ's calling and our being called in Christ to salvation and to a life in the world, to the honour of God. Auer himself offers an excellent theology of profession "from below", from the experience of modern people in their activity and profession, bringing everything finally into the vision of faith, of God's creation, and finding in Christ its Omega point, its unconcealment and salvation.[128]

Dietrich Bonhoeffer, while bringing the vision down to earth, never loses sight of the centrality of Christ. "Speaking on the world without Christ is mere abstraction. The world stands in a relationship to Christ whether it knows it or not. This relationship to Christ becomes concrete in certain *mandates* of God in the world."[129] For Bonhoeffer, the main mandates are: work, marriage, authority, church. Professional activity of every kind has clearly the character of a "divine mandate for the conservation of the world for the sake of Christ and in view of Christ."[130]

Here, then, we ask: how does modern man see "work"? Does he discover a "vocation", a "divine calling" or a "mandate"? As a consequence of industrialization and assembly line production of what sells rather than of what is needed, together with a consumer society mentality, work is, for many people, merely a "job". For "job", two considerations predominate. The first is to earn enough for the "real life", family life and/or prestigious consumption, leisure time, pleasure. The second is self-affirmation and social status by achievement and monetary earnings. In a capitalist system (whether private or state capitalism), work becomes an article to be sold, something not belonging to the person as person, within the "Thou-I-We relationships". Add to all this what Luther so forcefully expressed: "Each profession has its meaning in the service of others", to which he adds: "We invert it".[131] We act in just the opposite way.

But what do we mean by work as a "mandate" or "vocation"? In "work" in its broadest sense, man discovers the potentialities of the created reality and participates in God's creative action. By doing so properly, he discovers and develops his own capacities. And if he does this in conscious social-mindedness, he also develops his own personality and precious social relationships while contributing to the creation of humane social-economic conditions. There is no need to exclude the average person's attitude to his or her "job" as a way to earn one's living, to support one's family and to affirm one's social status, so long as these dimensions are integrated in the broader vision.

It is one of education's most neglected yet most important tasks to lead people to an integrated understanding of work in

general and of one's particular "job". Each of us should see
clearly what function we fulfil in the whole process of social
services and production. For some professional workers this is
easier than for others whose job seems rather irrelevant or
socially less appreciated. An education such as we describe would
probably change society. People would not so easily accept (for
payment) activities that are degrading or socially insignificant or
even valueless or detrimental.

D. von Hildebrand studies the question of how one's work or
job can be integrated in the original vocation of being called by
God and for communion with God. One may simply neglect the
immediate significance of one's work and accept one's condition
as "God's will". Or a person coming into contact with other
people through his or her activity may profit in order to manifest
justice, appreciation and love to them, or may through team-work
become able to exercise the apostolate "on such an occasion".
The third and ideal approach is, however, to discover the
imminent value of one's work and of social relationships in work,
and to honour God first of all by giving work its proper meaning
Then, the other motivations too become more authentic.[132]

The normal development that makes the job a response to a
divine mandate is the openness to the needs of others, and one's
response to the whole realm of personal relationships and to the
kind of relationships within the world of work. The response to
God's calling is thus transcendentally present and can come to the
foreground in an explicit vocational motivation.[133]

6. The arduous professions-vocations

There are professional activities that, by their very nature, are
humanizing and at the same time serve mankind's basic needs, for
example, farming, gardening, the healing professions. Many
activities in the industrial sector serve basic needs but are
frequently organized in such a way that the worker is
dehumanized although, through his help, the materia is made
beneficial. In these cases it would be futile to call just for a better
work ethics in the individualistic sense if nothing is done to
change the social and economic conditions.

Here I want to call special attention to the arduous professions
which, by their very nature, can become in an excellent way
"vocation" or "divine mandate". At least partially, they fall under

the category "authority", as understood by Bonhoeffer. I mean leading professions, key positions that allow substantial and beneficial influence for improvements, yet can also be terribly abused.

These professions were strangely neglected in a time when Catholic moralists were saying not one word about their being outstanding vocations but rather were treating them only under the heading, "proximate occasion of sin". Karl Rahner speaks of the pietistic mentality that kept the "pious" aloof from political activity, in the hope that others would do this "dirty work" for them in a way that would allow them a quiet and secure life.[134]

The professions which are especially arduous today, and decisive for the present generation and the future of the world, are among others, the political, artistic, and journalistic professions. But we should not forget the importance of the pioneers in the fields of medicine and the social and behavioural sciences, the experts in urban renewal, the genius that promotes authentic alternatives to the present socio-economic structures and mentalities, the novelists who help discover the disorders and hopes of the present world, the lawyers who know how to make law and courts effective services of human rights and dignity.

Society is urgently in need of men and women who can offer a vision for the organization and best use of the mass media. Furthermore, the world of today is in need of courageous and creative philosophers and theologians who break new ground, even at the risk of being considered "not safe". And we need creative people like Mahatma Ghandi to teach humanity the force of non-violent participation for peace and justice.

What we need are not just "professionals" but men and women who fulfil these "mandates" as an embodiment of "sanctity in the world". They need proper spiritual as well as professional preparation. Käsemann expresses beautifully this spirit which makes people pioneers in history and in the world, and witnesses for the beatitudes: "Those who hunger and thirst for righteousness that is nothing else than the reverse of Christian freedom in its reality on earth, and of genuine sanctification that must be practised every day."[135]

V. CONSERVING OR CHANGING THE WORLD?

1. Orientation towards the future and its implications

One of the reasons for the great impact of Marxist ideology on several generations is its radical orientation towards the future. In spite of its rigid scientific-analytical vestment, it belongs to "prophecy"; it shows a way out of the unacceptable present. It had its main impact on those parts of the world that were once Christian, chiefly because Christianity, at its heart and in its great tradition, was future-oriented, dynamic, governed by the divine promises and by corresponding goal commandments. But bourgeois Christendom, and especially legalistic moralism had betrayed that essential heritage that accords with the heart of man created by God. So Marxism could easily steal the Christian impetus.

In a conference on Christian-Marxist dialogue, Y. Congar dares to say: "Frequently theologians simply justify the given conditions; with arguments they consider sacred, they underpin the existing situation."[136] The great Protestant scientist and philosopher, Carl Friedrich von Weizsäcker, comes to the same conclusion: "The need of reassurance in our old traditions is a nostalgic anguish-reaction against the reality lying ahead of us. Indeed, problems that could be resolved become irresolvable through this flight inspired by anguish."[137]

J. Gremillion gives the following evaluation of the changes in the official church's attitude: The aggiornamento documents mark "a radical departure from status quo models of society which blemished and bemused Catholic social thought since Leo XIII tried to revive medieval guilds, and Pius XI and Pius XII espoused a preconceived corporative order. John XXIII began the 1960s by praising modernization[138] and socialization; by 1970 the church took on the ecclesial role of promoting deep and rapid change. Paul VI has gone so far as to affirm the value of 'utopias' ". . . to provoke "the forward-looking imagination. . . to direct itself towards a fresh future".[139]

Meanwhile, the traditionalist rebel-bishop Lefebvre reminds us of the worst of a once widespread mentality, the symbol of which is Lot's backward-looking wife: "The wife of Lot looked back, and was turned into a pillar of salt" (Gn 19:26).

May I remind the reader here of what I have said on other pages: that this orientation towards the future has its solid basis and inner force in a grateful memory. But it must at the same time be a critical memory. Only thus can it play "an important role in man's hermeneutical enterprise to seek for light for future actions".[140]

J. B. Metz feels that Christian theologians should be "alarmed about the loss of eschatology" and "disturbed about the neglect of the future in theology. This neglect is so persistent that, for example, the so-called *existential* interpretation of the New Testament involves only the re-actualization and the representation of the past in the present moment of religious decision. There is no real future!".[141] The response is, however, not a merely theoretical eschatology but one that urges us to take on our responsibility for the future.

2. The ideology of progress and Christian sobriety

Elements in any realistic assessment of our present world are nuclear stock piling, increasing criminality and terrorism, ecological waste and an endangered biosphere. Humankind, so far progressed yet so immured in the various mythologies about progress, is less happy and more anguished than ever. The Marxist gospel has become, for many, a nightmare, and the same is true for western materialism and reductionism. It is time for Christians to give witness to the world that the humanization of our societies is possible only by turning to the ever greater God, the Lord of history.

Mankind is irreversibly and urgently confronted by the question about the human shape of this world constructed by men. How can we overcome the "ethical lag, the disparity between the growth curves of technological achievements and ethical behaviour"?[142]

A certain incarnational optimism in theology must finally ask whether it is not contaminated by the secular myth of progress. The world is not to be divinized, nor have we a right to bedevil it. The absolute hope in the final victory must find us vigilant and sober in the midst of the present tension and combat. The clear orientation and the goal commandments are best observed by those who take the ever possible next step, even though it be a modest step, in our endeavour to make the world less inhumane and, bit by bit, more just.

3. Spearhead or rearguard of history?

Sobriety must not be confused with laziness or lack of creative courage. If Christians are faithful to the Lord of history and vigilant for the signs of the times, they will be the spearhead of genuine human progress. Our relationship with the world and history is marked by a creative and militant hope. This, however, may not be confused with "militant optimism".[143] Christian hope is prophecy and becomes proleptic action in doing, in the radical decision never to deny love of neighbour. But then we keep firm our hope that love does change the world. This love tends to express itself also through responsible and shared action in all realms of life.

"The hope of the gospel has a polemical and a liberating relation to man's present and practical life and to the social conditions in which man leads his life."[144] Christians and the church in its official representatives have the strongest motives to withstand the temptation of "eternalism" that all too easily tends to sacralize the inherited formulations and structures. "In biblical thought there is a co-existence of eternity with creative and innovative time. Time is not only the recurrence of what is timelessly predetermined, which would allow a timeless vision to grasp what once and forever exists. Time is really the spiritual realization of the new that cannot be foreseen."[145] It is our task not just to let God be God in his eternity but to let him be God in us and through our participation in history.[146]

Not infrequently, people of this modern world find it difficult to believe in God. For them, it is as if "God were the symbolic representative of those social systems which keep man immature in order to dominate him."[147] This is one more reason for Christians and the official church to liberate themselves from a one-sided "knowledge of dominion" that so frequently has made them the rearguard or even the last trail in historical development.

H. D. Wendland insists that we can preserve the world only by changing it. Church and individual Christians are to be committed not only to preach individual conversion but to strive mightily for on-going renewal. Should they, could they not do it so effectively that they would outpace the threatening revolutions and make them superfluous? "State and marriage cannot be preserved if the political and juridical ordinances are equated with the mandates of God, and if the historical reality is declared sacred and unchangeable."[148]

4. Promoting favourable conditions for creative liberty and fidelity

God's liberty to love the world reveals itself in his admirable fidelity to world and history, thus writing straight even with crooked lines. In spite of rebellion in the world, God remains faithful to his original design, setting man free for free and responsible participation. Our freedom is a participation in God's creative act and a presence in the true sense if it is also a participation in his faithfulness to every person, to community and society.

What the modern world needs is, above all, this faithfulness. We can maximize the creative attributes of man in responsible participation only if we maximize his rootedness and a corresponding fidelity to persons and to the living tradition. To reinstate tradition in its best sense and "to counter the increasing loss of memory and history in the self-awareness of our modern planned society are undoubtedly among the most important social critical tasks precisely of the church."[149]

Remembering, in common celebration and in one's personal life, Him who offered and still offers himself as "the bread of life for the life of the world" (Jn 6:51) we find courage and strength to commit ourselves to one another and to the cause of all people. And through such a commitment we shall discover ever new possibilities to actualize our freedom and to invite others to responsible participation. A faithful and grateful memory that makes us sharers in Christ's acceptance of the world can bring forth the true revolution of freedom in faithfulness to the beatitudes, freedom from lust for power, freedom for initiatives in non-violent strategies, freedom from guilt complexes and anguish, freedom for the ever new venture that discovers and uses the present opportunities.

NOTES

[1] Cf. R. Völkl, *Christ und Welt nach dem Neuen Testament*, Würzburg, 1961; J.B. Metz (ed.), *Welverständnis im Glauben*, Mainz, 1965; Id., *Theology of the World*, New York, 1969; J. Olinger, *Christliche Weltverantwortung. Die Kirche in der Welt von heute*, Köln, 1968; P. Schoonenberg, *Ein Gott der Menschen*, Einsiedeln, 1970; K. Rahner, "Welt und Kirche", in *Sacramentum Mundi* II, 1336-1357 (bibliography); G. Haeffner, "Welt", in *Sacramentum Mundi* II, 1300-1311 (bibliography); U. Duchrow, *Christenheit und Weltverantwortung*, Stuttgart, 1970³; J. Fuchs, *Human Values and Christian Morality*, Dublin, 1970; W. Kasper, *Glaube und Geschichte*, Mainz, 1970; P. Kerans, *Theology of the World*, New York, 1974; G. Bauer, *Christliche Hoffnung und menschlicher Fortschritt. Die politische Theologie von J. B. Metz als theologische Begründung gesellschaftlicher Verantwortung*, Mainz, 1975; Ch. Duquoc, "Presenza cristiana nella comunità umana. Una problematica morale inedita", in T. Goffi (ed.), *Problemi e prospettive di teologia morale*, Brescia, 1976, 315-332; F. Schlösser, *Thema Welt. Ja zur Welt. Schöpfungsglaube. Zukunft der Welt. Neues Weltverhältnis. Spannungsfelder*, Wien, 1976; B. Welte, *Die Würde des Menschen und die Religionen*, Frankfurt, 1977.

[2] *Gaudium et spes*, 2.
[3] *Gaudium et spes*, 1.
[4] Cf. R. Völkl, l.c., 18ff.
[5] Cf. A.V. Bauer, *Freiheit zur Welt. Zum Weltverständnis und Weltverhältnis des Christen nach der Theologie Friedrich Gogartens*, Paderborn, 1967, 229-233.
[6] Cf. J.B. Metz, *Theology of the World*, 51ff.
[7] K. Rahner, l.c., 1338.
[8] On the complexity of our age cf. R. Guardini, *Das Ende der Neuzeit*, Würzburg, 1950; Id., *Die Macht*, Würzburg, 1952; B. Häring, *Macht und Ohnmacht der Religion*, Salzburg, 1956².
[9] *Gaudium et spes*, 4-10.
[10] *Gaudium et spes*, 3.
[11] *Gaudium et spes*, 4.
[12] *Gaudium et spes*, 10.
[13] *Gaudium et spes*, 9.
[14] K. Rahner, l.c., 1339.
[15] Cf. B. Häring, *Manipulation. Ethical Boundaries of Medical, Behavioural, and Genetic Manipulation*, Slough, 1975.
[16] P.-R. Régamey, *Pauvreté chrétienne et construction du monde*, Paris, 1967, 59.
[17] Cf. G. Haeffner, l.c., 1308f.
[18] K. Rahner, l.c., 1355.
[19] Medellin Documents, On Justice, text in J. Gremillion, *The Gospel of Peace and Justice. Catholic Social Teaching since Pope John*, Maryknoll, N.Y., 1976, 446f.
[20] N.A. Luyten, "Der Mensch als Selbst- und Weltgestalter", in N. Luyten (ed.), *Weltgestaltung als Herausforderung*, Freiburg and München, 1973, 34.
[21] J. Moltmann, *Die Zukunft der Schöpfung*, München, 1977, 14.
[22] G. and P. Mische, *Toward a Human World Order. Beyond the National Security Straitjacket*, New York, 1977, 230f.
[23] D. Bonhoeffer, *Ethics*, New York, 1955, 291.
[24] R. Völkl, l.c., 153, cf. 19.
[25] G. Haeffner, l.c., 1304.
[26] J.B. Metz, l.c., 45, cf. 92.
[27] C. F. von Weizsäcker, *Deutlichkeit. Beiträge zu politischen und religiösen Gegenwartsfragen*, München, 1978, 102f.

28 *Gaudium et spes*, 39.
29 *Gaudium et spes*, 72.
30 H.-D. Wendland, "Die Welt verändern. Zur christlichen Deutung der marxistischen These", in F. Karrenberg and J. Beckman (eds.), *Verantwortung für den Menschen*, Stuttgart, 1957, 27ff.
31 K. Marx, *Die Heilige Familie* (1945), in Marx-Engels, *Werke*, Berlin, 1957, 40.
32 E. Schillebeeckx, "Questions on Christian Salvation of and for Man", in Tracy/Küng/Metz (eds.), *Toward Vatican III. Work that has to be done*, New York, 1978, 34-35.
33 J.B. Metz, l.c., 55.
34 D. Bonhoeffer, l.c., 25.
35 l.c., 192.
36 A. Köberle, "Das Weltbild des Glaubens", in *Der Auftrag der Kirche. Festschrift zum 70. Geburstag von E. Brunner*, Zürich and Stuttgart, 1959, 65f., 69.
37 H.U. von Balthasar, *Verbum Caro*, Einsiedeln, 1960, 67.
38 Cf. W. Zimmerli, *The Old Testament and the World*, Atlanta, 1976 (original German title: Die Weltlichkeit des Alten Testaments).
39 D. Wiederkehr, "Die Wirklichkeit Christi im Horizont des Weltverhältnisses Gottes und des Gottesverhältnisses der Welt", in *Mysterium salutis* III/1, 1970, 520-648, quote p. 643.
40 J.B. Metz, l.c., 22.
41 l.c., 30; cf. 46.
42 Cf. J. Moltmann, *Die Zukunft der Schöpfung*, München, 1977, 35.
43 E. Käsemann, "Die Versöhnungslehre im Neuen Testament", in E. Dinkler (ed.), *Zeit und Geschichte*, Tübingen, 1964, 52.
44 J. Moltmann, *Mensch. Christliche Anthropologie in den Konflikten der Gegenwart*, Stuttgart and Berlin, 1977, 34.
45 D. Wiederkehr, l.c., 520f.
46 K. Barth, *Kirchliche Dogmatik* IV/3, 383.
47 K. Barth, *Auferstehung der Toten. Eine akademische Vorlesung über 1 Kor 15*, München, 1924, 122.
48 A. Schmemann, *For the Life of the World. Sacraments and Orthodoxy*, New York, 1977², 68.
49 Cf. J.B. Metz, l.c., 93.
50 *Gaudium et spes*, 44.
51 *Lumen gentium*, 8.
52 O. von Nell-Breuning, *Soziale Sicherheit? Zu Grundfragen der Sozialordnung aus christlicher Verantwortung*, Freiburg, 1979, 202.
53 l.c., 224. It seems to me that it is mainly because of his rather individualistic concept of sin and redemption that Nell-Breuning is extremely critical of "political theology" altogether and not only against some false accents.
54 *Letter to Diognetus*, especially chapters 5 and 6.
55 J. Gremillion, *The Gospel of Peace and Justice*, 4.
56 In this section I follow above all U. Duchrow (ed.), *Zwei Reiche und Regimente. Ideologie oder evangelische Orientierung?*, Gütersloh, 1977; cf. H.H. Schrey (ed.), *Reich Gottes und Welt*, Darmstadt, 1969; K.H. Hertz (ed.), *Two Kingdoms and One World. A Source Book in Christian Ethics*, Minneapolis, 1976.
57 Cf. F. Gogarten, *Die Schuld der Kirche gegen die Welt*, Jena, 1928; Id., *Politische Ethik*, Jena, 1932; Id., *Ist Volksgesetz Gottesgesetz?*, Hamburg, 1934; Id., *Die Kirche in der Welt*, Heidelberg, 1942; Id., *Der Mensch zwischen Gott und Welt*, Stuttgart, 1956²; Id., *Verhängnis und Hoffnung der Neuzeit*, Stuttgart, 1958²; Id., *Jesus Christus, Wende der Welt*, Tübingen, 1966; cf. A.V. Bauer, *Freiheit zur Welt. Zum Weltverständnis und Weltverhältnis der Christen nach der Theologie Friedrich Gogartens*, Paderborn, 1967.

58 Cf. U. Duchrow, l.c., 282.
59 l.c., 18-20, 25, 287f.
60 Cf. l.c., 22, 25.
61 l.c., 278, 282f, 288.
62 Cf. E. Käsemann, *An die Römer*, Tubingen, 1974².
63 U. Duchrow, l.c., 275ff.
64 l.c., 302f.
65 Cf. U. Occhiali, *Presenza a Dio e presenza al mondo*, Milano, 1974.
66 Synod of Bishops, Rome, 1974, *Evangelization of the Modern World*, Declaration, n. 12, in *Word and Worship*, Jan-Feb. 1975, 100.
67 J. Desrochers, *Christ the Liberator*, Bengalore, 1977, 47.
68 John Paul II, *Redemptor Hominis*, esp. nn. 13-15.
69 Cf. K. Rahner, l.c., 1337, 1341, 1349.
70 *Redemptor hominis*, 11.
71 J. Gremillion, l.c., 132.
72 R. von Thadden, "Wie Reformen verfehlt wurden, am Beispiel der Hoch-schulen und Kirchen", in *Evangelische Kommentare* 12 (1979), 450.
73 R.L. Shinn, "How Control Technology? Faith-Science Conference: An Overview", in *Christian Century* 39 (1979), 268.
74 *Ad gentes*, 1.
75 Synod of Bishops, Rome, 1971, *Justice in the Modern World*, 39-48, in J. Gremillion, l.c., 522-523.
76 U. Duchrow, l.c., 276ff., 294, 297ff.
77 J.B. Metz, l.c., 94, 97.
78 D. Bonhoeffer, *Widerstand und Ergebung* (letters of July 18 and 21, 1944), Neuausgabe, München, 1970, 395, 402.
79 Y. Congar, "Der christliche Mensch im Spannungsfeld der Geschichte und Gesellschaft" in E. Kellner (ed.), *Schöpfertum und Freiheit in einer humanen Welt*, Frankfurt and Zürich, 1969, 93.
80 C.F. von Weizsäcker, *Deutlichkeit*, 153.
81 O. von Nell-Breuning, l.c., 204, 212.
82 W. Simpfendörfer, "Ökumene lernen", in *Evangelische Kommentare* 12 (1979), 461.
83 On Pluralism, cf. *Free and Faithful in Christ* II, 159-165, 301-304.
84 On Secularism, cf. *Free and Faithful in Christ* II, 350-353.
85 *Gaudium et spes*, 5.
86 Cf. G. Altner, *Zwischen Natur und Menschengeschichte. Perspektiven für eine neue Schöpfungstheologie*, München, 1975.
87 Cf. J. Moltmann, *Mensch*, 44.
88 G. and P. Mische, l.c., 6, 17, 31.
89 P.-R. Régamey, l.c., 9ff.
90 Cf. Chapter Nine of this volume.
91 Ayatollah Khomeini of Iran will, for a long time, be a symbol of this kind of out-dated "religion". Probably nobody can manifest better than he has the absurdity of an ecclesial system where lust of power and wealth go hand-in-hand with an inhuman fundamentalistic use of holy books and legalism close to "lawlessness" (anomia).
92 K. Rahner, l.c., 1349; cf. B. Häring, *Faith and Morality in the Secular Age*, Slough and New York, 1973.
93 J.B. Metz, l.c., 55.
94 Pius XI, *Casti connubii*, AAS 22 (1930), 545.
95 l.c., 546, 577.
96 l.c., 547, 557, 560, 563.

[97] l.c., 583.
[98] F. Gogarten, *Die Kirche in der Welt*, Heidelberg, 1948, 127.
[99] J.B. Metz, l.c., 34, cf. 64.
[100] l.c., 27.
[101] l.c., 47.
[102] K. Rahner, "Frömmigkeit früher und heute", in *Schriften zur Theologie* VII, Einsiedeln, 1971², 11-31, quote 25-26.
[103] K. Rahner, *Grundkurs des Glaubens*, Freiburg, 1976, 391-392.
[104] J.B. Metz, l.c., 47.
[105] Y. Congar, l.c., 92ff., 96.
[106] *Gaudium et spes*, 22,5; cf. *Lumen gentium*, 16.
[107] *Gaudium et spes*, 26 (towards the end); cf. 38, 41,1; 57,4.
[108] J.B. Metz, l.c., 45.
[109] l.c., 75.
[110] Cf. A. Auer, *Autonome Moral und Glaube*, Düsseldorf, 1971; Id., *Weltoffener Christ*, Düsseldorf, 1962².
[111] Decree on *Lay Apostolate*, 7.
[112] *Gaudium et spes*, 36, cf. 41.
[113] *Redemptor hominis*, esp. 8.
[114] A. Köberle, "Das Weltbild des Glaubens", 70, cf. 66.
[115] K. Rahner, *Sacramentum Mundi* IV, 1342, 1349.
[116] A.V. Bauer, *Freiheit zur Welt*, 43ff., 59, 187ff.
[117] U. Duchrow, l.c., 277.
[118] C.F. von Weizsäcker, *Deutlichkeit*, 157ff., cf. G. Schnellmann, *Theologie der Technik. 40 Jahre Diskussion um die Technik, zugleich ein Beitrag zu einer Theologie der Technik*, Köln and Bonn, 1974
[119] Cf. D. von Hildebrand, *Katholisches Berufsethos*, Augsburg, 1931; A. Auer, *Christsein im Beruf. Grundsätzliches und Geschichtsliches zum christlichen Berufsethos*, Düsseldorf, 1966; H. Asperger, Ch. Leitmaier, F.A. Westphalen (eds.), *Ein Chor der Antworten. Glaube und Beruf*, Wien and München, 1969; M. Oraison, *Berufsfindung und Berufung*, Frankfurt/M., 1972.
[120] Cf. A. Auer, l.c., 56ff.
[121] S.Th., *S. contra Gent.* III, 21; Pseudo-Dionysius, *De coel. hier.* 3.
[122] A. Auer, l.c., 64.
[123] M. Luther, *Predigten, Weimarer Luther Ausgabe* 15, 625.
[124] M. Luther, *Ob Kriegsleute auch im seligen Stand sein können*, WA 19, 656.
[125] Cf. K. Dunkmann, *Die Lehre vom Beruf. Eine Einführung in die Geschichte und Soziologie des Berufs*, Berlin, 1922, 92f.
[126] Cf. *Gaudium et spes*, 48-51; cf. B. Häring, *Free and Faithful in Christ* II, 493-542.
[127] Cf. U. Sanchez, *La crisis sacerdotal según la Gaudium et spes. Actitudes y caminos de superación*, Caracas,1977 (with preface of B. Häring).
[128] A. Auer, l.c., 108f.; cf. 203-310.
[129] D. Bonhoeffer, *Ethik*, München, 1953³, 70.
[130] l.c., 257.
[131] See fn. 123.
[132] Cf. D. von Hildebrand, l.c., 19-22; A. Auer, l.c., 290-307.
[133] Cf. M. Oraison, l.c., 108.
[134] K. Rahner, *Schriften zur Theologie* VII, 26f.
[135] E. Käsemann, *Jesus Means Freedom*, Philadelphia, 1970, 143.
[136] Y. Congar, "Der christliche Mensch im Spannungsfeld der Geschichte und Gesellschaft", in E. Kellner (ed.), l.c., 90.

[137] C.F. von Weizsäcker, l.c., 153.

[138] When John XXIII, on several public occasions in 1959, said: "Fr Häring has modernized moral theology", some would reply; "Fr Häring is a modernist." Many could never distinguish modernity from modernism.

[139] J. Gremillion, l.c., 2; quote from Paul VI, *Octogesima adveniens*, 37.

[140] E. Schillebeeckx, l.c., 36.

[141] J.B. Metz, l.c., 86.

[142] Cf. G. and P. Mische, l.c., 203, 213; J. Moltmann, *Mensch*, 42f.

[143] J.B. Metz, l.c., 87.

[144] J. Moltmann, *Theologie der Hoffnung*, München, 1964, 304.

[145] Cl. Tresmontant, *Essai sur la pensée hebraique*, Paris, 1953, 41.

[146] Y. Congar, l.c., 102.

[147] C.F. von Weizsäcker, l.c., 164.

[148] H.-D. Wendland, "Die Welt verändern", l.c., 33.

[149] J.B. Metz, l.c., 155.

Chapter Five

Ecology and Ethics

No part of our social ethics reveals more clearly the interdependence between human health and the commitment to work for healthy conditions of life than this central chapter on ecology.[1]

Ecology, as we treat of it here, is a relational concept and reality. Is man's way of dealing with his environment healthy, gentle, thoughtful, responsible? Does he establish a relationship with the world around him that fosters genetic balance, reflects healthy human relationships and a healthy system of economics and politics? Are our basic attitudes, our present system of economics, our societal organization able to face the already tangible ecological crisis which finally may be a question of survival for humankind?

An ecological problem is a special type of social problem. It can reveal the deepest disturbances of social conditions, processes and relationships. Carl Amery may well touch the meaning of the ecological crisis when he says that politics, up to now dominated by an irrational economic science, should rather be based on a rational science of ecology.[2]

What we have said about man's responsibility towards the world, and Heidegger's description of human existence as "Being-in-the-world" receive new relevance by insight into the present ecological situation. For the rational human being, to-be-in-the-world truthfully means having that wholeness of vision that allows a caring and responsible relation to things and the world.[3]

The support system of life, including human life, was and is the earth. In its relation to the solar system and especially to all the life processes on earth - processes that are always relational - the earth can be called the Biosphere.[4] The motor of the evolution of all life is the never ceasing interaction between species and environment. For man, this interaction is one of nature and culture. "The human environment is a matrix of elements derived by evolution through nature and contrived by man through culture."[5] It becomes ever clearer that man's cultural level depends on and reveals itself in the way he respects and develops the totality of interactions which determine the quality of his environment and indirectly the quality of his life.

The focus is on the dynamic relationship between man and environment. The goals of an ethics and the strategy of ecology would be "to formulate the principles by which, through the various means, the multitude of man/environment relationships could be guided."[6] Man has to explore carefully his dependence on the surrounding ecosystem for the support of life itself. Then it is a matter of purposefully adapting the environment to best serve his real needs. By shaping his culture, he best reshapes his environment.[7] It is a matter of a moving and always delicate equilibrium, or "dynamic homeostasis".

Ethical thought sees ecology as a "middleman" science that brings together the respective results of the physical and biological sciences and the social and behavioural sciences. These sciences become ethically relevant in a vision of wholeness that see the real needs of humankind. The encounter with the sciences is especially complex in this regard. I agree with Charles Birch's observation that "The critical social context for science and religion is not the world of the factory but the world of ecological crisis. Yet the dominant scientific-technological world view is not an ecological model at all. It is anti-nature."[8]

Our present ecological knowledge and crisis show us the "cosmic" dimension of sin and redemption in a new light. In theology, we always knew that our failure to respond faithfully to God, who calls us in Christ and through all his work, word and revelation, is not just a personal deficiency. But today we can better understand that "it is a cosmic tragedy."[9] And we can no longer ignore the fact that the proper response to God and responsibility towards humankind must be manifested in our ecological consciousness that nature, which is the support system of all life, must be respected; it cannot be ruthlessly exploited without sinning against the essential cosmic dimension of creation and redemption.[10] It is an undeniable fact that the unwise *homo faber*, lacking the wisdom of *homo sapiens*, has been not only a desert-maker but a disturbing factor in biological stability.

I. HISTORY AND THE NEW SITUATION

1. History teaches us

Through thousands of years, humankind has lived in many separate histories. What people of one culture did directly affected only their own environment. Margaret Mead and Walter Fairservis show us that, among the great cultures of the past, there were some that undermined their future by irresponsible attitudes towards nature.[11] The aggressive Mesopotamian culture disappeared almost completely because of the ecological decay they caused, while the ancient Egyptian and Chinese cultures showed a much more gentle and respectful attitude towards their environment, and therefore could last longer. The Roman empire, marked as much by exploitation as the Sumerians, caused its downfall by extreme materialism that did violence to nature - for instance, by far-reaching deforestation.[12] Plato had already commented in his *Kritias* on the deforestation of Attica;[13] and the Mediterranean countries suffered disastrous ecological crises for the same reason. Many tribes destroyed the basis of their own subsistence by over-grazing.

"The desert is the dominant landscape of our solar system."[14] That whole regions of the earth which once were fruitful have become desert wastes is at least partially the fault of man. But what happened in past history usually affected one relatively small area. Today, man is about to be a desert-maker in a way that disturbs the global ecological system.

2. Man the maker-manipulator and the loser

Today's scientific, technological man is the most skilled

manipulator of nature. There is nothing wrong with shaping and refining things. But while modern man is building up an enormous monetary capital and ever more industrial plants and highways, he forgets to administer wisely the much larger and most precious "capital" provided by nature, although he does not even recognize it as such. "This larger part is now being used up at an alarming rate. The main symbol of this historical process is the 'fossil fuels'. They are not made by men; they cannot be recycled."[15]

Man is the loser, for the ruthless exploitation of indispensable and irreplaceable resources goes hand in hand with the exploitation of man by man. Modern industrial man invades the tolerance margin of nature and of human subsistence. He exploits nature in a way that blocks the path to a healthy future for humankind.

3. The magnitude of risks and dangers

Ecological consciousness is gradually resulting from examination of past environmental errors, but even more from a "growing awareness of the probable consequences of present environmental decisions."[16] Since humankind has emerged into a single history, in which the relationship between man and nature takes on global dimensions, we cannot allow ourselves such miscalculations as those of some tribes and empires of the past.

Some authors have tried to calculate in billions of dollars the measurable damage done to the human environment. But besides the fact that the damage done is beyond expression in material terms, man the maker has reached the point where, either by nuclear weapons or by environmental pollution and reckless exploitation, he can poison the whole earth and make questionable human survival. Unwise ecological behaviour "in ordinary affairs" can finally lead to the same results as a dramatic nuclear holocaust.[17]

It is not the individual factor alone that has to be considered but the combination of all the disturbances of the human environment by air and water polution, by destruction of indispensable resources, by poisoning the very genes. A worldwide use of DDT (a persistent insecticide), millions of tons of dust of lead, mercury, and cadmium, have caused not only a frightening increase of cancer but also a no less frightening increase of genetic mutations of all kinds.

The margin of tolerance of ionizing radiation by industry and armaments has been exceeded in many parts of the world. Asbestos is produced and used in increasing quantities although it is one of the principal causes of cancer, preceded only by excessive cigarette smoking. A study supported by the Health Research Council found that heavy smokers have a frequency of lung cancer 92 times that of persons who neither smoke nor have contact with asbestos.[18]

Besides all this, industry is hurrying to exploit, as soon as possible, the recombinant DNA that might well lead to a disastrous poisoning of the environment as an unwanted by-product of technology. There is much speculation on genetic manipulation. In principle, insofar as this is meant for therapy, no objection can be made. But we must not "lose sight of the agents that caused the damage in the first place: mutagens, carcinogens, radiation, etc. Our problems are not in our genes; they are in recreating a society in which the genes of individuals are protected from unnecessary damage. It is critically important that, wherever possible, the ability to identify genetic damage becomes also a first step in identifying the cause of the damage and removing it from the human ecosphere."[19]

We can agree with Konrad Lorenz when he stresses the point that one of the deadly sins of civilized man is not only in destroying the world around him, but even more in destroying man himself, his sense of beauty and his reverence for creation.[20] Man who, for his selfish goals, destroys for himself and posterity the world we live in, has already destroyed the best in himself - the sense of responsibility.

4. Ecological knowledge and resolution

The magnitude of the problem lies, most of all, in our unreadiness to study the whole and its parts with a firm decision to act upon it systematically and coherently. In the USA, about fifty thousand people die each year as a result of car accidents, and about fifteen thousand in each of the major West European industrial nations. Yet all these countries continue to foster the car industry and the private car. Each year, millions of acres of arable land are taken from agriculture for expressways. Furthermore, the private car produces the most dangerous air pollution and smog in the urban areas.

The present habit of driving one's private car unnecessarily consumes fossil energy that cannot be replaced and will be exhausted in the foreseeable future if nothing changes. Yet the car owners and manufacturers are the only arbiters in this matter. "If private cars were banned from the inner city, the speed of public transport could increase so dramatically that travellers would enjoy a cut of about seventy percent of the time of their journey across the city."[21] This is just one example of cases where enough knowledge is available but does not cause the moral shock so necessary for a profound change on a large scale. Besides the vested interests, there are our established habits that hinder a realistic assessment and the courage to look for the appropriate change.

Another major problem is the limited resources of certain minerals and, above all, fossil fuels. If all nations were to use them in the same way as the USA and the other major industrialized countries do, these treasures would be exhausted in one or, at most, two generations.

We can agree with Carl Friedrich von Weizsäcker, the director of the Max Plank Institute, that the totality of possible energy resources would be sufficient for any world population and for any meaningful use. But the concrete problem is the limited accessibility (because of the high cost or the too high risks).[22] It is not hard to foresee that the use of fossil fuels at the present pace will lead to an enormous impasse before new technologies are developed to make other energy sources truly accessible. If humankind does not come to drastic decisions, enormous social and political conflicts and psychological problems must be expected.

All the ecological facts and implications must be studied and made accessible to the widest possible audience, so that steps may be taken on the most solid ground of knowledge and careful evaluation. Mere cries of alarm - necessary as they may be - do not change the situation.

What we especially need to explore and to evaluate are the variables of our ecosystem's tolerance and its elasticity to regenerate itself, the quality of behaviour that is hostile to our human environment, and the attitudes that were and are the main causes of the situation.

The ecological problem is deeply rooted in a number of complex social conditions. After a serious evaluation of risk and chances, we have to ask ourselves whether there is, or can be awakened, a readiness to change our attitudes and to look for political initiatives which will enforce, gently but also firmly, the necessary measures. Besides the overall and long-term solutions, there must be a convincing and realistic catalogue of things to be done as soon as possible.[23] "The basic task is to learn what environmental adaptations are required in order to meet those human needs that can be demonstrated and evaluated, not merely those that are asserted."[24]

II. CHALLENGE TO THEOLOGY AND ETHICS

The magnitude of the ecological problem does not allow moral theology to confine itself to recipes or a mere casuistry of immediate duties. The stress, caused mostly by the industrial countries of Christian background, must find Christians, and especially theologians, ready to examine their conscience not only about wrong deeds or disastrous omissions, but about the attitudes and/or ideologies that might help to explain the deeper causes of the symptoms. The purpose is a conversion and renewal in depth.[25]

1. Our basic relationship to nature - creation

Ecology is a relational science. Among all the interactions and interdependencies in the human ecosystem, man's conscious and unconscious attitudes towards nature are the most decisive. What should be the vision and attitude of Christians, and especially of theology?

Not only outsiders and enemies of Christianity but also earnest Christian theologians feel that, in this respect, something went wrong in the thought patterns of the Judeo-Christian tradition. They give credit to Christianity for the kind of demythologizing of nature that allowed the development of modern science and technology in the western world. But they charge that either

Christian theologians and traditions which the church upheld, or even the biblical teaching, played at least a part in the lack of reverence for nature: a lack that, in the long run, has led to ruthless exploitation.[26] Paul Erlich's expression is typical. "Our dilemma is an unfortunate outgrowth of Judeo-Christian heritage which has produced a blind science and technology and a beserk econo-centric culture."[27]

Margaret Mead and John Passmore see the causes, not in biblical and typical Judeo-Christian tradition, but in either the special character of people and cultures[28] or in thinkers who influenced the western world in a way that does not correspond with the Bible. John Passmore notes the influence of Aristotle. Speaking of those who think that all of nature is specifically designed for man the user, there are striking texts from the Stoics, Cicero for example. "If, then, one can speak of 'Christian arrogance' in supposing things are made for men, it must be with the proviso that it is not Hebraic-Christian but Graeco-Christian 'arrogance'".[29]

Most typical of the western thought that does not reflect biblical revelation are the works of Descartes and Bacon. Descartes distinguishes man as the thinking thing and nature as the mechanical thing (a "mere machine") for use. He sees as the scope of science: "to render ourselves the masters and possessors of nature".[30] He does not think as 'piously' as some stoics that all of nature is specifically designed for man, but he is convinced that "there is nothing created from which we cannot derive some use".[31]

In the Old Testament, while the liberating action of God is in the foreground, it must not be overlooked that God, who liberates his people and teaches them to see history in this light, is also the One who manifests his glory, the splendour of his might, love and beauty in all of creation. God's blessing action (comprising all things) has an independent value side-by-side with his liberating action. The saving and the blessing action of God complete each other, and Israel praises him for both.[32] God's blessings teach us how to respect nature and to use it in a way that all may experience his blessing.

The great economist E. Fritz Schumacher sees modern man's attitude as in striking opposition to the biblical vision. "Modern man does not experience himself as a part of nature but as an outside force to dominate and conquer it. He even talks of a battle with nature, forgetting that if he won the battle, he would find himself on the losing side."[33]

In the light of the Bible we see man's relationship with nature as that of a co-creator who can be constructively creative only if he adores Him who has created all things. Man will make beneficial use of nature for himself and others only if he learns to admire God's works and to render thanks to him. Whoever knows and lives biblical piety will realize that when man reduces himself to only a user and exploiter of nature, he not only degrades himself but also sins against the Creator and his creation.[34]

2. The God-given dominion over nature, and knowledge of dominion

The ecological crisis caused by man the maker-manipulator forces theology to reflect on the meaning of the dominion God entrusted to man in his design of creation. "God blessed them and said to them, 'Be fruitful and increase, fill the earth and subdue it' " (Gn 1:28). This dominion, entrusted to the privileged creature, must be seen in intimate union with man's dignity as created to the image and likeness of God (Gn 1:27). God, who blesses those made to his image, entrusts them with the garden of Eden "to till it and to care for it" (Gn 2:15). Man should reflect the caring love of God in the wonderful world entrusted to him. Those who refuse to honour God as God and to honour each other as his image, involve nature, too, in their catastrophe. Their dominion over the world is no longer beneficial, as it could have been according to God's blessing.

Gerhard Liedke considers God's covenant with Noah and the renewed blessing given to Noah as a key for understanding the whole teaching of the first chapters of Genesis on man's dominion over the earth. He would explain Gn 1 and 2 in the light of Gn 6-9. "God is not seen here as *causa prima* but as He whom all creation confronts, He who creates, suffers, destroys and yet preserves."[35]

While the first covenant - with Adam - was one for a peaceful garden with peaceful adorers, Noah's blessing is a gift and an ordinance for a fallen world with conflicts not only between man and man but also a conflict between man and animals, in which the rights of man prevail but only if he is caring for animals as God and Noah did during the flood. This new ordinance is a constant call to conversion, to peace and to moderation in the conflicts.

Hugo of St Victor proposes the authentic tradition, insisting that man can exercise his dominion over the earth only by acting as God's image and receiving his dominion as an undeserved and gracious gift. He is one of the first writers who (in his Didascalion, written around 1120) connects new technologies with the restitution of the dominion over the earth by a merciful God. Everything aims at its re-installation in the blessing through an intimate knowlede of God's love.[36]

Quite different is the view of Francis Bacon who, in 1597, proclaimed that "knowledge is power".[37] Passmore rightly qualifies Bacon as a Pelagianist. Bacon asserts that it is not God's gracious gift but man himself who, by his knowledge of dominion, restores the original dominion over the earth. Passmore notes: "What sin had shattered, science could in large part repair. . . This was by no means the orthodox Christian teaching."[38]

Bacon wrote, "The empire of man over things depends wholly on the arts and science".[39] Here we are at the crossroads of a knowledge of dominion that has caused and continues to cause the ecological turmoil. Not that knowledge of dominion and control in itself is bad, but it becomes so when that knowledge is influenced by the powers of greed, predominion and ruthless exploitation, because it is a knowledge not acknowledged as gift of God, a knowledge that makes itself independent of wisdom, severed from the knowledge of salvation.

Modern science, as such, is good. "Man's dominion over nature must continue to be exercised, and with greater skill and wisdom than in the past."[40] Schumacher, who is particularly sensitive to the pitfalls of disintegrated science of dominion and exploitation, writes about the genuine meaning of science and technology: "This truthful knowledge, *as such*, does not commit us to a technology of giantism, supersonic speed, violence and the destruction of human work-enjoyment."[41]

Only if man learns to integrate his new knowledge of dominion in that service that comes from knowledge of salvation, from a vision of wholeness, will nature not be ruthlessly altered and destroyed. When man gives contemplation its place he will be a faithful steward of his brethren also by his care for conservation, for preservation of the beauty and goods of nature.[42]

3. Resacralization?

In the ecological disturbance that can lead even to a planetarian ecological collapse, many correctly see a profanation of nature. This injury to the ecological balance is indeed a blasphemy against the Creator. However, we cannot follow those who believe in an innocence of nature, as such, and seek the remedy in a "new remystification of that natural world, a design which reads holiness in untouched nature"[43]

We cannot return to a kind of primitive animism with its taboos or new artificial taboos. Nor can we renounce all manipulation of nature if we want to live a civilized life and to feed the 4.5 billion people today and the six or seven billion at the beginning of the next millenium. We shall not renounce our freedom and task, given us by the Creator, to subdue the earth to our real needs. "Christian theology is not committed to a blind obedience to nature or to the notion that nature handles all things for the best. Man has the right and the power to modify nature. But reckless intrusion into nature combines arrogance with the practice of virtual destruction."[44]

We surely can say with P. Teilhard de Chardin, "Everything is sacred", but not in the sense that it cannot be touched for change. Rather, in a more profound sense, we see everything as a gift of God, a sign of the ongoing creation and a call to creative and responsible cooperation in it. And this cooperation will be beneficial if, in adoration, we learn that kind of purpose and action that we can offer God, Creator and Redeemer. The believer who sees nature still in the making feels himself called to faithfulness in cooperation.

4. Process theology and ecology

Process theology, in a surprising alliance with orthodox sacramental theology, manifests a strong and specific commitment to an ecological theology and ethics.[45] This current of thought focuses on the "indeterminacy" (Heisenberg) in an unfinished, evolving creation, a "nature" full of creative energy. It is the opposite pole of deism. God is not aloof, not just watching the functioning of a machine-like nature. He is involved with all his love and presence in an ongoing process. And we, as co-creators should, by our responsible creativity, reflect him who has created us to his image.

We honour God and serve his design for nature, not by passivity or by tabooed limitations on our freedom, but by responsible, solidaric participation. God does not want us to be either idle spectators or ruthless users. We honour God's transcendence by adoration and by courageous and discerning self-transcendence, in dedication to our fellowmen and to the whole of creative and redemptive history.

Werner Heisenberg, the genial discoverer of the indeterminacy factor in evolution, strongly believed in a transcendental God, but not one who is a mere spectator. Even natural science should reflect God's creative presence and contribute to mature, dynamic response. "Natural science stands before nature no longer as mere observer, but recognizes itself as a part of this interaction between man and nature."[46]

5. A dynamic sacramental view

The best of Orthodox theology and our own tradition can lead us to a spirituality (ethics) that is both reverent and creative-responsive. We should forever refuse any kind of sacralization that practically closes the way to *creative* liberty; yet we cannot follow that kind of desacralization that left us only the meagre vision of a nature to be used. Theologically, we prefer to speak of "creation" or "created universe" rather than merely of "nature", to remind us that God wants the created reality to be transparent, to reveal him or point to him.

A Christological-sacramental vision is dynamic. It sees everything as created by the Word that became flesh in the midst of history. But it knows that the created world is involved in that shocking catastrophe of which today's ecological crisis is a real symbol. And it remembers that this world is yearning to receive its share in the liberty of the sons and daughters of God, already potentially present yet still to be revealed (cf. Rom 8:21).

A "reverent, receptive attitude" corresponding to this sacramental vision allows and requests responsible participation.

Thus false sacralization yields to discernment in creative liberty and fidelity. It is significant that leading Protestant theologians who are particularly committed to ecological consciousness meet the orthodox approach and stress the ecological fruitfulness of sacramental symbolism and celebration.[47]

We celebrate the origin and goal of our life "by taking as symbols of the divine presence in the world those elements of the natural environment appointed by its Lord: bread, wine and water. The Christian's sacramental life, in which is gathered up all his life in the world, is a living testimony to the love of God for both man and his environment."[48] The sacramental symbolism, pointing to the highest mysteries of salvation, does not allow us to ignore the humble earthly symbols. And a life coherent with the sacraments cannot blaspheme God by misuse of the earthly environment.

If, through the piety of Old Israel and the Christian liturgy, we learn to contemplate God's might, beauty and wisdom in creation, then we see in the world around us more than articles for production and consumption; but we also learn to give natural sciences and technology their fitting place. The sacramental people of God will not spurn usefulness but will give it its integrated meaning within the knowledge of salvation, in solidarity, service and mutual love. Then the earthly things enter into adoration of God in Spirit and truth. Ecological responsibility is a part of our praise of the Creator and Redeemer.

6. Human ecology and our final hope

The biblical and sacramental symbolism points not only to the past and the present but equally to the future. The divine promises of final salvation express themselves by image, through a reconciled ecology. How can we, when we destroy the God-given things, the beauty and the health and harmony of the human ecology, then use all these biblical pictures as signs of our hope? Besides, our hope and the hope of the created universe cannot be truthful unless we express it, symbolize it constantly by our responsible conduct and an environment that gives testimony of it.

God's promises and blessings for men and nature (cf. Is 11:1-9; Rom 8:19-22) proclaim the Lordship (Col 1:15-21) and the redemptive, healing power of Christ in a way that, seized by these truths, we can no longer be indifferent about the ecological equilibrium for the benefit of the present and future generations. The sacramental symbolism and the ecological symbolism of the divine promises tell us clearly that, for the believer, nature is not neutral and "value-free". Also, through our creative, responsible cooperation, nature displays the Creator's goodness and care to sustain human life.[49]

Our present world experience shows us that ecological irresponsibility has caused and will cause enormous suffering for our neighbours and for those who come after us. In biblical language, creation (nature) itself protests against this misuse that contradicts its origin and destiny. Redeemed humanity alerts us and calls us to join in a healing solidarity in the struggle between man and the created universe. It is as if God himself, through all these ecological insights, calls us to a renewed cooperation with nature, to a "planetarian solidarity".[50]

Christian hope and the ecological reality are not in an unbroken harmony. The biblical and liturgical symbols of hope tell us that neither man nor nature can produce that final peace and harmony which God promises as his undeserved gift. But grateful and hope-filled faith encourages humanity to resist sin and decay and to raise real symbols of hope, albeit of a transitory character.[51]

A shared commitment for a healthy human ecosystem is a sign that we endow our life's efforts to the present and future generations. This hope-filled love allows us to proclaim our final hope with greater trust and trustworthiness. It is in this perspective that I would say with Theodor S. Derr: "Long range policies are crucial. In order to avoid disaster by postponement of consequences, our notion of the proper care of the earth has to reach imaginatively into the future."[52]

7. For a sober and chastened anthropocentrism

A Christian anthropocentrism is totally different from anything unbelievers propose. We look at Christ, the Omega point of all creation and of history: "All things are created through him and for him" (Col 1:16). He is the adorer of the Father in Spirit and truth. If we say that the emergence of man is the great moment in evolution, then our interest is not first in man the maker but in man the adorer who, in his relationship with all of nature, honours the Creator and renders thanks. He is the image of God in his capacity to love his Creator and to join the Creator in his love for fellowmen.

At the heart of the Creation-Salvation plan is a humankind that honours God through mutual love and reverence and by grateful care of all of his gifts. Those who accept their calling to be a mirror image of God's love for their fellow-travellers will also mirror God's care for all of nature.

"The biblical view of man's relation to nature is, then, definitively anthropocentric, but devoid of false confidence in the results of man's mastery. . . From Genesis onward, man is conceived as a unity of the biological and the spiritual, always both at once, never separable from nature, and never without his unique dominance over nature."[53]

With all our reverence for whatever God has created by his almighty Word, we cannot overlook the levels of Being, the grades of significance, and above all, the position of man in the universe.[54]

A chastened, sober anthropocentrism implies a consciousness of our belonging to the whole. In a certain sense we can say, "We are members of one another", also in view of the sub-human reality. "All created entities from protons to people are like fountains; they perform their existence."[55] But our consciousness of these dynamic, life-supporting interactions and this sense of solidarity with the created universe are strengthened and heightened by our covenant relationship with all of humankind.

Our ecological responsibility, then, is a central act of justice and love for God and for our fellowman. "An earth which is so managed as to be ecologically sustainable is of more value to humanity than one which is ecologically unsustainable. An ecologically sustainable earth is a necessary requirement for distributive justice."[56]

Man, as co-creator under God, has a right to manipulate the processes of nature wherever he can judge with moral certainty that his action is beneficial for the present generation without jeopardizing the future one. But as soon as he realises that his manipulative interventions do more harm than good to humans, he is bound in conscience to change the course of his actions. He may or must, then, also use science and technology to repair the damage and diminish suffering.

The present frightening ecological crisis is, no doubt, to be interpreted prophetically as a call to conversion, to a renewed relationship with God-given nature - but always with and through renewed relationships within humankind.

8. Ecology and a new understanding of property and ownership

The new forms of socialization, conditioned by modern science and technology, have made evident the evils caused by an individualistic concept of private ownership. It is not only a matter of finding new and diversified forms of ownership, but there is an urgent need of new thinking and new attitudes. Nothing proves this better than the ecological crisis.

In his message to the first world conference on ecology, Paul VI wrote: "The environment is *res omnium*, the patrimony of mankind."[57] In justice, everyone individually, and private and public agencies, must cooperate in preserving this common heritage. Wrong concepts of property have led to a grave social malaise; but only the present malaise of the biosphere's ecosystem manifests the gravity of the errors that allowed a vast abuse of the God-given resources and man's accumulated capital, to the detriment of whole social classes and, indeed, of all humankind of present and future generations. Thus we see more sharply the truth of the Psalmist: "The earth is the Lord's and all the fullness thereof" (Ps. 24:1-2).

We cannot meaningfully assert equality and freedom among men without urging a solidaric responsibility for our ecosystem and the irreplaceable resources of the earth. Social and legal justice forbids everybody to receive honours and power by methods that damage the human ecosystem. And allowance of any of the manifold aggravations of the ecosystem - as, for instance, air pollution - should be tolerated only to the extent that it provides for real social needs.

No private person and no economic corporation should consider the human biosphere as his or its domain. The very context of this biosphere and the limitedness of important material resources urges humankind not only to strengthen local responsibilities but also to provide international agreements and organizations to guarantee the security of this, our most precious patrimony. With authentic internationalization of the problems of environmental health, energy and resources - and careful respect for the principle of subsidiarity - "the national production of weapons of mass destruction could not make any sense."[58] And that would be the greatest contribution towards removing the most horrifying threat to human survival and the accompanying threat of catastrophic deterioration of the biosphere.

9. *From a culture of wastefulness to a new asceticism*

The eminent economist E. Fritz Schumacher, who sees the solution of the ecological crisis in simplicity, beauty and joy that are accessible to those who creatively detach themselves from greed, lust for power, giantism and senseless status symbols, comments on Keynes, the father of the "constant growth" theory. Keynes holds that the time has not yet come "to return to some of the most sure and certain principles of religion and traditional virtues - that 'avarice is a vice, the exaction of usury is a misdemeanor, and love of money is detestable'". He suggests instead that the desired economic progress is "obtainable only if we employ the powerful human devices of selfishness". Indeed, the vast communication systems owned by the powerful, ever-expanding corporations and their politicians convey constantly the imperative, "Thou shalt covet".

Schumacher rightly observes, "If human vices such as greed and envy are systematically cultivated, the inevitable result is nothing less than the collapse of intelligence."[59] Thus man loses sight of beauty and healthy relationships, and human ecology must reflect this collapse of truth.

Conversion to the liberating truth and to beauty requires a creative detachment that has little to do with the old Puritan austerity that looked only for one's own predestination. Capitalism which, according to Max Weber, grew under the auspices of Calvinist doctrine and a corresponding puritan ethics, has unfortunately disowned what was good in that austerity. The remedy does not lie in going back to the poisoned roots. What we need are new models of simplicity that typify the beatitudes, joy, fullness of life, social responsibility.

Those groups of anti-culture protesters who separate themselves from the rest of society - as the sect of Qumran did at the Dead Sea - do not help us. We need élites that exercise a convincing influence by their creative liberty and fidelity to the true values. We do not aim at a culture of harsh deprivation or joyless puritanism. An "ascetical world culture" of which the great physicist and philosopher Carl Friedrich von Weizsäcker speaks, needs social élites who are "salt for the earth, yeast in the dough". We need a constructive critique united with a convincing new life-style, integrated groups, new social goals, but not flight from the world.[60] We need a radiating asceticism based on solidarity on all levels.

The mere endeavour to master the world is disastrous without man's mastery of himself, mastery of his desire to exploit the environment and one's fellowmen.[61] "Although there is considerable debate about the imminence of serious, even irrevocable threats to the ecosphere, it is clear that constraints on our wastefulness and pollution will need to become part of modern industrial life."[62] But constraint, self-mastery, mastery of greed, covetousness, wastefulness, will not work without high ideals and a solid ground plan, and not without groups that are able to offer convincing alternatives.[63]

III. ECOLOGICAL CONSCIENCE AND ITS OBSTACLES

New knowledge about the ecological relationships and dynamics brings new moral responsibilities. The well-documented insights should produce a profound shock as the first step towards a new consciousness and the formation of conscience. However, the causes of wastefulness and ruthless destruction of the ecosystems are deeply rooted in many structures of our western thought, economy, politics and established habits. And the courage to face the truth requires another type of knowledge - a knowledge of salvation.[64] If we want a change and want to commit ourselves to work and fight for it, we have to be aware of the main obstacles.[65]

1. The ideology of constant growth and expansion

The megalomania of Alexander the Great, of the Roman warriors, of the conquistadors after the discovery of the new world, of Napoleon, of the nineteenth century's national states, of Hitler, and Russian imperialism have brought unspeakable suffering to humankind. The chief cause of the imperialistic and colonial wars was the ideology of economic expansion.

Today, behind the ecological crisis and many political tensions and social evils, there is the ideology of constant growth of the national production, to such an extent that in spite of good will and considerable knowledge, political leaders remain prisoners of this trend and mentality. In democratic countries re-election depends greatly on the GNP figures (gross national product), and in authoritarian countries heads roll if a five-year-plan for growth is not fulfilled. But the time has come to realize where this trend will lead if humanity does not liberate itself from this "bigger is better" ideology.

Where would the process lead if the U.S.A. model of economic growth were to continue and be exported beyond the already industrialized countries of the western world and Japan? The 5.6 percent of the world's population that lives in the United States requires about 40 percent of the world's primary resources and causes almost 50 percent of its air and water pollution.[66]

The seriousness of the situation is largely the result of the influence exerted on politics and public opinion by economists. Their single viewpoint becomes the public viewpoint, so that it is much easier to "sell" high-growth than low-growth programmes to the voting public and the labour market. The Keynes school of "constant growth" is still predominant. In the highly industrialized countries, the consumption of energy doubled[67] between 1960 and 1975. The growth rate of waste was almost equal.

The statistics of the GNP that so impress public opinion are not measured by the fulfilment of human needs or improvement in the quality of life. What is not quantifiable does not count. The costs of covering car accidents (besides all the suffering), the money spent on alcohol, nicotine and hard drugs, are all part of the GNP success. "What is worse and destructive of civilization is the pretense that everything has a price, or in other words, that money is the highest of all values."[68] The way progress and "growth" are measured is a sign of the "underdevelopment of economics" that has lost the vision of wholeness.

Our statistics fail to show us the relationship between GNP and the damage done to the biosphere and to the health of present and future generations, the amount of dangerous mutagens, the price we pay in rapidly increasing criminality and for increased security services, the alienation of workers in the production process, loss of creativity, emptiness of leisure time: all this is not quantifiable, and so does not "count".[69] All that counts seems to be just the "throughput", as Dolan expresses it: "As long as we base our national goals on a number which measures throughput rather than welfare, you can be sure that the government will do everything in its power to maximize the growth of throughput, regardless of the effect on welfare."[70]

The decision to ignore the quantifiable and, even more, the non-quantifiable damage inflicted on the biosphere and on human health by this megalomania for "biggest is best" is a value-decision of tragic consequence. The report to the Club of Rome on the Limits of Growth draws attention to criminality in the overcrowded cities, psychological stress, lack of privacy, and above all, danger of war. In the extreme case we can say: "Maximizing the growth of the GNP is tantamount to maximizing the growth rate of ecological damage".[71]

Fighting against the powerful ideology of constant growth of the GNP has nothing to do, however, with opposing progress. With so many human needs that deserve better attention, so many dimensions of humanity crying for better development, the systematic cultivation and expansion for material needs in the service of growth of GNP "is the antithesis of wisdom. The exclusion of wisdom from economics, science and technology was something which we could perhaps get away with as long as we were relatively unsuccessful; but now that we have become very successful, the problem of spiritual and moral truth moves into the central position."[72]

The task is gigantic. The education of the citizens of our consumer societies has to be totally transformed; there is a need for new and persuasive ideals and patterns for individuals and for society. The problem in the profit-oriented, so-called "free" countries is not made easier by the conflict with the Marxist ideologies in state capitalism, where the megalomania, giantism and uncreative bureaucracies make a new thinking and restructuring difficult.[73] But a systematic, objective, well-documented formation about the ecological relationships can become an important start for global rethinking in West and East.

2. Established habits and patterns

The ecological problem is gaining ever broader attention. But since the remedies impose noticeable strictures on almost everyone, the fight is not only against power-structures but, first of all, against our own established habits and patterns of thought and practice. They are the allies of the integral system of a profit-oriented economy and a consumer culture. Barbara Ward describes the situation realistically: "The relentless pursuit of separate national interests by rich and poor alike in a totally interdependent biosphere produces global disaster of irreversible environmental damage."[74]

As long as the egoistic individual is not tangibly and immediately touched by the threat of a disturbed and poisoned ecosystem, he is not easily motivated to impose constraints on himself for the benefit of the present and future generations. We can unite in the saving struggle against the power of the vested interests only when we fight also against our own egoism, against individualism and particularism. The individual herdsman, for instance, faced with a serious situation of overgrazing in the whole tribal area, may still think that he can make some profit for himself by adding one more animal; and similarly, a Western man may think one more incinerator makes no great difference. When everyone thinks this way, catastrophe is unavoidable.

3. Vested interests

The encyclical *Mater et Magistra* of John XXIII, that touched on some aspects of the energy and environmental crises, could not yet quite realize the magnitude and urgency of the problem as we must see it today - and no wonder, when the pope could not yet foresee the immense difficulties involved in breaking open the way to reason and justice.[75]

One of the greatest powers that can block the proper solution of the environmental crisis is the nearly sixty multinational economic empires with their experts in all fields of related sciences and their tremendous power to influence public opinion. Great accountability should be attributed to the big oil companies, the automobile industry and the chemical industry. Those who add the greatest hazards to the biosphere are not motivated to study the problem objectively. On the contrary, just as the tobacco industry has been able to profit for a long time from scientific ignorance about how cigarette smoking increases the risk of cancer,[76] so it is consciously or unconsciously, with the chemical industries. Their experts play down the data of proven hazards and question their interpretations. This does not mean that they are consciously lying or trying to deceive. It is mostly the mechanism of a selective memory, the focus and thinking, under the impact of the prevailing motives and influence of their group.

We have seen that environmental damages do not enter the statistics of the GNP. This is even more the tendency of the profit-centred company. It is not only the power of the capitalists but also a certain group "solidarity". According to the ideologist of enterprise and management, C. C. Parkinson, the manager who takes common welfare into account, where law does not force him to do so, neglects his duty towards the enterprise.[77]

The selective principle of knowledge and attention is particularly operative when responsible action to avoid or reduce drastically environmental hazards would require considerable expense. In the cost-benefit assessment there is normally no place for the "goods" of health and a healthy human biosphere, unless there is law enforcement or strong pressure by way of public opinion and citizen initiatives.

Trade unions have not yet become sufficiently aware of or alert to this new and burning social issue, although it is as pressing today as the major issues of the fight of the working class were in the past. The direct result of this blindness is that the price of the product is a deceiving one. Enterprise and workers share the benefit while the public at large suffers the environmental losses.

All this happens not only where it is "merely" a question of long-term risk but even where suffering follows almost immediately. "The major breakthroughs have led to the recognition by a sector of the scientific community that much of human cancer is preventable. But there are powerful economic forces that have a vested interest in the continuing production and sale of these agents. so the prevention of cancer involves a social struggle not so different from the ones earlier in the century for better working conditions."[78]

The highest percentage of qualified scientists is employed either by the arms industry or by mighty industries that cause the major environmental damages. This leads to a deplorable situation of "benign neglect" of the environmental issues by those most responsible for them.

Moreover, the same powers that manipulate scientific research (at least in its goals and emphases) resort to all sorts of manoeuvres to prevent fair legislation aimed at the common good. By buying television time, by lobbying, bribery, blackmail, and especially by the argument that the jobs of thousands of people depend on them, they manipulate legislators and public opinion. Yet democratic societies "provide mechanisms of protest and agitation which are absent in any of their actual alternatives."[79] But without more forceful and intelligent initiatives from citizens we cannot get the scientific and political input that would enable the legislators and governments to deal responsibly and effectively with these grave problems.

The task is immense, for it is a matter of reconciling a great diversity of interests and duties. The solidaric effort must be equal to the task.

4. Nationalism and hegemonism

The pressure and the struggle becomes particularly intense because of new forms of nationalism, the conflict of opposed ideological groups, and especially because of hegemonic tendencies in the economic and political fields. Cannot the burning ecological threat become a motive for all people of good will finally to renounce nationalism and the hegemonism that lead to a senseless arms race involving the whole political and economic spectrum, and the piling up of arsenals of weapons that could make the earth forever uninhabitable?

5. The megalopolis

The idolatry of giantism, one of the most serious deviations of modern technology, has led to the megalopolis that not only lacks the human dimension of neighbourliness and rootedness but is in many ways a sick and sickening environment. Not human needs but transport and communication facilities - together with lucrative land speculation - determined the disproportionate growth of some industrial and commercial centres.

There is much talk about urban planning. But besides the persuasive conditionings by the economic and political powers, there is the question of why wisdom and foresight were driven out in the planning. There is a limit beyond which an urban and industrial agglomeration can no longer be under ecological control; the level of air, water and noise pollution becomes intolerable. The cost of efforts to avoid the worst damages to the human environment indicates only a small part of the iceberg. In the Ruhrgebiet in northwest Germany, with its 5.5 million inhabitants, the cost of a law-enforced diminution of air pollution comes to between five and fifteen percent of the total cost of the industrial plants.[80] The adverse physical and psychological effects of noise pollution should also be considered.

The economist E. F. Schumacher and the ethologist Konrad Lorenz both come to the conclusion that the modern megalopolis causes appalling problems of stress, alienation, violence and all kinds of crime.[81]

In his letter, *Octogesima Adveniens*, Paul VI calls attention to the increasing ecological and human problems of the megalopolis, and gives a pertinent suggestion about the humanization of life in our big cities.[82] This huge human problem should receive much greater attention and effort for wholesome change.

6. *Science and technocracy*

Ecological ethics is unthinkable without a thorough-going revision of the basic presuppositions of modern natural sciences and of technological and economic behaviour.[83] Our critique, however, is not directed against science or technology as such; but the trend of reductionism among scientists and in modern technocracy must be scrutinized in the context of the whole system of education. "The roots of economics and its carelessness toward the biosphere lie outside the economic sphere in education, organization, discipline. . . ".[84] The search for a vision of wholeness, ultimate meaning and wisdom was and is so greatly neglected that many "intellectuals", specialists in science and technology, "have not even the faintest idea what the term (wisdom) could mean."[85]

The consequence is that technology has become an end in itself;

it has lost direction. It develops as if persons do not matter. Science and technology are beneficial within their proper limits - that is, within a vision of wholeness and wisdom. What we need first of all is careful consideration about the direction and purpose of research, and then to find how to apply the available sciences and technologies most beneficially.

The "modern world is shaped by its metaphysics which shaped its education which, in turn, has brought forth its science and technology."[86] Economics as science and applied economics should not be a matter of exact science alone but, above all, an expression of wisdom. For this, the behavioural sciences could be helpful. But care must be taken to guard against the reductionism that not infrequently gains ground even in a behavioural science when it makes itself an absolute, isolated from the rest of human experience.

To make everything that technically is possible contradicts the purpose of technology "and is childish". Technology as an agent of culture is not possible "without the ability to exercise asceticism in the very field of technology."[87]

But the problem is not in an abstract technology, and not merely in the technocracy exercised by a few; it is ingrained in modern man. Helmut Schelsky writes: "Modern man, as social and psychic being, has become for himself a technical and scientific task of production."[88] It follows that a technology that has lost integration and direction, and as a consequence destroys the creativity of the work of most people, upsets the biosphere at the same time. It is inimical to man and his environment.

Technocratic man scientifically analyzes the last elements and constructs a synthesis of them in view of the highest possible efficiency.[89] What we plead for is not a renunciation of science and technology but for wisdom that allows us to transform, direct and control it for the benefit of rational man and his environment: a task which is not possible without asceticism in the use of technology.

Is it not evident that it is *not* the biblical revelation that has led to the chaotic and destructive technocracy, but unfaithfulness to its basic principles?[90] The present situation is a call to radical *metanoia*.

7. What kind of radicalism?

For disillusioned radicals, the ecological crisis can become a central political issue to justify even violent revolution, "to destroy the whole system". If the unredeemed powers of which we have spoken oppose sound and strong measures, this might well lead to more and more violent conflicts.

The radicalism I have in mind is of a quite different kind. It does not follow the patterns of those who want to begin from nothingness, and hope that everything will come automatically from different economic and political structures, the nature of which they cannot tell us. What is needed is a totally new thinking and new patterns of behaviour. And in this context we need a critical attitude towards the whole frame of a profit-oriented economy, nationalism and hegenomism and a directionless technocracy.

Social conflicts in the struggle for a healthy environment are unavoidable, but they must be carried out in a way that makes evident how the man/environment relationship is thoroughly linked with healthy human relationships.

The "radical" struggle for a good biosphere is a matter of social justice, and must therefore go hand in hand with the promotion of justice, love and peace on all levels and in all areas of life.

IV. ECOLOGICAL STRATEGY

1. Ecological education

The basic condition for healing the ecological malaise is a solid education and consciousness raising. But since the deplorable situation is, as we have seen, the result of the whole pattern of a profit-oriented consumer society with its horrifying reductionism, the ecological education can be successful only where salvation knowledge prevails and is able to chasten and integrate the knowledge of dominion.

A civilized society must know and love the goods that are beneficial - such as a healthy environment - which make it worthwhile to renounce the "goods" that are inimical.[91] Further, in order to be motivated and competent, we must see that in order to actualize a new society and to heal the human ecosphere, we need a new humanity by inner change. The two go hand in hand; but the inner change is primordial.

There must be cooperation among the various sciences and a special discipline of ecology in our educational system. Ignorance is enemy Number One. But the remedy is only in an integrated knowledge. Ecological education has to be all-pervasive, an integral part of social and political formation.

Without concerted political action by competent and responsible people, we will never get a participatory decision in all matters concerning the human environment. People who want to be active in this indispensable struggle should be informed about the social cost of a polluted environment but also should realize that the quantifiable facts are only the tip of the iceberg. It is a question of a qualitative evaluation.

The contribution of the church ought to be a clear vision of this problem within salvation knowledge and a corresponding motivation. All the salvation truths of creation, Christology, eschatology and anthropology can illumine and move us to that exemplary ecological conduct that the world should expect from Christians.

2. Personal and shared initiatives

The discovery of what we can do as individuals and groups should coincide with our ecological consciousness-raising and education. Competent critique is effective if whole groups offer convincing initiatives and make them credible by their life style. Good leadership is of paramount importance here.

Joint action by concerned citizens can force or persuade enterprises of some size to assess constantly their interaction with the environment. In this, not only private and group interests should be kept in mind but the good of society as a whole. There is a need to give ethical classifications an effective role. Citizens should give preference to those companies that satisfy legitimate needs, avoid waste of irreplaceable resources and use the best recycling methods that do not burden the ecological equilibrium.

3. Ecological politics

Ecology becomes a political issue - that is, an unavoidable task for governments and political parties - if enough citizens understand the importance and urgency of the situation, and realize that there is need of political decisions. In Sweden and West Germany, new political parties make ecology the main part of their programme; and since they find public support, they force the other political parties to convince the citizens that they, too, are willing to take equally good care of the issue.

Our biosphere must not be abandoned to economists and economic powers. This is a primary responsibility and competence of legislators and government, and indeed of all democratic forces.

To bring forth a qualitative growth, away from the heresy of the GNP quantitive growth, is a complex and long-term process. Only an interaction of legislation and public attitudes can face it in such a way "that the former may lead the latter but not at too great a distance, and the latter must ultimately support the former".[92] We cannot blame our legislators and governments if we do not do everything in our power to strengthen the consciousness and attitudes of all citizens.

Political action must not exhaust itself in a "permanent crisis management".[93] What is needed are long-term programmes that stress prevention more than simply repairing the worst damage. The prevailing tendency still seems to be to deal with ecological problems segmentally instead of planning holistically according to the nature of our biosphere and of the various conditions and actions that are inimical to it.

On the one hand, we must allow legislators and governments to be realistic, to provide intermediary programmes and structures. Political leaders have to look for ways acceptable to this particular population - certainly, ways that promote consciousness and prepare future steps, but not programmes that perhaps are the most ideal but are not feasible. On the other hand, "if a strategy for survival is to have any chance of success, the solutions must be formulated in the light of the problems and not from a timorous and superficial understanding of what may or may not be immediately feasible."[94] And what is urgently needed for the health and welfare of people, and perhaps for survival, may become feasible by changing the government and/or by thoroughly restructuring institutions - not, however, by opting for a totalitarian régime.

Political decisions can be made only after weighing the various alternatives and taking into account all the foreseeable consequences. For instance, a nation which wants to make itself more independent of political pressure and to avoid the risk of loss of liberty while looking for new resources that might diminish the beauty of the countryside and add to environmental pollution, must ponder all the values and dangers before making its decision. Compromises may be inevitable, and it is the task of Christian ethics to explain how such compromises must be honest and dynamic, ever tending towards the next possible step in a clear direction.

The past decade has shown encouraging signs that much is possible. London got rid of its smog; the fish in the Thames and the Rhine are alive again; the environmental condition of the 5.5 million inhabitants of the industrial area of the Ruhr are much healthier than fifteen years ago.

The magnitude of the problem, however, requires actions beyond the boundary of a nation-state. It is important to keep to the principle of subsidiarity that allows creative and organized participation by all. But we need new structures responding to the fact that our biosphere and our economic and political fates are indivisible.

The 1974 Report to the Club of Rome, "Mankind at the Turning Point", calls for "a new economic order and a global resources allocation system". This is in the programme of the United Nations since 1975, but its realization is not easy. What is required is nothing less than a radical conversion to a worldwide solidarity in economics, and a minimum agreement about the scale of values.

A new world order in liberty is thinkable only if there is no hegemonism and if local and national initiatives are showing the way to the best possible international solutions. But everyone should realize that "if we want clear air over our land and clean seas washing our shores, we shall have to play our part in worldwide pollution control."[95]

One of the big questions is: who pays the costs of restoring and preserving human ecology?

Many legislators, for instance in West Germany, have established the general principle that the producer has to pay the damage, or rather, bear the expenses necessary to prevent pollution. However, there are goods indispensable for common needs, for which it is fair that a part of the environmental cost should be borne by the taxpaying community. Wherever manufacturers of indispensable goods would be unable to compete if they had to bear the whole cost of preventing ecological damage, there is need for political action, even across national frontiers.[96] But the manufacturers of unnecessary products should not be absolved from paying the full cost, insofar as it can be assessed. Already half a century ago, A. Pigon wrote about the problem of "external costs": "Smoke in large towns inflicts a heavy uncharged loss on the community, in damage to buildings and vegetation, expenses for washing clothes and cleaning rooms . . . and in many other ways."[97]

4. Reconciliation between man and technology

With the second industrial revolution, humankind is reaching a turning point. It is being forced to decide either to follow the path of a technology of giantism, of massification, followed by destruction of creative work and increasing unemployment, or to reconcile itself with technology by creating a "technology with a human face".[98]

The manipulation of nature, necessary as it is, will be more cautious, following its rhythms whenever possible. There must be a transition from the principle of profit to a caring stewardship and meaningful parsimony in methods and the use of resources. Schumacher writes on this point: "There is a measure in all natural things - in their size, speed or violence. As a result, the system of which man is a part tends to be self-balancing, self-adjusting. Not so with technology, or rather, with man dominated by technology and specialization."[99]

Man is a being with brains and hands, and work should give a chance to both brains and hands to be creative, not only for small élites but for as many as possible.

A technology with a human face, fostering everyone's creativity and healthy human relationships in the working process, must also be friendly to the human environment. The change begins with our courage to doubt the normalcy of the present technical development towards both giantism and wastefulness. It is, indeed, abnormal and unhealthy in the eyes of those who care about the person and a healthy society.

So we need a new "technology assessment" with emphasis on the importance of studying alternatives in an all-inclusive way. No technocracy should be allowed to take the unnecessary risk of harming human relationships or human ecology. For technology to take risks that burden the human community or society at large is much worse than what cigarette smokers do by risking their own health - although, unfortunately, they also pollute the air that others breathe.[100]

Ecologists speak of intermediate, small scale, "soft" technology adapted to the particular culture and avoiding centralization and mass technology. The idea, if not the concrete practice, follows the example of Mahatma Ghandi and Julius Nyerere (Tanzania). The intermediate technology is especially important for the developing countries with tremendous labor surpluses. But it should also be promoted in the industrialized countries for many reasons, including providing more numerous and more satisfying jobs. Small scale and ecologically "friendly" technology can and must be applied especially for gaining energy from sun, water, wind and other resources wherever available.

If this were done, humanity one day will bless the Lord for the oil shortage. No time should be lost. We need a lead time between creative impulse and final, broad-scale availability. But this lead time, necessary for small-scale technology, is not comparable to that required, for instance, for implementation of massive nuclear energy.

In his world best-seller book, "Small is Beautiful", E. F. Schumacher emphasizes the dimension of beauty, creative work and art which I consider one of the indispensable gateways to liberating truth.[101] Descartes' dualism between "thinking thing" (man) and spacial thing (*res extensa*) could not at all foster a healthy relationship between these two "species of things".

Schumacher synthesizes his proposals well: "Wisdom demands a new orientation of science and technology towards the organic, the gentle, the non-violent, the elegant and beautiful." The soft and elegant technologies, reconciled with the human ecology should be "cheap enough so that they are accessible to virtually everyone, suitable for small-scale application, compatible with man's need for creativity."[102] If the soft technology gives special attention to creativity and beauty, then the real reconciliation between technology and man begins.

5. Global development

Many people of the Third World are rather suspicious when they hear or read the words of churchmen from the wealthy industrial countries about the strictures necessary for the sake of environment and resources. They fear that the westerners, who have all they need, want to restrict the hope of the developing countries to reach a reasonable standard of living.

The church documents on development give strong support to the right of the poor in general, and of the poor in the developing countries in particular, to have their share in the goods of the earth and in the beneficial advances of science and technology.[103] But the model delivered and used by the western industrial countries and Japan is not suitable for the poor countries just as it was not helpful and sound for the rich. We all have to learn to see development more in being-becoming than in having-consuming.

The most frightening prospect is the spiral of quantitative growth. The lower classes of the rich countries tend to orient their life style and aspirations according to the wealth of the rich and privileged part of society. Similarly, there is the danger that the highly industrialized countries export not only their goods but also their covetousness. Their movies and advertisements do the most and the worst in this direction. If all countries were to reach the present level of the United States' consumption and its actions hostile to human ecology, the fossil energy resources would be exhausted almost immediately, and the biosphere irreparably damaged.

The wealthy countries can afford the tremendous costs of repairing and/or diminishing the anti-environmental output; but the developing countries importing western technology cannot afford it. When, for instance, the pernicious consequences of the insecticide DDT were clearly known, it was eliminated in the rich western countries but still was exported in huge quantities and used in the developing countries.

The developing countries have a right to the scientific and technical tools essential for feeding their ever-increasing populations and reaching a decent standard of living. We can hardly preach to them that the ideology of GNP's constant quantifiable growth is a heresy and a threat to survival if the powerful countries do not change their dangerous course.

Both faith in one God and fraternal love oblige us to harmonize justice to the poor nations with a common sharing of irreplaceable material resources. If things continue as they are now, ten percent of the people will have seventy percent of the world's income by the end of the century - with all the hazards for peace and for the biosphere entailed in such a situation. Yet "it would be an ethical disaster if we were to allow ecological concerns to be expressed in a way that directly thwarts the need of the poor for material improvement."[104]

First, we all have to learn together that development does not begin with goods and profits but with people and their education, respect for their dignity and equality, organization and discipline. Secondly, the rich can help development of the poorer countries in many ways without either exporting their growth-ideology or thwarting genuine progress. For instance, much cooperative work could be done for afforestation to block everywhere the advance of the deserts.

The developing countries have a right to join in a common cause in order to obtain a just price for their raw products. And the wealthy countries have to limit waste of precious food so necessary for the hundreds of millions of children and adults who are starving. In France in 1970, no less than two million tons of excellent food were bought for dogs and cats, the equivalent of the amount necessary to feed twelve million Asian children; and the expenses for an average North American housedog were higher than the median income of an Indian worker.[105]

The Food and Agriculture Organization (FAO) is an important agency of the United Nations. It should be strengthened. Equally needed is a new international order, with agencies and international agreements that assure a just allocation of energy resources and important raw material for all nations, especially the poorest. Like air, water and quietness, these resources of the earth are not private property but the common heritage of humankind.

We need that "kind of Christian ethic which is critical of the consumer economy while pressing the claims of the poor to greater material benefits."[106]

The developing nations could well make an important contribution to genuine progress everywhere by developing and creatively using the small-scale, gentle technology so much recommended by Schumacher and many ecologists and development experts. All cultures need mutual help to free themselves for the cult of higher values such as greater appreciation of contemplation and quiet enjoyment.

For all this and above it, a real revolution towards a worldwide solidarity is needed.[107] Then the industrial countries would not just export for profit but would evaluate carefully, in cooperation with the people of the developing countries, what really fits into their culture and ecosystem. This applies particularly, for instance, to the new explosion of knowledge about the recombinant DNA for food production. All this will "require substantial biological education and an investigation of environmental and occupational health."[108]

6. Nuclear energy and alternatives

One of the hottest issues in ecology is the question of nuclear energy. It imposes hard decisions on political leaders - decisions in which well-informed citizens should participate. The opinions of experts about the hazards vary enormously. It is not only an ecological but also a highly political issue and a problem of security against terrorists and, in case of war, the enemy.

It is estimated that at the beginning of the next millenium, about 25,000 plutonium breeders would be necessary to provide sufficient energy (also for the now developing nations) if there is not in the meantime a radical change in economy and style of life.[109] Six kilograms of plutonium are enough to produce an atom bomb. Would not the atom state almost unavoidably become a police state? And, with nuclear energy, will not the production of nuclear weapons gradually spread all over the world?

Schumacher warns drastically against such a development. He is convinced that a "solution" of the energy crisis by nuclear power is tantamount to creating "an infinitely greater problem." It is a question of "salvation or nuclear damnation". "Ionizing radiation has become the most serious agent of pollution." And Schumacher fears that the decisions will follow the patterns of scientists of the nuclear industry and of economists to whom it matters only "whether it pays" according to "the religion of economics".[110]

The Boston meeting on "Science and Faith", organized by the Council of Churches in July, 1979, proposed a five-year moratorium until we can see more clearly. In the debate, most of the Russian and North American participants spoke in favour of nuclear energy, while many European and Third World representatives warned strongly against it.[111]

The famous Russian scientist Sacharov, who is known for his independent thinking, speaks favourably for nuclear energy both on the issue of responsibility for the environment and on the possibility of sufficient security.[112] Friedrich Weizsäcker, a renowned scientist, reliable for balanced evaluation, is cautious in his assessment and, envisaging all the alternatives and dimensions, does not oppose a careful and moderate political decision in favour of nuclear energy. Although a "world asceticism" and small-scale solutions with solar and other forms of energy would be more ideal, political leaders have to take into account the still prevailing trend of the consumer society and the difficulty of gaining sufficient lead time for other solutions.[113]

Those who protest against all production of nuclear energy - and to my mind they have good reasons - must realize under what presuppositions they can do it coherently and honestly. Humanity can do without nuclear power stations if it returns to simplicity and renounces wastefulness. If we refuse to make a conscious choice of a simple life style as presupposition of our action, then the others are right who tell us that industrial growth cannot go on without nuclear power.

Sociologist Hoefnagels, who emphasizes the hazards, would take nuclear energy into consideration as a limited interim solution, while doing everything to provide "clean" energy sources.[114] I tend towards approximately the same "solution". But the churches and every sensitive person and group should do their utmost to bring the nuclear arms race to an end, not only in view of horrifying wars but also in view of the unheard-of "danger to our genes from plutonium and other deadly by-products of the production of nuclear weapons."[115]

7. Limits of population growth

At the present time the world population is close to 4.5 billion. Carl Friedrich Weizsäcker makes a well-founded assessment:

"Those who want to plan economy responsibly must do it in view of a coming world population of at least eight billion. What amount of energy will these people need per capita? If today's way of thinking perdures, it is unacceptable to respond that, in the world average, each person will need as much as today. It seems to be still a modest extrapolation to say twice or three times as much as today's world average."[116]

Those who say that population control is not urgent, because the earth can produce enough food (which is true) and energy and all else needed for a growing mankind, must radically examine their presuppositions and the coherence of their life style with their thesis. Again I refer to such a reliable authority as Weizsäcker: "Population growth and unemployment are met by further economic growth: the environmental damage is met by technology, the violence by control, the war by arms-race deterrence, psychological disturbance by psychoanalysis. The existing system of this kind to solve problems means to programme problems."[117]

Here again it becomes evident that these problems cannot be solved segmentally. They call for a holistic vision as part of a radical conversion and profound societal-cultural change. Whoever preaches morality, simply applying traditional moral solutions outside the new total context - for instance against family planning and population control - with no intention to change his own life style and to cooperate generously for the necessary economic and societal changes, is incoherent, if not a hypocrite.

J. Gremillion notes how absurd it is, in such a situation, to stick to a population policy inspired by the motive, "as many as possible of our own kind".[118]

8. Creative liberty and fidelity

Radical environmentalists use the danger of a planetarian ecological collapse as an argument to justify any kind of coercion and manipulation of people's minds. They do not know or do not believe in the power of creative liberty. What they do know is the concept and practice of the liberty to make profits, to be a part of the consumer society, and to enjoy other individualistic freedoms. The freedom they renounce, and of which they would like to deprive others, would not be the most terrible loss. But the remedies they propose would drive out any kind of true liberty.

However, in view of the interaction between economic life and all the other dimensions of our existence, we should highly evaluate the right kind of economic freedom. Human freedom and responsibility make economics different from physics. Liberty makes predictability impossible. The only thing that should be almost predictable is growth in creative liberty and responsibility. This is possible only in a participatory society and economics based on mutual respect and the art of dialogue which leads at least to a minimum of common convictions.

E. F. Schumacher feels that man's activities are so predictable "because most people, most of the time, make no use of their freedom and act purely mechanically". This is so also because the present technocratic, gigantic and centralized system does not foster initiative. Schumacher believes, however, that things can be changed. He hopes for a new direction in economics, favourable for creativity and a healthier ecosystem, if intelligent and joint initiatives are undertaken in many places. Usually the most important innovations and substantial changes start from tiny creative "minorities who do use their freedom".[119] The Report to the Club of Rome on "The Limits of Growth", which has shaken the ecological conscience of many people, also stresses the need for imagination, creativity and courage.[120]

John Passmore makes a strong point about freedom. Faced with the proposals of those who think only about survival, we make clear our point: we do not sacrifice the future of freedom for a future without freedom and the most basic capacity of man to love and to be faithful to the fundamental requirements of love and freedom. "To surrender our freedom, to abandon all respect for persons, in the name of control over population growth, is to make sacrifices which our proper concern for posterity cannot justify."[121] But other sacrifices can be made. "If we are really convinced that unless we take steps *now* to recycle metals and to cut down the consumption of fossil fuels, freedom will not survive, then we can fairly easily convince ourselves, without invoking any novel principles, that we ought to be prepared to make such sacrifices and to demand them from others."[122]

So the question is not survival but the survival of *homo sapiens*, faithful to creative freedom and true humanity, and at the same time, faithful to the earth. It cries and yearns to have its share in the freedom of God's children.

Any proposals on how to resolve the ecological problems have to be assessed in this light. We must renounce that "freedom" of competition and profiteering that threatens disaster for us. "Is the note of freedom that is absolutely indispensable for a truly humane society nothing else than a guarantee of an individualistic conception of freedom? This is the great question which decides about our future."[123]

It should be clear to every believer that Christians and other adorers of the one God and Father of all cannot be "salt for the earth and light to the world" unless they know and make known to others by word and example what creative freedom is and what it means for human ecology.

NOTES

[1] R.L. Carson, *The Silent Spring*, New York, 1962; C.R. Taylor, *Das Selbstmordprogram*, Frankfurt, 1970; H. Weinzierl, *Das grosse Sterben. Umweltnotstand-Wege in eine heilere Welt*, München, 1971; B. Commoner, *The Closing Circle*, New York, 1971; E. Weizsäcker, *Humanokölogie und Umweltschutz*, Stuttgart, 1972; B. Ward and R. Dubos, *Only One Earth. The Care and Maintenance of a Small Planet*, Penguin Books, 1972; F.W. Dahmen/W. Heiss, *Umwelt - ein Schlagwort oder rettende Einsicht?*, Salzburg, 1973[3]; H. Liebmann, *Ein Planet wird unbewohnbar. Ein Sündenregister der Menschheit von der Antike bis zur Gegenwart*, München, 1973; H. Siebert, *Das produzierte Chaos. Ökonomie und Umwelt*, Stuttgart, 1973; R. Dumont, *L'utopie ou la mort?*, Paris, 1973; G. Altner, *Schöpfung am Abgrund*, Neukirchen-Vluyn, 1974; H. Gruhl, *Ein Planet wird ausgeplundert: Schreckensbilanz unserer Politik*, Frankfurt, 1975; H.D. Engelhardt (ed.), *Umweltstrategie*, Gütersloh, 1975; E.F. Schumacher, *Small is Beautiful*, New York and London, 1975; G. Remmert, "Umwelt und Gesellschaft", in *Stimmen der Zeit*, 196 (1978), 85-94; E. Pies (ed.), *Überleben wir die Zukunft? Umweltkrise - materielle und ethische Aspekte*, Stuttgart, 1979.

[2] C. Amery, *Natur als Politik. Die ökologische Chance des Menschen*, Reinbeck, 1977, 36f.

[3] Cf. G. Liedke, *Im Bauch des Fisches. Ökologische Theologie*, Stuttgart and Berlin, 1979, 101.

[4] G. von Wahlert, "Der Mensch als Bestandteil der Evolution" in Aichlein/Liedke (eds.), *Naturwissenschaft und Theologie*, Neukirchen, 1974, 239.

[5] L.K. Caldwell, *Environment: a Challenge for Modern Society*, Garden City, 1970, x.

[6] l.c., 66.

[7] Cf. l.c., 89.

[8] Ch. Birch, "Nature, God and Humanity in Ecological Perspective", in *Christianity and Crisis* 39 (1979), 261.

[9] l.c. 265.

[10] G. Altner, *Zwischen Natur und Menschengeschichte. Perspektiven für eine Schöpfungstheologie*, München, 1975, 91.

[11] M. Mead and W. Fairservis, "Kulturelle Verhaltensweisen und die Umwelt des Menschen", in D. Engelhardt (ed.), *Umweltstrategie*, l.c., 15-32.

[12] l.c., 24f; 30f.

[13] Th.S. Derr, *Ecology and Human Needs*, Philadelphia, 1975[2], 31.

[14] R. Gore, "The Desert: An Age Old Challenge Grows", in *National Geographic*, 156 (Nov. 1979), 585-639.

[15] E.F. Schumacher, *Small is Beautiful. Economics as if People Mattered*, New York and London, 1975, 15f.

[16] L.K. Caldwell, l.c., 21.

[17] l.c., 81.

[18] G.R. Taylor, *Das Selbstmordprogram*, 144.

[19] "Prospects and Hazards of New Genetic Technologies, in *Christianity and Crisis*, Oct. 1979, 247-252 (quote: p. 251).

[20] K. Lorenz, *Die acht Todsünden der zivilisierten Menscheit*, München, 1974[7], 107.

[21] J.V. Taylor, *Enough is Enough*, London, 1976[7], 24.

[22] C.F. von Weizsäcker, *Deutlichkeit. Beiträge zu politischen und religiösen Gegenwartsfragen*, Munchen and Wien, 1978, 54.

[23] Cf. C.F. von Weizsäcker, "Die Rettung der Lebenswelt und der Erwartungshorizont der Zukunft", in *Universitas* 34 (1979) 897-904; Engelhardt, l.c., 225.

[24] L.K. Caldwell, l.c., 134.

[25] Cf. to Section II: J. Sittler, *The Ecology of Faith*, Philadelphia, 1970[2]; A. Portmann, *Naturschutz wird Menschenschutz*, Zürich, 1971; *United Nations Conference on the Human Environment. Panel of Experts on Development and Environment*, Genf, 1972; C. Amery, *Das Ende der Vorsehung. Die gnadenlosen Folgen des Christentums*, Hamburg, 1972; M. Schmoemann, *Wachstumstod und Eschatologie. Die Herausforderung christlicher Theologie durch die Umweltkrise*, Stuttgart, 1973; F. Cramer, *Fortschritt durch Verzicht. Ist das biologische Wesen Mensch seiner Zukunft gewachsen?*, München, 1975; Th. Sieger Derr, *Ecology and Human Need*, Philadelphia, 1975; G. Altner, *Schöpfung am Abgrund. Die Theologie vor der Umweltfrage*, Neukirchen-Vluyn, 1977[2]; O.H. Steck, *Welt und Umwelt* (biblische Konfrontation), Stuttgart, 1978; J. Renker, "Umweltfeindliche Moral? Zur Weltverantwortung der Christen, in *Theologie der Gegenwart* 22 (1979), 11-18; *Herderkorrespondenz* 33 (1979) 91-94: "Theologie und Naturwissenschaft; zu einer Tagung der Evangelischen Akademie Arnoldheim"; K.A. Wohlfahrt, "Die Umweltkrise als Bewertungsproblem", in *Stimmen der Zeit* 197 (1979), 173-182 (with well selected bibliography); K.M. Meyer-Abich (ed.), *Frieden mit der Natur*, Freiburg, 1979; G. Liedke, *Im Bauch des Fisches. Ökologische Theologie*, Stuttgart, 1979.

[26] Th. S. Derr, l.c., and G. Liedke, l.c., refer frequently to authors who intend to make not only Christianity but even the Bible accountable for irresponsibility in ecological problems.

[27] P. Ehrlich, *How to be a Survivor*, Ballantine Books, 1971, 129.

[28] M. Mead, l.c., 17ff.

[29] J. Passmore, *Man's Responsibility for Nature*, New York, 1974, 17.

[30] R. Descartes, *Discourse on Method*, bk. 6, in *The Philosophical Works of Descartes*, trans. by E.S. Haldane, Cambridge, 1931, vol. 1, 119.

[31] R. Descartes, *The Principles of Philosophy*, Works, vol. 1, 271.

[32] Cf. Ch. Westermann, *Der Segen in der Bibel und im Handeln der Kirche*, München, 1968; Id. *Schöpfung*, Stuttgart and Berlin, 1971; Id. *Ertag der Forschung: Genesis 1-11*, Darmstadt, 1972; G. Liedke, l.c., 85ff.

[33] E.F. Schumacher, l.c., 14; in the same sense C.F. von Weizsäcker, *Der Garten des Menschlichen*, München/Wein, 1978⁵, 94.

[34] Cf. F. Blanke, "Unsere Verantwortung gegenüber der Schöpfung", in *Der Auftrag der Kirche in der modernen Welt*, Festschrift für E. Brunner, Zürich and Stuttgart, 1959, 194.

[35] G. Liedke, l.c., 114.

[36] l.c., 66.

[37] F. Bacon, "Religious Meditations", in *Works of Francis Bacon* (ed.), Spedding, vol. 7, 253.

[38] J. Passmore, l.c., 19.

[39] F. Bacon, *Novum Organum*, Aphorism 129, Works, vol. 4, 114.

[40] Th.S. Derr, l.c., 77.

[41] E.F. Schumacher, l.c., 151.

[42] Cf. G. Altner, *Zwischen Natur und Menschengeschichte*, 170.

[43] Th.S. Derr, l.c., 44.

[44] R. Shinn, "Ethics and the Family of Man", in M. Hamilton (ed.), *The Little Planet*, London and New York, 1970, 138.

[45] It is not my intention here to venture an evaluation of the whole and the details of modern (especially North American) process theology based to a great extent on the process philosophy of N. Whitehead. Without being an adept in process theology, I think that its affinity with a dynamic ethics of ecology is worth being taken into serious consideration. Cf. G. Liedke, l.c., 103ff., and *Evangelische Kommentare* 12 (1979) 438-439: "Demütige Wissenschaft"; Th.S. Derr, l.c., 27; 38-42.

[46] W. Heisenberg, "Das Naturbild der heutigen Physik", in Bayerische Akademie der Schönen Künste (ed.), *Die Künste im technischen Zeitalter*, 1956, 45ff.

[47] Cf. G. Liedke, l.c., 107, 153, 177.

[48] Th.S. Derr, l.c., 158.

[49] Cf. Derr, l.c., 23f; Liedke, l.c., 155-162.

[50] Th.S. Derr l.c., 175.

[51] Cf. H. Westmüller, in H.D. Engelhardt (ed.), l.c., 321.

[52] Th.S. Derr, l.c., 89f.

[53] l.c., 17f.

[54] E.F. Schumacher, l.c., 96.

[55] Ch. Birch, "Nature, God and Humanity in Ecological Perspective", l.c., 264.

[56] l.c., 266.

[57] Text in J. Gremillion, *The Gospel of Peace and Justice*, Maryknoll, 1976, 109.

[58] G and P. Mische, *Toward a Human World Order*, New York, 1977, 256.

[59] E.F. Schumacher, l.c., 31.

[60] Cf. C.F. von Weizsäcker, *Deutlichkeit*, 58, 69, 74, 80ff.

[61] L.K. Caldwell, l.c., 108.

[62] A.J. Dyck, *On Human Care*, Nashville, 1978², 46.

[63] Cf. H. Hoefnagels, *Die neue Solidarität*, München, 1979, 192.

[64] K. Polanyi has made a great contribution in his reflections on existential knowledge.

[65] For this section, see the various reports to the Club of Rome, beginning with D. Meadow, *The Limits of Growth*, etc.; P. Bohm and A.V. Kneese, *The Economics of Environment*, London, 1971; Der Rat der Sachverständigen für Umweltfragen. *Umweltgutachten*, 1974, Stuttgart, 1974; P.O. Barkley and D.W. Seckler, *Economic Growth and Environmental Decay. The Solution Becomes the Problem*. New York, 1972; G. Myrdal, "Ökonomie in einer verbesserten Umwelt", in H. von Nussbaum (ed.), *Die Zukunft des Wachstums: Kritische Antworten zum "Bericht des Club of Rome"*, Dusseldorf, 1973; D. Gabor, U. Colombo, A. King, R. Galli, *Das Ende der Versschwendung. Zur Materiellen Lage der Menschheit. Ein Tatsachenbericht an den Club of Rome*, Stuttgart, 1976; H. Swoba, *Die Qualität des Lebens. Vom Wohlstand zum Wohlbefinden*, Stuttgart, 1973; E. Eppler, *Masstäbe für eine humane Gesellschaft: Standard oder Lebensqualität*, Stuttgart, 1974; E.F. Schumacher, *Es geht auch anders. Jenseits des Wachstums*, Basel, 1974; J.V. Taylor, *Enough is Enough*, London, 1975, I. Illich, *Selbstbegrenzung. Eine politishce Kritik der Technik*, Hamburg, 1975; M. Linquist, *Economic Growth and the Quality of Life. Analysis of the Debate Within the World Council of Churches, 1966-1974*, Helsinki, 1975; O. Jensen, *Unter dem Zwang des Wachstums. Ökologie und Religion*, München, 1977; H. Siebert, *Ökonomische Theorie der Umwelt*, Tübingen, 1978; H.Ch. Binswanger/W. Geissberger/Th. Ginsburg (eds.), *Der NAWU-Report: Wege aus der Wohlstandsfalle; Strategien gegen Arbeitslosigkeit und Umweltkrise*, Frankfurt, 1978.

[66] Cf. E.F. Schumacher, *Small is Beautiful*, 119, 121; H.D. Engelhardt, l.c., 349.

[67] Hoefnagels, l.c., 33.

[68] E.F. Schumacher, l.c., 46.

[69] Cf. H.D. Engelhardt, l.c., 76.

[70] E.G. Dolan, *The Economic Strategy for Environmental Crisis*, New York, 1971, 9

[71] U.E. Simonis, "Lebensqualität: Ansätze zur Gewinnung sozio-ökonomischer Ziele", in H.D. Engelhardt, l.c., 352.

[72] E.F. Schumacher, l.c., 33.

[73] Cf. H.D. Engelhardt, l.c., 326.

[74] B. Ward, "Only One Earth", in *Anticipation*, N. 11 (July 1977), 31.

[75] John XXIII, *Mater et Magistra*, 188, 189, 192; Cf. J. Gremillion, l.c., 99

[76] J. Passmore, l.c., 62.

[77] C. Cortecote Parkinson, *Big Business*, London, 1974, 217ff., 228ff.

[78] J. King, "Prospects and Hazards of New Genetic Technologies", l.c., 248.

[79] J. Passmore, l.c., 62.

[80] Cf. L. Wierling, "Die Grenzen des Wachstums", in H. D. Engelhardt, l.c., 379-392.

[81] E. F. Schumacher, l.c., 70; K. Lorenz, *Die acht Todsünden der zivilisierten Menscheit*, München, 1974[7], 21

[82] Paul VI, *Octogesima adveniens*, 10, 11, 12; cf. J. Gremillion, 109.

[83] Cf. H. Westmüller, "Die Umweltkrise - Eine Anfrage an die Theologie", in H. D. Engelhardt, l.c., 344.

[84] E. F. Schumacher, l.c., 204.

[85] l.c., 38.

[86] l.c., 146.

[87] C. F. von Weizsäcker, *Deutlichkeit*, 91.

[88] H. Schelsky, *Auf der Suche nach der Wirklichkeit*, Düsseldorf and Köln, 1965, 449.

[89] Cf. H. Schelsky, *Der Mensch in der wissenschaftlichen Zivilization*, Köln and Opalden, 1961.

[90] Cf. J. Ellul, *The Technological Society*, New York, 1971, 32.

[91] C.F. von Weizsäcker, l.c., 69; H.D. Engelhardt, l.c., 56.

[92] Th.S. Derr, l.c., 146.

[93] A.J. Moore, "Meeting on 'Science and Faith' Debates - Ethics and Technology", in *Christianity and Crisis*, 1979, 245.

[94] J. Passmore, l.c., 58

[95] Th.S. Derr, l.c., 90f.

[96] l.c., 145.

[97] A. Pigon, *The Economics of Welfare*, London, 1932⁴, 184.

[98] Cf. E. F. Schumacher, l.c., 146-159.

[99] l.c., 146.

[100] Cf, J. Passmore, l.c., 50.

[101] Cf. *Free and Faithful in Christ* II, ch. II on Beauty and Art; cf. O. Jensen, *Unter dem Zwang des Wachstums*, 97.

[102] E.F. Schumacher, l.c., 34.

[103] Paul VI, *Octogesima adveniens*, 21, John Paul II, *Redemptor hominis*, 8, 16.

[104] Cf. Th.S. Derr, l.c., 136.

[105] R. Dumont, *L'outopie ou la mort?*, Paris, 1974, 59.

[106] Th.S. Derr, l.c., 148.

[107] Cf. E. Laszlow and others, *Goals for Mankind: A Report to the Club of Rome on the New Horizons of the Global Community*, New York, 1977, 387, 451ff.

[108] J. King, "Prospects and Hazards of New Genetic Technologies", l.c., 252.

[109] Cf. H. Hoefnagels, *Die neue Solidarität*, München, 1979, 35.

[110] E.F. Schumacher, l.c., 19 and 134-145.

[111] Cf. A.J. Moore, l.c., 224-227; H.N. Janowski, "Für eine Ethik des Lebens. Von der ökumenischen Weltkonferenz in Boston", in *Evangelische Kommentare* 12 (1979), 514-517.

[112] A.D. Sacharow, in *Neue Züricher Zeitung*, May 3, 1978.

[113] C.F. von Weizsäcker, *Deutlichkeit*, 43ff.

[114] H. Hoefnagels, l.c., 197, fn. 28.

[115] J. King, l.c., 252.

[116] C.F. von Weizsäcker, *Deutlichkeit*, 48.

[117] l.c., 74; K. Lorenz, l.c., 37, expresses this thought even more dramatically; cf. R. Jungk, *Atomstaat, Vom Fortschritt in die Unmenschlichkeit*, München, 1977.

[118] J. Gremillion, l.c., 94.

[119] E.F. Schumacher, l.c., 230f.

[120] D. Meadows, *Die Grenzen des Wachstums*, Stuttgart, 1972, 172f.

[121] J. Passmore, l.c., 170.

[122] l.c., 95.

[123] H. Hoefnagels, l.c., 57.

Chapter Six

Culture and Ethics

One of the most important signs of church renewal is the present keen awareness of the interaction between religion and culture and between morality and culture. In the Second Vatican Council, a church document speaks systematically, for the first time on such a level, about the Christian's duty to foster the progress of culture, in openness to all that culture means for persons and for the very mission of the church.[1]

Only an individualistic narrowness in moral theology could overlook the importance of culture for moral development and responsibility. In *Free and Faithful in Christ*, important dimensions of culture are treated in various contexts - for instance, education for the sense of beauty, art, feast, play and sense of humour, in Chapter Two of Volume 2. And in our previous chapter on Ecology and Ethics, we constantly met with the interaction between nature and culture. Nevertheless, an effort towards a certain synthesis of the fundamental theme of culture and ethics seems to be an indispensable part of a comprehensive text on Christian ethics. The question is not only the general relation between culture and ethics but also the specifically Christian encounter between culture and gospel, culture and a fully Christian life.

Here we not only deal with a general concept of culture but give special attention to the diversity of cultures. We speak on culture in view of the self-actualization of persons and communities and persons in communities, but also on culture that transforms the environment. The Second Vatican Council gives a good description: "The word 'culture' in its general sense indicates all those factors by which man refines and unfolds his manifold spiritual and bodily qualities. It means his effort to bring the world itself under his control by his knowledge and his labour. It includes the fact that by improving customs and institutions he renders social life more human both within the family and in the civic community. Finally, it is a feature of culture that throughout the course of time man expresses, communicates and conserves in his works great spiritual experiences and desires, so that these may be of advantage to the progress of many, even of the whole human family.

Hence it follows that human culture necessarily has a historical and social aspect. . ."[2]

I. THE RELEVANCE OF CULTURE FOR MORALITY

In view of crying injustices and political crimes, of the sickness of a consumer society and of frequent reductionism, moralists can easily come to a biased vision, insinuating that the moral person has to acutalize himself or herself in a constant struggle against an immoral culture. Typical of such a one-sided perspective is the interesting book, *Moral Man and Immoral Society*, by a great Christian ethicist, Reinhold Niebuhr.[3]

It is my conviction that our faith in the goodness of creation and the superabundance of redemption, together with a profound sense of gratitude to past generations and to our contemporaries, make it appropriate to discover first what is good in our culture and, indeed, in all cultures. Then we shall be able to face the evils courageously and to offer constructive critique. If we always point first to the dark side, our own relation to culture will be disturbed and our cultural mission will be handicapped.

First of all, we think of the wealth and beauty of our language, reflecting the experience and wisdom of many generations and the achievements of the great geniuses. Language leads us to the whole of tradition that speaks to us and enriches us by so many monuments of art, craft and, above all, by the wisdom expressed in mores, institutions, proverbs, and so on. Mores and customs embody an ethos, a basic relation to decisive values. All this reaches the human person from the very beginning of life in family and society. "Culture is based on an all-inclusive reality of convictions and attitudes towards life and world, which the child receives from the first infancy and that begin to shape him spiritually."[4]

From these cultural roots, law and order develop which regulate and protect fundamental relationships in family, society and the economy. Law and order are an essential part of culture but not the summit; their strength and helpfulness depend on the whole of the culture.

All this makes evident the fundamental role of culture in man's moral growth and self-realization. Because of this role, culture must be an important object of ethics.

Even the religious and moral genius, the saint, the prophet, the hero are not thinkable without the support and stimulation that comes from culture. George Gurvitch criticizes Henri Bergson's famous work on "The Two Sources of Morality and Religion" because it does not at all do justice to the promordial importance of culture, with its ethos, juridical expression and the whole wealth of embodied values.[5]

Jürgen Moltmann warns about the narrowness of a merely "ethical anthropology."[6] "Biological anthropology" elaborates the distinction between man and animal. "Cultural anthropology" arises from the study of the encounter of various cultures, and unmasks the underdevelopment of an ethnocentric vision in which only people of one tribe or culture count, and where so many things are absolutized. "Religious anthropology" cannot ignore cultural anthropology (comparative culture). "There are many links between the message of salvation and human culture. For God, revealing himself to his people to the extent of a full manifestation of himself in his Incarnate Son, has spoken according to the culture proper to different ages."[7] And so does the church act whenever she faithfully follows the divine example.

The objective culture - the whole of tradition, mores, ethos, law - is indispensable for the awakening of the individual's conscience, but it cannot guarantee the development of a sensitive, mature conscience. On the contrary, there are certain cultures, forms of traditions and mores which, especially under the impact of unfortunate authority structures, so strongly enforce the external assimilation that it becomes difficult for the conscience of the individual to transcend the phase of mere conformism. Josef Messner gives a significant example: Within tribes that frequently had to travel to other, sometimes distant places in search of food, and had to carry everything on their neck or head, the conviction easily arose that it was their duty to kill the old who were unable to march with them.[8]

Such a traditional praxis, which we in our culture consider intolerable but which came into being under the pressure of a whole economic and cultural situation, tends then to persist afterwards when the causes or "reasons" no longer exist, unless the cultural development favours growth of discernment. In the absence of a critical spirit, tradition becomes traditionalism. If such a tribe enters into friendly relations with other tribes in which the practice is considered appalling, it becomes psychologically easier to consider it anew and to make the appropriate change.

We live in a pluralistic culture. Not only do we have the opportunity to know about various now-existing cultures; we can also compare distinctive past cultures. This knowledge can enrich us. Not everything that is beneficial in another culture is fitting in our own, but if we are mature, we shall critically choose from other cultures whatever is good, healthy and beautiful. This can be done in creative fidelity to one's own culture and tradition. The Second Vatican Council exhorts the faithful to live in close union with the people of their time, and to try to understand "their ways of thinking and feeling as expressed in their culture."[9]

The many forms of communication among the various cultures, and the many ways to foster dialogue, open gateways to a kind of "universal culture" in which all cultures are enriched by sharing and discerning. The greatest risk, however, is unrootedness and superficial selection, with consequential insecurity and/or scepticism. The trend towards a universal and unifying culture needs constant effort, with special care to come to a vision of wholeness and synthesis and a deeper understanding of the richness of diversity. This enables people to synthesize rootedness in their own culture with creative openness towards the other cultures.[10] A "universal culture" understood as uniformity contradicts the very essence of culture and conscience.

II. RELEVANCE OF MORALITY FOR CULTURE

1. *The creative power of religion and morality*

The power of faith not only allowed Abraham an exodus, a creative detachment from the inherited culture and its taboos, but was also a continuing source of new ways of thinking and acting. It allowed fruitful contact with other traditions. Rooted in faith and trust in Yahweh, the Mosaic law with its covenant morality inspired all kinds of arts and shaped the cultural cohesion of the twelve tribes.

An ethical anthropology and a purely imperative morality, where everything is based on abstract principles, are culturally sterile. But enthusiastic faith, a sharing of one's trust in God and a common search to know God and his design can impregnate all expressions of personal, social, cultural life. Faith lived in a faith community gives the wholeness of vision and the clear direction that distinguish a healthy culture. A morality rooted in faith, symbolized in manifold religious expressions and articulated in the faith community creates those healthy, cooperative relationships which are at the heart of both culture and morality.

Morals alone do not create a culture. This must be said pointedly against any kind of moralism that is alienated from the inner sources of life and wants to impose its dictates without regard for the cultural background and psychic orientation of the people. Genuine morality, constantly nourished by religious symbols and celebrations, is marked by that creative liberty and fidelity that allow both temperance and courage, wisdom and objectivity.

Each culture as a whole, and each of its dimensions, follow their own dynamics where faith and faith-morality are present as yeast in the dough, working for consistence and synthesis. Thus morality is not a mere spectator nor a dictator. The Second Vatican Council was convinced that religion and morality do not lose but gain by respecting a certain autonomy of the temporal sphere, and especially of culture.[11]

2. *The impact of the moral genius*

The genius, the great artist, the prophet, the saint, are the discoverers of new values and new opportunities. They open new directions and gateways, bring traditional values and forms of ethos to new life, and open the eyes to values not yet realized. They do not disdain the many silent and humble people who, day by day, keep values and forms of wisdom alive.[12] The closer they are to the people, the more creative will be their impact on the whole culture. Mahatma Ghandi and Martin Luther King are examples of the genius close to the simple people, yet courageous enough to challenge them and to lead to new paths.

It is a most tragic situation when the genius or the people's hero has not sound vision and judgment of values. It is an even greater tragedy if the authentic prophets and saints are not listened to or are outrightly rejected. The heinous murder of the two modern prophets of non-violent and creative commitment to peace, justice and liberation, sad and bitter as it is, might be a lesser loss than the unwillingness of so many to act according to the message and witness of the great prophets.

3. Conscience and culture

The most precious thing on earth is a healthy, alert and faithful conscience, free for the others, free for all moral values, and able to discern the scale and urgency of values. The healthy conscience reflects the vision and experience of wholeness that create healthy relationships, a true co-humanity. These foundations of a truly developed culture are surely the forces most urgently needed by our modern cultures. Today's pluralism becomes a cultural dynamic for creative liberty and fidelity through the reciprocity of developed consciences, where absolute faithfulness to one's own conscience is harmonized with a deep respect for the other's conscience and a readiness to share and to learn together.[13]

III. THE CULTURAL MISSION OF THE CHRISTIAN

1. A mission and a conscious task

The greatest contribution Christians can make to their culture is to be fully Christian and fully human. However, the insights into the profound interaction between culture and religion, culture and morality, makes the mission, "You are the light to the world", a conscious mandate to participate actively in the promotion of culture. This is especially true in our modern society in which many ideological forces strive to mould the culture according to their alienating ideas.

Although the content and form of the culture cannot be altered concretely by our faith or by church authority, the cultural responsibility has to do with eternal salvation. Therefore, the Christian's best possible contribution will be inspired by Christian love and justice, and for the sake of salvation.

The Second Vatican Council sees a conscious participation in the promotion of culture as a sign of growth: "There is an ever-increasing number of men and women who are conscious that they themselves are the artisans and the authors of the culture of their community. Throughout the world there is a similar growth in the combined sense of independence and responsibility. Such a development is of paramount importance for the spiritual and moral maturity of the human race. This truth grows clearer if we consider how the world is becoming unified and how we have the duty to build a better world built upon truth and justice. Thus we are witnesses of the birth of a new humanism, one in which man is defined first of all by his responsibility towards his brothers and towards history."[14]

2. The values without which a culture must wither away

All great world religions cultivate values which are truly universal, such as the primacy of the human person over and above things, the actualization of true co-humanity over and above the cultural transformation of things, and this latter transformation only or mainly in the service of persons, universal justice and solidarity. Therefore, the Christian's prime commitment must be to bring these values home into his culture in a lively synthesis and, last but not least, to strengthen the meditative dimension of life.[15] The Christian should be an expert in and a credible witness to these values without which there is no culture with a truly human face.

Beyond these points, the believers, as such, and the church have no official competence for matters of culture, and do not automatically have special expertise. Religiosity and moral sense alone do not make a culture; hence, Christians, both lay people and clergy, like other citizens, have to acquire the necessary qualifications. For this, the behavioural sciences can be of great service.[16]

Without arrogating to himself false certainties, the believer will bring home into his culture the dedication to truth and the tireless common search for fuller truth and a life in truth. Cardinal Henry Newman expressed this forcefully in his "The Idea of a University". From this follows the task of promoting the art of dialogue, the communication of truth and the search for truth.

3. Broadening the space for creative liberty

Following the insights of ethicists and sociologists who have focused particularly on the interdependencies of culture and morals,[17] Vatican II emphasizes, along with a sense of continuity and fidelity, the necessity to guarantee the space for freedom so indispensable to creativity in the realm of culture.[18] It is interesting that, in the chapter on promotion of culture, the Council makes it clear that lay people and priests engaged in bridging the gap between theology and culture "possess a lawful freedom of inquiry and of thought, and the freedom to express their minds humbly and courageously about those matters in which they enjoy competence".[19]

4. The right of all to share actively in the goals of culture

In a humanistic culture, especially if it is of Christian inspiration or promoted by Christians, there should be no doubt about the right of all to participate not only as recipients but also as promoters of culture. The Second Vatican Council is very specific on this point. It gives a kind of programme for a respective conscientization but also requests planning, so that in all fields, in politics and economy, on the national and international levels, basic decisions will be made whereby the rights of all to participate in human culture will be guaranteed. It also deplores the fact that so many are deprived of the possibility to develop responsible initiative and, as a consequence, cannot truly contribute to the common good.[20]

This is a basic principle of Catholic social doctrine as it has developed since the encyclical *Rerum Novarum* of Leo XIII. The goal is a participatory society and culture in *solidarity* and *subsidiarity*. What the individual can do responsibly should not be taken over by the community, and what the more fundamental communities can achieve by themselves should not be arrogated by the larger organization. The higher level should supply where the lower one is unable to do so, but principally with the intention to enable and encourage all to fulfil their own functions by creative participation in culture.

This vision applies also to the problem of *ownership*. The meaning and justification of private property goes only so far as *all* benefit in its purpose, namely, the creative and responsible use of things for one's own person-culture and needs, and for the common good.

Gratitude to the Creator and Redeemer oblige us to cooperate so that the conditions of life, and especially of work,[21] may allow all to develop their cultural capacities. For the Christian, this is included in our common, total vocation to become ever more an image and likeness of God. The way man subdues the earth and organizes the conditions of work is as much a cultural as a socio-economic question.

Christians should be creatively present in the whole field of education, and should give particular attention to a vision of wholeness in order to overcome the dangerous trend of our culture towards reductionism, superficial pragmatism and one-sided specialization.

A school monopoly by the state, especially if it is banning all religion from its educational system, is culturally a disaster. State and society should not only tolerate but greatly encourage church-related and other educational agencies that creatively offer alternatives.[22] The state schools at all levels should try to compete with the "alternative" schools in a spirit of mutual enrichment and innovation. But the state schools will scarcely be able to match the educational purpose to form the whole person as a person. The very pluralistic character of our society makes this difficult if the parents and children have not the right and the real possibility to choose a school which guarantees basically the same vision and purpose of life and education.

5. Culture and politics

Good politics is an indispensable service to culture. But the other way around is even more fundamental: the promotion of culture is an indispensable precondition for fruitful politics. This is to be said against the temptation of a superficial "political Catholicism". In the past, churchmen and laity not infrequently tried to obtain too much (for good and less good purposes) directly through politics or by pressure on politicians, while neglecting the cultural sector. Our responsibility for the promotion of culture is fundamental.

Sound politics is one way of promoting culture and trying to create the best possible conditions for the preservation and growth of culture. Vatican II has pertinent principles on this point: "It is not the function of public authority to determine what the proper nature of forms of human culture should be. It should rather foster the conditions and the means which are capable of promoting cultural life among all citizens and even within the minorities of a nation. Hence in this matter men must insist above all else that culture be not diverted from its own purpose and made to serve political or economic interests."[23]

To use cultural activities just as means for political ambition or economic utility is a kind of rape.

IV. ENCOUNTER OF RELIGION AND GOSPEL MORALITY WITH CULTURES

Since we live in a time of deep and rapid changes in our own culture and of encounter with many other cultures, we have to ask ourselves pertinent questions: Is our religion, with its culturally conditioned forms of organization, its conceptual framework and symbols, simply the same as the gospel and faith in it? How do our faith and our morality grounded in it reach the present scientific, technical, urban culture without loss of integrity and without remaining strangers to it? What about the encounter of the western church with the cultures of Africa, Asia, Oceania and so on? Christians and other religious people of the Third World are critical of the way the latin church organized their religious expressions and structures and, above all, the way it taught them morals according to the western "classical" manuals. Did we not hide from them, rather than unconceal for them, the newness of gospel morality?

1. Fidelity to the mystery of the Incarnation

The whole history of creation and salvation has its summit in the incarnation of the Word of God. He not only took the flesh of humanity, but became a Jew for the Jews while being equally free for the Samaritans and Gentiles.

The church ought to remain thoroughly faithful to this basic orientation, wonderfully demonstrated by the Apostle of the Gentiles.[24] This implies a courageous and never ceasing effort to incarnate the abiding truth of gospel and gospel morality in the living traditions, the forms of ethos, the mores, and in the whole of the cultures of the various people, tribes and subcultures.

The Second Vatican Council's decree on missions, and many pre-conciliar and especially post-conciliar decrees of the popes and the Holy See, have fully adopted this incarnational principle, although it is easier to affirm it in general terms than to apply it to urgent problems: "The work of planting the church in a given human community reaches a kind of milestone when the congregation of the faithful, already rooted in social life and considerably adapted to the local culture, enjoys a certain stability and firmness."[25]

This incarnation and implantation imply - as the apostolic exhortation of John Paul II on catechesis affirms - a certain "cultural dialogue" that must keep contact with the manner in which, from its beginning in Jesus, in the Apostles and then in the course of history, the gospel incarnated itself in the various cultures. If this occurs faithfully, "the force of the gospel brings forth everywhere a transformation and regeneration. If the gospel is a yeast within the culture, there is no wonder when it corrects some elements."[26] In this incarnational encounter it is not the gospel that changes; rather, a change occurs in the culture, but from within.

This courageous adaptation to new cultures is in no way a lack of fidelity to the church. Until recently, the church itself was almost exclusively a latin, western church marked by the cultural patterns of the Greek, Roman and Germanic world; and the very adoption of these patterns had been an incarnational process in the past. Genuine fidelity to the past is not a repetition of the results of a past creative event but rather the courage to undertake new forms of incarnational encounter with other cultures.

The encounter with so numerous old and new cultures helps to preserve the purity of faith in the mystery of salvation, for the mystery of God and of a truly Christian life is infinitely richer than the expressions in only one culture. The incarnational processes prevent heretical deviations when there is a sharp consciousness that the same faith and the same moral message are being articulated in many languages and cultures. It is like a magnificent orchestra where each voice and instrument has its full truth in the whole. To identify Christian faith and morality simply with their time-bound expression in one culture would be tantamount to heresy. That is what traditionalists do unconsciously.

The message of salvation, including the moral exigencies of faith, must always and everywhere manifest its newness and freshness. This important dimension is concealed and betrayed whenever, with cultural arrogance or in alien cultural patterns, people are offered the gospel message in such a way that assent to it seems to require the adoption of alien cultural patterns.

The decree of Vatican II on missions stresses this experience of newness and its presuppositions for people of another culture in their encounter with the Good News. "They must give expression to this newness of life in the social and cultural framework of their own homeland, according to their own national traditions. They must be acquainted with this culture. They must heal it and preserve it. They must develop it in accordance with modern conditions, and finally perfect it in Christ. Thus faith in Christ and the life of the church will no longer be something extraneous to the society in which they live, but will begin to permeate and transform it."[27]

2. The exodus

The incarnational evangelization[28] we speak of requires faithfulness to the exodus paradigm which has reached its fullness in Jesus Christ. This is particularly painful for a church which, for a long time, made no protest against colonialism and frequently nourished a superiority complex about its western and especially its latin culture. When the unfortunate document, *Veterum Sapientiae* was issued, which John XXIII signed and then deeply regretted, the *L'Osservatore Romano* spoke triumphantly several times of the Romans' "latin superculture" which the church treasures and uses "in order to cultivate the barbarians".

The Second Vatican Council brought - not without a heart-searching examination of conscience and violent opposition - a turning point which, however, like the breakthrough of the Apostle of the Gentiles, must be defended against ever new temptations and reactionary attempts. In a decisive intervention, Cardinal Lercaro dealt with these problems through the paradigm of evangelical poverty.[29] He insisted that the culture is the basic medium, a pattern present in each word, symbol, rite and every message. However, the latin church had tied up the mediation with an exclusively occidental "organon". The Cardinal called for a conversion to evangelical poverty by returning to the simplicity of the Bible and renouncing all boasting in the flesh, boasting in its "higher" culture.

On the basis of the poverty and simplicity of the gospel, it will be easier for the missionary church to reach a genuine dialogue with the various cultures of the world. I suggest that the older generation should apply this same vision and attitude also to its dialogues with the younger generation.

3. The universal reign of God

The church would be unfaithful to her main mission - to proclaim the universal kingdom of God by word and action, by liturgy and organizational structures - if she were to give to any one culture a kind of monopoly in her life, her institutions and moral teaching. She must not even dream of a universal culture where one culture would swallow up the others or impose on others its language, thought-pattern, symbols, and so on. This would be tantamount to an abominable cultural colonialism. If religious and moral teaching were used for this purpose, it would be nothing less than sacrilege.

The true "universal culture", prefigured by the Pentecost event, is marked by many languages, symbols, customs that, in one great symphony, play their proper part. All contain precious elements, a millennial heritage ever renewed and enriched. Through their diversity which, under the impact of the gospel fully incarnated in them, tends towards a truthful unity, they can proclaim the reign of God and point to his mystery much better than one culture alone. Indeed, if one culture were to claim a monopoly, it would be absolutely a counter-sign of God's kingdom.

The great moral task common to all people does not only allow but actually requests a diversity of mores, customs and forms of ethos "in a kind of historical partition of different roles within the total moral endeavour of humankind, the result of which will be unique and much greater than what mortal eyes have seen thus far"[30]

4. Meta-ethics

The incarnation of the one faith, with its moral implications, in an enormous diversity of constantly changing cultures is somehow disquieting and, indeed, most disturbing for those who are mainly concerned with security and/or knowledge of dominion and control. But even where there is no insane security complex and no wild-running knowledge of dominion, the incarnational view poses a great challenge to Christian ethics and ethics in general. Because of the manifold interdependencies between culture and morality, "ethics has to scrutinize with sharpened alertness what, in the relationship between both, belongs to the realm of the essential-abiding and what to the realm of the historically-conditioned."[31]

From the diversity of moral manifestations among so many cultures, philosophers like Plato, Aristotle, Thomas Aquinas, Kant and Hegel have tried to crystalize a universally valid meta-ethics. But in this philosophical enterprise there was manifested time and again the temptation to ignore or to minimize the historicity of man. As a consequence, the constructed meta-ethics did not really speak on historical man, and even less on the complexity of a fallen and redeemed humankind.

In newer times, sociologists of mores and morality have tried in their own way to reach a kind of meta-ethics by methods of comparative culture. Thus they took the cloak of the philosophers. A great sociologist warns, "What escaped them is, however, the irreducible multiplicity and diversity of moral styles which co-exist under the same sociological conditions, and even more in the whole society."[32]

There is so much in common flowing from human nature and the moral giftedness of humankind, that it is reasonable and even necessary to reflect on the possibility, purpose and meaning of a meta-ethics. However, it should not be forgotten that this can be thought of and spoken of only with the cultural tools of a concrete language and of thought-patterns that cannot be translated literally into a distant culture.

And one thing more must be understood: as long as persons, whether in the same or different cultures, sincerely and freely seek what is good and truthful, and put it creatively into practice, there can never be a monotonous and tensionless universal morale. Sincere and mature people will be able to agree on basic values, rights, duties, but not even the life of a saint and not the best *Summa Moralis* can bring home the full richness of moral values and their incarnations. A meta-ethics must content itself with the basic truths and values.

The history of treatises on natural law shows clearly the temptation to absolutize what is common to a certain group. The famous texts of past centuries on natural law allow us to reconstruct to a great extent the mores, the forms of ethos and the deficiencies in the milieu of the philosophers, on the basis of what they present as absolute. This should suffice to make us cautious when it is a matter of generalizing. And this caution should also allow us to meet other cultures with greater openness and respect, and to learn from them and with them.

5. The proprium of Christian morality

At this point we can come back again to the much-discussed *proprium* of Christian ethics. It can be expressed in a way that does not separate us from other cultures and religions, but unites us in the sincere search and realization of what is good, true and beautiful.

As we have seen, the *incarnational* aspect belongs essentially to the Christian moral message. Equally emphasized must be the historical dimension of salvation and a life responding to the salvation message, the universality of God's kingdom on earth, the power of the content and attitude of faith to mould and enrich the moral insight and character. Central is faith in the Easter mystery of the death and resurrection of Christ and the coming of the Holy Spirit to reveal the true countenance of love. Also essential are the all-embracing dynamics of love of God and

of neighbour articulated in all Christian virtues, the pre-eminence
of the eschatological virtues reflecting the dimensions of history,
and last but not least, appreciation of the redeemed human
intelligence, the constant readiness to share experience and
reflection beyond the boundaries of one's own culture and
subculture.

V. CONFLICT AND BLESSINGS

1. Avoidable conflicts

The history of all major religions, including Christianity,
records tragic conflicts, frequently leading to persecutions, which
were caused by unfortunate religious teaching and especially by
inculcating moral norms and imperatives in the name of religion
when, in reality, social conditionings and unhealthy authority
structures played a major role in establishing these norms.

A classic example is the dispute about Chinese and latin rituals.
The question was not only - as might appear to a superficial
observer - the uniformity of the "sacred language" and rituals,
but equally the quest for complete uniformity in matters of
mores, customs, traditions and forms of ethos. This practically
meant an attempt of one culture to overpower and to eliminate
others in the name of religion. Many schisms within Christianity
were occasioned by an ambiguity about cultural differences, and
more deplorably, by a combination of cultural superiority
attitudes and the arrogance of religious circles.

Already in the very beginning, Christianity's mission to
evangelize all nations found an almost insurmountable obstacle in
the firm conviction of most Judeo-Christians that conversion to
Christ implied essentially a full acceptance of the Mosaic laws.
That would have meant practically the acceptance of the whole
Jewish culture, with the result of a total estrangement from one's
own culture. This error was, at that time, almost natural, because
of a false concept of Jewish chosenness and the total lack of
reflections regarding the interdependence between religion and
culture. Through divine revelation, the Apostle of the Gentiles
could break the barrier, but not without most painful conflicts.

The first great missionaries of the Far East, Matteo Ricci and

DeNobili, had the broad vision of St Paul, helped by solid reflection on the legitimate diversity of cultures and the necessity for the gospel to take root in the culture. The Roman decision against their ideas and work erected a latin wall which, for a long time, made evangelization almost fruitless. Today the systematic research of ethnology, cultural anthropology, sociology of culture and mores makes unfaithfulness to the example of St Paul even more unforgiveable. The central government of the church should make generous use of experts in these sciences whenever the question arises about whether a certain moral norm must or can be imposed on all regardless of cultural differences.

2. Blending the old and the new

The complexity of the problem must be clearly faced. In spite of a given good will and scientific competence, there remain enough occasions for perplexity and conflict. The present reflections intend to help prevent avoidable conflicts and to make the unavoidable clashes fruitful or at least less harmful.

To dramatize this burning issue, I want to confront the reader with these questions: Do not the responsible leaders of a tribe or nation have the right and duty to prevent a cultural estrangement and uprootedness which they foresee or actually experience as a result of alienating methods of evangelization? Can the principle of religious liberty be invoked when foreigners, in the name of God, impose new moral norms and customs that dissociate the cultural unity? Can churchmen who, because of a false traditionalism, reaffirm moral norms taught in past times under vastly different historical conditions, without taking into account new knowledge and urgent new needs, expect the *reaction* to be more discerning than their *action*? For me, the response cannot be a theoretical "yes" or "no". The existential response is that Christians must do everything possible to avoid any form of cultural estrangement or any undermining of legitimate structures of existing cultures.

A genuine teaching of gospel morality by Christian leaders well instructed in the sacred and humane sciences will always be directly or indirectly also a service to cultures, although temporary tensions and conflicts may not be excluded.

A useful paradigm for approaching this problem seems to me the distinction between the "sacred ethos" and the "sanctioned ethos" proposed half a century ago by Rudolf Otto.[33] For him, "sanctioned" ethos means almost the same as for Alfons Auer, a world-ethos of a Christian or another believer.[34] It is the ethos existing in the culture and/or professional group, not arising from faith as such, while the "sacred" ethos is inherent in the religious experience. The sacred ethos determines our relationship in the sphere of the sacred - with God and what directly points to him or belongs to him in a special way. While it is not totally independent from the existing culture, it transcends it essentially; it is more than a cultural phenomenon. In the basic experience of the sacred and its ethos, there are differences but also important similarities in Eastern and Western religiosity. As Christians, we synthesize the sacred ethos in faith, hope, love and adoration.

Many of the conflicts between different religions or religious people of different cultures directly concern dimensions of the sacred ethos. An important example is the cult of the ancestors.[35] In many African and Asian cultures, the sacred ethos has its central expression in the memorial cult of the ancestors. The deeply-felt gratitude and the solidarity with them gives motive and sanction to traditions, and especially to the family spirit. The spirits of the ancestors are trusted and feared as mediators between God and their progeny. People feel that the ancestors are unhappy and unsettled in the assemblies of the honoured ancestors if their offspring are unfaithful to the inherited mores or do not properly fulfil their role in the human community.

Christian missionaries and church authorities who condemned the cult of the ancestors in general terms not only hurt deep religious experiences but also seriously undermined the social and moral fabric of these cultures, or else made it impossible for the people to accept the Christian message. There is so much truth and beauty in the cult of the ancestors that it can well be brought home and re-affirmed as an experience of saving solidarity beyond death, as part of the memorial of our real ancestors, Jesus Christ and the saints.

The "sanctioned ethos" is that part of the people's total ethos that is most intimately attached to the culture and the whole human experience in family and society. It guides the attitude towards the world. According to Otto, the great religions like

Islam and Christianity did not create this ethos but met it as a given, firmly rooted reality. What religion does, then, is to give this ethos sanction, as expression of the divine will, or to eliminate what contradicts the "sacred ethos" of these religions.

The first purpose of the messengers of Christ's gospel is not at all to teach a new "world ethos" or a kind of new code of morals. First is to communicate the experience of the newness of faith in Jesus Christ, his death and resurrection, the mission of the Holy Spirit and the expectation of the final coming of Christ. A part of the message is, then, the newness of a "life in Christ Jesus" with its direct call to love of neighbour and to universal solidarity as a sharing in the love of Christ and his Father for all the children of God. The new experience of the all-embracing love in Christ surely does not, of itself, lead to conflicts with the given culture or with traditionally good people. It could stir up only those who try to justify hatred and enmity. The cross-fertilization or the clash comes mostly when the religion deals with vital issues of the inherited ethos and mores.

3. Process of integration

What Otto calls "sanctioning" might better be understood as integration in the happy case where it is not only a matter of approving and strengthening the ethos but of bringing it home into a vital, deeply-felt synthesis. But a first step is to discern in the ethos and mores what is right, good, honest, gracious (cf. Phil 4:8) and to keep it; and then to make it consciously a part of fidelity to Christ.

Paul did not have to invent or to import the virtues of the household (Eph 6:5ff; Col 3:18ff); he found them as a part of the mores of the Greek culture. "Point of departure is the given, historically-grown, culturally-determined ethos of the milieu. Paul's letters to the communities, to a great extent do not contain materially new, concrete norms of action, but take this from the Judaic proverbial wisdom and the popular Greek philosophy."[36] For a fruitful encounter and discernment, the mores and morality of the people are more relevant than philosophical systems that did not and do not reach the average person.

Whatever the newly converted believers with upright consciences consider valuable from their past experience receives sanction not just from an external religious authority but from their own conscience illumined and purified by faith. It is not added sanction as motive for hope of reward or fear of punishment, but sanction by the very integrity of the believer's conscience. What happens in the best event is an organic integration that gives also a sense of continuity with the past, an experience that makes the freshness of the Christian message even more fruitful.

What can be "sanctioned" and integrated by the conscience of the faithful and approved by the faith community becomes normally clear through the conduct of the most outstanding members and groups. In this process, the religious leader may sometimes feel the need to alert influential groups to a greater sense of responsibility, as Paul did with the "strong" of Corinth (1 Cor chs. 8 and 9). The whole of revelation, together with rational arguments, offers criteria - not, however, applicable in totally different situations.

In the Old and New Testaments we find many cases of a "sanctioned ethos", that is, of ethos forms and mores not revealed but met or inherited by those who came to faith in Yahweh and/or in Christ. And if we compare them with each other, we see that what was sanctioned as God's will in one situation received no attention or was even disapproved of in another era or culture. If we ignore the historical process of encounter and integration, it might appear that God commands in one case what he forbids in another situation, The fitting explanation is that each community of believers, at a given time and in a given culture, has to search and discern in a spirit of openness.[37] And what may be acceptable at one stage of growth of faith, may not be acceptable at a higher stage, and what may be helpful in one cultural context can be disruptive in another.

Not only what is good in all cases but also time-bound mores can receive authentically religious sanction. A classic example is Paul's order, given to the women of Corinth, to observe the custom of their culture not to appear unveiled in public, The reason was the good name of Christians and sensitivity to the feelings of the co-citizens.

4. Purification

Frequently, the process is not so much a simple and clear integration as a gradual purification of a custom that then finds "sanction" in its modified form. The faith of the individual and the community, if it is strong and illumined, operates gradually but thoroughly as yeast in the dough. Hence the duty of evangelizers is, above all, to strengthen faith and the virtue of discernment while, for a certain time, tolerating some more or less imperfect mores and forms of ethos.

This must not be misinterpreted as a foul compromise. Call it compromise if you want, but be sure that it is a most dynamic process of an ever more intense education in faith and discernment. The attitude of the Apostle of the Gentiles in the question of slavery illustrates this aspect. The epistle to Philemon indicates the goal. The first letter to the Corinthians (1 Cor 7:20-24) and the table of virtues of the household in the community letters show the graduality or temporary tolerance. Only a naïve way of thinking could confuse temporary tolerance with sanctioning and integration.

In my opinion, this vision could be helpful, for instance, for facing realistically the problem of baptizing African polygamists without destroying a healthy and socially approved and sanctioned family unit. Cannot the levirate marriage, which in the Old Testament was one of the most "sanctioned" moral duties, be temporarily tolerated in newly converted African communities in which this institution has the same function and the same sense of obligation as in Old Israel? The same is true for the stages of the customary marriage, which cannot be changed suddenly without damage to all involved and to the life of the young church.[38]

5. Process of elimination

Faith education and moral teaching can and must sometimes lead to the disapproval and gradual but firm elimination of certain forms of ethos, attitudes and practices which are part and parcel of an existing culture but which strikingly contradict the moral implications of faith.

I can refer here to an example which I studied before and during my activity with the Bemba tribe in Zambia. The practice is called "pupyani". While in the neighbouring tribe the levirate regulates the marriage of a widow with a brother or relative of the late husband, the Bemba have twisted this custom in a strange way. The widow must undergo sexual union with a member of the departed husband's clan, and then may return to her clan and family, where she is free to marry whom she and her family want.

The missionary church tried to abolish this abominable practice by severe prohibitions and sharp sanctions against the man and woman transgressors, but without success. The hypothesis I reached, and which seemed probable to many people with whom I spoke or corresponded, is this: the pupyani practice reflects a two- or three-centuries-old conflict between the older and peaceful indigenous matriarchal culture and the hunter-warrior tribe which conquered the area. The Bemba men, who came with a strong male-centred patriarchalism, demonstrate by this practice their superiority over and against the former local matriarchal family structure. In this way they symbolize that the husband's clan owns the woman but does not feel obliged to take loving care of the widow through the normal process of the levirate marriage.

The women disliked and still do generally dislike this reinforcement of male domination, but they were finally induced by a mythos, a typical superstructure: a belief that the women who refuse the pupyani, and her family, will be severely punished by the spirit of the deceased husband.

My pastoral proposal was not to try to eliminate this by threats and punishment but by instructing people about the origin and ideological character of the practice. The following is very important: by highly honouring those men and women who courageously refused this sexual exploitation in spite of severe treatment, they become the true ancestors and heroes of a new era, to be honoured by the young generation.

6. Critique of the existing culture

The complex process of integration, purification, elimination implies a highly developed level of discernment, and should lead to a constructive critique of the culture by the Christian community. Here, however, some dangerous misunderstandings have to be avoided. The critique has to be uttered at the proper time, with a proper rhythm and by the appropriate people.

From beginning to end, there should be a learning process of discernment about the various elements and the composition of the culture in which we preach the gospel and its moral implications. But the first thing we preach or utter is not a critique of cultural shortcomings but the gospel and those dimensions of morality that arise immediately from faith. Then the integrative and purificative process must come before the process of elimination.

It is frequently useless and even dangerous for a small and young church to criticize publicly the prevailing culture. The believers need time to reach a certain maturity of faith and discernment, besides the need for rootedness in and knowledge of the culture. Public criticism of a culture by foreign missionaries is normally not well received; it smacks too much of a superiority complex. The church can usually fulfil the task of culture-criticism through well instructed and culturally competent lay people. The Second Vatican Council stresses the point that the promotion and critique of culture, in the spirit of religious and human responsibility, is part of the total vocation of the laity.[39]

This difficult task, like others, must never be approached with a pessimistic and negative attitude. Everything that is purely negative provokes repulsion and leads to unnecessary conflicts without accomplishing anything good. The proper place for culture-critique is within an activity that promotes and vitalizes the given culture. This important contribution can best be understood and fulfilled in the light of Christ, the Prophet and Healer. It is participation in his prophetic and healing mission. A church that can decipher the signs of the times in this spirit is a great blessing for the human culture.

VI. IN THE LIGHT OF SOCIOLOGY OF MORES AND MORALS

The various parts of empirical sociology illumine many aspects of the interaction and interdependence between morals and cultures. They can demonstrate how structures of a society, the social processes and relationships, can favour or obstruct the knowledge of religious and moral values. Sociology of sexuality, marriage and family shows the respective values and virtues, hazards and vices in interaction with the various facets of culture. Comparative sociology of cultures helps us to grasp more concretely the historicity of cultures, their ascent and decay, in interaction with all of the social, economic and political realities of their times.

For us in this context, the sociology of mores and morals holds special interest. The concept of morality is broader than that of mores. However, sociology frequently studies both phenomena together, since they are in many ways interrelated.[40]

The sociology of morals studies the functional (in contrast to causal) interdependencies of the expressions and doctrinal systematizations of moral attitudes on the one hand, and on the other, the types of social organizations (classes, groups and other manifestations of man's social nature) whereby the dynamic processes and interactions can be observed.

This sociology proceeds by way of comparison, for only by comparing the various types of social organization with the different kinds of mores found in them can we obtain fruitful insights. Further, there is interest in the origin, development and disposition of certain tendencies, attitudes and mores within the individual culture and its subculture.

Studying the occidental cultures, sociology is making a typology of morals and mores within the various social classes and groupings. As a result, it is asserted that farmers tend to prefer a tradition-bound morality, the bourgeois a pragmatic approach, the typical middle class a morality in terms of duty, while a self-conscious proletariat inclines towards a morality of high aspirations and creative innovation.[41]

G. Gurvitch offers an interesting typology of basic attitudes and forms of ethos: 1) the tradition-bound morality; 2) a pragmatic morality with inclination towards utilitarianism; 3) a morals of virtue; 4) the morals of control and subsequent judgment; 5) the imperative morals; 6) a morality of ideal symbols and images; 7) a morality of high aspirations, a morality of new departures; 8) a morality of liberty and innovative activity.

Within each type there can be a tension between: a) a more mystical and a more rational orientation; b) a more intuitive and a more reflective mode of knowledge; c) a morality of rigid imposition and one of natural gifts; d) an opening and a narrowing morality; e) a morality that easily gains followers and one that does not appeal to many; f) a morality emphasizing the collective dimension and one preferring the individual aspect.[42]

With Gurvitch, I want to make clear that the relativism of sociology that discovers the functional relativity of interactions and interdependencies has nothing to do with a philosophical relativism. The task of ethics begins where sociology ends. Thus we ask ourselves how the scale of values and the moral perspective of culturally-conditioned forms of morality can be reconciled with, integrated with, or purified by the Christian moral message.[43]

1. Encounter with a tradition-bound morality

We should not confuse rootedness in tradition with traditionalism in a pejorative sense. A tradition-bound morality can be mystical and intuitive and can contain precious elements of most of the other types of ethos. It can be a morality of ascent, opening to new horizons, and finding fellowship, but it can also be a narrowing morality of harsh controls and little free fellowship. This depends on the kind of tradition and how much its values are internally assimilated, appreciated and creatively developed.

Within the same culture there can co-exist and conflict with each other the most different types of tradition-bound ethos. It suffices to remember the priestly and the prophetic traditions in Israel. We can compare the tradition-oriented morality of Israel with those of African and Asian cultures, most of which are community oriented. An individualistic morality cannot foster the same values of continuity and fidelity as the community-oriented, and in order to continue it needs more controls.

History and sociology can teach us a great deal about healthy and unhealthy relationships to tradition, and about their social-cultural presuppositions and consequences. As Christians, and especially as Catholic or Orthodox Christians, we do value highly a tradition which embodies the shared moral experiences and reflections of many generations and the wisdom of the genius as well as that of humble people. Our gratitude is best expressed by our creative fidelity.

Dealing with a tradition-bound morality which shows decay, narrowness and shallowness we shall not try to impose a totally different type, but rather to make clear that genuine fidelity to tradition and a healthy rootedness are something different. The first thing is not changing traditions but discovering the real meaning of the tradition in the light of the whole wealth of history.

When dealing with people of cultures undergoing profound changes and innovations, it would be a disaster to teach only in terms of a tradition-bound morality characterized by individualism and corresponding narrowness and control. The paradigm of the prophetic tradition and of the Exodus can be far more helpful.

Our society is one of new departures and, at the same time, of many groups and social mores which are tradition-bound. In a reaction against an excessive traditionalism in one part of society and church, some easily lose the sense of tradition. Moral pedagogy must not only meet the ethos of each social class and group, but also aim at mutual enrichment and complimentarity. To proclaim the Christian moral message to different cultural sub-groups requires a high degree of artistry in communicating from various perspectives and with various emphases.

2. Encounter with a pragmatic morality

A certain type of higher middle-class, the so-called "bourgeoisie", tends towards a pragmatic morality with strong emphasis on reward and punishment, a morality of merit. The good is done mainly for eternal and temporal reward. The pragmatic evaluation looks to purpose and result more than to abiding values and meaning. Frequently a utilitarian overtone prevails.

If it is a religiously-coloured morality, motivation for the afterlife may lessen plain egotism; but as soon as the religious dimension evaporates, the pragmatic character gives way to egotistic utilitarian evaluation for either the self or the group. Theoretically, the talk may be about the highest possible good for all, but practically - as is evident in classical liberalistic theory for the socio-economic life - the "highest possible good" is interpreted as allowing each to seek his own advantage.

A certain pragmatism, if it is moderated by moral and religious motives which transcend the realm of naked purpose, can prevent the danger of a fanaticism obsessed by abstract principles. But a pragmatism without a clear scale of values blocks the normal development of a mature conscience.

The worst deviation of pragmatism is the Skinnerian proposal to manipulate people's conduct scientifically and thoroughly by the twin masters of pain and pleasure, reward and punishment. Such a theory can easily find followers only in a utilitarian culture or sub-culture.

Christian education, meeting such a type of morality, does not need to eliminate all pragmatism but ought to integrate it and heal it by a higher and fuller vision and motivation. This cannot be done by teaching a morality of naked duty or of authoritarian imperatives which, in such a culture, will be either rejected or will simply turn towards a utilitarian security. Neither can a "morality of virtue" help, for taken up by such a culture, it will be a self-centred business of self-fulfilment.

The remedy is integration with a morality of gratitude, a deeper insight into the inner fruitfulness of good, as we see it classically in John, chapter 15. This is not a matter of utilitarian pragmatism but of making good the tree, expecting moral health and salvation from dedication to the good, and from grateful, joyous faith in Christ and surrender to his kingdom. A genuinely Christian teaching and the example of a morality of responsibility[44] can use the energies of a pragmatic culture, transform and ennoble them, and prevent them from deteriorating into a plain utilitarianism.

3. Encounter with a morality of virtue

Gurvitch thinks that a morality of virtue (like that of control and of imperative imposition) tends to narrowness, ossification and/or rigorism, and does not appeal today to the more dynamic part of youth and adults.[45] Evidently, he found in various cultures a morality focusing starkly on virtue, where the leitmotif is self-fulfilment, self-realization, or a self-conscious morality similar to that of the Stoics, not to speak of the ostentatious virtues of the eternal pharisee.

Totally different is the Christian morality of the eschatological virtues: gratitude, hope, vigilance, discernment, serenity. Such a biblical morality is bearer of the dynamics of the history of salvation. It can easily find a fruitful synthesis with a form of morality in which the ideal symbols, high aspirations, creative activity and new departures are culturally alive.

The history of Catholic moral theology shows that the encounter of the Christian moral message of the Bible with an ethos of self-actualization by virtues could deeply transform the concept and style of virtues. They became a part of the loving faith response to God, a part of the dedication to the kingdom of God. But all too often, especially in the last centuries, under the impact of an individualistic culture, the morality of virtue practically forgot the central position of the eschatological virtues, and centred instead on the idea of self-perfection.

There is a most striking contrast between the morality of virtue described by Gurvitch and the morality of the Bible. To all people of all cultures we should be preaching the morality of the Paschal Mystery, of the beatitudes that warn us that those who selfishlv seek themselves can - even in and through their "virtues" - lose themselves. Those who leave the selfish self are the ones who find their true self.

The morality of Confucius, with its four cardinal virtues, does not fall under Gurvitch's categories, for they are not conceived as means of self-perfection but essentially as gifts of heaven. It is an ethics of gratitude for the heavenly gifts; and this comes closer to the eschatological virtues. "The most precious share which Tao (Heaven) grants to the wise are the attitudes of benevolence, justice, gentleness and prudence. They have their roots in the heart. Their fruits radiate on the countenance."[46] The missionaries' effort to teach Chinese Christians the four stoic or aristotelian cardinal virtues was an exercise in futility and an insult to the wonderful cultural heritage of the Chinese.

4. The morality of subsequent judgment

Gurvitch considers a morality of subsequent judgment as practically a morality of control and success, and the most unfruitful of all types, a sign of a low-level person-culture. It is totally opposed to a morality of the "heart", of inner conviction and resources. He sees a certain type of tradition within the Catholic church, which overemphasizes control and sanction, as similar to the kind of "official" practice in communist parties and régimes.[47] Such a morality has no place for a creative élan, courageous innovations, or for sensitivity to the signs of the times. It must make place for the Christian morality of grace and of the freedom of the children of God.

Such a transformation or, indeed, re-education, helps us to understand better the biblical concept of a "new creation". The process requires time. And Christians deformed by the controlled kind of moralism must be helped to experience the newness of gospel morality. Simply to tear down the multiple controls and reinforcements does not suffice. As in the education of children, controls must be diminished gradually as the new vision and motivation grow. But then they, too, must be remodelled, even at some risk, to make place for the growing maturity.

5. Imperative morality

The wild, warlike tribes, brought into a covenant-morality by Moses and his successors, needed moral guidance by clear direction and strong imperatives. Indeed, we see that the very nucleus of Israel's morality was an imperative one. And Israel's history, especially the prophetic part, gives us a paradigm on how to meet similar cultural conditions. The imperative accent - the guidance from without - yields gradually to the morality of the "heart of man", a morality of high aspirations and expectations and of vital symbols.

In the history of the Occident, there was a long period when the old-Germanic morality of absolute allegiance to the chiefs or princes was combined with the imperative tendency of Roman "right". The evangelization of the Gemanic (and Celtic) tribes could make use of the ethos of absolute allegiance, for when the tribal leader was baptized, his subjects almost automatically followed his example and command.

Quite different, however, was a true conversion to Christ in the new fellowship. The best of missionary theology and practice, classically expressed in the old Germanic hymn "Heliand", made the principle of absolute allegiance a good point of departure, but in a way that warned of its dangerous aspects. The nucleus of the new transforming message is: "Thee alone, Christ, we follow in absolute allegiance, and the earthly leaders insofar as they follow you."

If the authority structures in the church and the moral teaching had folllowed this approach, the sixteenth century would not have proclaimed and practised the principle, "cuius regio, eius et religio", which means that the chiefs determine the religion (the denominational status) of their subjects. Moreover, there would not have been, in our own times, the slavish obedience-allegiance of so many Catholic and Lutheran Christians to their chief, Hitler. No bishop would have been found to bless the warriors and weapons of the senseless nationalistic and colonial wars.

6. The morality of inspiring symbols and ideal images

Gurvitch is convinced that a morality that lives by inspiring symbols and ideal images, speaking to the "heart" of people, is a sign of a high human culture. Symbols can unite people more fundamentally than dry concepts and raw imperatives. He thinks that, especially in a time of profound changes, of new opportunities and new risks, this kind of moral orientation and motivation is most appropriate and fruitful. It allows constant growth and renewal, and helps people to discover their own inner resources and, consequently, new opportunities.

After all that has been said and printed about the technological urban society of our time, one might be surprised to learn from Gurvitch that "we live in an era in which the morality of ideal symbols has a prominent place in moral life".[48] Here we might discover the best chances for the rejuvenating powers of the moral teaching of the church, but a teaching not by mere concepts and laws.

It is no less surprising that a leading Protestant theologian of North America - the continent most typical of the modern technical culture - comes independently to a similar conclusion. Langdon Gilkey expresses the hope that the renewed sacramental theology and liturgy of the Catholic church can contribute greatly to building bridges between the most vital expressions in today's life and the heart of religion. He presupposes that the symbols and images of the celebration of the mysteries of faith, hope and love will point effectively to the reality of our life and our culture, in such a way that we can discover there the signs of God's dynamic presence. The liturgy can and must bring the decisive points of life and culture into the presence of God, and give direction to life.[49]

Those who want to return again to a stereotyped liturgy where all its forms are controlled by a central government should carefully reflect on these realities. Creative liberty is indispensable for liturgy and theology to fulfil their noble tasks, and for nourishing a vital morality guided by symbols and ideal images.

The theology of the Second Vatican Council has re-integrated the sacramental vision of faith and life which was so central and fruitful in early Christianity. The church understands herself principally as a sacramental symbol of union with God and of the unity of humankind.[50]

The moral pedagogy and spirituality of the oriental churches were distinguished by a sacramental vision that opens the mind to the signs of God's presence in the world. It is my firm conviction (strengthened also by Gurvitch) that many cultures of Africa, Asia and Oceania invite the church to a synthesis of their own vital symbols and ideal images with the sacramental understanding of Christian life. So often when I participated in the celebration of liturgy or paraliturgy in various African cultures, this became evident to me. There is a creativity and strength of a culture and morality that have their main sources in vital symbols and the simplicity of creative expression. Of course such a vision, bridging faith and life, will be fully fruitful only if liturgical forms are not imposed by an alien culture.

7. A morality of aspirations

The morality of a part of the modern proletariates, and even more of parts of the Third World, fits into this type which Gurvitch characterizes as "morality of new departures and high aspirations".

The great movement of the worker class in Europe began with a kind of faith that the conditions of life and the social structures could be changed radically. Therefore, the philosophy of history, especially in the form proposed by Karl Marx, could appeal much more to the proletariat, students and many intellectuals, than would a static philosophy of the social order and a morals of static norms.

Christians don't need to seek salvation in a philosophy of progress put forth by Auguste Comte or K. Marx. A Christian morality characterized by the dynamics of salvation history, the eschatological virtues and the goal commandments, is the preeminent embodiment of a morality of aspirations and new departures. With a more creative fidelity to the gospel, the church would not have lost the working class in Europe. Now again today, the church has a great opportunity, especially in the new nations of the Third World.

From the farthest village of Africa to the Latin American theology of liberation, we find this sense of new departures, of almost prophetic aspirations. Who will channel them if the church does not, in her whole life, meet them by blending old and new, the old and ever new gospel message with the new awakening of cultures and nations?

What we need is the great biblical vision of ongoing conversion and renewal, in the clear direction of God's promises expressed in terms of the various cultures, and marked by aspirations which do not contradict the gospel or at least can be redeemed by it.

8. The morality of creative activity

In communities where a genuine democracy prevails there can develop a morality of creative liberty and activity tending towards an ever more responsible participation. It is not the morality behind military coups and infighting between authoritarian circles, but it can be a moral attitude and action in revolutionary epochs, among those who creatively seek a new participatory society. Gurvitch thinks that the social group of researchers, pioneers in the various fields, and artists can form a milieu in which a morality of creative liberty can find a strong echo.[51]

Such a morality, like that of ideal images and symbols, implies the capacity to celebrate, to play, and to manage life's troubles with a sense of humour. In this light we ought to give more attention to the play-age of children and to parents' play with their children. It is in this kind of cultural milieu that the morality of creative liberty and fidelity can best serve as leitmotif.

In moral teaching, careful attention and a constructive response to the types and cycles of cultures and sub-cultures is a sign of fidelity to the Lord of history, the Saviour of all cultures.

NOTES

[1] *Gaudium et spes,* 53-62. In the same sense speaks the fact that in the first consultative Consistorium convoked by John Paul II with the Cardinals, the most evident result was the participants' strong conviction that much attention must be given to the task of discerning the modern culture and the diversity of cultures. General bibliography on culture and ethics: M. Scheler, *Soziologie und Weisheitslehre,* vol. I, *Moralia,* Leipzig, 1923; J. Dewey, *Freedom and Culture,* New York, 1939; R. Guardini, *Die Kultur als Werk und als Gefährdung,* München, 1948; S. Niebuhr, *Christ and Culture,* New York, 1956; B. Häring, *Macht und Ohmacht der Religion. Religionssoziologie als Anruf,* Salzburg, 1956[2], 276-316; "Religion and Culture" (pp. 314-316 bibliography) D.D. Lee, *Freedom and Culture,* Englewood Cliffs, N.J., 1959; J. Messner, *Kulturethik mit Grundlegung von Prinzipienethik und Personlichkeitsethik,* Innsbruck, 1959[2]; G. Gurvitch, *Morale théorique et sciences des moeurs,* Paris, 1961[3]; Id., "La science des faits moraux et la morale théorique chez E. Durkheim", in G. Gurvitch, *La vocation actuelle de la sociologie,* Paris, 1963[2], vol, I, ch. X; K. Brockmüller, *Industriekultur und Religion,* Frankfurt, 1964; P. Tillich, *Theology of Culture,* New York, 1964; Id., *Die religiöse Substanz der Kultur,* Stuttgart, 1967; H. Freyer, *Schwelle der Zeiten. Beiträge zur Soziologie der Kultur,* Stuttgart, 1965; L. Huber, *Prinzipien und Möglichkeiten christlicher Kulturpolitik,* Würzburg, 1965; A.F. Bednarski, *Église, culture et promotion humaine,* Paris, 1970; Id., *Introduzione alla teologia della cultura,* Rome, 1973; J. Habermas, *Kultur und Kritik,* Frankfurt, 1973. Various authors, *Cristianesimo e cultura,* Milano, 1975; Th.M. McFadden (ed.), *America in Theological Perspective,* New York, 1976; L.J. Luhetak, *The Church and Cultures: An Applied Anthropology for the Religious Works,* South Pasadena, 1977[2]; J. Senior, *The Death of Christian Culture,* Arlington House, 1978; Ch. Lash, *The Culture of Narcisism,* New York, 1979.

[2] *Gaudium et spes,* 53.

[3] R. Niebuhr, *Moral Man and Immoral Society,* London, 1963; New York 1934[1].

[4] J. Messner, l.c., 331.

[5] G. Gurvitch, "Sociologie de la morale", in Gurvitch (ed.), *Traité de sociologie,* 1968[3], 137; H. Bergson, *Les deux sources de la morale et de la religion,* Paris, 1934[16].

[6] J. Moltmann, *Mensch. Christliche Anthropologie in den Konflikten der Gegenwart,* Stuttgart and Berlin, 1977[2], 24.

[7] *Gaudium et spes,* 58, 1.

[8] J. Messner, l.c., 357.

[9] *Gaudium et spes,* 62,8.

[10] *Gaudium et spes,* 56,1; 61.

[11] *Gaudium et spes,* 36, 58; on the abiding values and the autonomy of culture, cf. J. Messner, l.c., 410ff., 425ff.

[12] Cf. J. Messner, l.c,, 359.

[13] Cf. R. Scherer, "Kultur", in *Sacramentum Mundi* III, 112.

[14] *Gaudium et spes,* 55,1; this is also a main concern and theme of John Paul's encyclical *Redemptor hominis.*

[15] Cf. C.F. von Weizsäcker, *Der Garten des Menschlichen,* München, 1978[5], 62.

[16] Cf. J. Messner, l.c., 425ff

[17] Cf. J. Messner, l.c., 351ff., 379; G. Gurvitch, *Sociologie de la morale,* l.c., 143.

[18] *Gaudium et spes,* 56.

[19] *Gaudium et spes,* 62, towards the end.

[20] *Gaudium et spes*, 60, 1.

[21] *Gaudium et spes*, 60, 3.

[22] Cf. the excellent study on alternative schools in Germany, France, Italy, Great Britain, and USA, offered by 30 experts: D. Goldschmidt and P.M. Roeder (eds.), *Alternative Schulen? Gestalt und Funktion nichtstaatlicher Schulen im Rahmen des offentlichen Bildungswesens*, Stuttgart, 1979.

[23] *Gaudium et spes*, 59, towards the end.

[24] Cf. "Tradition und Anpassung im Lichte des Geheimnisses der Inkarnation", in B. Häring, *Die gegenwärtige Heilsstunde*, Frieburg, 1964, 73-86.

[25] *Ad gentes* (On Mission), 19.

[26] John Paul II, Apostolic Exhortation on Catechesis, *Catechesi Tradendae*, 53.

[27] *Ad gentes*, 21.

[28] Cf. B. Häring, *Evangelization Today*, Slough and Notre Dame, Ind., 1974; B. Bühlmann, *The Coming of the Third Church*, Slough and Maryknoll, N.Y., 1976.

[29] Cf. Lexikon für Theologie und Kirche, *Das Zweite Vatikanischen Konzil*, III, 263.

[30] M. Scheler, *Der Formalismus in der Ethik und die materiale Werethik*, Halle, 1927³, 565.

[31] J. Messner, l.c., 388.

[32] G. Gurvitch, *Traité de sociologie*, 139.

[33] R. Otto, *Das Heilige*, München, 1936²⁵; Id., *West-Ostliche Mystik. Vergleich und Unterscheidung zur Wesensdeutung*, Gotha, 1929²; Id., *Freiheit und Notwendigkeit. Ein Gespräch mit Nicolai Hartmann über Theonomie und Autonomie der Werte*, Tübingen, 1940; B. Häring, *Das Heilige und das Gute. Religion und Sittlichkeit in ihrem gegenseitigen Bezug*, Krailling, 1950, 167-187.

[34] A. Auer, *Autonome Moral und christlicher Glaube*, Düsseldorf. Auer, however, never refers to the works of R. Otto.

[35] Cf. C. Kalisa, *Le culte et la croyance aux ancêtres au Rwanda confrontés avec le message chrétien*, unpublished dissertation, Academia Alfonsiana, Rome, 1972; J.R. Goody, *Death, Property and Ancestors*, London, 1962.

[36] F. Böckle, *Fundamentalmoral*, München, 1977, 229.

[37] Cf. Lopez Aziparte, SJ, "Etica humana y moral christiana", in *Studia moralia* 15 (1977), 53.

[38] I have treated this question more explicitly in my book *Evangelization Today*, and in the last chapter of *Free and Faithful in Christ*, II.

[39] *Gaudium et spes*, 43, and *Ad gentes* (On Mission), 21 and 41; Decree on *Lay Apostolate*, 7; Decree on *Social Communication*, 21.

[40] This relationship is more thoroughly treated in *Free and Faithful in Christ* I, Chapter Seven.

[41] Cf. G. Gurvitch, *Traité de sociologie*, Paris, 1968³, 145.

[42] l.c., 146.

[43] Cf. l.c., 171.

[44] Cf. *Free and Faithful in Christ* I, Chapter Three.

[45] G. Gurvitch, l.c., 160.

[46] *Les quatre livres de Konfucius*, Ho Kien Fou, 1895, 616.

[47] G. Gurvitch, l.c., 151, 158-160.

[48] l.c., 164.

[49] L. Gilkey, *Catholicism Confronts Modernity*, New York, 1975, 198, cf. 22.

[50] *Lumen gentium*, 1; cf. B. Häring, *The Sacraments in a Secular Age. A Vision in Depth and its Impact on Moral Life*, Slough, 1976.

[51] G. Gurvitch, l.c., 155.

Chapter Seven

The Ethics of Socio-Economic Life

The integration of economic life into the whole meaning and dynamism of society and community, and even more, its integration into a holistic ethical vision is a fundamental task. The lack of a truthful solution and the ideologies that, as a consequence, severed economics from the ethical challenge have troubled the world during the last centuries and are at the roots of some of the gravest evils. Christendom, too, has its share in this disorder.

According to Max Weber and others, a false vision of economic activity, within the disquieting religious question about one's own predestination, had much to do with the rise and specific development of capitalism. For many Catholics and pietists, their ethical questions about socio-economic life were imprisoned in an individualistic ethics. Moralists tended to approach this realm with a static natural-law theory while being blind to the dynamics of history and of economy itself. Overlooked also was the tension between sin and redemption which not only affected people's mentality but also took root in the very structures, dynamics and relationships of socio-economic life.

Hence we consider here: what the socio-economic realm and dimension of life have to do with salvation, liberation, and the "economy of the beatitudes" (I); what relation the economy has with the totality of social, cultural and religious reality (II); how the church is a social actor and teacher in the fields of economics (III). In a dialogue with a philosophy of history, and especially with regard to historical and dialectical materialism and the

243

historical dynamics, we consider the role of conflicts, the challenge of socialization, and whether there is a possibility or even a need for a socialism as an expression of Christian responsibility (IV). We explore a broader vision within which we can discover the dimension of economy as an ethical task (V). Beyond the various ideologies of capitalism (including state capitalism) we ask questions about a free market economy, the need and limits of politics of economy, the role and ordering of property, especially of productive property in relation to labour, and the various functions within the economic enterprise (VI). Discerning the signs of the times, we face the striking problems of economy and ethics (VII).[1]

I. THE ECONOMY OF THE BEATITUDES

Redeemed humanity, experiencing the liberating power of the Holy Spirit in a life according to the beatitudes, shares in the Paschal mystery of death and resurrection.[2]

A theological ethics of socio-economic life considers the order of creation in the tension between sin and redemption which is present in the dynamics of all relationships and processes throughout history. It is appropriate, therefore, that the Second Vatican Council should conclude its chapter on socio-economic life by bringing everything home into the perspective of the beatitudes. Only thus will the example of the disciples of Christ "be a shining one". In faithfulness to Christ and his gospel, having acquired the necessary skills and experience, they will observe the right order of values in their earthly activities. Their whole lives, individual and social, will be permeated with the spirit of the beatitudes, notably the spirit of poverty.

Whoever, in obedience to Christ, seeks first the kingdom of God, will receive a stronger and purer love for helping all his or her brothers and sisters, and for "perfecting the work of justice under the inspiration of redeemed love".[3] Here we can see that the Council's message on the spirit of the beatitudes is not at all disincarnated. It does not dispense us from skills and experience or from shared reflection on the "right order of values". Receiving everything as a gift of God, the disciples of Christ will not exploit others but will put themselves, their skills, experience and their earthly goods at the service of others whom they will recognize as their brothers and sisters.

The great economist, E. F. Schumacher, echoes the vision of the Council, translating it into more specific appeals and a more concrete vision of a healthy economic order. "We are poor, not demigods. We have plenty to be sorrowful about, and are not emerging into a golden age. We need a gentle approach, a non-violent spirit, and small is beautiful. We must concern ourselves with justice and see right prevail. And all this, only this, can enable us to become peacemakers."[4]

The spirit of the beatitudes concerns not only individual morality; it concerns also communities and societies, economics and politics. It is the challenge coming from the Saviour of the world, a goal-commandment arising from the fact that Redemption is all-embracing. Economic man and his society need redemption too. Commitment to the spirit of the beatitudes in economic activities, in relationships and structures not only gives convincing witness to the gospel but also opens us to a deeper knowledge of God and prepares the way to true "knowledge of salvation".[5]

Sinful man in a sinful world needs the radical conversion granted and expressed by the beatitudes if he hopes to make the fruits of the Spirit visible in the economic and social reality. The Medellin document on justice expresses this powerfully: "The uniqueness of the Christian message does not so much consist in the affirmation of the necessity of structural change as it does in the insistence on the conversion of men which will, in turn, bring about this change. We will not have a new continent without new and reformed structures, but above all, there will be no new continent without new men who know how to be truly free and responsible according to the light of the Gospel."[6]

The church has again to become more aware that a static and abstract ethics of natural law cannot meet the conflict situation of a sinful world. We need a keener realization of the tension between the powers of sinfulness and redemption, as expressed in Rom 7:14ff.[7] An optimism about a better world[8] cannot be based on a philosophy of history as an immanent law of historical development, but only on the power of redemption offered to those who are accepting the grace and call of conversion and shared commitment to renewal.

As John XXIII constantly insisted, the church, sent to be a church for the poor, must know that she can proclaim the good news to the poor and freedom to the oppressed only while living according to the Paschal mystery, converted to the absolute gift and demand for justice and love.[9]

This radical conversion to the spirit of the beatitudes, this hunger and thirst that God's saving justice may prevail is part and parcel of genuine evangelization. Conforming with the mission of Christ (cf. Lk 4:18), prompted by the love of Christ and illumined by the gospel, "the church, as a truly poor, praying and fraternal community, can do much to bring about the integral salvation or, rather, liberation of men. She can draw from the gospel the most profound reasons and ever new incentives to promote generous dedication to the service of all - the poor especially, the weak and the oppressed - and to eliminate the social consequences of sin which are translated into unjust social and political structures."[10]

Christ, the Servant of God, is anointed and sent by the *Spirit*. His disciples can share in his mission for integral liberation only when renewed by the Spirit and trusting in Him. "Faith in renewal by the Holy Spirit, and hope for the coming of God's kingdom grants believers the freedom to refuse the existing structures and relationships of power and to initiate instead courageous steps to change them in favour of those who suffer misery."[11]

Philipp Schmitz suggests that the point of departure for a distinctively Christian solical ethics should be the poverty in the world, in the light of that new sense and dynamics of poverty which is visible in Christ and is his gift to the blessed ones. We are confronted with complex realities and dimensions of poverty: first, poverty as a radical experience of "loss and alienation. In its final consequence, it is the symbol of obstacle and resistance against that human self-realization that can be understood only as grace."[12] And this makes apparent the second perspective: the blessed poverty of believers who honour, as a gift of the One God, Creator and Redeemer, all good things that help people's liberation and self-realization in mutual love and justice.

In the same sense, John Baptist Metz writes, "Poverty as a virtue is the protest against the dictatorship of having, of possessing, and of pure self-aggrandizement. It presses towards solidarity with those for whom poverty is precisely not a virtue but a dire life situation and a societal imposition."[13] Poverty as a gift of the Spirit and a sign of the coming of God's kingdom is a liberation from the covetousness and greed (Col 3:5) that makes its poisonous investment in human relationships and in socio-economic structures.[14]

The poverty that means lack of the goods of this world necessary to live worthily as human beings is an evil, especially if it is due to unjust structures and people. The prophets denounce it. At the opposite pole is poverty as a gift of the Spirit, which is the distinctive characteristic of "the poor of Yahweh". This gift is unthinkable without an ever increasing commitment to help the poor and to remove the unjust causes and practices that afflict them.[15]

It is a part of the prophetic ministry of theologians, and of all whose competence gives them authority, to unmask and denounce the ideologies that again and again provide "a rationale for the advantaged to act in their own interests and to choose not to yield to the demands of the poor for a share in the resources they need."[16]

Through the good news of the beatitudes proclaimed and interpreted by living example, the church can and must "add the light of revealed truth to mankind's store of experience, so that the path which humanity has taken in recent times will not be a dark one."[17] A personal "yes" to the economics of the beatitudes does not, however, dispense us from sharing experience and actively cooperating with all who have special competence in this field.

II. ECONOMY IS MORE THAN BUSINESS

Two widespread ideologies correspond to an ever more widespread mode of behaviour: isolation (lack of integration) and the absolutizing of economic activity.

Classical liberalism (with Adam Smith as chief ideologist) considers economy as autonomous, with a self-regulating mechanism, which is mostly the self-interest of the economic man. Philosophically, this establishes and/or justifies an economic system and behaviour independent of any ethical norms beyond the "laws" of the market and the motive of self-interest. It does not scrutinize, as later scientific sociology does, the interdependence between economy and the other dimensions and spheres of social and individual life.

This ideology affects many people, Christians among them, who live their lives in separate departments, where religion, family life, culture, political reality and responsibility show no integration. Not only economy but equally the other domains of life, including morals and art, are characterized by a "loss of the centre".[18]

The second phenomenon, related to the first, is the tendency to absolutize economy in one way or another. Karl Marx, at least in Frederick Engels' interpretation, and many "orthodox" Marxists make economic relationships and processes the determinant for all the other dimensions of social, cultural, political and religious life. And who can deny that not only Marxists but many other people allow economic thinking and activity practically to determine most of their life?

The Second Vatican Council put its finger on this frightening phenomenon. "Many people, especially in economically advanced areas, seem to be hypnotized, as it were, by economics, so that almost their entire personal and social life is permeated with a certain economic outlook. These people can be found in nations that favour a collective economy as well as in others."[19]

As science, economics has a relatively broad and over-privileged place. What is more serious is that many economists tend to explain all cultural and social life in the key of economic concepts.[20] The reductionism of these economists is quite evidently related to the thinking and practice of people of a "one-dimensional culture".

"Wherever economy becomes the only interest, economic life is bedeviled, and conflicts of economic interests lead to tragic class struggles."[21] Here also is a main cause of wars.

1. Economy and society

One of the greatest sociologists, Max Weber, who began his career as an economist, wrote the groundbreaking work on the interdependence of economy with all the main features of society.[22] Another notable economist, Werner Sombart, came to the same conclusion that economy cannot be understood in merely economic terms. Economy is more than business; profit is not all that it means and not all that moves it.

Karl Marx was acutely aware of the impact of economic relationships and processes on the whole fabric of social and cultural life, on political organization and on religious institutions and thought. Although he tends to absolutize the determinant power of economic dynamics over all the other historical realities, he is concerned about the economy's social basis and organization. No individualistic ideology can compete with the insights of Karl Marx. His one-sidedness can be corrected only by those who are fully attentive to the social and cultural dimensions of economy itself and its various interdependencies with the structure and dynamics of family, community and society.

Ethology easily shows how, among animals, social organization and behaviour is to some extent conditioned by the economic situation.[23] For humans, it is more characteristic that other factors influence economy as well as social organizations.

To treat economic life as a self-contained entity or as the single key to everything else is destructive of society, culture and politics, as well as of "economic man". It also contradicts historical insight. "When all is said and done, it may well be that historical circumstances and culturally inherited values and beliefs have more to do with the shape of the economic life than do any universal economic motives."[24] It has been said on good evidence that, in primitive cultures, people dedicated relatively more time and work than modern man does to activities that had no economic purpose.[25]

A free society and freedom in economic relationships are related to each other, and both depend on how culture and religion understand and embody the basic values of freedom and fidelity. A "free enterprise ethic"[26] needs this clear vision of interaction and integration; otherwise it will be unrealistic and ineffective.

The Medellin Document on "Family and Demography" (September 6, 1968) is a good example of an ethical and pastoral approach based on a new awareness of the complex interdependencies[27] which was heretofore lacking in so many ethical writings and church documents. By the very title of its chapter on "Socio-Economic Life", the Second Vatican Council has expressed the same awareness.[28]

2. Economy and the person's total vocation

The Second Vatican Council begins its reflections on socio-economic life by emphasizing "the dignity and total vocation of the human person". The "welfare of society as a whole" cannot be truly advanced when socio-economic life (the organization of productive forces and the ordering of productive relationships) does not give witness to the basic truth that "man is the source, the centre and the purpose of all socio-economic life."[29]

There should be no dichotomy between the realm of personal culture and the mastering of nature. In economic activities and relationships, the person expresses and develops his or her own creative capacities and co-responsibility, or else degrades self and hurts others. In and through economic activities - in works and work-relationships - the person can express, communicate and conserve "great spiritual experiences and desires, so that these may be of advantage to the progress of many, even of the whole human family."[30]

The "economic man" is, at the same time, a social person. And only by ordering his economic activities and relationships with social responsibility and cooperation can he integrate this realm of life into his total vocation, and build up his own spiritual and psychic health. One's use of material things is even the test of one's highest vocation to love and to act in solidarity, the test of whether one knows and honours Christ, the Redeemer of the whole person and of all persons (cf. Mt 25:31-46).

Although Marxism does not discover the transcendental relationship of human economy, it does see some important aspects. Against "liberalism" that cuts economy off from the rest of life, and against disincarnate use of material things for "charities", young Marx insists that "the essence of man is to be creative and social. Man is self-creating."[31] Consequently, he decries as alienation all structures of productive forces and relationships that block man's creativity and healthy social relations. For Marx, the alienation of the worker and of those who exploit him in the economic realm is the root of all other forms of alienation - we might say, a kind of original sin. Thus the abolition of such exploitation is also the basis, *sine qua non*, for rooting out all anti-social behaviour.[32]

It is a pity that blind anti-Marxism has hindered for many

people the discovery of what is true in this description of alienation, its causes and its remedies. But it is equally regrettable that Marxist theory tends to insinuate that structural changes alone could overcome the evil. Economic relationships cannot be healed without a change of heart, of people's inner core, in a reciprocity of consciences.

If we Christians give priority to this change of heart, it will not weaken but rather strengthen our commitment to those structural changes that contribute to overcoming all forms of alienation.[33] The proper ordering of the productive forces and relationships can be approached realistically as an integral part of person-culture and the nurturing of healthy and peaceful human communities and societies.

3. Economy as an all-pervasive reality

Economy is more than business. It begins with the proper ordering of the household (oikonomia). In a healthy family the relationships are mirrored and sustained by shared economic productive activities and by the kind of distribution that makes evident the fact that economy is for the family, and not the family for the economy.

In oriental, and partially also in occidental theology, the ideal ordering of all economic activities and usages in a healthy household is used as symbol: the "economy of salvation" gives meaning to laws and institutions, and not the other way around. In the Lord's prayer, after the petitions about God's name, reign and will, the first request for his family is, "give us this day our daily bread". The way we use the earthly things - the bread for all and of all - reflects our earnest effort to honour God's name, to expect his reign and to conform with his loving will. Whoever refuses to consider *our* bread - food and all the other things that earth has given and human hands have made - as gifts of the One God for all his children cannot truthfully pray, "lead us not into temptation but deliver us from evil".

Sociology of religion has offered abundant evidence of the interdependence of economy and religion.[34] There the oversimplified and polemical theories of Karl Marx have given way to a nuanced consideration. The strength or weakness of religion influences the economic outlook and relationships in one direction or the other. Dangerous ideologies about "the economic man" falsify religion and lead to a confused mix of religion, religious ethics and ideologies. Eros and civilization, revolutions and counter-revolutions cannot be understood without relating them also (but not exclusively) to the prevailing economic structures and behaviour.[35]

Religious people and religious institutions do not escape the influence, good or bad, of the economic reality. The less consciously and deliberately they face these problems, the more effective will be the hidden ideological investments of the economic reality. All the great world religions have condemned the cult of greed and the lust for power; but all too often throughout history we have found in them foul compromises with these unredeemed and insatiable powers.

Everyone who has some knowledge of history and of the present situation will agree that "politics and economics affect each other profoundly".[36] But conclusions have not been drawn. There is not enough concrete inquiry and watchfulness, not enough consistent efforts to cleanse this interrelationship by structural changes and clear ethical education.

The emergence of the multinational corporations, with all the conflicts they are producing, highlight the problem of the relation between culture and economics. "Can a single institution, the corporation, flourish in a plurality of cultures, each with distinctive ethical traditions?"[37] A sharper awareness of this phenomenon would lead to greater sensitivity and could help to avoid many regrettable errors.

Deeper insight and clearer knowledge about the multifaceted relationships between culture, ecosphere and economics can make understandable the ethical appeals of such great economists and conservationists as E. F. Schumacher, who tells us time and again that "what is at stake is not economics but culture". He shows us an economic model that points to the beatitudes and teaches us "to live within the limitations of our nature and the physical world".[38]

4. Economy and philanthropic activity

The noted economist and sociologist, Werner Sombart, has given great attention to the problem of altruistic motives in economic life, and to philanthropic activities.[39] Altruism is not only relevant "for explaining certain allocations of resources, especially those outside the market; altruistic phenomena are equally crucial for the functioning of the market".[40] In primitive societies, economic activities, after first serving the needs of the family, serve mostly for exchange of gifts. This expresses a basic altruism, the consciousness of mutual dependence and solidarity, the joy of giving and belonging and, of course, the realization that those who give generously will receive generous gifts and, what is most important, social recognition.

"In a democratic society, the voting of expenditures for the benefit of others plainly constitutes an institutionalization of giving."[41] In today's free world, through charitable and other non-profit organizations, organized philanthropy constitutes a sizable voluntarism that gives away without economic profit. Many modern states acknowledge by tax deductions this service for the common good and for urgent needs.[42]

Philanthropy through churches and other voluntary organizations expresses and fosters altruism in a way that not only enriches the spiritual and/or social life of those who are sensitive to concrete needs and who give generously, but also humanizes society and the economy, if it is carried out as an integrated dimension of solidarity. The sad "fact that many nominally philanthropic organizations have been used to varying extents for tax avoidance and other purposes"[43] does not allow all voluntary giving to be considered in terms of "utility function" or "consumer choice", as if the philanthropist had nothing in mind but "to gain utility from the act of foregoing consumption opportunities without receiving *quid pro quo*. A more systematic analysis of underlying motivation is called for."[44]

The ethics of the state tend to favour philanthropic activities and organizations only in its own self-interest; but this, too, serves the common good and is more than financial gain. Preventing abuse and avoiding incentives to mere utilitarianism render a service to the common good, since philanthropy, as a genuine expression of altruism, is the more humanizing influence on society and culture. This consideration is ethically important also for those who organize philanthropic activities. What counts is not only the success in collecting and administering funds for good purposes, but also and especially the promotion of authentic altruism and solidarity.

III. THE CHURCH AS ECONOMIC SOCIETY AND AS TEACHER IN THE SOCIO-ECONOMIC REALM

The church of the Word Incarnate, too, experiences her interwovenness with the economic reality. The changing economic forces, structures, processes and relationships affect her life. And in turn, the whole life of the church (not only her economic needs and activities) affect the economy as well as the outlook and behaviour of the economic person. The church can be in many ways a model and teacher of sound economic goals, structures, relationships and behaviour.[45]

1. Model or scandal?

There were times and places in which the church was a dominant economic power, the greatest landowner with thousands of farmers dependent on dioceses, parishes or monasteries, the greatest builder, the most influential promoter and supplier of education and of all kinds of art.

At all times, the church needs enormous financial resources for those who work for her in parishes, seminaries, missions, administration, and so on. She is one of the world's leading employers, giving work and some kind of remuneration and financial security to more than a million priests and religious, and to even a greater number of laypeople in the various pastoral, cultural and administrative offices.

How the church understands and fulfils her role in her own economic practices and relationships is highly relevant for her credibility in both her specifically religious mission and her liberating influence on the socio-economic life. On all economic levels, the church has to ask herself a number of ethically pertinent questions about the methods of collecting funds, the priorities in allocating and spending them, the principle of subsidiarity and participation in the decision making processes, the intrinsic justice of contracts, remuneration and outlay, her special obligations to the poor and marginal people, and her observance of all the just laws of civil society.

The church's structures and practices do not necessarily serve as a model just by copying the economic society's prevailing trends and customs. Surely she should not cling to past methods if those of secular society are more adequate; but in this field, should we not expect creative innovation from the leadership of the church?

Those Christians who enter the service of the gospel for pastoral and cultic purposes do not present a helpful model if they want to be paid for everything according to the principles and expectations of the competitive economic society. Church authorities render poor service if they intend to promote priestly vocations by offering economic privileges or assuring candidates that in this "job" they will be socially and economically as well, or better off, than in a secular profession. Clergy and laypeople give scandal if, for religious services, they make economic claims equal to those of the ten percent of the world's population who consume two-thirds of the world's resources. Those who are dedicated to the service of the gospel, on whatever "hierarchical" level, should be models in their economic requests and behaviour, witnessing to the "economy of the beatitudes" by being at least on the road to this ideal.

Churchmen who live above the standard of average people are surely not entitled to ask others to render gratuitous or underpaid economic services to church enterprises. On the other hand, there is not necessarily any injustice or bad example if economic services are freely offered without any form of pressure, and accepted by the church for remuneration below the economic society's standard - provided that families do not suffer by these practices.

As employers, church institutions must surely be outstanding examples by putting into practice the social doctrine of the church, and by exemplary human relations, especially in covenant fidelity. The same must be expected from those who seek church employment.

In today's critical world, it is counterproductive if church institutions do not fulfil the expectations of an economic society in which states and corporations give public account. To adjust the church's economic legislation and practices to the new needs and legitimate role expectations, the clergy needs the cooperation of competent laypeople. Thus many role-conflicts can be avoided or lessened.[46]

Conscious of today's worldwide economic interdependence, the church can set up models of mutual assistance that fully respect the economically weaker partner. *Actio Misereor*, initiated about fifteen years ago by the West German bishops and followed by similar organizations in various local churches and denominations, can be counted as such a model. It has influenced political action also in the same direction. A purpose is to inspire society itself to foster the development of a deeper understanding of the world's needs and to "promote a readiness for worldwide cooperation. In this endeavour, the churches consider the realization of partnership among equals as a requirement for international social justice."[47]

2. Teaching with authority

As institution, the church needs economic means and, by exemplary moderation, can somehow offer models. However, she has no authority or power over political and economic society. Her authority is within the realm of the gospel and the appeal to people's consciences.

As sacrament of salvation who finds her own identity in the gospel of the Paschal mystery of Christ, the church is "present in the heart of the world by proclaiming the Good News to the poor, freedom to the oppressed, and joy to the afflicted. Action on behalf of justice, and participation in the transformation of the world appear to us as constitutive dimensions of the preaching of the gospel or, in other words, of the church's mission for the redemption of the human race and its liberation from every oppressive situation."[48]

This well-formulated text of the 1971 Synod of Bishops suggests that the church's authoritative teaching cannot be severed from convincing action. Only thus does the church bring the "joys and sorrows, the griefs and anxieties" of the people home into the liberating light of the gospel. And only thus does her teaching reach the individual conscience and the collective consciousness. The humble confession of her own shortcomings is an integrated part of the church's authority to form and inform people's consciences.

It is not enough for believers to assent to the general principles of the church's social teaching. They truly accept her authority if, in the light of her doctrine and example, they conscientiously apply these principles in their personal conduct and in their influence on the ordering of life conditions. With John XXIII, this has to be said emphatically to those Christians who think that only the norms for individual morality are binding in conscience.[49]

The social doctrine and practice of the church are expressions of her being the church of the Word Incarnate. She must "bring the social realities, experiences and expectations into the realm of the salvation wrought by Christ, and the final salvation. Consciousness of this relationship must be kept alive in her social moral teaching. Whether this has to be done through social prophecy, through the call to social *metanoia*, through liberating social critique or through social doctrine is another question. What matters first is that the social phenomena be seen in the light of the salvation message."[50]

3. Within the limits of competence

The church's moral authority emanates from gospel authority. Its effectiveness will correspond with the purity and depth of the salvation-knowledge of those who speak and act for her, their good reasoning, and the integration and subordination of knowledge of dominion in their global vision of the gospel.

The teaching authority of the church has direct competence only for those who, by faith and baptism, are her members. But as a part of the proclamation of the gospel and of gospel morality, her social teaching, prophecy and critique intend to reach the upright conscience of all people. The church is *Mater et Magistra*, Mother and Teacher of those who know her as sent by God; but she is sent to proclaim the Good News to all. Hence her every effort must be to proclaim social doctrine in a way that all can recognize it as a part of the whole gospel and as convincing for sincere consciences. Moreover, she must be aware that she can be a moral authority and can convince consciences in these matters only insofar as she relates to the experience and co-reflections of all, and gives good reasons for everything that she proposes as "law".

Public policy and effective participation by responsible people require that three factors be reconciled: "social needs, political feasibility and value preferences. . . It is in the area of value preferences that the church can - and should - play an important role."[51]

For the church to address socio-economic realities effectively, her competence of office has to be wedded to professional competence and to the direct experience of the people. The scientists exploring the socio-economic processes and relationships can help to measure the needs and can point to the most urgent problems. However, on the basis of their professional competence, they cannot define the value-choices that make policies appropriate or disastrous. In the church, all are learners; and whoever has competence of office or professional experience will exercise moral authority to the degree of the individual's effective listening and sharing in the common effort to come to an integrated and incarnated vision.

Whenever church authorities refer to the natural law, they will try to give convincing reasons, proposing not only abstract philosophy but offering a picture where historical and actual experience meet honest and shared reflection, always open to new insights.[52]

Knowing that the Spirit works wherever he wants, and believing in Christ's presence to all people, the church will enter into dialogue with people of other religions and convictions, listening and learning, and thus sharing her own experiences and vision in a forthright manner. On all levels of this dialogue and teaching, "the most urgent asceticism is the radically honest use of one's reason."[53] Needless to repeat that absolute honesty, the very complexity of the situations and the diversity of cultures will lead to a pluralism even within the realm of the church when it comes to specific approaches to concrete socio-economic questions.

4. A prophetic ministry

The church's mission in this field is, above all, a prophetic ministry in the service of believers, and a prophetic reaching-out to all people. For this, there must be a radical openness to the Spirit and readiness to suffer and to accept the risk and pain of ongoing conversion and renewal.

The prophetic dimension is indicated in the emphasis which John XXIII, his successors and the Second Vatican Council give to examine the "signs of the times" in the light of the gospel.[54] This liberates the social doctrine of the church from the more static and abstract approach that previously prevented a worldwide echo. John XXIII suggests following the method of Joseph Cardijn: "observe, judge, act". Immediately the realization follows that norms have to be expressed in view of the new situation, with an evident readiness to "adapt traditional norms".[55] This method also enabled John XXIII to speak in a different key, addressing the general public no longer as "leader of society" but with awareness that, as a member of the worldwide society, he had to use arguments and a tone acceptable to all men of good will while speaking also with the frankness and broad vision of the great prophetic tradition of the Old and New Testaments.

The prophet speaks to the consciences of all, and especially to those in authority. But he seeks the needed change not by reinforcing ecclesiastical norms through power but rather by working for a new consciousness and a consensus about basic values in view of the present needs and opportunities.[56]

The prophets act and speak in favour of the powerless while in no way seeking power for themselves. They follow Christ in the way he proclaimed the Good News for the poor, making evident that those who accept God's liberating reign will no longer exploit or degrade others but will be free for universal brotherhood and justice. By proclaiming the message of grace that frees people for God and for each other, the prophetic ministry in the churches confronts the consciences of all with the requests and norms of justice, peace and love.

The declaration of Vatican II on religious liberty is a cornerstone in the church's new awareness of the exigencies of her prophetic ministry. This ministry is distinguished by a global vision of mankind and of society, which is not the same as offering a systematic doctrine for all ages and cultures. Its social critique is not an application of a static doctrine but a wholesome shock for consciences awakened to the dignity of the poor and downtrodden, and to the all-embracing solidarity of humankind. Thus it unmasks the ruthlessness and stupidity of greed and lust for power (cf. James 2:5-6; 4:2).

The prophet does not offer recipes or magic solutions but he does proscribe the deviations, the dehumanizing errors and practices. He points to corporate sin in the light of a "powerful doctrine of corporate grace".[57] The prophet is willing to care personally for the victim of the robbers; but the present prophetic ministry awakens the collective consciousness about structures, situations and widespread practices that do the terrible work of the robbers. The purpose is to free and heal as many as possible[58] and thus to prevent wounds and murder.

Authentic social critique as prophetic ministry is marked by a balanced vision of socio-economic life in the light of creation, sin, the incarnation, death and resurrection of Christ, and our resurrection destiny. "The failure to incorporate all these aspects stands as a negative criticism of such past approaches as Catholic natural law, Lutheran two-realm theory, liberal Protestantism and Neo-Orthodoxy."[59]

It is in the shocking and liberating perspective of these dimensions that Christians offer clear goals and binding ideals, and call for the constant effort to humanize socio-economic life. All this is an integral part of a distinctively Christian social doctrine and prophetic critique. It is in this light, too, that we have to understand documents like the encyclicals *Pacem in Terris* of John XXIII, *Populorum Progressio* and *Octogesima Adveniens* of Paul VI, the Second Vatican Council's Pastoral Constitution, *Gaudium et Spes*, and the whole ministry of John Paul II.[60]

There are good reasons to consider the Secretariate for Peace and Justice, with its worldwide ramifications, as an organ of prophetic vigilance and frankness.[61] It is a ministry for freedom for all, for unmasking lies about freedom, in favour of structures and practices that favour true freedom. It is a modern ministry of the merciful Samaritan.

IV. HISTORICITY AND CONFLICT

The "Restoration" and the "Sacred Alliance" of the church (church state) with the reactionary empires and kingdoms favoured an unhistorical and anti-historical natural-law thinking, strongly represented by the French school of the "Ordre Social". Although contradicted by balanced Catholic thinkers like Montalembert, it seemed to receive final doctrinal confirmation in the Syllabus of Pius IX (1864). Gustav Gundlach, the influential adviser of Pius XII in socio-economic matters, was one of the last representatives of this frozen current of thought.[62]

However, if we look at the overall tradition and today's Catholic thought, we find them well described by Johannes Messner: "Human nature and human reasoning are changeable, and consequently so are natural law and right. . . The natural law doctrine, like science, is always on the move."[63] Oswald von Nell-Breuning takes the same view. "Social ethics inquires what should be and what should be changed. It needs both the science of being and the empirical sciences. . . Tell me what image of man you have, and I shall tell what kind of social ethics corresponds."[64]

If change of consciousness is a decisive factor in today's culture, Christians who consciously live salvation history will not be strangers to this dimension of culture. It is, however, badly in need of integration, especially in regard to socio-economic life.

1. Confronting "historical materialism"[65]

It was a unique tragedy that, apart from a reactionary static natural law theory, the decisive leaders of the workers' protest and of socialism heard little or nothing from the church about her social teachings. Prophetic voices like that of Bishop Emmanuel Ketteler of Mainz were not finding the ears of the official church or of the moralists who claimed to be the church's faithful interpreters. Karl Marx, therefore, could win many young intellectuals and a great part of the workers' movement because his thought - based on the French school of philosophy of history and on Hegel - was thoroughly dynamic.

Marx's "historical materialism" is more concrete and incarnated than that of other thinkers. He calls for attention to the role of the socio-economic infrastructures in the historical dynamism and struggle, while not decreasing the "idealistic" hope promised by earlier representatives of the philosophy of history. In his "scientific socialism", he tries to show that, in spite of all the dire conflicts, injustices and alienation, the history of economics and of social man is intrinsically directed towards a liberating synthesis in the classless society. There, the productive forces and relationships would foster mankind's solidarity in economy and society, and consequently in all structures, processes and human relationships.

Already in Hegel's historical dialectic, the master-slave relationship, imperfect as it might have been, constituted an advance over the previous situation where the "other" was destroyed as enemy. Hegel saw the slave in a better situation than the slaveholder, because he is productive for others and knows his finiteness, and in the final analysis it will be the slaves who will overthrow this "order", thereby liberating both slaves and slaveholders from a situation that cannot be a final relationship. "Thus the slaves of today are the bearers of tomorrow's history."[66]

Like the judeo-christian tradition which is essentially dynamic and hope-filled, Marx's "historical materialism" reveals an undisturbed faith in the final meaning of history. But it is not, as in Hegel, a history moved mainly by thought; it is a history of flesh and blood, of the economic and social man who *discovers* that history works through him in his collective solidarity. Hence, the purpose of history will be realized not from "above" but from "below", by the oppressed and exploited taking their turn through a radical change in the productive forces and relationships.

The church has learned anew that she must humbly confess that her practice is not identical on all levels with the teaching of Christ. Confronted with the various forms of socialism, and particularly of Marxism, we know that we must not identify "false philosophical teaching regarding the nature, origin and destiny of the universe and of man with historical movements that have economic, social, cultural or political ends. . . Movements, being concerned with historical situations in constant evolution, cannot but be influenced by these latter, and therefore cannot avoid being subject to change even of a profound nature." Furthermore, there is frank acknowledgement that these movements, "insofar as they conform to the dictates of right reason and are interpreters of the lawful aspirations of the human person, contain elements that are positive and deserving of approval."[67]

Beginning with Leo XIII, the social doctrine of the church has gradually grasped the historical, dynamic dimension of socio-economic life and has offered respective ethical teaching. The very richness of the gospel and the historical experiences enable the church "while continuing its permanent preoccupations, to undertake the daring and creative innovations which the present state of the world requires."[68]

Cardinal Roy, as president of the Secretariate for Peace and

Justice, well describes today's Catholic thought and teaching: "Anthropology and theology, in their indispensable development, must constantly preserve the twofold dimension of being and becoming, identity and renewal."[69]

The emphasis in *Pacem in Terris* and *Gaudium et Spes*[70] on examining and discerning the signs of the times is not a dimension besides natural law; the very law of the nature of historical man is to respond faithfully to the opportunities and needs arising ever anew. It may be an exaggeration to formulate, "Just as the figure of this world, so the figure of morality passes", but it is true that "the tasks which realize human conditions undergo modifications."[71] Today it can well be said that "the abiding character of Catholic social teaching is the openness of its ethical perspectives."[72]

Faithfulness to the Lord of history, and vigilance for the "signs of the times" help us to prevent or to overcome the cultural lag. Guided by the vision of the history of salvation, grateful for the past heritage, and rooted in the prophetic tradition, Christians should be the best qualified interpreters of those significant images and symbols that stimulate the social imagination and call for a renewed fidelity to the Lord of history.

An authentic Christian outlook is more dynamic than the Marxist ideology of "historical materialism" which could attract so many people only because Christians failed to be faithful to the Lord of history by interpreting the signs of the times in thought and action. We are bound to whatever is good in the past and to what now responds to the real needs and the dignity of the human person. We must not be controlled by economic trends. Man's question today focuses on his place in the social reality: "How much can he control it? How much must he be controlled by it? To what extent must he simply find a place within it?"[73]

If the "laws" are to be taken from within the economic forces and relationships, or if there is simply blind trust that economic life brings forth final liberty, then the space left for man's control is all too limited. The Christian outlook focuses on fidelity to salvation history and thus to the Lord, to be fulfilled in an unstable society and in view of deeply disturbed and disturbing economic structures. This vision puts believers over and above economic trends and realities, although they have to study carefully the dynamics of the past and present socio-economic life in order to discern the next step in the right direction. The direction, however, and the means are determined by truths that thoroughly transcend the socio-economic situation.

Technological progress and the power of state capitalism and big business increase human dependence on the technological and socio-economic processes. This is still further enforced by the various forms of reductionism that propose a false autonomy in the socio-economic realm. Man can make beneficial use of socio-economic forces only if he regains the strength to give prime importance to truth, to salvation knowledge, and to acts that accord with a clear orientation to ultimate meaning.[74]

2. Dialectic materialism and the role of conflict

Marxism calls itself also "dialectic materialism". Its interest is not in matter, as such, nor in the theory that matter alone is at the origin of everything. Atheism and the negation of the Spirit is not so irrevocably a part of Marxism as, for instance, of Feuerbach's materialism. The Marxist's focus is on the conflicts in the economic infrastructure which most decisively affect human relationships, societal life, culture and religion.

Characteristic of Marx's dialectic thought is, first, that in comparison with Hegel's dialectic explanation of history, Marx turns the priorities upside down. The dialectic dynamism arises not from thought but from the tensions in the economic forces, processes and relationships. Second, Marx is as optimistic as Hegel that the dialectic goes from thesis, through antithesis, to a more satisfactory synthesis, and finally even to a perfect synthesis in the classless society. There the solidarity and dignity of all people are embodied in socio-economic life. Third, Marx's emphasis is on economic alienation and injustice as the source of class hatred and class struggle, and on the struggle as creative in forming a better synthesis. From there, in "orthodox" Marxism, follows the tendency easily to justify violence and to recur to it as an unavoidable step in the dialectic progression towards a better world.

Heated discussions arise today among Christians (including liberation theologians) about whether the model of dialectic materialism can be used for analysis of the historical situation and foreseeable processes. The decisive points are: first, whether one agrees with rigid Marxism that hatred and hateful fight are necessary and therefore morally indifferent or even good; second, whether, in one's analysis, one tries to explain *everything* on the basis of the economic reality - as if the God of love does not exist or at least is nonexistent in the socio-economic realm, and as if the power of nonviolent commitment for justice, peace and love had no chance.

As proved by many of his texts, especially "Das Kapital", Marx's analysis of the role of religion is based on the sad fact, frequently experienced, that religious establishments tended to justify and "sanctify" as the God-given order, even for children and mothers, the existing, frequently inhuman working conditions. Where this was or is the case, we can agree with Marx that those who act thus are indeed determined by the economics of greed and lust for power or are totally lacking in discernment, and that the workers who accept the dehumanizing conditions and relationships as "willed by God" are speaking of a "God" in whom a critical person cannot believe.

To realize the historical situation analyzed by Marx, one needs only to read the writings of the rebel Bishop Lefebvre and his followers, and to observe the readiness of some rich "Christians" to spend lavishly for this traditionalism. Marx had not the good fortune to meet a genuine Christian practice and way of thinking in the environment in which he lived and by which he was suffering.

Although he considered his analysis as merely "scientific" and not as "ethical", it is in fact a strong prophetic protest against injustice not only of individual acts but of a whole socio-economic system. The "ethics" rejected by Marx are not, however, the genuine Christian and humanistic ethics but a disincarnated (and enchanting) imperative of "love" that should not denounce inhumane conditions.

The church of the Second Vatican Council and the World Council of Churches are as critical of unjust, alienating socio-economic conditions as Marx was. In line with the great prophetic tradition they summon awareness to conflict situations.[75] The protest is truly prophetic because it is inspired by faith in God, Creator of matter as well as of spirit, in God the Redeemer of the whole man and the socio-economic man, and in the Holy Spirit who wants to renew hearts and the face of the earth, including the socio-economic realm.

The Christian vision does not accept a fatalistic mechanism of hatred and violent struggle, but it does warn those who cling to the unjust order - those who do not use the resources of nonviolent, creative action - that they are delivering themselves to the "fateful mechanism" of greed, lust for power or lazy and cowardly passivism.

The churches' protest is truly prophetic because it does not accept the theory that the unjust economic conditions and relationships constitute a "law of progress". Rather, the churches denounce them as originating from sin and perpetuating and increasing sinfulness. The great sin is that this continues in spite of God's offering us a liberating justice and peace.

On the other hand, today's theologians and scientists inquire also into the dimensions of conflict that are not necessarily or not totally due to sin.[76] Conflicts can be used creatively if we refuse to explain everything as caused by bad will and sinfulness by others. Christ, the Saviour of the world, is also the Saving Conflict.[77] He sharpens the conflict by unmasking man's sin and the sinfulness of the world; but he also prays, "Father, forgive, they do not know what they are doing" (Lk 23:34).

The church does acknowledge the necessity of conflict and consciousness-raising about conflict situations, but not the necessity of violence, or at least not violence as a normal means.[78] The disciples of Christ, the Prophet, speak a frank language that cannot please the unconverted rich and powerful. "While an enormous mass of people still lack the absolute necessities of life, some even in less advanced countries live sumptuously or squander wealth. Luxury and misery rub shoulders."[79]

To the fatalism of hatred and violence, the moral message of the gospel contraposes the good news of reconciliation. But it would be a disastrous misunderstanding to confuse genuine reconciliation with passive acquiescence and acceptance of an unjust status quo. It is by redemption and reconciliation that the disciples of Christ become prophets, yeast in the dough, working for profound changes.

What is most needed is a careful psychology, ethics and art of conflict-solution, the courage to face the conflict and its roots, to discern what can be changed and what has to be accepted or can be tolerated for the time being. Charles Curran speaks for many today when he writes, "In general, Catholic social thought, in my judgment, must give more importance to conflict, with a somewhat decreased emphasis on order and harmony."[80]

We need a strategy for meaningful reconciliation as expression of authentic justice and love. A part of this is an ethics and art of compromise which rejects any foul compromise but favours the dynamic, open-ended concession that promises the next possible step towards a less inhumane and somewhat more just situation. The concession is accepted as the lesser evil while the fight against evil continues. "If compromise is understood as 'settlement' in spite of conflicting views" (Messner), then the decisive effort is to arrive at an agreed arrangement even though noticeable disagreements of opinions exist in some matters and may persist after reconciliation. In any case, the open-ended compromise is a decisive alternative to violence; therefore it ranks high for solving conflicts.[81]

Compromise is possible and frequently morally necessary even if the conflicts concern not only means and interests but also basic goals and ideals.[82] In the strategy of honest, open-ended compromise, both sides realize and let each other know that reconciliation is an ongoing task and that the compromise they have reached should open the way for further dialogue and prepare a better basis for more satisfying solutions.

3. Christians and socialism[83]

From the beginning, a mentality marked by defensiveness and one-sided "knowledge of dominion" tended to condemn as Communism every movement that emphasized social ties and certain forms of socialism. Moreover, anyone who favoured any kind of socialism was equally stigmatized.

Today's official church is far more discerning. The most significant expression of the present nuanced approach is probably in the apostolic letter of Paul VI, *Octogesima Adveniens* (May 14, 1971): "Some Christians are today attracted by socialist currents and their various developments. They recognize therein a certain number of aspirations which they carry in themselves in the name of their faith. They feel that they are part of that historical current, and wish to play a part in it. Now this historical current takes on, under the same name, different forms according to different continents and cultures, even if it drew its aspiration, and still does in many cases, from ideologies incompatible with faith. Careful discernment is called for."[84]

Here, it is indirectly recognized that not all forms of socialism have drawn their aspirations from ideologies irreconcilable with faith, and that some others no longer do so. We cannot judge simply on the basis of the name "socialism" or even "Communism". The text continues, warning against oversimplification: "Distinctions must be made to guide concrete choices between the various levels of expression of socialism: a generous seeking for a more just society, historical movements with a political organization and aim, and an ideology which claims to give a complete and self-sufficient picture of man. Nevertheless, these distinctions must not lead one to consider such levels as completely separate and independent. The concrete link which, according to circumstances, exists between them must be clearly marked out. This insight will enable Christians to see the degree of commitment possible along these lines while safeguarding the values, especially those of liberty, responsibility and openness to the spiritual, which guarantee the integral development of man."

This official guideline, which avoids any kind of simplification or formula, deserves the most careful reflection and acceptance.

The history of socio-economic life offers many models. Besides the various primitive societies marked by solidarity, sharing, collective ownership and general participation in decision-making processes, there are models of a kind of state-capitalism. We remember the story of the patriarch, Joseph, in Egypt. Herodot reports that "in the cities of Persia there was no market".[85] The king organized the distribution of goods. The sect of Qumran, early Christianity in Jerusalem and religious communities were, to various degrees, models of socialism wherein the people's solidarity in spiritual values was reflected in the socio-economic life and structures.

The great socialist movements of the last and the present centuries have had, as one common source, the consciousness that modern technology and the means of communication multiply social ties and socio-economic dependencies.[86] The concentration of productive forces and goods for distribution in the hands of private persons and groups has tended to exclude the masses from ownership and from the decision-making processes that vitally affect their lives. "It should be obvious that great concentrations of wealth have always influenced the democratic process disproportionately."[87]

For hard-line marxists-leninists-stalinists, no synthesis can be made between scientific socialism and a socialism based on ethical appeal (their "utopian socialism"). Yet many times, communists recur to ethical reflections quite different from the hard position that "everything that favours our communism is good". While Russian Communism bears the imprint of the heavy authoritarianism and centralism of the Czar's era, Chinese Communism is frequently influenced by the great ethical history of confucianism, and makes effective use of direct moral appeal. At least one current bears a resemblance to the Dubcek experiment in Czechoslovakia, seeking a socialism with a "human face".[88]

Today's African socialism, especially that inaugurated by Julius Nyerere, president of Tanzania, is based on the best of African traditions and Christian aspirations. "'Ujamaa', then, or 'familyhood', describes our socialism. It is opposed to capitalism which seeks to build a happy society on the basis of exploitation of Man by Man; and it is equally opposed to doctrinaire socialism which seeks to build its happy society on a philosophy of inevitable conflict between Man and Man. African socialism regards all men as brethren - as members of his ever extending family".[89]

A very decisive criterion is the kind of authority envisioned or produced by socialism: is there maximum participation in important decision-making processes? Or is economic, cultural and political power in the hands of a few or of an alienated bureaucracy?

One of the basic functions of Catholic social doctrine is the ministry to genuine liberty, to the education of people for freedom, its liberating use to the benefit of all, and concern for institutions that preserve and favour freedom for all.[90]

V. ECONOMY A COMMON ETHICAL TASK

1. The great heresy

Greed and lust for power can become the main forms of idolatry (Col 3:5). In modern times, these false gods have found ideologies that make them appear reasonable. Machiavellianism had justified a politics of power that bears its justification in itself. Adam Smith (1723-1790) and his school, under the influence of deism (with a God far away), taught that economy and the economic man need no ethical imperatives, but can rely wholly on the self-interest of the individual. Their thesis was that the mechanism of the free market and the sum of the individual interests would grow into a harmonious whole. "Every individual is continually exerting himself to find the most advantageous employment for whatever capital he can command. It is his own advantage and not that of society which he has in view. But the study of his own advantage naturally, or rather necessarily, leads him to prefer that employment which is most advantageous to the society."[91]

In our time, a consciously value-free and self-sufficient economics - with its reductionism - comes to practically the same over-optimistic conclusion as Adam Smith about the automatically harmonious outcome. The neoliberal Ludwig von Mises writes: "Liberalism is derived from pure sciences of economics and sociology, which make no value judgment within their own sphere and say nothing about what ought to be, and about what is good and what is bad; but, on the contrary, only ascertain what is and how it comes to be."[92]

"Scientific socialism", although it comes to quite different practical results, adopts this same, seemingly value-free scientific approach. For its supporters, it is not the task of ethics ("wishful utopian thought") but of exact, scientific analyses about the inborn law of economic history to determine what socio-economic life will be. This does not, however, hinder them from combining "their economic analyses with expressions of moral outrage"[93] and sharp imperatives which make their analyses compulsory law.

The social teaching of the popes, beginning with *Rerum Novarum* of Leo XIII, has to be seen against the background of these heresies of liberalism and "scientific socialism".[94] The church consistently denounces ideologies that deny the possibility of recognizing the basic requirements of truth and justice, and all tendencies to "sacrifice the reasons for living".[95]

Modern man, who creates his world without clear ethical purposes, cannot feel at home in it and must experience a senselessness that borders on nihilism. If thought patterns prevail which deny a conscious ethical orientation in the socio-economic world, then it is no wonder that this modern world is unable to put its tremendous technical development to the service of all people and the wholeness of each person. Without value-judgment there cannot exist a truly human and ever more humanized economy. To eliminate value-judgment from social sciences, and particularly from economics, while at the same time making these sciences the norm for the socio-economic area of life, is to miss nothing less than the human dimension.

"The economics of the laissez-faire school purported to abolish the moral problem by showing that the pursuit of self-interest by each individual redounds to the benefit of all. The task of the generation now is to reassert the authority of morality over technology. The business of social scientists is to help them to see both how necessary and how difficult that task is going to be."[96] It is surely not easy to offer concrete ethical norms for economic activity. But economic man can acquire the basic virtues, can deepen the knowledge of such basic values as the dignity of each person, genuine freedom, fidelity and solidarity, and can look at his socio-economic task in the light of the total vocation of humankind.[97]

Fundamental criteria for ethical judgment on economic theories, structures and modes of behaviour are: 1) the dignity, well-being and development of all people; 2) the solidarity of humankind; 3) active and creative participation by all who are willing and able to build authority structures that will foster these values.

Not only are there more and more people who propose a socialism based on ethics, there are also defenders of the free market who emphasize ethical conviction and behaviour as absolute conditions for the functioning of freedom in the socio-economic world. "To the ardent free enterprisers I say: 'quit kidding yourselves; quit giving up a little more freedom for a little or even a lot of short-term money. If you really believe in a competitive open market economy, if you believe in the worth of your own product or service, then be honest'."[98] One is surely not honest and does not know the exigencies of honesty if he does not know and cherish the basic values of solidarity, co-responsibility and respect for every person's dignity.

2. God's saving justice and people's solidly united response[99]

a) God's justice and our faith response

All articles of Christian faith call urgently for human solidarity, and particularly for active and solidly united social justice for the weak and oppressed. The biblical concept of God's justice (*dikaiosyne*) can serve as focal point. Especially in Paul and Matthew, the emphasis is on God's *saving* justice. God, being just and faithful to his own name, Father, takes the initiative in seeking the lost one, justifying the sinner by sheer grace.

The Pauline doctrine on justification by faith and grace must not be misunderstood as individualistic or as entitling one to boast over others, as Calvinists did who looked upon economic success as sign of their own predestination. God's saving justice is a rallying call. He who saves me is the Saviour of the world. He who calls to salvation calls me to communion with himself and with all people. Accepting God's undeserved grace, praising his justifying action, imply essentially the readiness to conform to this very truth of God's saving justice. It becomes the law written into our hearts.

A Christian cannot confine himself to commutative justice ("you give and then I give"). If we, in grateful faith, realize how graciously God has acted and still acts in saving us by undeserved justice, then we also realize that the downtrodden, the exploited, the marginal people and "hopeless cases" can make a strong claim on our individual and solidaric actions on their behalf. Anyone who does not perceive this from within, and in communion with his fellow-believers, still lives in an alienated religion.[100] Genuine faith widens one's horizon and strengthens one's energies for social justice. Here the faith of individuals and of the faith community meet their test. Fidelity to God's action issues in a corresponding fidelity between persons, and especially in fidelity to the needy.

"The biblical notion of justice may be summed up in the principle, 'to each according to the measure of his need', not because of anything human in the needy, but because of his need alone as the measure of God's righteousness toward him."[101] Carl Friedrich von Weizsäcker is convinced that these qualities of social justice are characteristic notes of a universal ethics, and fruits of the meditative experience of all great religions. He is also convinced that many young people are yearning for this kind of experience. [102]Lawrence Kohlberg too, in his cross-cultural research, comes to the conclusion that everywhere the virtue of universal justice is latent in the child's thought. "The problem is to draw the child's perception of justice from the shadows of the cave, step by step, toward the light of justice as an ideal form."[103]

b) Dimensions of social justice

The expression "social justice" has become especially prominent in Catholic social teaching since the encyclical *Quadragesimo Anno* of Pius XI (1931). It is that kind of justice that befits humankind as the family of the One God. Radically transcending the dimension of self-interest, it makes the common good or public welfare the central focus. Oswald von Nell-Breuning writes: "For Catholic social doctrine, the common welfare is simply the supreme and all-inclusive norm of all of social life and societal order. . . therefore social justice requires no more, no less than what is necessary to preserve the common good where it exists, and to bring it into existence or at least to come closer to its realization where it is lacking."[104] "The common good embraces the sum total of those conditions of social living whereby men are enabled more fully and more readily to achieve their perfection."[105]

The model is a solidly united family where the common interest prevails and where it is self-evident that the weaker members have a just claim on the stronger ones and on the solidarity of all. This experience and this education in the basic social virtues in the family are of paramount importance for the building up of the common welfare. And on the other hand, a society permeated by social justice brings great moral benefits and moral examples to families.[106]

While there cannot be the same kind of relationship in a modern enterprise as in a family, there should be, beyond the common work and economic goals, a feeling of common life purpose, of co-responsibility and care for the weaker ones. That is what social justice, as virtue, brings about. But it does not bring forth its fruits without the constant effort to develop structures that favour this solidarity.

Social justice tends towards equality of chances and life conditions, at least, this is the initial presumption and dynamic; deviations must bear the burden of proof. However, "there is no injustice in the greater benefit being earned by a few, provided that the situation of persons not so fortunate is thereby improved."[107]

The virtue of social justice goes beyond the possibilities of a social market economy and social legislation to which it gives vision and efficiency. The welfare state cannot give what can be freely offered by people who practise this virtue: for instance, personally caring for law-breakers, hoping to heal them and restore their dignity, and welcoming marginal people into one's own respected environment. This kind of acceptance, respect and care can and must be favoured by institutions and laws, but society will remain disordered if social justice, as virtue, is not deeply rooted in people's hearts. If it truly forms the hearts and minds of believers, its horizons will be worldwide and all-inclusive.

Social justice is not merely a matter between employer and employee; it deeply influences the conditions under which people are productive and distribute the products of their work. It touches everything, fostering the development of person-culture, and extends also to international relationships, particularly between the powerful and rich industrial nations and the poor, developing nations.

Mahatma Gandhi speaks the prophetic language of the church Fathers, unmasking the sins against social justice. "I suggest that we are thieves, in a way. If I take anything I do not need for my own immediate use, and keep it, I thieve it from somebody else. . . . If only everybody took enough for himself and nothing more, there would be no pauperism in the world, there would be no man dying by starvation in this world. But as long as we have this inequality, so long we are thieving."[108] This applies as well to relations between social groups and nations. But it has to be added that those who refuse to make their own contribution for the common good, while requesting the help of others, equally are sinning against social justice.

Social justice makes absolute and immediate claims, but in its perfect form it is a "goal commandment" that calls us to remain always on the road to better understanding and realization.

c) Distributive justice in the light of social justice

The modern welfare state realises that distributive justice is expressed by a balanced system of taxation whereby all bear, according to their abilities, the burden for common tasks, with notable fairness to the weaker ones. Further, a good part of the gross product is distributed by the state to those - the sick, the handicapped, victims of discrimination, the uneducated and other unfortunates - who have little or no possibility to obtain their share in the market.

There is a new consciousness of rights that legislators and administrators cannot ignore. The United Nations' declaration on human rights (1948) says in Article 25: "Everyone has the right to a standard of living adequate for health and well-being for himself and his family, including food, clothing, housing, medical care and necessary social services, and the right to security in the event of unemployment, sickness, disability, widowhood, old age, and other lack of livelihood in circumstances beyond control." This vision reaches international dimensions through the United Nations' General Assembly's declaration, in April of 1974, of a "New International Economic Order", and the "Charter of Economic Rights and Duties", issued in September of 1975. Although the United Nations has no power to enforce these rights, the declaration expresses and promotes a new collective consciousness.

Cardinal Roy, president of the Pontifical Commission of Justice and Peace, sees "some movement towards a new consensus in which earlier concepts of economic growth are complemented by new ideas of social justice. . . Economic man is beginning to give way a little to the full vision of man as a responsible agent, creative in his action, free in his ultimate decisions, united to his fellows in social bonds of respect and friendship and co-partner in the work of building a just and peaceful world."[109]

This is a vision quite different from that of David Ricardo, expressed in the preface of his famous work, "The Principles of

Political Economy and Taxation" (London, 1814). There he speaks only about the distribution of the products of the earth, of labour and of machinery and capital among "the three classes of society", the owners of land, of capital and of work. For him, the main task is to study the laws determining the distribution.

Social justice not only regulates the distribution of economic aid to the poor; above all, it responds to the dignity and liberty of man and respects people's "aspiration to equality and the aspiration to participation."[110]

Distributive justice, inspired by social justice, intends not only a fairer distribution of goods but also the correction of the enormous inequality of power which allows a minority to make decisions that clearly affect the life of the many. Justice and equity demand vigorous efforts "to remove as quickly as possible the immense economic inequalities" which frequently "are connected with individual and group discrimination".[111] Only in the last decade has the world become uneasy about the enormous injustice of discrimination on the basis of race and sex. It is an urgent challenge to the church to give women a fully proportionate share in its decision-making processes in order to make credible its call to society to overcome "as quickly as possible" the discrimination against women.[112]

To overcome past injustices to particular racial, sexual or minority groups, certain countries have proposed or already adopted a quota system as a way of assuring for minorities a better access to certain jobs or to certain places in schools. Distributive justice, which recognizes the fundamental criterion of human need and is based on a proportional rather than a arithmetical equality, is definitely open to such proposals as a way of compensating for past discriminations.

3. Economy at the service of human needs

Against a merely profit-oriented economy, social justice requires that the purpose and organization of human economics are oriented to serve authentic human needs. "The fundamental purpose of this productivity must not be the mere multiplication of products. It must not be profit or domination. Rather, it must be the service of man, and indeed of the whole man viewed in terms of his material needs and the demands of his intellectual, moral, spiritual and religious life. . . we mean *every* man whatsoever and *every* group of men". Only thus is economic activity carried out "within the limits of morality, so that God's plan for mankind can be realized."[113]

Different kinds of needs must be distinguished: first, what people need simply for a secure and dignified life; second, what one "needs" because others have it; third, what one *wants* to satisfy his feeling of superiority over others. While the second category of want or need is understandable as a desire for equity, the third is a main cause of disturbance in social life and in personal growth. The first kind of need should have absolute priority in production and distribution of goods.

Education, too, befitting the kind of culture and economy in which one lives, is a basic need. Unfortunately, a great deal of education today, especially informal education through the mass media, is determined by market-interest. People are urged to want to possess more instead of to *be* more. This tendency fosters materialism and violence in society and world.

The chief obstacles to a need-oriented instead of a one-sided profit-oriented economy are: big industry, big labour, big government. "The bigger has claimed to do the job more efficiently. Quantity and practicality prevail over quality and meaning."[114]

In today's world, especially in the developing countries with high birthrates, a most urgent need is employment. Balance must be sought between the goods for consumption and the investment necessary to guarantee a "sufficient income for the people of today and of the future."[115]

Profitability cannot be excluded from economy, but it must be moderated and superseded by care for the common good. Political economy must see that services and functions important for society or for certain groups are not sacrificed to mere profitability.

4. Responsibility and subsidiarity

Social justice requires and promotes the responsible participation of all. The basic principle of subsidiarity is a call to guarantee a space for both personal and solidly united responsibility.

It is against social justice if a society's whole organization and conduct suffocate the responsible creative capacity of individuals and intermediary groups. A higher organization must not claim for itself the functions which lower organizations can perform adequately. If, in a case of disability, the higher organization takes over, then the main purpose should be to enable the lower organization to resume its role as soon as possible. On the other hand, it is equally against social justice if a lower organization arrogates to itself functions that can be fulfilled for the common good only by a higher organization.

The doctrine of subsidiarity was set forth in the encyclical *Quadragesimo Anno* of Pius XI. Its aim, constantly inculcated and gradually applied to the church institutions, is to maximize individual participation in decision-making and to strengthen the intermediary organs in order to avoid a suffocating centralism.[116] "The legacy of Catholicism's concept of subsidiarity is a loud cry for liberty, freedom of choice, voluntary association, local community and pluralism of custom and manner."[117]

The social doctrine of the church applies this principle of subsidiarity which calls for responsible initiative and cooperation on all levels. Although a certain gradualism for its application is indispensable, this is the optimistic vision of John XXIII: "There will soon no longer exist a world divided into people who rule others and people who are subject to others."[118] A concrete application which is especially urgent today is a certain autonomy of ethnic minority groups within sovereign nations.[119] Another is the readiness of nations to give up certain rights and functions that can be adequately administered only by international organizations. The social efforts of the church during the last decades "attempt to create participatory forms of interaction instead of the more formal patterns of social contract, the hierarchical society, or a pattern of *quid pro quo* exchange".[120]

E. F. Schumacher explains the strength and functioning of subsidiarity by the "principle of vindication". "The burden of proof lies always on those who want to deprive a lower level of its functions and thereby of its freedom and responsibility." And he pointedly applies this to government interventions. "Good government is always government by exception. Except for exceptional cases, the subsidiary unit must be defended and upheld."[121]

The implementation of subsidiarity meets many and formidable obstacles. In the first place, many people were not at all educated for personal responsibility and co-responsibility. In our society there is a trend to anonymity of decision-making. Increasing specialization makes the grasp of the whole more difficult. Church and society must make studied and unceasing efforts to give proper education and to foster structures which encourage people's readiness and capacity to accept responsibility. The church has to make clear that "by grace, man is not only called to his worldly responsibility; he is also empowered to assume it."[122]

5. Creative liberty

All these reflections lead us again to a basic leitmotif for our approach to moral theology. The principle of subsidiarity gives space and opportunity for creative liberty. It will fulfil its role if enough people discover their vocation for creativity and take initiatives that are honest, fair, mutually respectful and faithful to the common purpose.

Paul VI, in praising creativity, went so far as to speak in favour of *utopias* which, however, make sense only in a spirit of courageous responsibility. The utopian perspective can be a form of "forward looking imagination both to perceive in the present the disregarded possibility hidden within it, and to direct itself towards a fresh future; it thus sustains social dynamism by the confidence it gives to the inventive powers of the human mind and heart; and it refuses no overture; it can also meet the Christian appeal. The Spirit of the Lord, who animates man renewed in Christ, continually breaks down the horizons within which his understanding likes to find security, and the limits to which his activity would willingly restrict itself; there dwells within him a power which urges him to go beyond every system and every ideology."[123]

Socio-economic life needs both "the orderliness of order and the disorderliness of creative freedom."[124] Space for creative innovation is particularly important today for solving the most urgent problems of ecology, and for the survival of authentic freedom. In view of shallow and erroneous ideas about liberty, in classical liberalism and elsewhere, the present discussions on the basic values for social life have, above all, to clarify what freedom means and intends.[125]

6. *Solidarity and fidelity*

Genuine freedom cannot survive without the basic covenant virtues of solidarity and fidelity. Psychology renders poor service when it focuses only on liberating oneself from the past and looking for self-fulfilment. It has to insist more than ever on "permanence, loyalty, fidelity and duty". And we would like to hope "that it will begin to see that limited, contained, rooted selves are the only kind capable of creativity and generativity".[126]

God's action in history manifests his fidelity to his own name as Creator of all. It is a call to covenant fidelity on every level including the socio-economic life. It is not, in the first place, fidelity to contracts we have shaped but fidelity to our intimate being, our belonging to each other.

Even the best laws do not help much unless people realize profoundly that solidarity is a part of the very essence of our humanity, of being created to the image of God, being loved by the Father of all, and being enabled by the Sprit to love all. This is what Christian education has to imprint in the heart and mind of everyone. "Without a renewed education in solidarity, an overemphasis on equality can give rise to an individualism in which each one claims his own rights without wishing to be answerable to the common good."[127]

Christian solidarity, understood as covenant fidelity, extends particularly to the poor and unfortunate. They belong to us as we belong to Christ who, without any merit on our part, identified himself with us. "In this we have come to know the love of God, that he (Christ) laid down his life for us; and we likewise ought to lay down our life for our brethren. He who has goods of this world and sees his brother in need and closes his heart to him, how does the love of God abide in him?"(1 Jn 3:16-17).[128]

The universal dimension of solidarity, as intrinsic implication of covenant fidelity based on creation and redemption, is strongly expressed in the social teaching of the church. "Man must meet man, nation meet nation, as brothers and sisters. In this mutual understanding and friendship, in this sacred communion, we must also begin to work together to build the common future of the human race." Here we see the obligatory concern of the wealthier nations. "Their obligations stem from a brotherhood that is at once human and supernatural, and take on a threefold aspect: the duty of human solidarity - the aid that the rich nations must give to developing countries; the duty of social justice - the rectification of inequitable trade relations between powerful nations and weak nations; the duty of universal charity - the effort to bring about a world that is more humane towards all men."[129]

No doubt we have to be prepared for a "sustained and convulsive change as the inescapable lot of the human society for a long period to come."[130] Preaching self-control will be ineffective unless the decisive groups recognize and confront the dimensions of solidarity as expression of covenant fidelity written into our very being.

7. Unethical conduct in business

a) What does unethical conduct mean?

Whatever we have said on positive duties could now be repeated in negative form. In economic life, there are sins which are transgressions against clearly defined obligations and sins of prohibited conduct. In the over-all, the harm done by neglecting the binding purposes, ideals or goal-commandments is no less serious. Those who constantly confine their conduct to a mere borderline morality lower the standards and frequently remain below minimal expectations. Others seem to have no moral conscience insofar as economic life is concerned. They try to avoid conflict with law, and if they are smart enough, they are "honest" insofar as this promises more for their profit-oriented business activity.

There are still quite a few who explicitly deny social responsibility in business. Economists tell them that this is reasonable and necessary. "The businessman should be the tool who responds to market demand by making what society shows it demands."[131] Then the conclusion is drawn that no appeal should be made to executives to show social responsibility, because this is the task of politics and because decisions inspired by ethical responsibility beyond the rules of profit and prosperity are a handicap in competition. Yet the unfair means by which business and industry try to block legislation designed to set a minimum of social responsibility are judged severely.[132]

There are surely many people whose "conscience" scarcely functions above the level of what is defined by law and penal sanctions as criminal conduct. One of the reasons is that education for honesty, as inculcated and exemplified in family and school, seldom extends to business methods.[133] Many who are otherwise ethically oriented have simply no criteria about ethical conduct in the economic realm. In business, they will generally avoid criminality but not what we call unethical conduct in view of moral norms.

b) A catalogue of sins and crimes

Not all sins must be considered by law as crimes. If legislators were to try to define all forms of unethical conduct and forbid them as crimes, the result would be a horrifying police state with intolerable forms of control, or else a catalogue of crimes so extensive as to be ineffective. Legislators have to select those forms of unethical conduct that greatly damage the public order and the common good, and which can be detected without intruding unduly on peoples' lives.

Even the effectiveness of criminal law in the socio-economic realm depends on ethical principles generally accepted, and on education for honesty beyond the level of criminal law and sanctions.

Here I try to point to the most frequent forms of unethical conduct which, in some serious cases, are also defined as crimes or may be so defined in the future.[134] Practically all are sins not only against truth and justice but also sins of exploitation of one's fellow men: swindling, cheating, fraudulent practices in thousands of ways; calculated gratuities, gifts, open bribery, the use of call girls; extortion, kickbacks, tax evasion, subvention frauds; violation of patent rights or rights of authors and artists; unfair credit and loan practices, fraudulent bankruptcy; dishonesty in advertising and selling; espionage on competing firms, cartel agreements to the detriment of others; neglecting safety measures for workers, adulteration of food, practices detrimental to ecological balance, endangering peoples' health and life; wastefulness of resources or goods, thus depriving people of necessary raw material and products.

In the area of employer-employee relationships, there can be sins on both sides; unjust recompense by the employer, unjust work response by the employee; unjust lockouts, unnecessary and wasteful strikes, and violence in either case. Lockouts and strikes can be in some instances grave sins of injustice to the public, for instance, strikes in the healing professions in hospitals, nursing homes, institutions for the mentally ill or for other helpless people, and strikes by public employees - firemen, police, teachers - which are practically strikes against the welfare of a whole community and not against profit-making employers.

c) The extent of business criminality

Sociology has studied business criminality and particularly "white-collar" criminality[135], but those moral deviations in business which are generally outside the realm of law and sanction have received only limited attention. There has been some focus on trade union officials and their opposites (associations of employers) regarding such unethical conduct as fraud, extortion, acts or policies that frustrate democratic procedures, acts influencing salary and work conditions unfavourably, shady manoeuvres against the benevolent purposes of their own organization (mismanagement of pension funds, for instance), or, more frequently, against the common good. But it is fair to say that "most union leaders worthy of the name believe the labour movement is inherently a moral and ethical force".[136]

Many see business executives on various levels as the villains. Worldwide attention has been drawn to some multinational corporations by the disclosure of economically and politically devastating bribes paid to the highest officials of foreign countries and their own country "to lubricate the decision-making machinery" in favour of their products. The fault in some cases is not so much with the ones who pay the bribes as with those who are bribed, who solicit or extort the bribes.

Opp asserts that business criminality is unusually high in countries like Germany and the United States.[137] Two-thirds of 1227 respondents among Harvard Business Review readers wrote that practices which they consider unethical exist in their industry, and one-half of them feel that one's superiors often "do not want to know" how results are obtained, so long as the desired outcome is achieved. "Respondents frequently complained of superiors' pressure to support incorrect viewpoints, sign false documents, overlook superiors' wrongdoing, and do business with superiors' friends."[138]

Estimates of the financial damages caused annually in West Germany by business criminality vary between ten and fifteen billion marks.[139] The immaterial damage - loss of mutual trust, need for offensive and sometimes degrading controls, and the tendency of the "normal" criminal to rationalize his own behaviour in view of the conduct of people in high social standing - is inestimably greater. This is especially so when business crimes are more or less condoned and less severely punished than the relatively small transgressions of petty thieves.

d) Main causes of business criminality

The chief cause of business criminality is surely not poverty. The psychological characteristics of the offender play some role. In many cases, a subordinate executive or clerk yields to pressure in order to keep his job or win promotion. Often the general unethical trend in the economy plays a part: if competitors profit from such methods, one does not want to be a loser. Almost half of the Harvard Business Review's respondents feel that "competition today is stiffer than ever. As a result, many in business find themselves forced to resort to practices which are considered shady but which appear necessary for survival".[140] The temptation increases when these practices are approved or easily condoned in the particular environment, and the offender can hope not to be discovered or not to be punished. Last but not least we have to recognize the impact of widespread greed and the general decay of morality.

It would be wrong, however, to think that businessmen, and particularly executives, are less ethically oriented today than those of previous decades. A comparison of the 1977 Harvard Business Review inquiry with an earlier one in 1961 seems rather to indicate an improvement in ethical consciousness. Sixty-five percent of the respondents in 1977 agree that social responsibility is an ethical issue for the individual business person, and eighty-three percent feel that it is an issue which concerns the role that corporations should play in society.[141]

e) Remedies

Marxists assert that it is impossible to fight business criminality effectively in a society with free market competition where profit is a main force and motive. Opp finds that sociological analysis does not prove this thesis. Neither can it be proved that state socialism, of itself, eliminates this plague.[142] Unless there is strong ethical motivation, only the forms will change.

Adherents of the *social* free market system underline the need for a strong ethical education. Without honesty, the free market cannot function for the common good. Profit is an absolutely inadequate measure of the social effectiveness of business.[143] Ethical codes alone are not sufficient unless people are thoroughly convinced that the collective conscience unambiguously condemns unethical conduct in business. In this latter case, it can be very helpful if corporations freely adopt and make known an ethical code and somehow enforce its observation.

If the collective consciousness and sensibility are fully awakened, and those who are tempted know by public disclosure that many offenders are caught and adequately punished, then many will resist the temptation. It is not helpful if the public is informed only about the high percentage of offenders; people also need to be aware of the background, prevalent motivation, disastrous consequences, and society's determination to fight the evil.[144]

Those who want to follow a career that carries difficult ethical responsibilities must not only shield themselves with clear ethical purpose but must also qualify professionally. "The socially aware executive must show convincingly a net, short-term or long-term economic advantage to the corporation, in order to gain acceptance for any socially responsible measure he might propose."[145]

f) Reparation

Moral education for justice includes a sharp awareness of the duty to repair and make satisfaction for the damage one has caused, whether law enforces it or not. To profit from wrongdoing because of a dormant conscience (a so-called "good conscience") means to be bereft of a moral conscience; and this paves the way to new unethical and even criminal offences.

Proper law enforcement serves also the purpose of educating the collective conscience. There is no serious objection to provisions in law that protect the good name and social opportunities of an offender who is not socially dangerous. But it is absolutely unacceptable if offenders in business, who have caused and may still cause enormous damage, are treated more leniently than the poor offender who, in need, has been thieving. The fact is, however, that governing bodies tend to issue less severe and non-stigmatizing laws against the kind of crimes or unethical practices of the more prominent members of society who have role connections with big business, big industry or big government.

In view of the many kinds of societal damages caused by most business crimes, it is proper to impose, besides punishment, tough requirements for reparation. West Germany punishes severely some transgressions of cartels and imposes reparation three times higher than the profit gained by the infringement.[146] This is no more than just.

VI. BEYOND CAPITALISM

For a nation and its international interactions, our fundamental quest is for the kind of economic order in enterprise, economic associations and unions that favours the nation's indispensable purposes of cooperation, personal and shared responsibility, social justice, liberty and fidelity, and peace. If these are the decisive criteria, then it can be definitely said that *laissez-faire* capitalism and "socialistic" centralized state capitalism have failed utterly. New models of socialism with a human countenance are still to be developed and proven in the dire reality.

What the western world, Japan and many developing countries are now living with is a mixed economy of all shades, depending on the form of government, the extent of socialized or nationalized industry, education and communication, along with large areas of private enterprise, a diversity of income distribution among the social classes and groups, and the powers and demands of various interests.

The welfare state has softened the harshness of naked capitalism. In most countries, capitalism is no longer the same as the one whose final decline Karl Marx predicted. Paul VI warned Christians who take the path of neo-liberalism and tend to idealize liberalism: "They would like a new model, more adapted to present-day conditions, while easily forgetting that at the very root of philosophical liberalism is an erroneous affirmation of the autonomy of the individual in his activity, his motivation and the exercise of his liberty. Hence, the liberal ideology likewise calls for careful discernment on their part."[147]

1. The free social market system

The free market can serve human needs and human growth only in an interdependence of forms and arrangements of state, society and economy. The concept, "free social market economy", is frequently used for the West German system introduced by Christian Democrats and carried on by Social Democratic governments. It means that a whole system of social measures has to modify the mechanisms of the market, guarantee fair competition, and put the economy at the service of the basic social, cultural and political needs, thereby contributing to the social peace and welfare of all.[148]

The idea and the purpose of the social free market system go far beyond the ideas of Lord Keynes,[149] whose main intention was to find those mechanisms and to advise those interventions which can overcome depression in economies whose chief concerns should be constant growth, full employment and monetary stability. An economic system can call itself *social* only if social justice is the heart of the matter. And it is surely not an easy task to harness the tool of a free market in this direction without jeopardizing the concern for freedom and creative initiative. The social objectives are to be "determined outside the market-place itself."[150]

The free, socially oriented and directed market system can function only if there are mutual trust, shared ideals and values, and a commonly accepted social ethics. If there is no basic consensus, it will be impossible to obtain just wages and prices, which are essential elements for a social market system. A consensus is even more needed when a good part of the gross income is assigned for cultural and social purposes which are not determined by market interests.

A market system can be called neither "free" nor "social" if the inequalities of property and economic power are so great that they constantly disturb justice in the market and block social legislation for its application. This problem appears insoluble unless the principles of free trade are integrated into an economic order on the international level where social justice has the highest priority.

The advantages of the rule of free trade "are certainly evident when the parties involved are not affected by any excessive inequalities of economic power: it is an incentive to progress and a reward for effort. That is why industrially developed countries see in it a law of justice. But the situation is no longer the same when economic conditions differ too widely from country to country: prices which are 'freely' set in the market can produce unfair results."[151] In other words, the rules of laissez-faire capitalism cannot serve international social justice. Just as the free market system within a national economy can and must be harnessed by social-political provisions, "there must be found analogous ways to reach something like the social market system on the international level".[152] This is surely not an easy task.

2. Politics and economy[153]

In view of the interdependence between economy and socio-political life, we have to inquire into the role of politics in and for economic processes, relations and structures. The free social market system seems best fitted for democratic governments. Ongoing political reform thereby becomes a prerequisite for healthy socio-economic conditions.

Catholic social doctrine emphasizes the role of economic politics on the level of intermediary institutions, states and international bodies. "Each man feels that in the social and economic field the ultimate decision rests with political power."[154]

The Second Vatican Council is critical of both a lopsided economic liberalism and "those theories which subordinate the basic rights of individual persons and groups to the collective organization of production".[155] Paul VI, referring to the encyclical *Mater et Magistra* of John XXIII, insists that in order to prevent an unjust accumulation of wealth in the hands of a few and domination by the strong, "programmes are necessary to encourage, stimulate, coordinate, supplement and integrate the activity of individuals and of intermediary bodies. It pertains to the public authorities to choose and even to lay down the objectives to be pursued, the ends to be achieved, and the means for attaining these. . . But let them take care to associate private and intermediary bodies with this work."[156]

With the increase of social ties in modern national and international economy, there is more need for regulation, protection against exploitation, and many other measures that can serve the cause of social justice and peace.[157] Economic politics should serve a *qualitative* growth of economy, particularly in the third-world market, making the third world more independent. Wherever political economy gives preference to certain goals and means, there enter - or should enter - "considerations and evaluation of ethical and moral order: is all this favouring the basic human values?"[158]

The ecological problems cannot at all be solved without ecological politics. It becomes ever more evident that the distribution of indispensable and non-renewable resources cannot be left to the free game of market interests. The legislator must create for the social market a carefully elaborated social right, while all of society should be concerned with those ethical convictions and criteria without which neither the free market nor social legislation can be effective.[159]

All should be alert to the trends which E. F. Schumacher calls "the planner's addiction to over-centralization" and the "constant unlawful confusion between politics and economy".[160] The politicians and legislators should not be owned by businessmen, nor should they own the state. Legislation and administration should, rather, make sure that the people, solidly united, own the state.

In its Godesberg Programme, the German Social-Democratic party, opting for a mixed economic system (the social market economy), state the sound principle, "as much competition as possible - as much planning as necessary".[161] There is an *a priori* case for using the free market system, "and there is a stronger case against interfering with it, unless careful scrutiny is made of the wider consequences of such interference".[162]

In view of the increasing imbalance and consequent disproportionate power of big business and big industry, there are compelling reasons for an economic politics to protect the small and medium-sized enterprises, handicrafts and family farms, thus manifesting the political decision for quality rather than for ever more quantity. There are many good reasons to limit the size of industrial firms. State subventions should be given chiefly in view of the common good, in favour of the middle classes, the weak and minorities.

The free social market is greatly jeopardized by the enormous expenditures for defence and the big industries that live for military purposes while acquiring disproportionate influence over the whole industrial system.

3. Ownership and labour

God, the Creator, has so offered to his people his abundant gifts that they bear the mandate to submit them, by labour, to the benefit of his whole family. Both the gifts and the mandate to submit them by individual and collective effort are a call to solidarity. Humankind acknowledges God's sovereignty over the earth by fulfilling the divine mandate with generosity and justice.

A western culture, marked by both individualism and a capitalistic liberalism, emphasized so much the institution of private property and the self-interest of individuals, that no abuse seemed bad enough to give reason for interfering with property titles. The state's main function in economy appeared to be to protect private property, and in such a way that its actual distribution was considered "sacred". "Christian ethics was not uncontaminated by this ideology."[163]

The official teaching of the Catholic church, as well as that of the World Council of Churches, has again brought to the fore the social dimensions of property as well as of work.

a) Private ownership and social purpose of earthly goods

"Whatever the forms of ownership may be, as adapted to the legitimate institutions of people according to diverse and changeable circumstances, attention must always be paid to the universal purpose for which created goods are meant. In using them, therefore, a man should regard his lawful possessions not merely as his own but also as common property, in the sense that they should accrue to the benefit not only of himself but of others."[164] This strong text of the Second Vatican Council refers to a text of Thomas Aquinas wherein he teaches, "according to natural law, all things are common".[165]

Consequently, any concrete order of private ownership and the use people make of their property have to be justified by this more basic purpose, the common good. This, however, does not exclude the right to private ownership, but its distribution belongs only to the "secondary natural law" and therefore is submitted to historical changes. The changes have to be evaluated by how the primary natural law is thereby observed.

The social purpose of all private property is so clearly perceived that the Second Vatican Council not only urges spontaneous sharing with the needy but also speaks of the absolute right of a person "in extreme necessity to take from the riches of others what he himself needs"[166] if he cannot obtain freely-granted help. The rich who use their riches selfishly in the presence of crying misery should hear the words of the Bible: "If someone who has the riches of this world sees his brother in need and closes his heart to him, how does the love of God abide in him?" (1 Jn 3:17).

The encyclical *Populorum Progressio* quotes one of the strongest expressions of Ambrose, typical of the teaching of the church Fathers: "You are not making a gift of your possessions to the poor person. You are handing over to him what is his. For what has been given in common for the use of all, you have arrogated to yourself. The world is given to all, and not only to the rich".[167] There can be no doubt that it is in the spirit of the Bible and of the church Fathers when, in our age of worldwide interaction, these texts are analogously applied to the relationship between the rich and the extremely poor countries.

b) Titles for ownership

The chief title for acquisition of land and resources is socially oriented work. In the original culture of gatherers of the fruits of the earth, there was no formal title to occupation. Rather, there was an agreement among groups about the areas where they preferred to collect their common sustenance. Unused areas were free for new formal or informal agreements. More complicated were the agreements about grazing grounds for the nomads' animals and about areas for organized hunters. Among the latter, the tendency was to regulate disputes by violence. Occupation of arable land by stable agricultural groups brought a new sense of claim to permanent ownership.

During epochs of mass migration and up to modern times, this kind of occupation was frequently not at all peaceful. The "right" of the stronger prevailed. The pioneers, in some cases, appropriated just as much land as they were able to cultivate. In other cases they disowned the weaker groups and made them slaves on their former land. The next generations then forgot the history of violent appropriation at the expense of others. This happened in a great part of the "new world", and the historical consequences still exist, especially in Latin America.

In our own time, there prevails more and more the ethical conviction that the continuation of actual occupation of land and resources, which one cannot or does not honour with his own work, is unjust. The land and oceans, the rivers and the earthly resources belong to God, and therefore to all his people. Again and again, private property has to justify itself by socially oriented work[168] and the existing social needs.

Heritage is a lawful title for private ownership because private property is family oriented from the very beginning. The right of heritage is not only an important incentive for responsible care; it also gives a sense of stability, permanence and fidelity to the basic community of persons. If, however, the accumulation of land, resources and means of production is the result of earlier exploitation or becomes an obstacle to subsidiarity, solidarity and participation by all, then justice calls for new provisions. Heritage should give the progeny the opportunity for socially oriented work but not a title to live idly from the work of other people whom they keep dependent by holding immoderate amounts of property. Therefore, legislation can impose laws of progressive inheritance taxes in cases of disproportionate wealth.

A transfer of property by a contract which conditions the work, independence and security of other people can be utterly unjust, even if commutative justice (equality of price) is observed by the contracting partners.

There are new forms of ownership such as systems of social security, life and other insurances, savings accounts, building and loan contracts and so on, which allow people "to look to the future with tranquillity".[169] The most valuable possession, however, for oneself and one's offspring, is a good human and professional education which no inflation can destroy. A holistic education - including the dimension of social justice - and a regulation of ownership which honours socially oriented work as the primary title for ownership, will contribute most to the realization that "work, properly conducted in conditions of dignity and freedom, blesses those who do it and equally their products".[170]

c) Necessary reform of right to property and distribution of property

The traditional arguments in favour of the institution of private property - human dignity, creative liberty, family spirit, fidelity, solidarity and subsidiarity - are all too often contradicted by the actual distribution and role of property in modern economy. Hence, the very meaning of this institution and natural right calls for a profound reform and sometimes for some kind of redistribution.

In the church, this consciousness came gradually to the fore despite the reluctance of those who wanted to see the church as an insurance for the status quo. Those interested in the existent distribution (and quoting church texts in their favour) frequently act in a way that contradicts all ethical reasons for private property. The discrepancy is so great as practically to justify those who, on principle, are opponents of the institution of private property.

The fight for freedom of human work and responsible participation by all begins with humanizing conditions of work and a just distribution of power, so vastly based on property. But the freedom and initiative which we mean do not include the right of everyone to set up his own factory or university, to the detriment of other people's participation.

According to serious studies, 1.6 percent of the adult population in America hold at least 30 percent of the wealth.[171] It is not difficult to see their disproportionate power in economic, cultural and political life. Such an accumulation of economic power, as well as the influence of socially uncontrolled cartels and monopolies, erode the foundations of political democracy and frequently deprive political institutions of the power to act in the service of the common good.[172]

What is most urgently needed in many parts of the world is a courageous and wise *land reform*. A number of papal documents and the Second Vatican Council are quite outspoken on this important issue. Oswald von Nell-Breuning considers the following text of the Pastoral Constitution as one of the most important statements of the Council.[173] "In many underdeveloped areas there are large or even gigantic rural estates which are only moderately cultivated or completely idle for the sake of profit. At the same time the majority of the people are either without land or have only small holdings, and there is evident and urgent need to increase land productivity."

"It is not rare for those who are hired to work for the landowners, or till a portion of the land as tenants, to receive a wage or income unworthy of human beings, to lack decent housing, and to be exploited by middlemen. . . Depending on circumstances, therefore, reforms must be instituted if income is to grow, working conditions improve, job security increase, and an incentive to working on one's own initiative be provided. Indeed, insufficiently cultivated estates should be distributed to those who can make these lands fruitful. In this case, the necessary ways and means, especially educational aids and the right facilities for cooperative organization must be supplied. Still, whenever the common good requires expropriation, compensation must be reckoned in equity after all the circumstances have been weighed."[174]

Unfortunately, most of the capitalistic countries have not yet been able to stop speculation on land which is badly needed for decent housing and urban planning. The consequences are disastrous for millions of families and for conditions in modern cities. Here the strong language of the prophets is needed (cf. Is 5:8; Neh 5:8-12). Our whole way of life is involved in the evaluation of the land. If it becomes an object of speculation in a culture, this is an alarming sign.[175]

Where flagrantly unjust landholders or land speculators have done great harm to many people and to the common good, living in luxury while exploiting others, compensation for the land may be nil or even subject to additional charges to be paid from the accumulated wealth of the exploiters. Where personal injustice cannot be proven, those who are expropriated should be compensated in a way that gives them a chance to use their capacities in economic life.

The ecological crisis and the foreseeable shortage of important resources force us to a deepened understanding of the truth that the earth and all that it contains belong to the Lord, and that means to all his children. The willingness to recognize him truthfully requires new and courageous expressions of solidarity which cannot be found in the market place alone.

A false concept of private property is also a main cause of our growing ecological misery. The adequate answer to the question, "who owns the earth?" cannot be, "the military national state" or "a monopoly of a rich and powerful few".[176]

d) Socialization or nationalization

The irresistible multiplication of social relationships as a consequence of modern science, technology, means of communication, and modern trade, make necessary more and more governmental interventions in the economic life, in order to insure public health service, education for all, free social communication, and some social organization of the means of production in key industries. This can and should be done in a way that the "precautionary activities of public authorities" not only avoid unnecessary restriction of freedom, "but also increase it, so long as the basic rights of each individual person are preserved inviolate".[177] For instance, legislators and governments can guarantee education and social use of the mass media without monopolizing them. Socialization must not be nationalization. Many countries have formed institutions for radio and television, representing the major cultural and social forces, while reducing direct political interference to a necessary minimum.

The church's social doctrine does not exclude socialization or even nationalization of key industries or indispensable resources if the common good and the proper participation of all require this. "The right of private control, however, is not opposed to the right inherent in various forms of public ownership. Still, goods can be transferred to the public sphere only by the competent authority, according to the demands and within the limits of the common good, and with fair compensation."[178] The encyclical *Quadragesimo anno* of Pius XI gives as the main reason for such transfer of goods to public agencies: "if these carry with them power too great to be left in private hands, without injury to the community at large".[179]

4. The key role of work

The intolerable error of naked capitalism was and is to consider work as just another element of cost: the capitalist wants to buy work at the labour-market, as he buys raw materials and machines. On principle, Catholic social doctrine agrees with a leading thesis of Karl Marx, that work has to be honoured as the preeminent role in socio-economic life, and this ought to determine all productive relationships and processes. "The history of liberation of liberty begins with the work,"[180] with its becoming fully human and humanizing. Work is to be organized in such a way that it plays its role in man's self-realization.

a) Greatest possible participation of the workers

The nobility of work and its expression of solidarity ought to determine the productive relationships on all levels. If work is something to be sold and nothing more, then it is alienating; work - and all too easily the worker - becomes only a "means of life".[181] What makes work truly human is not the mere production of material goods but the intersubjective relationships in the process of production and distribution. Therefore, it is not indifferent to the one who owns the means of production, and the one who effectively manages them and thus decides the conditions of work.

There is something healthy in the private property of the *working* proprietor in the small-scale, personal, local enterprise. In the medium-size enterprise, private ownership is functionally unnecessary; the idea of ownership is already strained. In large-scale enterprise, private ownership becomes more and more a fiction that allows the passive owner to live "parasitically on the work of others".[182]

It is useful to consider roughly a typology of productive relationship. (1) The private owner of a small-size enterprise has co-workers who, although not sharing in his ownership, are honoured as co-workers. Their creativity is appreciated; their "payment" is seen as a fair share in the common work. (2) The opposite model is the "passive" owner who hires workers, allows them no participation in any important decision concerning work conditions, and pays for work as a thing, as one of the factors of cost, among others. (3) The extreme case, then, is that work itself is organized to such a degree that it becomes boring, stultifying or nerve-racking for the worker. The products count more than the person in his or her work-conditions and relationships.

In the whole of economic life, there are many degrees and forms of workers' participation in small, medium-size and large enterprises, and on the regional, national and international level.

In classical capitalism, the owners of capital hire workers and purchase work like old-time lords. But through workers' organization in powerful trade-unions, owners and employees become partners bargaining not only on wages but also on the organization of work and work conditions. Increasingly, the consequence is that management (the executives) become concerned as much or more for the contentment of the workers as for financial profit for the shareholders.[183]

It is not enough, however, to look solely at the frequently conflicting "partnership" of employees' and employers' organizations. Very important are the more direct relationships in the enterprise itself. From profit-sharing to co-partnership in all decisions which concern the dignity and security of work conditions and the future of the enterprise and the employees, there can be varying degrees of participation whereby common ownership or common wealth is a natural development. What is decisive in the arrangement conceived as "common wealth" is not so much formal titles of ownership as "specific rights and responsibilities in the administration of assets".[184]

New forms of organization, participation and ownership alone do not suffice; they simply create more favourable conditions for higher purposes and ideals of socio-economic relationships. Hence the building up of new structures ought to go hand-in-hand with a renewed vision of the meaning and purpose of economy in the whole of human culture. The purpose of participation is not to increase material productivity but to heighten morality in human relations.

The church's doctrine on an overall participation of workers in economic enterprises and in national and international socio-

economic life has developed from a constructive expression of
Pius XI in the encyclical *Quadragesimo anno*, followed by some
cautioning but also some encouraging words of Pius XII. Then
came the clear vision of John XXIII in his encyclical *Mater et
Magistra*, and finally the strong statement in the Pastoral
Constitution of the Second Vatican Council: "In economic
enterprises it is persons who work together, that is, free and
independent human beings created in the image of God. Therefore
the active participation of everyone in the running of an
enterprise should be promoted. This participation should be
exercised in appropriately determined ways. It should take into
account each person's function, whether it be one of ownership,
hiring, management or labour. It should provide for the necessary
unity of operations. However, decisions concerning economic and
social conditions, on which the future of the workers and their
children depend, are rather often made not within the enterprise
itself but by institutions on a higher level. Hence the workers
themselves should have a share also in controlling these
institutions, either in person or through freely elected
delegates".[185]

John XXIII has given an inspired response to discussions on
whether the right of the worker to greater participation and
responsibility is a right belonging to natural law or only an
acceptable response to historical conditions. It "not merely
accords with the nature of man but also is in conformity with
historical developments in the economic, social and political
fields."[186] This is an approval characteristic of Pope John's whole
emphasis on deciphering the "signs of the times" as an essential
element of historical man's nature, and especially of man's
redeemed nature.

Already at the beginning of the workers' and socialist
movements, Bishop Wilhelm Emmanuel von Ketteler agreed with
his friend, the early socialist leader, Ferdinand Lassalle, that the
alienation of the proletariate cannot be overcome without the
fullest possible participation by the workers. The difference was
only that Ketteler considered this idea so convincing that a moral
appeal should move everyone to put it into practice, while
Lassalle, more realistically, put strong emphasis on political action
to enforce this approval.[187]

If Christians, including the official body of the church, had listened to these men, history would have taken a quite different course. But even today, many Christians, even among those most insistent on "obedience to the church" (for instance in matters of sexual morality) seem to have no intention to give obedient attention to the now clear doctrine of the official church in the socio-economic field.

The idea of the greatest possible participation of workers and employees in economic enterprise would fill the gap between such socialist countries as Yugoslavia and Tanzania, and the countries with an advanced concept of the free *social* market system.

b) Just wages

It should be clear that social justice concerns not only prices and wages. Above all, it is a question of dignifying human relationships. But by that very fact, it applies also to prices and even more to just wages for the workers. And by "workers" we understand here all who contribute to economy by their own work, whether manual or intellectual.

Catholic teaching from the time of Pope Leo XIII has insisted on the right of the worker to a just or living wage. Today it is recognized that such a wage must be sufficient to raise one's family. This teaching recognizes that work is something more than a commodity to be bought and sold at the going rate. A living wage is based on the fact that through one's work one has a right to what is economically necessary to support one's family in basic comfort.

One of the main problems concerns the balance between merit or incentive wages and wages that take into consideration not only the personal contribution to production but also the social position and function (allowed by wages) that give the worker and his or her family "a standard of living in keeping with human dignity".[188]

The economically just wage has to correspond to the available resources, the economic situation of the enterprise, and the overall productivity. The family-oriented wage is a socially oriented and determined income. Mothers, for instance, who raise little children are not "productive" in a business enterprise but make a most important contribution to society in all its dimensions, including the economic. It cannot be expected that the enterprise alone will be able to afford the socially just wage. This must be supplemented, especially for larger families, by some socio-political efforts such as tax-exemption and other aids.[189]

During a course which I gave for trade-union officials, I sometimes heard the opinion that getting higher wages is a question of power and not of moral considerations of justice: an opinion, however, always contradicted by other officials or by members of the unions. The first consideration must be one of social and distributive justice, of the foreseeable consequences for the enterprise, the national economy, the stability of currency, and so on. Then, of course, there enter also considerations of the power to get what is just or only a reasonable compromise on the road towards a more just distribution of the social product.

Negotiations about wages ought to take into consideration the limits of economic growth, the purpose of full employment, and should avoid a "cost-push-inflation outside the normal supply-and-demand relationships".[190] This is an urgent problem, especially in times of recession.

c) The right to work

Man has a duty to work for his own and his family's sustenance and to contribute to the common good. The idle must hear the word, "If anyone will not work, let him not eat" (2 Thess 3:10). The readiness to work is necessary for a person's own self-realization as a social being, giving and receiving.

Corresponding to the duty to work is the right to work under adequate working conditions "in which physical health is not endangered, morals are safeguarded and young people's normal development is not impaired. Women have the right to working conditions in accordance with their requirements and their duties as wives and mothers".[191]

Work ought to be a source of joy, of creative initiative, and an occasion to manifest responsibility, solidarity and fidelity. Whoever radically destroys the joy inherent in dignifying socially-oriented work jeopardizes the bliss of leisure.

d) Strike and lock-out

Catholic social teaching asserts the right of workers to join associations (unions) through which they are able to achieve justice for themselves in wages, working conditions and other benefits.

Trade unions and employers' associations have important social functions. Their arrangements not only affect material profit; they ought also to guarantee loyalty and fidelity to each other. Their agreements and performances can contribute much to social peace and justice.

But time and again there arise conflict situations. After having praised the role of labour unions for helping the working class to feel and act as "associates in the whole task of economic and social development and in the attainment of universal good", the Second Vatican Council warns: "When, however, socio-economic disputes arise, efforts must be made to come to a peaceful settlement. Recourse must always be had, above all, to sincere discussion between the parties. Even in present-day circumstances, however, the strike can still be a necessary though ultimate means for the workers' own rights and the fulfilment of their just demands. As soon as possible, however, ways should be sought to resume negotiations and the discussion of reconciliation."[192]

Unions as well as employers must recognize their solidarity with all other human beings, and avoid the temptation of power to push their own cause at the expense of others. Union members and other workers have to form their consciences judiciously about whether a strike is just and justified, particularly whether the suffering it causes to innocent people and the damage to the common good are in proportion to the rights and advantages for which the union wants to strike. Members should raise their voices if they feel that not enough has been done to avoid the strike or that the cause is not just.

Strikes that deprive people of important public services - schools, transportation, postal service, fire and police protection, and especially hospital and other services for the helpless, the injured, the sick and dying - should absolutely be avoided. The author of this book has had personal experiences that make him sensitive in this respect. One of his best friends was brought to the airport in Rome for flight to Zurich for urgent surgery. A sudden strike called at the airport made the transport impossible, and the man died because the surgery was too late. The author himself had to wait for cancer surgery for some weeks during a strike of hospital personnel throughout Italy. Besides the immediate risk of life, the consequence was complete loss of his larynx and voice. Thousands of sick people are the "hostages" in a quarrel that, with the help of appropriate laws, patient dialogue and conscientization of public opinion, could be resolved peacefully.

If laws or government orders forbid strikes in vital public services, of course provisions must be made that those workers and employees who are deprived of the sharp weapon of strike will not be worse off than others who could win their just cause by strike. Submission of such disputes to impartial binding arbitration seems to be the most fair and just way to provide for the needs of all concerned.

It is surprising that the Council has said nothing about the weapon of lock-out, used not infrequently and sometimes ruthlessly by employers' associations. There is need of political legislation and action to limit the right to lock-out, at least to the point where parity between the partners is guaranteed. Many countries have laws about strikes in order to protect the common good and social peace against excessive forms of strike.[193]

5. The function of capital and interest

The Old Testament forbade the Israelites to take interest for a loan granted to members of their own people, but allowed them to take interest from alien people (Ex 22:25; Deut 23; cf. Ezek 18:8, 13). Until the encyclical *Quadragesimo anno* (1931) the official doctrine of the church forbade taking interest, under grave sanctions and without any distinction between loans to the poor and loans in the modern economy. Moralists and confessors were constantly in conflict between the doctrine and the people's conscience. A great deal of responsibility falls on those theologians and canonists who boasted about their allegiance to the magisterium by repeating the old formulas and attacking those who were aware of the new situation. As a consequence, the church's doctrine could have no constructive influence on the new forms of economy.[194]

Tradition frequently recalled the authority of Christ's word as recorded by Luke 6:34: "And if you lend only where you expect to be repaid, what credit is that to you? Even sinners lend to each other to be repaid in full." This teaching has abiding force in its original sense and in circumstances similar to those presupposed. It speaks about a loan of perishable goods or money to those in need. How can a disciple of Christ lock his heart when confronted with dire need? And how can he dare to act only for gain, to the detriment of the needy?

But in modern economy, as it developed especially since the twelfth century and even more since the sixteenth century, loans have a totally different meaning. Money loaned to business brings the businessman a considerable "interest" (the original meaning of "interest") out of which he gives a part to those who have lent the money ("interest" in today's meaning of the word). Without this system, the development of modern industry and trade, the growth of population, and multiplication of jobs would not have been possible. The method of teaching without first analyzing the historical situation and concrete meaning was disastrous for relations within the church and between the official church and modern society.

Loans given in the form of fruitful capital to a trustworthy enterprise at a decent rate constitute a moral question totally different from the loan given to help those in dire need. We can apply the distinction somehow to the loans given to the poorest developing nations, if they are actually used to relieve extreme poverty.

Interest as an incentive for saving has high relevance for investment urgently needed for full employment and peaceful development of industry, agriculture and trade. The interest is a just recompense for renouncing goods for immediate consumption. Moreover, it can serve for the security of the one who lends as well as for the increase of production and employment.

The percentage of just interest cannot be determined in the abstract. Among other aspects, the rate of inflation and its impact on economic development have to be taken into account.

The real problem of capital and interest begins with the excessive accumulation of capital and the corresponding power in the hands of a relatively small minority. It is true that the greatest part of the wealth of the rich is productive capital investment, a wealth held in trust for the benefit of the common good. However, it cannot be denied that an all too high percentage of the sometimes too high interest goes into luxury consumption, and this understandably irritates the lower and poorer classes. Even more serious is the fact that wealth held in trust becomes dangerous power, upsetting the democratic balance and depriving many workers of a just part in the decision-making processes. Political economy and public opinion have to watch these dangers and look for remedies.

Paul VI stigmatized one of the selfish abuses of capital which, in recent times, has inflicted deep wounds on national economies and upset international economic balance: the "flight of capital". "The available revenue is not to be used according to mere whim, and no place must be given to selfish speculation. Consequently, it is unacceptable that citizens with abundant incomes from the resources and activity of their country should transfer a considerable part of this income abroad, purely for their own advantage, without care for the manifest wrong they inflict on their country by doing this."[195] However, one cause of these abuses and disorders can be an economic policy of banks and public authorities.

A most difficult problem of modern times is the rate of inflation. It damages the economic processes and relationships, and is frequently a crying injustice against lower and middle-class people whose modest savings are gradually expropriated. Government and legislators are adding new injustices if these people have to pay income tax on interest which does not even equate the loss suffered by inflation. We have to remember that inflation rarely, if ever, hits proportionately the great capitalist whose wealth is invested in productive goods. The high rate of inflation, which economic policies have allowed in many countries, is an exceedingly unjust redistribution of income and wealth which disorganizes economic activity, discourages needed saving and its proper allocation, and gravely damages many families.[196]

6. The role of management

The thorniest ethical and social problems concern, above all, the executives of modern enterprises and of government.[197] They have a key position for the better or worse course. They can mediate between the interests of the shareholders (stockholders) and those involved in the work processes (stakeholders). And the more influential their role in the decision-making process, the more they can become vulnerable to conflicts between their private interests and their obligation to objective service. The same is true also for members of boards of directors who set the general policies of the enterprises.

It depends greatly on the management, and especially on high executives, whether or not an enterprise undertakes an economic policy which meets moral and social needs and the just expectations of the society which it is supposed to serve. Management's main tasks are: to keep the enterprise going, to preserve the jobs it creates, arrange the conditions of work according to the best findings of the sciences on work, and care for maximum security for the workers. It should promote a constructive partnership and good human and public relationships, guarantee a decent interest for the stockholders, maximize production and services, guard against waste of raw material and energy, and promote and enforce healthy ecological conduct. It should observe the rules of fair competition, give truthful information within the enterprise and to the public through honest advertising, be loyal to legislation and government, and make the activities of the enterprise transparent to the workers, the shareholders and the public.[198]

A clear role-definition in the contract should set forth the conditions for planning and initiative as well as for dynamic participation of the workers in management-decisions which concern all.

It is interesting to note that modern business executives are becoming more sharply aware that their corporation is not only an economic unit but also a social entity, and that they "rank responsibility to customers ahead of responsibility to stockholders and employees".[199] In the long run, the employees will surely gain the most benefit from good service and good relations with the customers. On the other hand, a monopoly that tends to exploit the customer will suffer from the customer's poor relations with the enterprise. The reason for the existence of the enterprise is to serve the needs and expectations of its customers.

7. His majesty, the customer, and just prices

On principle, the customers in a free market system decide what should be produced, what needs should be served and how they should be met. Many professional groups have set up ethical codes that oblige them to give reliable and faithful service to the customer.[200]

If each citizen were to choose services and products judiciously this would be one of the most important contributions to a healthy socio-economic life. Customers can join together to boycott poor services, unreliable products and unjust prices. There are, however, power blocks that impose unfair prices which normally can be changed only by political measures and the alerting of public opinion.

The actual forces influencing prices are treated by economists, and this can be very useful for controlling the mechanism in the sense of commutative and social justice. The relation between supply and demand surely plays an important role, but the rules of the market can be falsified by such unjust practices as unfair competition, reckless abuse of monopoly, the monopolistic functioning of cartels, manipulation of prices by powerful groups, deceptive advertising, mass-psychological manoeuvres to stimulate false needs, and so on. Unsettling also is the fact that, too often, agricultural products are underpaid in comparison with industrial products and wages. There can be, in some cases, good reasons for price protection through public authority.[201] Just laws that limit prices oblige in conscience. Gains by unjust prices cry out for restitution.

VII. SHIFTING SOCIO-ECONOMIC PROBLEMS

At all times there have been unacceptable flaws and shortcomings in the existing socio-economic order, but only a critical age brings the situation to full consciousness. The question is one of diagnosis and therapy. The lack of a radical diagnosis leads to an inadequate approach to therapy, alleviating only the symptoms without removing the causes.[202]

1. Liberation of slaves

For thousands of years a vast percentage, if not the majority, of the world's population were slaves. Sensitive people everywhere tried to alleviate their condition and appealed for more humane treatment of slaves while, at the same time, accepting slavery as "given", as a part of the social order.

The approach of early Christianity was similar. Slaves should be honoured in their human dignity, and especially as brothers and sisters in Christ, if they were believers. They should be evangelized and thus made conscious of their highest dignity as children of God. Frequently, Christians and others granted liberty to individual slaves, but scarcely dreaming that this should be a duty of all and for all. It was normal that the apostles and the Christianity of the first centuries did not realize that slavery should be radically abolished, since there was no chance at all to accomplish this. Even slaves themselves, when they joined in insurrections, did not demand the abolishment of slavery as a social institution, but only reacted against intolerable abuse.

If however the symptomatic therapy had been faithfully applied by all Christians, then early prophetic voices like that of St Chrysostom's would have been followed and slavery would have been abolished a long time ago. Only under the pressure of the humanist movement and changing socio-economic conditions did slavery become a *conscious* social problem calling for radical therapy to remove the causes by absolutely abolishing and by proclaiming the equal dignity and right to freedom of all people.

For believers, it is humiliating to know how irrelevant in this social process was the contribution of the official church and the theologians.

2. The liberation of farmers

As in other cultures, in western Europe and many other parts of the world where the Conquistadores exported their system, farmers were made bondsmen, serfs, belonging to noblemen and, in great part, to church institutions. Not only were they obliged to compulsory work for their "lords", but their freedom to move or to choose another professional occupation was usurped. They could not change their inferior social status. Yet those farmers who, during the early period of reformation, joined in a concerted insurrection did so not in order to win their freedom from serfdom but only to claim better protection of their rights as bondsmen.

Only during the eighteenth and early nineteenth century did this situation become a "social question" in the qualified sense: a public consciousness that this institution had to be abolished or radically changed. In Latin America and the Philippines the process of liberation is only under way. The first step is consciousness-raising (conscientization).

In today's world, there exists again a serious social problem in the agricultural world. In several of the rich industrial countries, farmers have no equal share in the affluent society. Not only are their products and labour frequently underpaid, but the farmers themselves are not awarded proportionate cultural opportunities. The situation is, of course, much more urgent in many developing countries where industrial growth is pushed and some farming is done with all the modern machinery while most of the sustenance farmers remain in absolute poverty and underdevelopment.

The social doctrine of the official church shows alert consciousness to this social question.[203] The neglect of the agricultural sector not only jeopardizes the nutrition of hundreds of millions of people; it leads also to great frustration among rural people, and flight into the urban ghettos.

3. New dimensions of the classical social question

Generous Christians responded to the enormous evils of exploitation and alienation of the working class by all kinds of "works of mercy": care for alcoholics, cripples, jobless, demands for improvement of housing and for higher wages. However, to those who were thoroughly dedicated to this symptomatic therapy, there gradually came the awareness that the causes had to be removed. Among Christians educated merely to obedience and allegiance to the given order, and among members of the teaching church (hierarchy plus theologians), a full consciousness of a social problem needing radical etiological therapy did not arise. Many did, however, promote social reforms which not only alleviated the situation but made more and more people aware that a new approach was needed for socio-economic change. The encyclical *Rerum novarum* of Leo XIII (1891) was a still cautious but decisive step towards a new analysis and constructive proposals.

Today there are similar new social problems which deserve immediate and positive attention, new analysis and synthesis.

a) New consciousness of women's role

In the first place, I mention the role of women in the industrial, democratic, scientific society: the participation of women as equal partners in the cultural, socio-economic and political life, without detriment to their role in family life.[204]

A document prepared for presentation at the 1980 United Nations conference on women notes that although females account for half the world's population, they put in two-thirds of the world's working hours, receive only one-tenth of world income, and own only one-hundredth of its property.

In many parts of the world, liberation theology cannot be effective unless women's equal dignity and equally important role in family, society and church life are acknowledged, not by mere words but by new and better-informed attitudes and new structures.

I do not think that there is, on all levels of the church, a realistic consciousness about the depth and breadth of this problem and its injustice not only to women but to the world to which they could contribute so much. As already noted, the church herself can appear to the world as model or scandal by the way she herself addresses various questions such as the role of women. The church must make sure that her own house is in order so that her word to the modern world will be backed up by her own witness.

We are not talking here about the question of ordination of women but about the many roles and functions that women can and should play in the life of the church. Great harm has been done and is still being done to woman and to the church by refusing any decision-making power to one-half of the human race. We thereby deny God's creative design and distort the "image of God" as shown by his creating "them male and female".

Women are not really consulted on social and ethical problems of church and society even when they are most vitally concerned and most knowledgeable. One glaring anomaly was the fact that the Vatican delegation to the 1980 United Nations Conference on

Women was headed by a man. We might well ask if future generations will have to say about sexism what we have said here about the institution of slavery: that it is humiliating to know how irrelevant the official church is in this social problem. Some high church officials seem presently to be more concerned to keep women completely out of the altar circle than to claim their proper contribution and right in socio-economic life.

b) Migrant workers and refugees

Another urgent problem concerns the millions of migrant workers in all parts of the world.[205] Frequently they are less than second-class citizens. Their situation is not solved by pastoral care that looks after them; a new thinking is needed. The first step is to insert the migrants and their families into the new environment while recognizing and favouring their own cultural and ethnic rootedness; the second is to bring forth that change in planning by which job possibilities are brought to people, and not workers sent to distant places and foreign countries.

There is, further, a growing public consciousness about the millions of refugees and displaced persons, but there is not yet a sufficient sensitivity to the problem or a sufficiently organized effort, first, to help these suffering people, and second, to remove the political, cultural and socio-economic causes of their shocking fate.

c) The social situation of the elderly[206]

The recent development, especially in the United States, of a new science, gerontology, is a sign of the growing perception of a new social need. This science studies not only the medical problems but also every cultural, social and psychological aspect of the aged.

In the year 1900, only 7 percent of the people in Germany were over sixty years of age. In 1964, the percentage was 16.4. The forecast for 1986 is 18.5 percent. Only 8 percent of those older than 65 are living in a family unit with children and grandchildren.

The increasing cult of youthfulness in the western world sharpens the psychological problem of ageing. It leads to a general attitude marked by neglect or repression of the aged, almost as if they did not exist. The prevailing model is not favourable. People retire or are forced into retirement when they still enjoy physical and mental strength. If they are not culturally and psychologically prepared for retirement, the sudden change can lead to a fateful apathy. They feel useless, with no purpose for their newly gained leisure.

Gerontology suggests important social tasks for the elderly. The person must prepare himself or herself for the art of making the best of the older years. Ongoing education, cultural and spiritual activity prevent or delay the more negative aspects of ageing; there can be a surprising freshness and alert wisdom well into a very great age. Many opportunities are opening up for the elderly. Interesting courses are offered to them in many schools and colleges, especially in the summer months when campus rooms are available. The churches, too, should realize the enormous potential of retired people for various forms of apostolate and charitable activity.

Retirement should not be abrupt and should not be enforced where the person is willing and able to carry on his or her normal activity or a new, more fitting one. If a community or a society simply sidetracks its elderly, it is not only the latter who suffer. The community or society itself loses the enormous potentialities of the ageing but still active population.

d) Integration of youth in socio-economic life

The cult of youthfulness does not, however, lead to a fruitful effort to integrate youth everywhere in socio-economic life. In many countries, although the educational system is success-oriented, it does not offer youth the kind of preparation which enables them to find their places in the world of work.

Even in the industrial countries, but much more in the developing countries with high birthrates, there are great masses of youth who, for long periods, are jobless. Many cannot find employment in the field for which they were prepared. For instance, in Africa and Asia, I heard strong criticism against the school system which was introduced by colonial powers in accordance with European models, but which is counter-productive for the cultural and socio-economic conditions of the country. This sharpens the already difficult problem of creating jobs for the numerous young people. A part of youths' criminality and drug addiction is the result of this unfortunate situation. It is, indeed, a most urgent social problem.

4. Ecology, megalopolis, urban ghetto

The list of new social problems would be grievously incomplete if we failed to include the ecological situation which humanity is only now recognizing as a social problem of enormous dimensions (see Chapter Five of this volume). The megalopolis and the urban ghetto deserve special mention, since in those areas there flow together the shades and threats of almost all the other social questions, along with the growing ecological difficulties. The irresistible decay of some of the proudest cities and the disastrous conflicts that explode in urban ghettos bring to public consciousness a number of social evils: racial discrimination, unhealthy housing conditions, lack of space for play and social leisure, a lack of integration of the young with older people in this unhealthy and socially deprived environment.

The right of free migration is not helpful if there is no corresponding urban planning, creation of meaningful employment in rural areas and smaller cities, agrarian reform, and a citizenry well informed about the situation of those who, without the necessary preparation, come to the urban ghettos and make things worse. Everyone should be alerted early in life about the complex problems of individuals, families and society-at-large, caused by massive migration to the big cities.[207]

5. From colonialism to a new world order

Colonialism is as old as the system of military states with ambitions to submit others to their interests. Again, it is shocking to realize that, in the mind of most Christians and of the official church, the modern, unbridled colonialism was not perceived clearly as a "social question" of monstrous proportions, requiring a thoroughgoing analysis of the deeper causes and a radical therapy.

Mahatma Ghandi contributed greatly to making colonialism a social question felt by every sensitive conscience and finally by world opinion. But the pernicious consequences of western colonialism are not yet overcome when many highly developed and freedom-loving countries are being submitted to a new ideological, economic and military colonialism. It is, however, a sign of the times that the new consciousness of these social problems has become "worldwide".[208]

a) Facing the heritage of colonialism

Colonialism cannot be considered as past. The consequences are a heavy burden on those who were under colonial régimes and on those nations which imposed it, approved it and profited by it. There is a need for a contrite memory and a firm purpose of solidly-united reparation. Respectful cooperation and bilateral and multilateral agreements should "allow the ties of dependence and feelings of bitterness, left over from the era of colonialism, to yield place to the happier relationships of friendship based on a footing of constitutional and political equality".[209]

Only a radical diagnosis of the various kinds of colonialisms and their misdeeds, looking for their deeper roots and causes and for the wrong mentalities still existing, can work effectively for genuine liberation and shared freedom.

The present imbalances among nations must be seen in the context of colonialism. Cardinal Roy, as president of the Pontifical Commission on Justice and Peace, has done this effectively. "The European peoples took over all the remaining temperate land of the globe after 1840. Forty million migrants left Europe in the nineteenth century for new lands and jobs in the new world. The Europeans could also complete the colonization of virtually the whole humanity. Their trade and investment gave them - although they made up less than twenty percent of the world's people - eighty percent of the world's resources and trade, ninety percent of the investment, one hundred percent of the services, banking, shipping, research."[210]

Profiting by the results of these past events, and trying to export western culture and political programmes in the context of trade relations and development, is frequently called "neocolonialism". This neocolonialism manifests itself economically in distortion of international commerce, flight of "economic and human capital" from the developing countries to the rich ones, enormous tax evasion through foreign companies which send their profits and dividends abroad, progressive debt, international monopolies and the imperialism of money.[211]

Transnational corporations comprise a focal point of apprehension. Their operations throughout the world depend greatly on decisions made in the United States, Japan and Western Europe. Some transnational corporations, and also some countries of the third world, propose codes of conduct for their activities.[212] Many of them operate in key economic sectors. These codes can provide an ethical setting within which the game is to be played. They are to regulate the ways to settle disputes, to guarantee the disclosure of indispensable information, and to assure honest dealings in general.

b) Shift from development to liberation view

The Pastoral Constitution of the Second Vatican Council, and *Populorum Progressio* of Paul VI reflect the then prevailing emphasis on the need for development in its integral meaning, and for corresponding development-aid by the rich countries. But hard experiences with many forms of neocolonialism and resistance by the overprivileged classes led to a new and more basic vision of liberation. It is characterized by a more vivid consciousness of the conflict situation, by prophetic protest and the quest of a spirituality and methods of solving conflicts. This does not, of course, devaluate the previous constructive proposals (such as a world fund and a world tax system) about mutual assistance in development and greater participation by the developing countries in the decision-making processes.[213]

Development is not just a matter of reducing poverty and eliminating hunger. "It is a question, rather, of building a world where everyone, no matter what his race, religion or nationality, can have a fully human life, freed from servitude imposed on him by other men. . . a world where freedom is not an empty word, and where the poor man Lazarus can sit down at the same table with the rich man." In this context, Paul VI alerts us to the possibility that the conflict may well have to be first overcome in ourselves by a firm decision for active solidarity. "Let each one examine his conscience, a conscience that conveys a message for our times. Is he prepared to support, out of his pocket, works and undertakings organized in favour of the most destitute? Is he ready to pay higher taxes so that public authorities can intensify their efforts in favour of development?"[214]

An important question of social ethics, and especially of the social question of development-liberation, is whether we are ready to renounce a part of our wealth - and especially our power - to the point that we leave the other a chance for that level of equality in the decision-making process and all socio-economic relationships which, in justice, would give a fair start for all. This surely implies a redistribution of power and, to some extent, of property.

6. *The end of an ideology of constant quantitative growth*

Capitalism, whether laissez-faire capitalism or socialistic state capitalism, is wedded to the ideology of constant quantitative growth and expansion. This is a frequent cause of increasing conflicts. The sharpness of the ecological crisis and the scarcity of energy and raw materials force humanity to rid itself of this dangerous ideology. This is probably the thorniest social question of the decades ahead of us.[215] There is not yet enough consciousness of the dimensions and foreseeable disastrous consequences of the present ideology. It is a question of spiritual health, of wholesome relationships and of peace in the world.

Even if the energy crisis were solved by new technical break-throughs - for example, by new methods of producing and conserving hydrogen[216] - there still remains the need for liberation from the quantitative growth mania. "When growth is directed away from the cultural and spiritual values, it becomes a cancerous quest for satisfaction in the mere accumulation of material goods."[217] If individuals, groups, corporations, nations, cannot curb the desire for ever more material goods, more expansion of business, more power, nothing can prevent constant conflicts and ruinous wars. A decentralization of power and a more balanced development of small and medium-size communities with integrated relationships are sorely needed.

The transition from a constant-growth economy to a qualitative and more humanized economy carries enormous difficulties. It cannot be resolved without a new spirit which has to move in the direction of what I have called "the economy of the beatitudes": but there must also be great competence among the people responsible for the various branches of the economy.

How can this qualitative change be reconciled with the magic quadrangle where full employment, stable currency and a balance between export and import has, as the main support, quantitative growth? The solution is in the direction of redistribution of time for work, for leisure and for cultural activities. If this is done, the prevailing concern for full employment must not be neglected.

Renouncing the growth mania should not be misunderstood as a choice for stagnation. Rather, it would liberate people's energies for a more creative ordering of a socio-economic life more fully integrated into a healthy cultural development, and would release their potential for the spiritual sphere of life.

To achieve this transition, great educational efforts must be made. The first step is to unmask the present ideology, freeing minds from the growth mania. We want to grow as human beings in healthy relationships instead of wanting constantly to sell, to purchase, to possess and to use more things.

7. How to control the national military state[218]

The present ideology and shape of the national military state constitute an almost universal problem of political ethics (see Chapters Eight and Nine). At the same time, they are a nodal point of socio-economic order or, more exactly, a main cause of many of the disorders in this field. In national states, politics is frequently so one sided in the service of economic expansion that the military industry can obtain a key position in research and planning. The export-import balance is reached by export of weapons. A great part of the so-called "development aid" is swallowed up by the sale of armaments. Early retired colonels and generals move from military service into powerful economic positions. The budget for defence modifies almost all social and cultural planning.

There can be no solution to these large-scale social problems of today and of the decades ahead, without a new world order in which the ambitions of the national states are bridled, and nations undertake solidly united, peaceful measures to solve them. For this, a new spirit, deeper insight, but also appropriate international organizations are necessary.

NOTES

[1] Cf. A. F. Utz, B. von Galen (eds.), *Die katolische Sozialdoktrin in ihrer geschichtlichen Entfaltung. Eine Sammlung päpstlicher Dokumente vom 15. Jahrhundert bis in die Gegenwart*, 4 vols., Aachen, 1976; A. F. Utz, *Bibliographie der Sozialethik*, 10 vols., Freiburg, 1964-1978; A. Tautscher, *Wirtschaftsethik*, München, 1957; O. Schilling, *Christliche Wirtschaftsethik*, München, 1959²; W. Künneth, *Moderne Wirtschaft, christliche Existenz*, München, 1959; N. Monzel, *Katholische Soziallehre*, 2 vols., Köln, 1965-1967; J. Kenneth Galbraith, *Economics and the Public Purpose*, Boston, 1973; Id., *A Contemporary Guide to Economics, Peace and Laughter*, Boston, 1971; H. E. Richter, *Lernziel Solidarität*, Reinbeck, 1974; H. Ludwig, *Die Kirche im Prozess der gesellschaftlichen Differenzierung*, Mainz, 1976; I. Hill (ed.), *The Ethical Basis of Economic Freedom*, Chapel Hill/N.C., 1976; R. K. Mueller, *Metadevelopment: Beyond the Bottom Line*, Lexington/Mass., 1977; J. Schwarte, *Grundfragen des menschlichen Zusammenlebens in christlicher Sicht*, Paderborn, 1977; J. P. Wogaman, *The Great Economic Debate: An Ethical Analysis*, Philadelphia, 1977; S. T. Bruyn, *The Social Economy: People Transforming Modern Business*, New York, 1977, W. Weber, *Person und Gesellschaft*, Paderborn, 1978; F. Böckle, F. J. Stegmann, *Kirche und Gesellschaft heute*, Paderborn, 1979.

[2] Cf. R. Régamey, *Pauvreté et construction du monde*, Paris, 1967; Ph. Schmitz, *Die Armut in der Welt als Frage an die christliche Sozialethik*, Frankfurt, 1973; A Rizzi, *Scandalo e beatitudine della povertà*, Assisi, 1975; E. F. Schumacher, *Small is Beautiful. Economics as if People Mattered*, New York, 1975; M.-D. Guinon (ed.), *Gospel Poverty, Essays in Biblical Theology*, Chicago, 1977; Sr. A. Niel, *A Sociotheology of Letting Go: A First World Church Facing Third World People*, New York, 1977; A. Cussianovich, *Religious Life and the Poor*, Maryknoll, N.Y., 1979.

[3] *Gaudium et spes*, 72. The footnote refers to many biblical texts such as Lk 3:11; 10:30; 11:4; et al.

[4] Cf. E. F. Schumacher, l.c., 156f.

[5] Cf. John XXIII, *Pacem in terris*, 45.

[6] Medellin document, *On Justice*, 3.

[7] Cf. *Gaudium et spes*, 10,2.

[8] *Populorum progressio*, 17.

[9] Synod of Bishops, Rome, 1971, *Justice in the World*, 5, 32-34.

[10] Synod of Bishops, Rome, 1974, *Evangelization of the Modern World*, 12.

[11] H. Kunst, H. Tenhumberg (eds.), *Soziale Gerechtigkeit und internationale Wirtschaftsordnung*, München and Mainz, 1976, 7.

[12] Ph. Schmitz, l.c., 64.

[13] J. B. Metz, "For a Renewed Church before a New Council: A Concept in Four Thesis", in *Toward Vatican III*, 140.

[14] Cf. V. Taylor, *Enough is Enough*, London, 1976, 4ff.

[15] Medellin document, *Poverty of the Church*, 4-7.

[16] Sr. A. Niel, "The Challenge of Sociobiology", in *Christianity and Crisis* 40 (Jan. 1980), 345. Augusta Niel draws our attention to that kind of sociobiology which, through biological theories, tries to discourage any help to disadvantaged individuals and groups; cf. E. O. Wilson, *Sociobiology: A New Synthesis*, Cambridge/Mass., 1975.

[17] *Gaudium et spes*, 33

[18] Cf. H. Sedlmayr, *Verlust der Mitte*, Salzburg, 1948.

[19] *Gaudium et spes*, 63, 3.

[20] Several highly renowned economists who are contributors to the book - *Altruism, Morality and Economic Theory* (ed.), E. S. Phelps, New York, 1975 - explain altruism and philanthropic activities exclusively in terms like "consumption".

[21] A. Tautscher, l.c., 42.

[22] Cf. M. Weber, *The Theory of Social and Economic Organization*, Glencoe/Ill., 1947 (this is part of his groundbreaking work *Wirtschaft und Gesellschaft)*; M. Scheler, *Die Wissensformen und die Gesellschaft*, Leipzig, 1926; K. Mannheim, *Essay on Sociology of Knowledge*, London, 1952; P. L. Berger and Th. Luckman, *The Social Construction of Reality*, New York, 1966; H. Schelsky, *Theorie der Institution*, Düsseldorf, 1970; J. Robinson, *Freedom and Necessity. An Introduction to the Study of Society*, London, 1970; G. E. Steiner, *Business and Society*, New York, 1975²; E. W. Böckenförde, *Staat, Gesellschaft, Freiheit*, Frankfurt, 1976.

[23] Cf. W. Wickler,"Ergebnisse der Verhaltensforschung - auch von Bedeutung für die Ethik?", in *Renovatio* (Regensburg) 32 (1976), 58-63.

[24] J. P. Wogaman, l.c., 164, cf. 151.

[25] Cf. J. Robinson, l.c., 18ff.

[26] W. E. Simon, "A Challenge to the Free Enterprise", in I. Hill, l.c., 406.

[27] Text to be found in J. Gremillion, *The Gospel of Peace and Justice*, Maryknoll, N.Y., 1976, 464-471.

[28] *Gaudium et spes*, 63-72.

[29] *Gaudium et spes*, 63,1.

[30] *Gaudium et spes*, 53.

[31] J. P. Wogaman, l.c., 59.

[32] Ibid., 61.

[33] Cf. John Paul II, *Redemptor hominis*, 15.

[34] B. Häring, *Macht und Ohnmacht der Religion*, Salzburg, 1956² (chapter on interaction between economy and religion); M. Weber, *The Protestant Ethic and the Spirit of Capitalism* (tr. T. Parsons), New York, 1958 (first published in German 1904/1905); K. H. Tawney, *Religion and the Rise of Capitalism*, London, 1926; A. Müller-Armack, *Religion und Wirtschaft. Geistesgeschichtliche Hintergründe unserer europäischen Lebensform*, Stuttgart, 1959; R. Niebuhr, *Man's Nature and His Communities*, New York, 1965; B. Häring, "Man in Quest of Liberation in Community", in L. Colonnese (ed.), *Human Rights and the Liberation in the Americas*, Notre Dame, 1970, 247-258.

[35] Cf. H. Marcuse, *Eros and Civilization*, Boston, 1955.

[36] J. P. Wogaman, l.c., vii.

[37] J. L. Peacock, "Ethics, Economics and Society in Evolutionary Perspective", in I. Hill, *The Ethical Basis of Economic Freedom*, 36.

[38] J. P. Wogaman, l.c., 145.

[39] Cf. W. Sombart, *Der moderne Kapitalismus. Historisch-systematische Darstellung des gesamt-europäischen Wortschaftslebens von Anfang bis zur Gegenwart*, München und Leipzig, vol. I and vol. II, 1902, vol. III, 1927; Id., *Studien zur Entstehung des modernen Kapitalismus*, München and Leipzig, 1913.

[40] E. S. Phelps, l.c., 3.

[41] K. J. Arrow, "Gifts and Exchanges" in E. S. Phelps (ed.), l.c., 15.

[42] Cf. W. Vikrey, "Private Philanthropy and Public Finance" in E. S. Phelps (ed.), l.c., 149-169.

[43] Ibid., 166

44 B. Bolnick, "Toward a Behavioral Theory of Philanthropic Activity", in E. S. Phelps (ed.), l.c., 197-223, quote pp. 197-198.

45 J. Stamp, *The Christian Ethics as an Economic Factor*, London, 1939; Id., *Christianity and Economics*, London, 1939; J.-Y. Calvez, *The Social Thought of John XXIII. Mater et Magistra*, Chicago, 1964; J.-Y. Calvez, J. Perrin, *Die Kirche als Wirtschaftsgesellschaft*, 2 vols., Recklinghausen, 1964/1965; H. Weber, *Theologie, Wirtschaft. Die Sozial- und Wirtschaftsethik in der evangelischen Theologie der Gegenwart*, Göttingen, 1970; J. C. Bennett, *The Radical Imperative: From Theology to Social Ethics*, Philadelphia, 1975; J. Gremillion, *The Gospel of Justice and Peace: Catholic Social Teaching since Pope John XXIII*, Maryknoll, N.Y., 1976; O. von Nell-Breuning, *Soziallehre der Kirche. Erläuterung der lehramtlichen Dokuments*, Wien, 1977.

46 Cf. H. Ludwig, *Die Kirche im Prozess der gesellschaftlichen Differenzierung. Perspektiven für eine neue sozialethische Diskussion*, München and Mainz, 1976.

47 H. Kunst and H. Tenhumberg (ed.), l.c., 9.

48 Synod of Bishops, Rome, 1971, *Justice in the World*, 5-6.

49 *Mater et Magistra*, 239.

50 J. Giers, "Der Weg der katholischen Soziallehre", in *Jahrbuch für christliche Sozialwissenschaft* 13 (1973), 11; cf. H. Ludwig, l.c., 187; L. Roos, *Ordnung und Gestaltung der Wirtschaft. Grundlagen und Grundsätze der Wirtschaftsethik nach dem Zweiten Vatikanischen Konzil*, Köln, 1971, 12ff.

51 P. S. J. Cafferty, "The Church in Public Policy Making: The Need for Professional Competence", in D. Tracy (ed.), *Toward Vatican III*, 297.

52 P. Knauer, *Der Glaube kommt vom Hören. Ökumenische Fundamentaltheologie*, Graz, 1978, 224; cf. *Mater et magistra*, 220; *Pacem in terris*, 36. This complementarity between the Pastors of the Church and competent lay people is classically expressed in *Gaudium et spes*, 43.

53 D. A. Seeber, in *Herderkorrespondenz* 33 (1979), 488.

54 This is a main dimension of the Pastoral Constitution *Gaudium et spes* in all its parts; cf. ibid, 14.

55 *Mater et magistra*, 236.

56 Cf. The common declaration of the Catholic Bishops' Conference and the Council of the Evangelical Church in Germany on "Grundwerte und Gottes Gebote", in *Herderkorrespondenz* 33 (1979), 561-571.

57 H. Cox, *The Seduction of the Spirit*, New York, 1973, 75.

58 "Lukas Vischer hält Rückschau auf 18 Ökumene-Jahre", in *Ut omnes unum sint* 42 (1979), 180-185.

59 Ch. E. Curran, "Social Ethics: Agenda for the Future", in D. Tracy (ed.), *Toward Vatican III*, 152.

60 *Pacem in terris*, 35, 38; *Populorum progressio*, 13; *Octogesima adveniens*, 50.

61 J. Gremillion, l.c., 129.

62 In the years 1949-1950 I had the opportunity to participate frequently in discussion groups with Gundlach where he most fervently rejected any connection between the biblical vision of the history of salvation and the dynamic concepts of historicity belonging to natural law. Other advisers of Pius XII, however, favoured a more dynamic vision.

63 J. Messner, "Aktualität des Naturrechts", in *Österreichische Zeitschrift für das öffentliche Recht* 27 (1976), 43-66.

64 O. von Nell-Breuning, *Soziale Sicherheit?*, Freiburg, 1979, 225, 227.

65 K. Marx, *Capital: A Critique of Political Economy*, (ed.), Frederick Engels, New York, 1967 (*Das Kapital*, vol. I published 1867, vols II and III edited after the death of Marx by F. Engels); J. Schumpeter, *History of Economic*

Analysis, Oxford and New York, 1954; Id., *Capitalism, Socialism and Democracy*, New York, 1950³; K. Polanyi and others, *Trade and Market in the Early Empires*, Glencoe/Ill., 1957; Id., (K. Polanyi), *The Great Transformation. Politische und ökonomische Ursprünge von Gesellschaften und Wirtschaftssystemen*, München, 1977; J. Habermas, *Zur Rekonstruktion des Historischen Materialismus*, Frankfurt, 1976.

66 Hegel, *Encyclopedia*, §§430-435.

67 Paul VI, *Octogesima adveniens*, 30, quoting John XXIII, *Pacem in terris*.

68 *Octogesima adveniens*, 42.

69 Card. Roy, *Reflections on the occasion of the tenth anniversary of the encyclical* Pacem in terris *of John XXIII*, April 11, 1973, 140.

70 Cf. *Pacem in terris*, 39-45, where among the signs of the times are underlined the ascent of the working class, the new consciousness of women, the longing of the people for independence, human experience of rights and duties; cf. *Gaudium et spes*, 5 and 6.

71 J. M. Pohier, Cl. Geffre, "Church Reform and individual Life", in D. Tracey (ed.), l.c., 108.

72 H. Zwiefelkofer, "Wandel der Gesellschaft und Pluralität der Erwartungen", in J. Wallraff (ed.), *Sozialethik im Wandel der Gesellschaft*, Limburg, 1974, 20.

73 H. Cox, l.c., 61.

74 Cf. D. A. Seeber, "Vakuum", in *Herderkorrespondenz* 33 (1979), 485-488.

75 Cf. D. Hollenbach, SJ, *Claims in Conflict. Retrieving and Renewing the Catholic Human Rights Tradition*, Paramus, N.J., 1979.

76 Cf. *Gaudium et spes*, 6-7, 9-10.

77 Cf. B. Häring, *Theology in Protest*, New York, 1970.

78 *Populorum progressio*, 32.

79 *Gaudium et spes*, 63,5.

80 Ch. E. Curran, "Social Ethics", l.c., 155.

81 A. Klose, *Die katholische Sozialethik. Ihr Anspruch, ihre Aktualität*, Graz, 1979, 45f.

82 E. H. Pless, "Wirtschaft und Ethik", in *Renovatio* 32 (1976), 53ff.

83 M. Harrington, *Socialism. The Accidental Century*, Baltimore, 1968; Id., *Toward a Democratic Left*, Baltimore, 1968; J. Eagleson (ed.), *Christians and Socialism. Movements in Latin America*, Maryknoll, N.Y., 1975; Cl. D. Kernig, *Sozialismus. Ein Handbuch*, 3 vols., Stuttgart, 1979/1980.

84 *Octogesima adveniens*, 31.

85 J. Robinson, *Die Gesellschaft als Wirtschaftsgesellschaft*, München, 1971, 43.

86 Cf. *Gaudium et spes*, 63,2.

87 J. P. Wogaman, l.c., 71.

88 Cf. J. Robinson, l.c., 101.

89 J. Nyerere, "Ujamaa": *The Basis of African Socialism*, Dar es Salaam, 1962, 8.

90 Cf. H. Ludwig, *Die Kirche im Prozess der gesellschaftlichen Differenzierung*, München, 1976, 190.

91 A. Smith, *An Inquiry into the Nature and Causes of the Wealth of the Nations*, 1776, Bk V, ch. II.

92 L. von Mises, *The Free and Responsible Commonwealth: An Exposition of the Ideas of Classical Liberalism* (tr. R. Raico), Princeton, N.J., 1962, 88-89; cf. G. Myrdal, *Value in Social Theory*, London, 1958; Id., *Against the Stream. Critical Essays on Economics*, New York, 1973.

93 J. P. Wogaman, l.c., 24.

94 Cf. *Mater et magistra*, 11.

95 Cf. *Populorum progressio*, 40; *Mater et magistra*, 206.

96 J. Robinson, *Freedom and Necessity*, London, 1970, 124.

[97] Cf. *Gaudium et spes,* 63; A. Tautscher, l.c., 81.
[98] I. Hill, "The Meaning of Ethics and Freedom", in I. Hill (ed.), *The Ethical Basis of Economic Freedom.* Chapel Hall, N.C., 1976, 19.
[99] Cf. J. A. Ryan, *Distributive Justice. The Right and Wrong of our Present Distribution of Wealth,* New York, 1927; E. Jacques, *Work, Creativity and Social Justice,* New York, 1970; T. Nagel, *The Possibility of Altruism,* Oxford, 1970; J. Rawls, *A Theory of Justice,* Cambridge/Mass., 1971; D. Miller, *Social Justice,* Oxford, 1976; P. Freire, *Pedagogy in Process,* New York, 1978; O. von Nell-Breuning, *Gerechtigkeit und Freiheit. Grundzüge katholischer Sozialethik,* Wien/München/Zurich, 1980.
[100] B. Häring, "Gottesgerechtigkeit und Lebensgerechtigkeit", in J. Feiner (ed.), *Mysterium Salutis V,* Zürich and Einsiedeln, 1976, 259-284; D. Goulet, *A New Moral Order. Development and Liberation Theology,* New York, 1974.
[101] P. Ramsey, *Basic Christian Ethics,* New York, 1950, 14.
[102] C. F. von Weizsäcker, *Der Garten des Menschlichen,* München, 1978⁴, 62.
[103] L. Kohlberg, "Education for Justice", in J. Gustafson and others, *Moral Education,* Cambridge/Mass., 1970, 81.
[104] O. von Nell-Breuning, *Soziale Sicherheit?,* Freiburg, 1979, 232, 235.
[105] *Mater et magistra,* 65.
[106] Cf. K. B. Clark, *Pathos and Power,* New York, 1974, 57-65.
[107] J. Rawls, l.c., 15.
[108] M. K. Gandhi, *All Are Brothers. Life and Thought of Mahatma Gandhi as told in his own Words,* Unesco, Geneva, 1958, 130.
[109] Message to U Thant, Secretary General of the UNO (November 19, 1970); text in J, Gremillion, l.c., 482.
[110] *Octogesima adveniens,* 22.
[111] *Gaudium et spes,* 66; cf. *Mater et magistra,* 82; *Populorum progressio,* 9; on racial discrimination, see G. Myrdal, *The American Dilemma. The Negro Problem in Modern Democracy,* New York, 1944.
[112] *Gaudium et spes,* 29.
[113] Ibid., 64; cf. *Populorum progressio,* 26.
[114] J. Gremillion, l.c., 117.
[115] *Gaudium et spes,* 70.
[116] Ibid., 31, 63, 65; cf. *Mater et magistra,* 61-67; *Pacem in terris,* 24, 34, 42.
[117] B. V. Manno, "Subsidiarity and Pluralism: A Social Philosophy Perspective" in D. Tracy (ed.), *Toward Vatican III,* New York, 1978, 319-333, quote 331.
[118] *Pacem in terris,* 42.
[119] Ibid., 43.
[120] Sr. A. Niel, "The Challenge of Sociobiology", l.c., 343.
[121] E. F. Schumacher, l.c., 244, 246.
[122] H. Cox, l.c., 75.
[123] *Octogesima adveniens,* 37.
[124] E. F. Schumacher, l.c., 243, 265.
[125] Cf. Ph. Schmitz, "Grundwerte Diskussion in den USA", in *Herderkorrespondenz* 33 (1979), 496-501, referring to G. Wills, *Invention America. Jefferson Declaration of Independence,* New York, 1978. The author thinks that already in that declaration the social dimension of freedom is not sufficiently developed.
[126] J. N. Kotre, "Of Human Fertility", in D. Tracy (ed.), l.c., 267.
[127] *Octogesima adveniens,* 23.
[128] John XXIII in *Mater et magistra* uses this text emphatically to assert an essential dimension of solidarity.
[129] *Populorum progressio,* 43-44.

[130] R. L. Heilbronner, *An Inquiry into the Human Prospect*, New York, 1975, 158.
[131] W. J. Baumol, "Business Responsibility and Economic Behaviour", in E. S. Phelps (ed.), *Altruism*, 45-46, quote 47.
[132] Ibid., 52.
[133] Cf. E. H. Sutherland, *White Collar Crimes*, New York, 1949 (new edition 1964), 247.
[134] Cf. D. F. Linowes, *The Corporate Conscience*, New York, 1974; G. A. Steiner and J. F. Steiner, *Issues in Business and Society*, New York, 1976²; N. H. Jacobi, P. Nehemkis, *Bribery and Extortion in World Business*, New York, 1977; G. Dworkin, G. Bernant, P. G. Brown, (eds.), *Markets and Morals*, Washington and London, 1977; C. van Dan and L. M. Sallaert (eds.), *Trends in Business Ethics. Implications for Decision Making*, London and Boston, 1978.
[135] Cf. E. H. Sutherland, l.c., K.-D. Opp, *Soziologie der Wirtschaftskriminalität*, München, 1975.
[136] K. Fiester, "How Labor Unions view and use Codes of Ethics", in I. Hill (ed.), l.c., 233-253, quote 242.
[137] K.-D. Opp, l.c., 84.
[138] St. N. Brenner and E. A. Morlander, "Is the Ethics of Business Changing?", in *Harvard Business Review* (Jan-Feb 1977), 60 and 62.
[139] K.-D. Opp, l.c., 31f.
[140] St. N. Brenner, l.c., 62.
[141] Ibid., 68.
[142] K.-D. Opp, l.c., 94; 121ff.
[143] K. C. Lodge, "Top Priority: Renovating our Ideology" in *Harvard Business Review* (Sept-Oct 1970), 50.
[144] Cf. K.-D. Opp, l.c., 94, 181, 190; St. N. Brenner, l.c., 66f.
[145] A. Z. Carr, "Can an Executive Afford a Conscience?" in *Harvard Business Review* (July-Aug 1970), 58; St. N. Brenner, l.c., 69.
[146] Cf. K.-D. Opp, l.c., 162, 150, 17.
[147] *Octogesima adveniens*, 35; cf. 26; cf. J. V. Robinson, *Accumulation of Capital*, London, 1956; Id., *Contributions to Modern Economics*, Oxford, 1978.
[148] Cf. F. U. Fack, *Soziale Marktwirtschaft*, Würzburg, 1979, 47.
[149] L. Keynes, *General Theory of Employment, Interest and Money*, 1936; cf. J. Hickes, *The Crisis in Keynesian Economics*, Oxford, 1974; H. E. Daly (ed.), *Toward a Steady State Economy*, San Francisco, 1974.
[150] J. P. Wogaman, l.c., 98f.
[151] *Populorum progressio*, 58.
[152] Cf. H. Kunst, H. Tenhumberg, l.c., 11.
[153] Cf. G. Myrdal, *Beyond the Welfare State. Planning in the Welfare States and its International Implications*, London, 1960; K. Bolz, *Grundfragen moderner Wirtschaftspolitik*, 3 vols., München, 1972; A. Campenhausen, *Kann der Staat alles besorgen? Zur Geringschätzung freier Initiative durch die öffentliche Hand*, Düsseldorf, 1976.
[154] *Octogesima adveniens*, 46.
[155] *Gaudium et spes*, 65,2.
[156] *Populorum progressio*, 33.
[157] Cf. C. F. von Weizsäcker, *Wege in der Gefahr. Eine Studie über Wirtschaft, Gesellschaft und Kriegsverhütung*, München, 1976, 39f., 47f., 80ff.
[158] A. Fazio, "Valori umani in economia" in *Parlamento* 25 (1979) N. 12, 20-24.
[159] Cf. H. F. Zacher, "Sozialrecht und Soziale Marktwirtschaft" in *Stimmer der Zeit* 198 (1980), 319-333.
[160] E. F. Schumacher, l.c., 269ff.
[161] J. P. Wogaman, l.c., 104 and 99.

[162] D. Munby, *Christianity and Economic Growth*, London, 1956, 303.
[163] Cf. E. Beutter, *Die Eigentumsordnung in der Moraltheologie des 19. Jahrunderts*, München and Paderborn, 1970.
[164] *Gaudium et spes*, 69.
[165] S.Th., II/II q 66, a 2: "Secundum jus naturale omnia sunt communia."
[166] *Gaudium et spes*, 69,2: The Council refers to the *Summa Theologica* II/II q 66, a 7, insisting: "Obviously for the correct application of the principle, all the conditions that are morally required must be met".
[167] *Populorum progressio*, 23; Ambrose, *De Nabuthe*, c. 12, n. 53, PL 14, 747.
[168] Cf. *Mater et magistra*, 43; *Gaudium et spes*, 34, 35, 67, 69, 71.
[169] *Mater et magistra*, 105.
[170] E. F. Schumacher, l.c., 55.
[171] A. B. Atkinson, *The Economics of Inequality*, Oxford, 1975, 38f.
[172] Cf. J. P. Wogaman, l.c., 96.
[173] O. von Nell-Breuning, Commentary on the chapter on socioeconomic life of Vatican II, *Lexikon für Theologie und Kirche* III, 513f.
[174] *Gaudium et spes*, 71; cf. *Populorum progressio*, 24.
[175] W. Kerber (ed.), *Eigentum und Bodenrecht. Materialien und Stellungnahmen*, Köln, 1972.
[176] Cf. the important document of the Pontifical Commission on Justice and Peace of August 6, 1977, on the universal destination of the goods of the earth; cf. R. Orfeo, "Vaticano: Parole nuove sulla proprietà", in *Rassegna di critica politica* 1 (1977) N. 5, 57-59.
[177] *Mater et magistra*, 55.
[178] *Gaudium et spes*, 71,4.
[179] *Quadragesimo anno*, AAS 23 (1931), 214; *Mater et magistra*, 116.
[180] W. Luijpen, *Existentielle Phänomenologie*, München, 1971, 173.
[181] Cf. K. Marx, "Kritik der Nationalökonomie", in Marx-Engels, *Kleine ökonomische Schriften*, Berlin, 1955, 104.
[182] E. F. Schumacher, l.c., 263ff.
[183] Ibid., 278.
[184] Cf. D. Clurman, *The Business Condominium. A New Form of Property Ownership*, New York, 1973; H. P. Steinbrenner, *Arbeitspartizipation. Modell einer neuen Unternehmensverfassung zur Emanzipation der Mitarbeiter*, Frankfurt and Zürich, 1974; G. D. Garson, *On Democratic Administration and Socialist Self-Management. A Comparative Survey emphasizing the Yugoslav Experience*, London, 1974; J. Vanek, *The Labour-Managed Economy*, London, 1977; J. C. Furlong, *Labor in the Boardroom. The Peaceful Revolution*, Princeton, N. J., 1977; B. Wilpert, A. Kudat, Y. Ozkam, *Worker's Participation in an Internationalized Economy*, Kent/Ohio, 1978; S. Pejovich (ed.), *The Co-Determination Movement in the West. Labor Participation in the Management of Business Firms*, Lexington/Mass., and Toronto, 1978; G. Fisher, *Ways to Self-Rule. Beyond Marxism and Anarchism*, Hicksville/N. Y., 1978.
[185] *Gaudium et spes*, 68,2; Pius XI, *Quadragesimo anno*, 65, 101; Pius XII, Allocution of June 3, 1950, AAS 42 (1959), 487; Allocution of March 11, 1951, AAS 43 (1951), 305; John XXIII, *Mater et magistra*, 84, 91-103.
[186] *Mater et magistra*, 93.
[187] W. E. von Ketteler, *Schriften*, (ed.), J. Mumbauer, Mainz, 1911, vol. III, 124, 134, 160.
[188] *Pacem in terris*, 20.
[189] Cf. A. F. Utz, *Philosophische Grundlagen der Wirtschafts- und Sozial-Politik*, Freiburg/S., 1961, 11-16; A. Tautscher, l.c., 114.

[190] J. P. Wogaman, l.c., 108.

[191] *Pacem in terris*, 19.

[192] *Gaudium et spes*, 68.

[193] Cf. H. Streithofen, *Wertmassstäbe der Gewerkschaftspolitik*, Freiburg/S., 1967; F. Hengsbach, SJ, "Die Kampfparität der Tarifpartner", in *Stimmen der Zeit* 198 (1980), 341-350; G. Radice, *The Industrial Democrats. Trade Unions in an Uncertain World*, London, 1978.

[194] Cf. J. Noonan, Jr., *The Scholastic Analysis of Usury*, Cambridge, 1957; Th. F. Divine, SJ, *Interest. An Historical and Analytical Study in Economics and Modern Ethics*, Milwaukee, 1959; W. Weber, *Geld und Zins in der spanischen Spätscholastik*, Münster, 1962.

[195] *Populorum progressio*, 24; cf. *Gaudium et spes*, 65.

[196] A. Fazio, l.c., 23; J. K. Galbraith, *Money: Whence it Came, Where it Went*, Boston, 1975; F. Beutter, *Zur sittlichen Beurteilung von Inflationen*, Freiburg, 1965; G. K. Kaltenbrunner, *Inflation ohne Ende. Wer verliert und wer gewinnt?*, Freiburg, 1977.

[197] Cf. J. Messner, *Der Funktionär. Seine Schlüsselstellung in der heutigen Gesellschaft*, Innsbruck, 1961; A. K. Rice, *The Enterprise and its Environment: A System Theory of Management and Organization*, London, 1963; R. W. Ackerman, *The Social Challenge to Business*, Cambridge/Mass., 1975; J. B. Condliffe, "Capitalist Enterprise and Bureaucracy", in I. Hill, l.c., 83-110.

[198] Cf. E. H. Plesser, "Wirtschaft und Ethik" in *Renovatio* 32 (1976), 56.

[199] R. C. Baumhart, *Harvard Business Review* (Jan-Feb 1977), 68.

[200] Cf. e.g., "Code of Ethics and Regulations of the Direct Selling Association", in I. Hill, l.c., 276-282; "Code of Ethics of the National Association of Realtors, l.c., 359-363.

[201] *Mater et magistra*, 137-140; K. Brunner (ed.), *The Economics of Price and Wage Controls*, Amsterdam, 1976; Th. G. Meyer, *Lohn- und Preiskontrollen als Instrument der Stabilitätspolitik, Begründung und Wirksamkeit*, Bochum, 1978.

[202] F. Tönnies, *Die Entwicklung der sozialen Frage bis zum Weltkrieg*, Berlin and Leipzig, 1919³; R. L. Camp, *The Papal Ideology of Social Reform: A Study in Historical Development 1878-1967*, Leiden, 1967; St.-E. Szyzik (ed.), *Christliches Gesellschaftsdenken im Umbruch*, Regensburg, 1977.

[203] *Mater et magistra*, 126-148; *Gaudium et spes*, 66; Paul VI to the FAO, November 9, 1974, 7 and 8; Text in J. Gremillion, l.c., 599-606.

[204] *Gaudium et spes*, 52; cf. *Octogesima adveniens*, 10-12.

[205] *Gaudium et spes*, 66,3.

[206] Cf. F. Coester, "Entscheidungsmöglichkeiten bei der Integration älterer Menschen", in H. J. Wallraff (ed.), *Sozialethik im Wandel der Gesellschaft*, Limburg, 1974; 82-106; D. C. Kimmel, *Adulthood and Aging. An Interdisciplinary Developmental View*, New York, 1974; A. Fontana, *The Last Frontier. The Social Meaning of Growing Old*, London, 1977; E. W. Marvin, *Planning for the Elderly*, Philadelphia, 1978; F. Mayer, *Schöpferisch alt werden*, Innsbruck, 1978.

[207] Cf. *Octogesima adveniens*, 8-10; J. R. Feagin, U. Hahn, *Ghetto Revolts. The Politics of Violence in American Cities*, New York, 1973; P. H. Furfey, *Love and Urban Ghetto*, Maryknoll, 1978.

[208] *Populorum progressio*, 3.

[209] Ibid., 52; cf. ibid., 7.

[210] Message to U Thant, Secretary General of the UNO, November 19, 1970, 9; Text in J. Gremillion, l.c., 479.

[211] Medellin document, *Justice and Peace*, 9, in J. Gremillion, l.c., 456-458.

[212] Cf. J. N. Behrman, "Codes for Transnational Enterprises" in I. Hill (ed.), l.c., 125-128; R. J. Barnet, R. E. Müller, *Global Reach. The Power of the Multinational Corporations*, New York, 1974; C. Hamelink, *The Corporate Village. The Role of Transnational Corporations in International Communication*, Rome, 1977; *Octogesima adveniens*, 44.

[213] Th. Dams, *Weltwirtschaft im Umbruch. Konfrontation oder Kooperation mit der Dritten Welt*, Freiburg, 1978; W. Brandt (ed.), *North-South. A Programme for Survival*. Report of an independent international commission offered to the Secretary General of the UNO, February, 1980.

[214] *Populorum progressio*, 47.

[215] Cf. R. L. Stivers, *The Sustainable Society: Ethics and Economic Growth*, Philadelphia, 1976.

[216] Cf. J. O. M. Bokris, W. E. Justi, *Wasserstoff. Energie für alle Zeiten. Konzept einer Sonnen-Wasserstoff-Wirtschaft*, München, 1980.

[217] M. Lamb in F. Lawrence, *Lonergan Workshop*, Missoula, 1978, 289.

[218] J. K. Galbraith, *How to Control the Military*, Garden City, N.J., 1969; G. and P. Mische, *Toward a Human World Order. Beyond the National Straitjacket*, New York, 1977.

Chapter Eight

The Ethics of Politics

We understand politics as organized, purposeful activity for the welfare of society and/or of particular groups in society in view of the common good. The innate purpose and meaning of politics is the common good of all people and all groups. Good political activity is a way of helping people to live faithfully in the freedom and solidarity that befit human dignity and make possible the attainment of social justice and peace.

The best possible result of political activity is to build up a public authority of freedom in covenant fidelity. It is not merely a question of how to protect my individual freedom and my interests; rather, it is to realize how to respond faithfully to that freedom which organized society makes possible, and to bring my freedom home into it as expression of solidarity and justice, for the benefit of others. It is an ongoing task, never done once-forever. Yet it implies also the willingness and capacity to make abiding investment of freedom in organized society for the benefit of family, small communities, the state and the world community.

For the authority of freedom, political ethics requests its genuineness, its power, its delicacy and strength in all spheres of political life, in the interaction between politics and culture, politics and economics, politics and family, politics and religion. Not only does political ethics ask generally for the requirements of freedom in these realms of life in view of the whole of human life in society, but in a fallen and redeemed world, it asks also for the requirements of conversion to genuine covenant morality.[1]

I. THE POLITICAL DIMENSION OF SOCIAL LIFE: ALL-PERVASIVE BUT NOT EXCLUSIVE

Those German citizens who, through their vote or through abstaining from voting or in any other way brought Hitler into political power, must realize how their political decision or irresponsible lack of it affected the life of nations, of churches, of families, and of the economic and cultural life almost everywhere. Of course, one of the reasons is the totalitarian and authoritarian character of Nazism. Therefore, we have also to think about the tragic consequences of the errors of other non-totalitarian political forces which allowed Hitler to become strong enough to enkindle a world war.

With the enormous growth of socialization and worldwide interaction, our political responsibility is constantly growing. Surely the gospel tells us that there is more than politics in our life and in the life of all people; but does this diminish our present political responsibility?

1. The politics of the Gospel

A first impression might be that the gospel is completely nonpolitical. Jesus is not a "politician" nor does he entrust political power to his apostles and disciples. There are no prescriptions for political activity for Christ's disciples, nor are they to be a political party along with others. Yet, divine revelation sheds its liberating light also on the political world, its misery and dangers, and shows the way of redemption and liberation from lust for power.[2]

a) Politics and the Kingdom of God

There is no doubt that the Old Testament, in almost all its parts and in its totality, deals with the political world. There is the paradigm of the exodus, leaving behind political security, the paradigm of the liberation of the oppressed who cry out to God, the conflict between the prophets and the political rulers whenever the latter contradict God's saving rule, the paradigm of the earthly kingdoms (including the dynasties of Israel) on the one hand, and on the other, God's own rule where there is no oppression and no exploitation. There are the promises of the coming Kingdom of God, expressed in political imagery, but promises not only for Israel. The new Israel will not follow the example of the ancient political powers with their oppression; it will be a servant to the nations, a sign that God cares for all of humankind.

Jesus, proclaiming the nearness of God's kingdom and his saving rule, frequently uses political imagery while making absolutely clear that the coming of God's kingdom is not the result of political power. One of the central and all-pervasive themes of the gospel is Jesus' conflict with a false messianic expectation. This should be seen in the light of the temptation paradigm. Political reductionism of the messianic expectation is the poisoned air around Jesus. He cannot allow even his disciples to call him publicly the Messiah, since the people, too, are contaminated by this dangerous spirit that would allow the privileged to draw power, wealth and first places from the coming Kingdom of God. When Peter refuses to accept the truth of the Servant-Messiah who renounces any political ambitions, Jesus calls him Satan: "Away with you, Satan; you are a stumbling block to me. You think as men do, not as God thinks" (Mt 16:23).

There is sometimes the impression that Jesus' chief enemies were the Pharisees, but this is an error, Jesus does everything to win them over, and finally many of them accepted his gospel and believed in his resurrection. His most fanatical enemies were the ruling class, most of them Sadducees, who did not believe in the resurrection and a life after death, and therefore were seeking "salvation" totally in the political realm. Luke especially is interested in showing that it was not the Jewish people, as such, who were guilty of Jesus' death. "Luke does not attribute significant responsibility to any Jewish group other than the chief priests and their allies."[3] They resorted to political manoeuvres to do away with him, and thus cooperated with the power of the Romans whom they hated. In their reductionism, they were totally a part of the political power game.

The gospel is not at all disinterested in political events. It puts the events of salvation emphatically into the context of political history (cf. Lk 1:5; 2:1; 3:1). The incarnation, the public activity of Jesus and his death are politically "dated". More than anything else, they concern world history.

Jesus' gospel about the coming kingdom of God is surely not a political manifesto. But it has enormous political implications. It is the fulfilment of the prophecies that, after the domineering earthly empire, the saving kingdom of God will come, where there will be no domination over others, where all will be servants of all, signs of God's love and saving justice, ministers of peace and solidarity among all men and women.

Where God's kingdom is accepted, there the poor will no longer be exploited and degraded; there healing mercy and saving justice will reign; there the blessed peacemakers will be; there even the persecuted will no longer hate but will demonstrate the power of reconciliation and love. The Beatitudes constitute the most revolutionary message and bring the greatest changes into the political realm wherever people live by faith.

This message has to do with those who are really poor and, up to now, downtrodden. And the "alas!" of Jesus points to those who possess the goods and the power of this world but who refuse the conversion made possible by the coming kingdom of God. It also implies a conversion not only to the transcendent God but to the God of history, and hence to the poor who then will be seated at the same table with the converted rich (cf. Lk 6:20ff).

By resisting the pervasive temptation to expect nothing other than a power-Messiah, and choosing the life of the suffering Servant of God, Jesus made a choice which was the most striking decision for world history and for the political realm as well. He could foresee the political implications: being put to death, death on a cross which was inflicted on slaves and political enemies, and death imposed by the political power of the Roman empire and the political abuse of religious authority. Jesus had acute judgment about the political situation. The fact that Christians confess One who is put to death by the Roman empire must have political implications.[4]

b) Jesus, the Prophet, denounces political abuse

Jesus calls Herod what he really is, a "fox", and denounces him as a bad political ruler who deserves contempt rather than deference (Lk 13:31-33). He frequently denounces the earthly rulers' ambition and lust for power, especially if they want, at the same time, to be religious leaders. In contrast to them, he defines the role and attitude of his disciples: they are not to act like "pagan rulers" (Lk 22:24-27; cf. Lk 9:47ff; 14:7-11; 17:7-10). He warns Pilate not to forget that his power over life and death comes from God (Jn 19:11). In the light of Jesus, his disciples recognized his mother as a prophetic sign that foretells the rule of the coming kingdom: "the arrogant of heart and mind he puts to rout, he has brought down monarchs from their thrones but the humble have been lifted high" (Lk 1:52).

If the disciples of Christ, especially the church authorities, had followed wholeheartedly the example and guidelines laid down by Jesus, this would have implied the most radical changes also in political life. His preaching of conversion, so explicitly in opposition to the demonism of abused political power, had to do with the redemption of the world. It remains a strong prophetic warning against those in power and those revolting who, like the Sadducees, expect everything from direct political action, and sacrifice for their political programme the transcendent dimensions of the eschatological preaching of Christ, and faith in resurrection.[5]

Jesus celebrates the messianic meal with outcasts, lepers, the downtrodden. He breaks the narrow national circle of the Jews by reaching out to the Samaritans and praising the faith of those who had no political or blood connection with Israel. He breaks political rules by the role he gives women, and his prophetic pattern opened the way to a new personal identity and social standing for women.[6]

By demythologizing political lust for power and the prestige of unjust wealth and success, Jesus gives true freedom for responsible political decisions and cooperation.

If the leaders of Israel had accepted Jesus' message of the coming kingdom, they would not have led the people into the catastrophe of civil war and destruction by the Romans. The same can be said about the later history in which, time and again, unprophetic and anti-prophetic churchmen opted for power, wealth, for the "two swords" of an earthly messianism. It is no wonder, then, that the revolt against a sacralized superiority remains in a vicious circle.

c) No political programme but a clear direction

Jesus did not enter the political arena as a part of it. His life and his message made him an outcast from the political game. Yet, as a prophet, he has spoken about the greatest evils in politics and, what is more, has given a clear direction for believers and for all people of good will. His goal-commandments of all-embracing love, service, reconciliation, absolute sincerity, healing and saving justice, would suffice to bring the reality of salvation also into the political reality. Docility to his Spirit and watchfulness for the present opportunities would ensure space for creative liberty and fidelity.

If humanity turns to Jesus wholeheartedly, then the promise of old, that the kingdom of God will bring oppressive empires and rulers to an end and bring forth an era of justice and peace, will manifest the true and strong political dimensions and implications of his gospel.[7]

Jesus truly wills and makes possible by his truth and the power of his Spirit a community built on love, solidarity, justice, sincerity and peacefulness. At the same time, he teaches us realism, the art of looking for the next possible step which, here and now, serves best on the road towards greater hope. In this realism, Jesus is paying for himself and for Peter the temple tax (Mt 17:24ff).

Jesus' message is eschatological and vertical: communion with God for everlasting life already beginning, while at the same time the salvation he offers implies a new fellowship, a new social life, which should prove here and now that we accept not only his promises but also the reign and rule of his kingdom.

His reign is not of this sinful world (cf. Jn 18:36); its renewing and transforming power may not be confused with the age-old means of political action. This is a warning for all liberation theology which neglects the eschatological dimension and expects almost everything from changed external structures. But it is equally true that the wholehearted acceptance of God's kingdom and, as consequence, the decision to seek first God's saving justice set free amazing energies for the political as well as the individual life (cf. Mt 6:33).

It is not a matter of equating political activity - giving "to Caesar what is due to Caesar" (Lk 20:24) - with faith and adoration, with paying God what is due to God. In the context, the word of Jesus means, rather, that only those who honour God as God and accept his saving rule can fulful their political obligation in the actual historical situation. Caesar will never get his due, nor will we ever understand the "politics of the gospel" unless we try, above all, to understand what is due to God, who sends us his only begotten Son as Saviour of the world.

2. Political theology[8]

a) A new consciousness

The numerous theologians who asserted simply that Jesus' mission was non-political, spiritual and eschatological, came to this conclusion because they had a rather narrow concept of politics. They did not find what they were looking for: direct political advice and Jesus' participation in a political career. In the light of the new consciousness expressed in political theology, and frequently even by opponents of political theology, we discover more easily the political horizon of Jesus' life and death and of the apostolic community, and the political implications of their original and authentic religious choices.

A political theology can be as false and one-sided as the theology of those who simply ignore the political dimension of redemption. It is lopsided and misleading when its main concern is political or when the political stance of the theologians decides, practically or theoretically, their theological concerns and vision. Political theology has a sound starting point when the first thing it seeks is God's kingdom, faith, hope, love and adoration in spirit and truth.

The limited and yet important purpose of a healthy "political theology" is the study of the interaction between religion, on the one side, in its truest and less true manifestations, and on the other side, the political dimension of human life, including the actual political situation.

We have seen that the parables and much of the message of Jesus are expressed in images taken from political experience of that time. Political theology is a "pastorally" oriented theology. First, it intends to sharpen the consciousness of the political consequences of each religious choice and style. And secondly, it calls for a sharpened critical self-examination about political ideas, ideals, ideologies and interests which might illegitimately determine the horizon of our religious and theological thought and practice.

When political theology and its practice sometimes give the impression of one-sidedness, then we should not forget the one-sidedness of an individualistic, pietistic, merely vertical thought-pattern and practice. The catechism of the community of Isolotto (Florence) evidently implies a certain direction of political practice; but those who, in the name of eternal truth, condemned it thoroughly might ask themselves whether their unchangeable formulas, their emphasis on mere theological opinions, their "spirituality", were not politically conditioned and still condition or favour a political option.

Political theology reminds us that, in the eyes of early Christianity, Jesus was conscious that faith in him and discipleship would cause conflicts within the clan and beyond it. Strictly theological truth can be formulated with a clear note of contrast with political situations. When Paul writes, "We, by contrast, have citizenship *(politeuma)* in heaven, and from heaven we expect our deliverer *(soter)* to come, the Lord *(kyrios)* Jesus Christ" (Phil 3:20), he is warning not only generically those whose minds are "set on earthly things", but he is opposing the religious-political claims of the Roman emperor to be the "deliverer and Lord". It implies the refusal of the cult of the emperor and any kind of practice that contradicts citizenship in the reign of Christ.

Theology and churchmen constantly have to test not only what they say and do but also what they omit to say and do in view of the often hidden interaction between political interests and religious structures and thought. We must ask how all this will influence or will omit to influence as it should, the political life in the strict and broadest sense.

The political theology of J. B. Metz centres on what rightly is considered the centre of our faith-practice, the memorial of our Lord's death and resurrection. He urges the wealthy, the powerful people who participate or refuse to participate responsibly in the political life (especially of the super-powers) to ask themselves, in the light of this memorial, why and how they cause suffering, and how this suffering is related to the passion of Christ.[9] This is surely not a flight from faith into politics, but the earnestness of faith in all realms of life and especially in politics.

Political theology does not intend to present us with an obliging model of integration of the European national state in a unified Europe, but it bids us to examine all possible models to find whether and how they foster worldwide solidarity, peace and reconciliation, and how they serve the cause of liberty and subsidiarity.[10]

It seems easy to show how church structures (monarchical or extremely hierarchical, collegial, centralistic or federal) have a political background and political implications. It is obvious that those who truly desire a participatory society will not continue to equate "church" with a centralistic church authority. But we ask whether the most intimate and direct expressions of faith, such as prayer, are also to be tested in the light of a political theology.

b) Politics and prayer

The two volumes of *Political Night Prayer in Cologne*,[11] edited by Dorothee Sölle and Fulbert Steffensky, surely make the connection between prayer and politics; but one must ask oneself whether prayer, here, is not "used" as political activity and weapon. Is it still prayer first and above all, prayer whose first purpose is to recognize and honour God as God? Are people turning to God, or are they turning him to their political opinion? But if we so ask, then we must also have the courage to face the other question: whether there are kinds of prayer, liturgical and other, that arise unconsciously from a false political option, or manifest a flight from political responsibility, and "use" God for private interests.

In authentic Christian prayer, we enter into the mystery of Christ, the Redeemer and Brother of all. We respond personally and in solidarity to God, *our* Father, who calls us his children and calls us to be his family. If, in prayer, we ask that God's name be hallowed, then those in the street who have no name are recognized as our brothers and sisters. Finding our own unique name, we shall not use others as a means, as political fanaticism and terrorism do so frequently and as political powers are constantly tempted to do. If, in prayer, we are truly longing for God's kingdom to come, then we are also desiring that all people - the powerful and rich, the downtrodden and exploited - may experience its coming by being drawn to each other in this experience of faith. "To pray is to seek the coming of the kingdom, the achievement of its values in the society in which we live. It is to accept our political vocation to help transform that society."[12]

The new identity which we find in prayer must take flesh and blood in social structures, in everything we can do "politically" so that God's will, which calls for brotherhood and reconciliation, may be done; that the bread of the earth may become "our" bread for all, and that institutionalized temptations may give way to healthier structures and relationships. But through genuine prayer, all this transcends the category of "must". It becomes an innermost need, an expression of a new freedom.

Joseph Gremillion, reflecting on the thoughts of Paul VI about the "rebirth of Utopias" (Oct. adv. 37), whereby the Spirit of the Lord who dwells in our heart urges man "to go beyond every system and every ideology", points to the many prayer groups around the globe that, in creative and shared prayer, open themselves to the great concerns of justice and peace beyond national borders.[13]

Christian liturgy, as proclamation of the word of God and school and practice of "adoration in spirit and truth", has an impact on the political reality not by political intention but rather by its very authenticity. "Whoever has had experience with totalitarian political systems knows that Christian worship, as such, even if no political word is to be heard in it, is a politicum of the highest rank. . . If one comes from a political cult assembly to a simple act of worship, then he may be touched by an atmosphere of freedom."[14] Men in political authority may frequently not realize what it means that the Christian community includes them in their prayer. "But if the victims of a depraved political power are remembered, it is quite different, since those who victimized them desire that their names should be forgotten."[15] For the community of believers, nobody is a non-person or an enemy to be annihilated.

3. Christian politics or politics of Christians?

In view of our own identity in our dialogue and cooperation with all people, it is important to consider the question; "Is there a 'Christian politics' or should we rather speak of a 'politics of Christians'?"

We may speak of a "politics of the gospel" as a direction or absolute "utopia", an obliging but never fully realized ideal which, time and again, produces relative utopias and liberates believers for realistic and discussible policies. But, for a number of reasons, we do better not to claim a "Christian politics".[16] First, Christians have no monopoly on politics. The Spirit of God can operate everywhere and grant wisdom and discernment. Secondly, no Christian should dare to call his political activity simply "Christian". It is always so imperfect that we must be most careful about identifying politics with the name of Christ. Thirdly, Christians, in faithfulness to their faith and conscience, can make choices for various political models.[17] Trutz Rendtorff will find agreement not only in his evangelical church but also among many Catholics when he writes: "There is a distinctively Christian ethic of politics only in the concrete form of a pragmatic, rational and humane politics. Such an ethic not only includes a pluralism in the political dispute, but this kind of pluralism makes possible also a vital rationality of such dispute; for Christian faith liberates us from the temptation to try to realize through political activity what we expect as content of faith and hope of salvation".[18]

Another Protestant theologian expresses the same conviction with the strongest words: "Just as there does not exist a Christian medicine, there exists no Christian politics, while there are Christians in politics; and, just as in the healing profession, they are needed in politics".[19] Jacques Ellul gives a convincing reason for these distinctions. The Christian "does not christianize the state. On the other side, he presents a series of demands based on another view of reality".[20] He emphasizes, possibly too strongly, the Christian's direct witness in political activity for the ultimate reality in which he believes. He tends to justify the presence of Christians in the political arena not so much by political concern as by the immediate intention to evangelize people. If, as we think, the Christian's presence in politics intends, above all, to contribute to beneficial political decisions, the Christian should be able to express his political options in a rational way.

When we speak here of the distinctive character of the political activity of faithful and enlightened Christians, we do not mean this in an exclusive way. Each of these notes can probably be found also among non-Christians.

The true Christian will do everything in that love which Christ has revealed and which is a fruit of the Spirit. If the Christian ought to act everywhere in love of God and neighbour, in solidarity with all of God's children, then this holds true, too, for his political choices. Of course, this does not mean that he can transform all of politics into pure love. Politics can no more be the full reign of love than the state can be the kingdom of God. But the political activity of Christians can qualify itself by the strength of their love. Where redeemed love is active, a politics of naked power cannot reign, nor can love eliminate the need of power.[21] Yet love can give meaning to the proper use of power. Christians who are nourished by the word of God and care for purity of intention should be best qualified to discern what love requires and what kind of means best embody it.

The Christian's contribution is one among many others. Do they make visible what a readiness to serve can do, over and above what particular interests can do? Do they draw attention to what the "reign of God" intends for humankind? In the best of Christian tradition, faith is much more than assent to a truth; it is, rather, a total openness for redeemed and redeeming love.

Christians whose faith and life bring everything home into the memory of Christ's death and resurrection will make their choices for the underprivileged in such a way that solidarity and dedication to the common good give place to everyone, and especially to those who cannot act as pressure groups.

A clear Christian vision liberates from exclusiveness and fanaticism, and makes one free for discernment and genuine dialogue. The authentic Christian will not bedevil his opponent but will discover his concerns and good reasons. Aware that a clear option for the ideals indicated by the gospel and by human experience does not confer any kind of infallibility, Christians can choose different parties with different programmes. Since the different positions are only human and partially conditioned by one's upbringing, social and cultural milieu and other factors, tolerant Christians can easily split into different groups and movements. This diversity, "far from manifesting the incompetence of Christian thought, will be a striking expression of Christian freedom".[22]

If they have the love, freedom and discernment befitting their faith, Christians will work for meaningful solutions to conflicts and thus bring fruitfully into politics the Christian vision of reconciliation.

A mature Christian will not allow anyone to patronize his political choices.[23] He knows that he cannot honour Christ and his church or serve the common good without being faithful to his own conscience.

A Christian who lives the dimensions of the history of salvation in gratitude for the past, vigilance for the present opportunities and in active hope for the future, will not be alienated by rigid schemes. His clear orientation to an abiding ideal will go hand in hand with a realistic assessment of the present chances and of the next possible step in the proper direction. He will never sacrifice persons to abstract ideals, nor will he try to impose particular solutions as if they were of universal validity. On this point, Paul VI remarks: "Such is not our ambition, nor is it our mission. It is up to the Christian communities to analyze with objectivity the situation which is proper to their own country".[24]

4. Church community and politics[25]

a) The new situation

From the time of Constantine the Great, the church organization (institution) tended to imitate the structures of empire. This led to a "monarchical episcopacy" and a centralized, monarchical, empire-like papacy. More and more, the bishops took over political functions. The bishop of Rome, with the legacy of the church-state met the political powers as one of them. The centralized church government called itself simply "the church". Its "diplomatic" representatives were simultaneously deans of the diplomatic corps in the various empires and kingdoms and supervisors of the bishops. This "church" was meant to guarantee the status quo of the political powers, and the latter were expected, in turn, to be the "secular arm" of the church, to enforce its moral and religious teaching, and all too often, its political positions.

This situation had an enormous impact on all relationships within the church, and even on theological concepts as, for instance, the concept of sin. For those "under the church" (subjects of the church) religion could and had to be privatized, since they had nothing to say about the public life which was in the hands of the earthly powers, including the earthly powers of a centralized church. It is one of the miracles of history that, in spite of this situation, prophetic charisms in the church did not die out, and that, throughout all times, prophets spoke in a way totally different from "knowledge of dominion".

The problem with which we are dealing here is no longer the historical model "church-state relationship"; rather, it is the relationship between the community of believers and the political community[26] which, becoming more and more democratic, emphasizes the participation of all citizens in policy-making decisions. The question arises immediately: What does it mean today if the pope or bishops address themselves to actual political questions without allowing the community of believers to participate in the evaluation? The new situation manifests itself when, for instance, before the Synod of bishops dealing with questions of justice and peace in Rome, their whole Christian communities were first consulted. This is an important sign of our times.

Nothing better can happen for the church, in her relations with the various political communities (from village to world-community) than a thorough-going reflection on her own *identity*, wherein the following main results become more and more visible and effective.

The church understands herself as a community of salvation gifted with salvation knowledge, a holistic vision with no political pretensions or political privileges, and giving most attention to the prophetic charisms within herself and even outside her visible boundaries. In renewing her institutional structures according to a more "sacramental" self-understanding (a visible sign of union with God and solidarity with humankind), she is realizing in a new way that she does not give to God what is due to him unless she respects fully the competence of the earthly political communities.

The Second Vatican Council expresses this programme emphatically: "The role and the competence of the church being what it is, she must in no way be confused with the political community nor bound to any political system. For she is at once a sign and a safeguard of the transcendence of the human person."[27] From this vision follows also that Christian citizens do not practise politics in the name of the shepherds of the church but in their own name as citizens.[28]

It is equally a blessing for humanity if the political powers confine themselves to their realm, renouncing all temptations to define the creed or religious activities of their citizens. For the political powers, it is a liberating event if, in sincere dialogue, they encounter a church-community that has no political self-interest but only an absolute dedication to salvation, the wholeness of people, and the unity of all in justice and peace.

b) Breaking the vicious circle of clericalism and anti-clericalism

Church and humanity have suffered terribly because of church authorities and political authorities overstepping the limits of their competence and intruding on each other's domain. Popes, bishops and priests as private persons, may have good political discernment; they may, in some extraordinary and dangerous situations, take over temporarily some political responsibilities. But they cannot do this as an act of their competence in their divine mission. They must terminate their subsidiary task as soon as possible, as an act of justice to both the church community and the political community.

From their habitual transgressions of the boundaries of religious competence, popes, the Roman curia, bishops and their curias, and priests acquired a bad habit that blinded them also to the limits of their competence in theological, moral and religious questions: limits arising from the very boundaries of the office and divine mission, from the limits of their acquired experience and knowledge, or self-imposed limits due to their refusal to dialogue or to discern the signs of the times. The clergy's transgression of the limits of their competence by intruding into the realm of political powers was labelled "clericalism". The inevitable reaction was an anticlericalism which was also unable or unwilling to acknowledge the limits of the state's competence.

The utterances, decisions and activities of churchmen must not only judiciously observe the boundaries of competence but must also display a historical memory that is sensitive to the other side, in view of a long history of damaging clericalism.

It seems to me that the programmes and activity of Pope John Paul II cannot be fully appreciated without giving attention to this need. If a priest, as a good citizen and competent in political science and practice, takes the seat of a congressman or senator, there is, in principle, nothing wrong so long as it is an exceptional case and everyone is aware that his political activity is carried on in his own name as a citizen, and not in the name of the church community. But it is dangerous if priests and religious feel that they are the ones most competent for political activities. In the given reality of history, this smells of clericalism. Therefore the warning, "You are ministers of the people of God, ministers of faith and dispensers and witnesses of the love of Christ for men . . . be priests and religious, and not social-political leaders or functionaries of an earthly power".[29]

If priests think that lay people are not equally qualified for political tasks they should ask themselves as priests whether they fully respect the role and mission of lay people, and whether they have done their best to help them to become religiously and morally competent in the exercise of their political competence. Priestly formation, although it should include social and political ethics, is not at all a school for politics.

c) Ministry of reconciliation

Popes, bishops and priests must in no way conceal the fact that their privileged mission is to be ambassadors of reconciliation, messengers of peace, servants of all of God's people. Therefore, they must not give the impression that they are part of a political faction or party. Of course, Christians should accept each other fully in the community of faith and worship, while belonging to different political organizations and adhering to different political, economic and cultural programmes; but the fact is that often they do not. The priest or bishop is not in a position to be an effective sign and minister of unity and reconciliation when he himself speaks and acts publicly as a party-man without making it very clear to everyone that he is not speaking as bishop or priest but strictly as a citizen only. But how can he make this clear when he speaks on political ethics where there are vested interests of one group, and he seems to be very much a part of that group?

The ministry of reconciliation and the proclamation of God's reign for all spheres of life, including the political dimension, require absolutely that those entrusted to such a mission seek no power, honour or wealth in the pursuit of their mission, neither for themselves nor for the church as institution. On this point, the Second Vatican Council, after an interesting debate, made a solemn pledge: "Still, she (the church) does not lodge her hope in privileges conferred by civil authority. Indeed, she stands ready to renounce the exercise of certain legitimately acquired rights if it becomes clear that their use raises doubt about the sincerity of her witness or that conditions of life demand some other arrangement".[30] This is a bill payable on sight. It surely includes renouncing, once and forever, the temptation to use the political powers as "brachium saeculare" (the secular arm) for enforcing the church's creeds and moral teaching.[31]

The church's prophetic ministry is for all people, peace and justice for all, respect for human dignity, justice and opportunity for the poor and oppressed, and all basic human rights. In the name of humanness and in the name of Christ the Reconciler, the church will urge the political powers to make only the most necessary use of enforcement and vindictive justice, and to do all that can be done for the healing of social wounds and for the rehabilitation of law-breakers.

d) The "diplomatic papal corps" and prophetic conflict

One of the most gigantic tasks of church reform today might be to harmonize continuity with healthy discontinuity in the institution and functions of the Papal Diplomatic Corps with the "Secretary of State of his Holiness" as head. Name and organization point to the past which, in this respect, is to be critically remembered and redeemed. The position of the Nuncios as deans of the diplomatic corps accredited to the various countries, the whole system of honours and promotion, the conjoining of diplomatic tasks with enormous influence on control and on the nomination of bishops, pose great problems and can constitute an outright institutionalized temptation to be less faithful to the prophetic mission of the servant-church.

On the other hand, it is all too easy to postulate a total suppression of this institution which does still play an important role in the church's endeavour for peace and for a world-community of nations. How can an appropriate education of those in the church's diplomatic service transform this service into a thoroughly pastoral ministry of a prophetic church without radically changing the structures? Are honours and promotions in the traditional form necessary or acceptable in view of motivation and prophetic credibility? Surely not for those who are guided by the Spirit!

The diplomatic corps seems to be necessary or at least useful for stable relations between the church-community, the states and international organizations, but is the identity of the church sufficiently evident in all this? The conflict of conscience with earthly powers, who intend to use the institutional church and its diplomatic representatives for their own goals, is the conflict between an all-too-institutional church and the great prophetic men and women. Is not this conflict more serious than that of those who, for the sake of the gospel, suffer persecution and discrimination through unjust political systems?

One thing is sure which the Lord predicted for his disciples, apostles and their successors: that faithfulness to his mission will bring them opposition and persecution from the powerful of this earth, including those who make religion a career for power, honours and wealth (cf. Mk 13:9; Mt 10:17ff).

5. The horizon of political interaction and responsibility

To understand better the importance of political education and the difficulties of political ethics, we can remember here what was an over-all theme in previous chapters: the interdependence between politics on the one side and, on the other, family, culture, economy, ecology. A political ethics isolated from the total context is no longer thinkable today. There has to be a profound recognition of the magnitude of the task of synthesis, coordination, integration, of temporary subsidiarity for matters which do not properly belong to the political power - all without falling into the traps of totalitarian or authoritarian systems.

Here, not only the state in its classical sovereignty and centralism is meant, but political responsibility of each citizen, of political bodies, townships, counties, provinces, states, federal governments and legislators, and last but not least, of world organizations.

a) Politics and family

The family is the cell of society. Its structure, whether the older patriarchal form with a more or less authoritarian *paterfamilias* as head of the three-generation family, the matriarchal structure or today's partnership pattern, will be almost unavoidably reflected in a society's political organization, or at least in strong political inclinations. And reciprocally, almost all political decisions affect family life in one way or another, in stability and health or in disorder and trouble. Therefore, many governments have a special department for family affairs, not only to prepare special legislation concerning families and to oversee their application if laws are passed, but also to study all political decisions in view of their impact on family life.

Societal upheaval and cultural and political insecurity tend to undermine, or at least to jeopardize, the stability of marriage and family. Unbridled capitalism has had devastating effects on the whole institution of marriage and family.

It is a matter of justice, and in the interest of the whole of society and the political communities, that politics should avoid everything that weakens the health, harmony, and especially the stability of families, while protecting very positively the rights and conditions of family life. The legislator can pass laws that favour stability or restrict divorce, but the political task is surely not fulfilled just by legally disallowing any divorce, while nothing positive is done about unfavourable economic, cultural and political conditions that contribute to the break-up of marriages.

Not only the external stability of marriages is at stake; politics has to be concerned with life conditions and laws that favour peace in families and the best possibilities for the family's educational tasks. The political communities at their various levels have to make their contribution to education and advancement of culture, but by doing so, they ought to be most careful of the principle of subsidiarity where the basic rights and duties of families and other educational entities are concerned.

All levels of politics have to take responsible positions in the various demographic situations. It is surely poor politics to fight overpopulation only or mainly by promoting means of contraception, sterilization, and the inhuman "right" to abortion by choice. Much more can be done by a general education for sexual responsibility and by promotion of equal rights and the best possible education for women. Where, as in Germany and several other highly industrialized countries, the population problem is the trend towards a one-child or no-child family, the offer of a certain amount of financial support for each child is not an adequate answer. A well-intentioned political promotion of this kind of solution arouses the selfish cry, "Let those who want many children bear the burden". In its very structure and in its explanation and application, legislation should make evident that it is not just a matter of helping poor families to raise their children; rather, it is a matter of the "generation covenant". Just as the aged, who have made their contribution to economic welfare, have a right to receive social security from what the present generation produces, so the covenant relationship should be extended to the coming generation through those families who are willing to educate children, and thus make a most substantial contribution to the future security of the present working generation.

To let families with three and more children bear the whole burden of education (or, as in the United States, even to impose on them practically a double educational tax if they do not yield to the state monopoly of education) is not only injustice to these families but disrupts the "generation-covenant".[32]

b) Politics and culture

Rational and wise politics is a part and important expression of culture. In all its dimensions, politics depends on the over-all health and growth of culture. One of the original sins of the so-called "nation-states" of past centuries was a tendency towards a cultural melting pot, disregarding or discriminating against certain social, ethnic or other sub-cultures.

The richness and diversity of a culture are, above all, a matter of the free society. The government should respect most carefully the cultural activities of groups and bodies other than political. But legislators and governments at their various levels should be aware of the interplay between the existing cultures and politics. The best contribution politics can make for the development of cultures is to assure an equal chance and freedom for all citizens in the realm of cultural initiatives and activities.

c) Politics and economy

The interaction between economy and politics differs widely, according to the ideology or the system that determines economic life. Extreme capitalistic liberalism not only restricts the state's economic politics but, because it divides the various social dimensions into self-regulating, autonomous spheres, it has little space for a constructive, integrated policy. According to Frederick Engels' and others' interpretation of Marxism, the economic forces and relationships determine all of the superstructures, including politics. Marxists see the politics of the capitalist society as nothing else than class-war carried on by the privileged classes; whereas in the future socialistic society, both politics and class-war would cease. They tell us that in a classless society with its scientific, self-regulating economy and where everyone seeks the benefit of all, there will be no need for politics. The state is expected to disappear.

The fact that this scientific prediction did not occur after the Soviet revolution was one of the great dilemmas. The answer seemed to be twofold: first, that the prophecies would come true when Communism was installed all over the world; and secondly, according to Stalin's theory, the social consciousness - itself a supra-structure of economic processes and relationships - was "lagging behind", and therefore it was the duty of the communist party (that is, the political power) to hasten this new consciousness by political enforcement.[33]

The mixed system of the social free market acknowledges the complexity of the interaction between the economic forces, relations and processes on the one side and, on the other, culture and politics. The role of politics for economic order and transformation ought to allow the principle of subsidiarity. Politics has a corrective and supplementary function. An example is the need for extensive research programmes subsidized or financed by governments when private enterprise does not or cannot carry on research for development of medium-size and labour-intensive technologies.[34]

d) Politics and ecology

The urgency of the ecological problems and the scarcity of indispensable resources have an enormous impact on and beyond the whole interplay of politics and economy. All political bodies, from the township up to international organizations, have to examine carefully the various economic processes and relationships with regard to their impact on the ecospheres and on human health. This new need and a corresponding consciousness make impossible for the future a laissez-faire capitalism and a merely national economy. Unless all social forces, cultural, religious and economic, show greater responsibility for these burning problems, we cannot avoid the probability that the ecological problems and the scarcity of resources will lead to wars and to totalitarian régimes.

6. The possibility and necessity of a political ethics

In politics, we encounter a great deal of distasteful moralism.[35] Politicians glorify or justify individual or group egotism. Ancient emperors, despite all their misdeeds, made themselves god-like and great benefactors. In democratic societies and elsewhere, moral judgments all too easily become tools of demagoguery or hostility. Politicians not infrequently use splendidly phrased moral principles as empty rhetoric. Regrettable as this may be, it points to an almost universal conviction that politics has to do with justice and injustice, with good and evil.

a) Negation of the possibility of political ethics

In politics, positivism, in its many shades, has no place for creative freedom and moral responsibilities. The methodology of a "value-free" empirical research by historians, sociologists and others has its justification within certain limits. In studying situations, interactions, trends, one should not try to use factual material to prove ethical principles or religious truths. But the very study of politics shows that people are convinced that some actions are just or unjust, and that some people act like evil persons while others deserve moral admiration.

From the methodology of objective, unbiased research it does not follow that there are no moral values involved, unless one indulges in a regrettable reductionism. Leaving space for creative freedom and taking seriously the claims of moral responsibilities do not exclude, however, the fact that many political misdeeds or crimes might be conditioned by prevailing ideologies, a low level of collective consciousness, or other causes.

The theories of Karl Marx were conditioned, at least partially, by the positivism prevailing in his time and by an ideal of science that wanted to explain everything by necessary causality.[36] "Scientific socialism", at least as Engels understood it, left no place for an ethics. The very nature of economic man and of economic processes would supposedly lead to the final classless society where morality would not be necessary because, given the saving economic structures after the proletariate revolution, everyone would care for the common good. Indeed, at any phase there need be only the appeal, "Be conscious of sociological conditions and act accordingly".[37]

At the same time, it cannot be denied that Marxism offers a vision of universal solidarity and justice which contains high moral values, even if their justification is offered as "scientific analysis" and if the means seem to us to be heretical and devastating.[38]

Niccolo Machiavelli was interested in morality and religion insofar as they help to produce subservient and loyal citizens. For the rulers, however, there was the first and supreme principle: to keep power. They could use means which up to now were labelled as immoral and criminal, if these were necessary for their purposes. The virtue of princes was to be brave in combat and successful in the use of power.[39]

b) The political ethics of conformists and non-conformists

A division into conformists and non-conformists is not so much a matter of systematic ethical thought as a result of presuppositions often accepted uncritically or even unconsciously. But looking critically at moral systems or treatises on political ethics, one has to inquire whether the one or the other tendency and mentality prevail. For the conformists, the emphasis is on conservation, security, stability of the given "order", and consequently a trend towards absolute allegiance and uncritical obedience or, on the side of the rulers, the trend to act just as the others do.

The Catholic tradition of natural law was sometimes dynamic enough to discern and to refuse conformism where political activity contradicted the principles of natural rights; but in other epochs, the natural law theory was conceived too statically and, therefore, did not favour a critical mind and responsible attitude of nonconformism.

Among Christians, since the time of Constantine the Great, there have been both conformists and non-conformists, and both sometimes have used religious arguments for their own ethics. But above all, there was and is the influence of interests, temperaments, the cultural environment, and the prevailing philosophies and world views.

c) The role of theology in public ethics

Whoever studies the history of the Old Testament prophets and of prophetic men and women throughout the history of the church and other world religions cannot deny the influence of faith on political ethics. We have already given attention to the "politics of the gospel", the direct or indirect teaching of the New Testament on political ethics. The fruitfulness of religious doctrine and symbols for the political realm depends, however, on the dynamics of faith. With Reinhold Niebuhr we can say: "The prophetic faith in God who is both the ground and the ultimate fulfilment of existence, who is both the creator and the judge of the world, is involved in every moral situation."[40]

But Reinhold Niebuhr believes at the same time that the basic insight into the over-all principle of justice is common to all humankind. "Every human society does have something like a natural-law concept; for it assumes that there are more immutable and purer principles of justice than those actually embodied in its obviously relative laws."[41] Improvement of civil laws and customs would not be possible if people did not have a deeper intuition about justice and fairness. "Every society needs working principles of justice as criteria for its positive law and system of restraints. The profoundest of these actually transcend reason and lie rooted in religious conceptions of the meaning of existence."[42]

The rights of the human person to be respected, honoured and promoted by political authorities, as expressed in 1948 and later by the United Nations Organization, comprise a good platform on which the great religions can meet with authentic humanists everywhere and define at least some basic principles of politics. The point of departure is, first and in all questions, the understanding of human existence in its We-Thou-I relationships.

In 1516 - at almost the same time as Machiavelli's writings - two great Christians and humanists published outlines of a humanist political ethics: Thomas More in his *Utopia*, and Erasmus of Rotterdam in his *Institutio principis christiani*.[43] Thomas More believes in the power of holistic formation of the public as guarantee of justice and peace. He believes that the conflicts of interests of individuals, groups and nations can be overcome on the basis of a fully human education. Erasmus' ideal is a Christian, humanistic pacifism: Christian insofar as it is based on the redeeming love revealed in Christ and on the common Christian conviction that justice and peace are the most urgent implications of love. He believes that Christians could win over all men of good will if they are on the road to a politics of the Sermon on the Mount and of genuine humanness.

d) Pluralism of political ethics

There is a possibility and even inevitability of a certain pluralism in political ethics, according to the diversity of cultures, religious and political needs and opportunities. A genuine pluralism would allow constructive dialogue and enriching cooperation if the art of dialogue in various "languages" (cultural expressions) were part and parcel of universal education.

However, history gives us the horrifying causes and results of a most heretical pluralism connected with political polytheism. In the pagan antiquity of Europe and the Middle East, every political entity had its own gods who patronized the conflicts and wars for each side.

When people truly believe in One God, Creator and Father of all people, then conflicts take on a different shape. Faith in God, of itself, will be the constant monitor for reconciliation. But in the sad reality of history, theological monotheism frequently went hand in hand with a practical "polytheism" of political ethics. Christians, Jews and Moslems were fighting "holy wars" in the name of God, monopolizing the "one" God for their national and ideological interests. What, for instance, was the image of God in the crusades for the sacred places? What were the hidden political interests that castrated monotheism and transformed it into a battle cry? And were not the nationalistic wars of the last centuries among nominally Christian nations with Christian rulers practically a heretical political polytheism? The humiliating fact is that powerful churchmen and church communities practically confiscated their God for their irrational patriotism.

The basis of this heresy was that kind of privatizing and ideologizing of religion which could not see directly and clearly the political implications of the creed and, on the other hand, the tendencies of divinizing political authorities in the nation-states to the point where allegiance to the rulers' heretical polytheism became a requirement of religious obedience. All too often, this process was linked to an earthly messianism whereby powerful nations felt divinely called to be God's instrument on the political scene.

Hitler and Rosenberg made their own brand of religion for justification of superiority over other nations and for elimination of Jews and Gypsies. So, at least, everyone could see the political heresy. In 1935, I heard Cardinal Faulhaber, then archbishop of Munich, telling a small group of students that Hitler's national socialism combined all the heresies of all ages in one great heresy.

National wars, especially colonial wars, made in the name of the One God of the Christian creed, were sacrilegious attempts to introduce political polytheism into the Christian religion.

II. POLITICS IN THE LIGHT OF THE HISTORY OF CREATION, SIN, REDEMPTION

Political ethics and activity cannot ignore the complexity of the history in which the main actor is God, the Creator and Redeemer, but which, concretely, is carried on by men and women who are God's masterpieces but at the same time are involved in the long history of collective sinfulness and personal sins. But for Christians, the last word is not sin but redemption, reconciliation, forgiveness. One of the reasons for the pluralism of political ethics among Christians is the different vision and emphasis in the tension between the fallenness and the redemption.

1. Redemption-liberation and forgiveness in the midst of conflict

The pessimist calls himself "realist" when he continually points to the sinfulness of the world and especially to the sins of the enemies. A superficial optimist has not the courage to face the evil in himself and in the world around him. The authentic Christian vision never forgets the cross of Christ, where the evil - including political evil - becomes most visible; but the decisive words on the cross are a promise of trust and a testament of reconciliation and forgiveness.

Responsible Christian politics faces the terrible evil perpetrated by politics and by the refusal to see political responsibility in the light of the resurrection. The resurrection is the absolute sign of reconciliation's final victory, the victory shared by those who seek wisdom and prudence in the light of both the death and the resurrection of Christ.

In politics, integralism is mostly a combination of self-righteousness and pessimism about sin in the world, especially in the world of enemies. The integralist tends to deny that there is any possibility of dialogue with the other. He anticipates already the final separation of sheep from goats. Redemption, in its all-embracing extension as explained by the Second Vatican Council, inspires the Christian realist to overcome the ancient "friend-enemy" mentality, and to seek whatever is good in the political opponent, in order to better understand him. For example, Christian humanists will meet the humanistic traits and trends in socialism and in Marxism, and pursue a patient dialogue in view of cooperation in the cause of justice, peace and human rights.

However, faith in the final victory of redemption does not authorize any ideology of necessary and constant progress of true humanism. There is always man's freedom that can betray the liberation offered by Christ, and there is always the massive investment of past sins in history which can be overcome only by that solidarity which is a central truth of Christian faith. The fight for the good and against the evil in us and in the world is a constant task. "Progress in good - say, in civilization considered as the diminution of the *traces* of 'original sin' - can never be guaranteed to be once-for-all; to believe otherwise is to accept the *myth* of progress."[44]

The distinctive Christian vision of the tension between sin and reconciliation imposes on Christians a distinctive presence in the political arena. They will confess their sins, expose and denounce the collective sins of their own group and nation: sins of nationalism, of an earthly messianism, accountability for war, war crimes such as bombing open cities, dropping atom-bombs on unarmed people, antisemitism, and so on. Thus they will seek forgiveness in solidaric contrition and, at the same time, humbly offer forgiveness to the other side.

The basic value of forgiveness in the light of redemption wrought by Christ would radically change the value-scale of politics. The order of justice and the quest for security will not be abolished but transformed and integrated in a liberating way. Something in us and in our collective consciousness dies: offended pride, resentment, the monster of "vindictive justice" which, in reality, often is nothing else than vindictive self-righteousness in disguise. Only thus can the circle of hatred be broken. "Hatred has no creative power", Father Kolbe told his fellow prisoners - and in this way also his torturers - in the concentration camp. His testament was one of forgiveness.[45]

2. The role of the state in a fallen-redeemed world

The role of the state cannot be exactly the same in all respects for all times and circumstances. Bible and tradition contain time-bound statements, but they also give valuable indications of abiding direction. It is always a fallen and redeemed world in which the state has to fulfil its role.

a) Some indications of the New Testament

What the New Testament says about the state and its role has to be seen in the eschatological perspective. "Those who, in the midst of the faith-community, have found their true *polis* (city) and live according to its laws can no longer consider the state or this earth altogether as the ground of their existence. As far as the state concerns us, it is only a tent that will be removed . . . Fatherland and state are not the soil in which we are rooted forever. State and politics are not, on principle, rejected or bedeviled but are deprived of divine appearance and thus relativized."[46]

The fact that early Christians expected the parousia in a not too distant future was not without influence on their understanding of politics or on their neglect to give proper attention to politics. However, for all times, the eschatological expectation has implications for our relationship with the state. The knowledge about the end of the earthly city allows us to recognize the world - including the realm of politics - in its true character as God's creation, contaminated by the "sin of the world" but also called back to the truth by redemption.

Christians do appreciate order and tranquillity guaranteed by good rulers; hence the exhortation: "First of all, then, I urge that petitions, prayers, intercessions and thanksgiving be offered for all men; for sovereigns and all in high office, that we may lead a tranquil and quiet life in full observance of religion and high standards of morality" (1 Tim 2:1-2).

The faithful are admonished to submit themselves to "every human institution for the sake of the Lord, whether to the sovereign as supreme, or to the governor as his deputy for the punishment of criminals and the commendation of those who do right. For it is the will of God that by your conduct you should put ignorance and stupidity to silence" (1 Pet 2:13-15). Here an intrinsic reason is indicated for the requested submission in view of the service the rulers render to order; but the main emphasis seems to be on the credibility and acceptability of Christians. Christians should be recognized as promoters of peace and of an orderly life (cf. Tit 3:1).

The most quoted text of the New Testament on duties to the state is Romans 13:1-7. This text is not simply an approval of politics as we encounter it, but a general recognition of the role of the state and the duties of political authorities insofar as they fulfil their task for justice and order as "God's agents". The text does not at all request absolute obedience but "submission", and forbids a rebellious attitude. "Every person must submit to the supreme authorities" (13:1). An anarchical attitude against the state and state authorities is surely rejected. But submission is not the same as an undiscerning obedience. Paul's letter to the Romans (13:8) brings home into the vision of the commandment of love the citizen's duties to the state. The submission is understood as recognition of the God-willed functions of the political authority. To recognize the purpose of the state and to acknowledge gratefully whatever is good in the exercise of political authority prevent the danger of bedeviling politics.

However, early Christianity was fully aware of the sinfulness of the concrete state, the Roman empire. Following the prophetic traditions, it denounced the idolatrous traits of the actual politics (cf. Rev ch. 13). Christians were to refuse participation in this idolatry in which one of the symbols was the cult which the Roman emperors requested for themselves. When Christians preferred tortures and martyrdom rather than to yield, this was not a lack of "submission" to the political authorities as such, but rather an indispensable service to the state, so that it might free itself from this perverse alienation.

b) For authority but against the totalitarian state

Aristotle defined man as *zóon politicón*, a political animal. He gave too much to the political dimension, and his commentators all too often yielded to the temptation to hand man over totally to the state or to measure his value according to his political activity. Against any kind of totalitarian interpretation, Thomas Aquinas wrote: "Man's ordination to the political community is not in his totality and not in everything that belongs to him".[47]

Catholic social-doctrine tradition balances the role of the state by the reciprocity of the two concepts of solidarity and subsidiarity. The role of the state and other political institutions is to coordinate activities whenever this is necessary for the common good. Especially in view of the many conflicts arising in the socio-economic field, this role is strongly felt today. Paul VI writes: "It is true that in the term 'politics' many confusions are possible and must be clarified, but each man feels that in the social and economic field, both national and international, the ultimate decisions rest with political power".[48]

Subsidiarity says, above all, three important things: first, the state should not arrogate to itself social, economic and cultural tasks which other groups can properly fulfil; secondly, within political life there should not prevail an overpowering centralism; the federal principle should favour the intermediary political entities; and thirdly, there must be space for liberty of the individual person and families. In our time, the principle of subsidiarity and the federal structure become vital in view of the necessity of world organizations and some kind of world authority.

The political community needs authorities able to represent it in its internal and external affairs. To function properly, they depend greatly on the consensus of those whom they intend to represent. The consensus has to be not only on their legitimacy but also on basic values that support solidarity and unity, and give meaning and purpose to politics. These values are especially the dignity of each person, and creative liberty and solidarity. The submission meant in Romans 13:1, or consensus in favour of the political community and its authorities, implies also the readiness to renounce those manifestations of freedom which would practically negate or irresponsibly diminish the equality, liberty and opportunities of other persons or groups.

Public authorities ought to show temperance not only by keeping their activity within the limits of their competence but also by not multiplying laws beyond what is strictly necessary or highly useful for the common good. Intemperate multiplication of laws leads either to an intolerant police state or diminishes the value of legislation. Thomas Aquinas warned: "Nobody can be obliged to impossible things; therefore, if an authority introduces or imposes so many laws that the citizen cannot fulfil them, he is excused from sin."[49] The "submission" or consensus to the political community does not include the willingness to be unnecessarily deprived of meaningful expressions of creative liberty or to be overburdened by unnecessary or useless laws.

c) The modern welfare state

The church of today affirms the modern welfare state which not only promotes the production of the most needed goods, and frequently can guarantee a certain affluence, but even more, cares for the underprivileged so that they, too, can have a fair share. John XXIII showed himself rather enthusiastic about the ideal modern welfare state, for the church "is also solicitous for the requirements of men in their daily lives, not merely those relating to food and sustenance but also to their comfort and advancement in various kinds of goods".[50]

Beyond the minimum necessities, the welfare state offers - or tries to guarantee - health services, education (although frequently with an unacceptable trend towards monopolization), housing, training in skills, social communication and social security.[51] Paul VI praises the welfare state when it promotes not only material development but an integral development which is for him "a new name for peace".[52]

3. Taxes

The modern welfare state, by implication, is also a tax state.[53] Taxes are a serious concern for most people. Over the centuries, the meaning, extension and modality of taxes and customs have changed greatly. Ethical consideration has to take note of this. The few things the Bible tells us about taxes have to be seen in the historical context.

In Israel, people had to pay in the form of a tithe which, in the theocracy, was at the same time church-tax and state-tax. The prophet Samuel severely judged the way the kings of the nations imposed on their subjects compulsory work and unbearable taxes, and warned that kings in Israel would do the same (Sam 8:10-18). From then on, the prophets of Israel frequently denounced the abuse of political power that exploited the citizens.

In Jesus' time, tax-collectors were considered public sinners, not only because they cooperated with the colonial power but because many of them enriched themselves by arbitrarily and immoderately increasing their own share. For Zaccheus, a superintendent of taxes, the faith experience was therefore also an awareness of having cheated people and of the need to repay (Lk 19:8).

For many of Jesus' contemporaries, the question was not only whether they were obliged in conscience to pay taxes to a foreign colonial power, but even more the sharper problem: "Are we or are we not permitted to pay taxes to the Roman emperor?" (Mk 12:14). The meaning of Jesus' response, "Pay Caesar what is due to Caesar, and pay God what is due to God" (Mk 12:17), has found various interpretations. Was it ony a rebuke to the inquirers, since they were not sincere in their question? It seems that the word implies somehow that, although the emphasis is on "giving to God what is due to God", Jesus also acknowledges the givenness of Caesar's political sovereignty and hence his right to request taxes.[54] Evidently, disputes about taxes are not meaningful in Jesus' eyes, if people do not really care to give to God what is due to God.

The apostle Paul, a Roman citizen, gives direct and emphatic advice about paying taxes. After having taught that "submission" to political authority is not just a matter of fear of punishment but an obligation of conscience, he continues: "That is also why you pay taxes. The authorities are in God's service, and to these duties they devote their energies. Discharge your obligations to all men, pay tax and toll, reverence and respect to those to whom they are due" (Rom 13:5-7). Through the payment of taxes the service of political officials is honoured and repaid.

The question of whether all the taxes were just was not approached. For the young Christian community, any effort to amend the tax-system was out of the question. They would surely have disapproved of the cheating of tax collectors, but they had no chance to reform the questionable system of tax-leaseholding which left ample freedom for the lessee to determine his own share as long as he paid the stipulated sum to the authorities. Today, in a political system where we can raise our voices, we would not be content only to warn the tax collectors not to exact too much; we would insist on changing the rules of the game.

From the seventeenth to the nineteenth century, moralists were, in their hearts, sharply critical of the tax system of absolutist rulers who had enormous income from their own holdings and, at the same time, used a great part of tax and custom income for their luxurious living and senseless wars. Since severe state censorship prevented an open statement about the crying injustice of this system, moralists took the side of the taxpayers, declaring that the laws of tax and toll were mere "penal laws" not binding in conscience, yet not allowing open rebellion by those who had tried to escape from tax or custom payments and had to pay a fine.

Today, at least in the democratic societies, the situation is different. The ethical question is no longer confined to whether the citizen is, in justice, held to observe just laws of tax and custom, but rather whether, by his vote and participation in the formation of public opinion, he cooperates in supporting just tax legislation. There is not only the sin of tax-evasion by trying to escape tax payments; there is frequently the greater injustice of blocking proper legislation through powerful pressure groups and through cooperation in these sins because of individual and group selfishness.

The most abominable tax crimes are committed by members of the legislating bodies who, for personal benefits, back the already over-privileged groups to the detriment of the less-privileged and of the welfare of all.

Whoever affirms the welfare state ought to be willing to pay the taxes decreed for guaranteeing the purposes of social justice. He should also, in conscience, feel obliged to cooperate responsibly in having just tax laws passed.

No responsible citizen can be indifferent to how legislators and administrators use the taxes collected. The burning question today seems to be: what can be done in the rich industrialized countries and in developing countries to prevent the rulers from spending more for armament than for education, medicare, rehabilitation of the handicapped and so many other humane purposes?

In a democratic welfare state where the rules of the tax game are fairly well observed, the very affirmation of democracy recognizes that tax laws must generally be observed in conscience. Of course, this does not exclude a critical mind and efforts to amend legislation and uncover frauds by legislators and the administration. There can arise extreme situations when, for instance, tax moneys are used for nationalistic military goals, where the defence budget grows because of an unjust power politics, or where tax money is used to finance abortions which have no serious therapeutic purpose. In such circumstances, public protest and eventually even tax strike cannot be categorically excluded.

Tax crimes committed by legislators and officials, as well as by taxpayers, require restitution in the best possible form.

4. Power, redeemed or unredeemed[55]

Decades ago my venerated teacher, Romano Guardini, wrote that the decisive question of the forthcoming era would be the question of power: will humanity be able to control it enough to guarantee its rational use for justice; or will the era be one of prepotent power, of man controlled by irrational power?[56] Jacob Burckhardt considered the power of the state simply as evil, while Friedrich Nietzsche glorified the will to gain power and to use it over others.[57] In their own way, both positions lead to the bedevilment of power.

a) The glory and the power

God is all-powerful. He reveals his power through the glory of his truth, goodness, love and beauty. Love between the Father and the Son in the Holy Spirit is the most intimate source of all power and glory revealed in creation and salvation history.

By creating woman and man in his image and likeness, God gives them power over the earth. He empowers them to discover and to manifest his glory by respecting each other's freedom and dignity, and by becoming for each other ever more an image of his love and beauty. But as soon as they eat of the forbidden fruit of power, making themselves independent of God, they will domineer over each other, and their power over the earth will bring disorder into their mutual relationships, into their environment, and into human history.

Men and women have to cultivate the power of their love: to love God with all their powers, including the power of their passions for what is good, honest and beautiful, and their wrath against evil, especially the evil of abusing others. And how could they learn to love God with all their powers unless they love and respect each other? The noble purpose of power - of people empowered by God - is for good, for love, for justice.

Redeemed power - power received gratefully from God and shared with each other - is the power to persist in truth and to preserve each other in truth. True human glory is earned by power used in the service of God and of one another. But this power, entrusted by God to human responsibility and co-responsibility, can be woefully perverted.

To resist the self-glorification of human power is an essential part of the first commandment, but also a part of the commandment of mutual love. "There is only one way to legitimatize power: to share it with others. Power that refuses sharing or, in other words, power not transformed into love, becomes mere domination and oppression."[58]

b) Demon power

Of itself, power - that is, power used in the truthfulness of its purpose and its divine origin - is good. It is the evil person who makes it a demon when he listens to the serpent and arrogates power to himself regardless of God and of fellowmen. Power as well as knowledge of dominion, is demonized by its divorce from love, service, knowledge of salvation.

The danger in church and world is the monopolizing of power.

Then it degenerates into tyranny. Where rulers are unwilling to share authority and power with others, where they refuse to seek with others the vision of wholeness and the rational use of power, the monopolizing monarchs or oligarchs try to impose on others their "truth" which is an ideology interwoven with their self-interest. Thus power, divorced from service to the common good and from the common search for truth, becomes prepotence, domination, oppression. Lord Acton said it well: "Power tends to corrupt, and absolute power corrupts absolutely".[59]

Consciousness of our collective sinfulness obliges us to control very carefully the use of our own power and especially that of those who are in power. The state needs power in order to diminish the ruthless power of evil; but if political power serves mainly the self-interest of the ruling class, it contradicts the power and reign of God, who is honoured if all use their capacities and powers in view of the whole, the common good.

A functioning democracy is best able to check political power, but even orderly democracies easily tend to become oligarchies, the rule of a minority for their own purposes which contradict the common good. A way to withstand more easily the danger of demonic prepotence is by division of powers among the state's legislative, judiciary and administrative realms.

But no political constitution or structure works automatically for freedom and justice. We all are in need of redemption from lust for power and self-glorification. The earthly city urgently needs those who, with all their heart and mind, believe in the Servant-Messiah, Jesus, who in his whole life and especially in his passion and death, unmasked the satan of prepotence and ruthless power.

Our battle is not against spirits and discarnate ideas or human foes but "against the authorities and potentates of this dark world" (Eph 6:12). The superhuman forces of evil militate against God's saving reign and against us through those who, in the exercise of their great power, pervert everything by their personal and collective egotism and lust for dominion. The person who abuses God-given power by trying to make others his slaves or tools falls under the power of the demons. Fighting against demons is fighting against abuse of earthly power.

c) Dealing rationally with power

Power is fully rational in the sense of redemption-liberation when it takes sides with the powerless of this earth. God has manifested his supreme power on the cross of Jesus, who made himself powerless even against those who misused their political authority and power. Blessed are the powerless if they refuse to be caught in the vicious circle of blind violence. Blessed are those who, by non-violent action, convert the powerful to the use of power in justice for all. And blessed are the rich countries which treat the developing poor countries as equals. But superpowers that think they can keep their superiority over others by threat of annihilation are surely not rational. The irrational display of superpowers in foreign politics unleashes also irrational tendencies inside their own countries.

To allow a powerful group of party-men or bureaucrats to plan and engineer the whole national industry and business gives them so much power that mere human beings cannot reasonably be expected to avoid the temptation to misuse their power and exploit people. Too great a concentration of power within the nation-state leads also to irrational conduct in the field of foreign relations.

Political power is rational if it submits to justice, law and order. A rational power uses force only where strictly necessary. Then the moderate use of force, which is not intended to break people's free will but only to prevent them from perpetrating unjust violence on others, can be, indeed, a paradoxical work of love.

Solidarity, expressed by consensus on basic human rights and duties and a common concern for social justice and fair processes, strengthens rationality in the use of power. The principle of subsidiarity, which forbids the concentration of power in one person or group, requires and assures the necessary harmony.

Rationality of power implies clear and just purposes and the use of means that best respect human rights and the common good. The purposes ought to be the most noble ones. But on the road towards a clear goal, rationality sometimes requires a compromise, In politics, the prudent compromise seeks the degree of power that can protect and promote peace and justice in an evil world. While the goal should always be to guarantee space for freedom, love and justice, political prudence may sometimes recommend the acceptance of allies of whom one cannot fully approve and temporary indulgence of distasteful displays of egotism. On the other hand, there can be sometimes the dire obligation to oppose people whose motives are quite worthy of respect.

A political career might imply compromises not only with other forces and people but even with oneself, by furthering one's own ambition through service to what one considers a good cause. But one becomes the slave of irrational ambition and power as soon as one compromises by betraying the clear goal of justice and truth and/or by using means that clearly contradict it.

d) Power versus violence

The state has not or should not have a monopoly of power. Its power should not try to make powerless as many people and groups as possible. But the legitimate political authorities have, in a certain sense, a monopoly on the use of violence where this is the only feasible way to check unjust violence. In other words, "they hold the power of the sword" (Rom 13:4). It is a sign of authentic authority if violent means, such as severe punishment of criminals and especially the death penalty, are almost unnecessary.

The common teaching of the church is that state authorities never, under any circumstances, have the right to torture people. The most atrocious use of violence is that of modern war. Can it ever be justified? (cf. Chapter Nine).

If restricted to the most extreme cases, violence can sometimes be an act of love, just as justice is a modality of love. However, the use of violence may never intend to break a person's free will or induce him to do anything against his sincere conscience. The purpose of legitimate violence is to hinder or prevent people from doing wrong against others or against the common good.

Police should receive the best possible training for temperance and non-violent action. But in dangerous situations, the principle holds that the condition of the forces of order must be better than those of the unjust offender-aggressors. If on one side the police are ordered to abstain from violence insofar as possible, it is only fair that criminals who violently attack them should receive particularly severe punishment.

The state may use violence only within the strict limits of justice, and according to well-defined laws.

The presence of Christians in politics ought to point to the ideal of non-violent use of power. Even when there is an extreme need to use legitimate violence against unjust violence, Christians should cooperate only with deep regret, clearly manifesting that they would surely prefer non-violent solutions, and that their love still reaches out to those whom they have to oppose by violent means.

If state authorities use violence or command its use for an unjust cause, everyone has to refuse cooperation and, if possible, to protest and try to persuade them to desist from the unjust use of violence. Every state needs people who foster non-violent use of power even if, in the eyes of the political authorities, this ideal cannot always be put fully into practice.

5. Criminal law, enforcement and rehabilitation[60]

a) Power and justice in a sinful world

In a sinful world where criminal elements threaten life, freedom, property and other rights of their fellowmen, a minimum of justice and security sometimes cannot be safeguarded without a political power able and willing to use even drastic means of criminal law enforcement. But Christian legislators and citizens should never forget that the decisive word of God for us and our sinful world is the word of redemption, forgiveness and reconciliation. And this must have its impact also on legislation, on courts, and especially on the system of correction and rehabilitation.

It is sad to observe that ultraconservative Christians of the various churches, who look to God mainly as judge, sometimes yield even more than unbelievers to the biological and tradition-based reaction of revenge. They put their trust more in vindictive justice than in constructive approaches. The consequences are disastrous for society and for the credibility of their faith-witness. Believers whose lives are deeply marked by faith experience of forgiveness and reconciliation through Christ will fulfil a therapeutic mission even in the realm of criminal law.

We distinguish three phases of criminal law: (1) legislation, (2) administration of justice, and (3) application of the court decision.

(1) Criminal legislation ought to manifest temperance and be combined with measures designed to remove the main causes of criminality. In order to be an effective deterrent, the laws must be clear, well motivated, and in no way heavier on the poor and powerless than on the rich and powerful.

(2) Administration of justice ought to be fair and to be guided by profound knowledge of psychology and of the impact of the social milieu. The main purpose is reconciliation of the offender with society, expressed through atonement (punishment). The court, which defends society's common good, ought to refrain when possible from unnecessary means of punishment such as "civil disabilities" and jail, insofar as these means make difficult or even impossible the reinsertion of the offender into society. In other words, they block a lasting reconciliation. Juvenile courts should be especially careful in this regard.

(3) The penal system should be thoroughly free from any sign of revenge. Imprisonment ought not to be considered as the most ordinary means of correction. If the United States of America paid 1.25 billion dollars on prisons and only about 30 to 40 million for rehabilitation,[61] this shows a tragic lack of imagination and purposefulness. By now, it is well known that in most cases the present system of prisons does not serve the purpose of correction.

Government should provide the best possible probation staffs. Christians who feel their vocation to be "ambassadors of reconciliation", and can acquire the necessary education for it, should be in the correctional system to humanize it from within, and to bring their direct experience to bear on public opinion and legislation. Here is a decisive test of whether we believe truthfully in the divine Healer who, through his disciples, reaches out to the outcasts. The inmates of our prisons need professional assistance and, most of all the friendship and presence of people who help them to discover their own inner resources for what is good.

b) Sin versus crime

Criminal law does not make saints. Conversion to the good cannot be obtained by law and even less by law enforcement. Politics surely has to do with socially desirable conduct, but for that purpose enforcement should take the last place, while constructive approaches for social justice, ethical education and environmental improvement can give far better returns. A police state, with too many and too severe criminal laws and a revengeful punishment system, may intimidate the less dangerous elements but will provoke more violent reactions and greater criminal skill in other offenders.

Law and morality are neither identical nor totally separate. There is a relation of polarity. Law should serve the self-realization of individuals in their social mutuality and solidarity. Citizens, legislators and political officers have a moral responsibility for good legislation and fair application of good laws. For this goal, it would be a disastrous illusion to dream of forming a perfect society by trying to enforce almost all of morality and good conduct by criminal law.

Criminal law should have as its object only socially *dangerous* conduct. And to be effective, it should include only those actions which are morally disapproved of and considered socially dangerous by a decisive part of the population. Legislators should be continually watched for whether or not their passing a criminal law is a kind of flight from passing constructive laws that tackle the deeper causes of crime.

c) Non-punishment is not the same as approval

Punishment ought to have only a subsidiary function in the fight against wrong and socially undesirable conduct. It is pitiful if ordinary citizens and even legislators think that everything is allowed that is not forbidden under criminal law. The legislator can strongly disapprove of a certain kind of conduct, or realize that it is morally unacceptable, yet for various reasons of political prudence, he may reject law enforcement.

This is the case, for instance, in the actual abortion law of the German Federal Republic. The constitution obliges the legislator to protect the unborn human life; but if there is a serious therapeutic reason or grave social distress, there is no prosecution if the woman has brought her case before a commission where she is instructed about alternatives and possible help. In all these cases it is not said that there is a legal right to interrupt pregnancy but only that, under the particular circumstances, the case does not fall under criminal law.

In the United States the legislation is evidently different. If the taxpayer has to pay for abortion on request, this seems to mean that the woman has a right to abortion. Does it not also mean that she has a right to irresponsible sexual activity and to successive abortions at the taxpayers' expense?

Several legislatures acknowledge exemption from punishment for those (especially youth) who use forbidden drugs. The purpose is to obtain easier cooperation for therapy. The same laws, however, make provisions for better information about the dangers of these drugs and the injustices that people commit against society when, by drug abuse, they risk becoming unable to work and expose themselves to the danger of committing crimes under the impulse of addiction. This is a clear case where exemption from punishment does not at all mean approval of the social conduct.

Recent legislation against drug addiction shows a growing worldwide consciousness that criminal law is not only ineffective but also unjust, if it is not integrated into a whole package of legislation that provides better therapy and removes, insofar as possible, the social evils that are the main causes of this pestilence.

In this context we recognize that most of the penal laws of the church are understood as therapeutic laws (*poenae medicinales*). They do not apply in cases where malice cannot be presumed; and those who fall under these punishments - normally, exclusion from the sacraments - have a right to be absolved as soon as they manifest good will. The so-called "vindictive punishments" (*poenae vindicativae*) are not meant as a kind of revenge but to underline the need of reparation. They are comparable to the "civil disabilities" of secular criminal law. In the life of today's church these punishments are becoming less frequent.

The exclusion from the sacraments (especially from communion) of divorced and invalidly remarried Catholics who, in spite of all good will, cannot in conscience dissolve a present stable and helpful union, is neither a vindictive nor a therapeutic punishment. It seems that this provision makes some sense only if it is a deterrent for others. Does it make sense at all when this function is no longer effective and, indeed, alienates many people from the church? Especially sad is the situation of parents who are trying to bring up their children as Catholics, but can never join them in receiving the Eucharist.

d) Fighting political corruption[62]

Although most citizens behave benevolently most of the time, David Hume argues that legislators are well advised to establish social control mechanisms as if people were self-serving egoists. If this postulate is realistic, it seems to apply even more strictly to the political actors who, all too frequently, pursue egoistic goals to the detriment of the common good.[63]

In the course of history, especially in eras of absolutism, ethical treatises tended to reveal extreme pessimism about ordinary people's moral qualities, but an even more excessive optimism about the moral standards and wisdom of the rulers. History proves how little ground existed for this optimism, especially when rulers sought no counsel from wise citizens, shared no power with others, and did not allow the control mechanisms to apply to themselves.

Today a worldwide conviction is growing that it is plain hypocrisy to apply criminal law to ordinary citizens where there is no legal provision to fight the corruption of the political actors. Asked for the name, the species and number of political crimes, this demon could well respond as the demons who begged to enter the swine: "My name is Legion, there are so many of us" (Mk 5:9). Throughout history, the worst of these demons were too seldom recognized in their unclean character while they sowed hatred against other nations, other ethnic groups or social classes, causing wars, senseless revolts, unjust revolutions, intrigues and lies that caused horrible suffering to many people and nations. Only recently, churchmen, journalists and Amnesty International have been publicly unmasking one of the ugliest political crimes, the torture of political opponents and the hiring of murderers to kill those who are working for a more humane world. The declarations of the UNO on human rights make it easier to call by name some of these demons.

Men and women in influential political positions are especially exposed to bribery and other forms of corruption in favour of big business and pressure groups. While powerless young men are being jailed for minor cases of larceny, legislators and other political actors, who give and take bribes for lobbying in favour of powerful groups or for blocking prosecution of gravely dangerous practices, are frequently exempt from punishment.

In June 1980, the West German Parliament passed a moral code describing a number of political crimes. Politicians accepting payment for lobbying in favour of business, industry or other powerful groups, get away with only the publication of this conduct if they are caught. Is this sufficient for fighting such abuses effectively, and is it at all proportionate with other provisions of our criminal codes?

Law and control mechanisms should remove, as far as possible, permanent causes of conflicts between private interests and the common good. "Regulation of conflicts of interest seeks to prevent situations of temptation from arising."[64] Hence, among other requirements, "officials in congress and the executive branch should be required publicly to disclose their financial holdings and activities".[65]

There should be international courts not only of arbitration but also for prosecution of governmental criminal conduct in international affairs and especially for war crimes. But it should not be "the victor's justice". A common decision of all nations for such an international, absolutely impartial institution would greatly contribute to sharpening the conscience of political and military actors. Such a criminal law is most necessary as a deterrent.

III. PARTICIPATORY SOCIETY

Creative liberty, creative covenant fidelity and shared responsibility are fundamental values not only for individual self-realization but also for all dimensions of social life. We have to study, therefore, how the political community should be structured to favour these qualities in individuals and groups, and how it can be sustained by them. "The concepts of participation, responsibility, conscience and freedom are interwoven."[66]

Documents of the World Council of Churches and of the magisterium of the Catholic church have increasingly proposed the ideal of the "participatory society". It applies to the development of the partnership structure in modern marriage and family life and, in its own way, to the economic, cultural and political realms. Everywhere the aim should be for the highest and best possible form of active participation by all the constituent parts and members. What has gradually been affirmed in Catholic social doctrine about an over-all participation on all levels of economy now comes more and more to the foreground also in political life.

Personal rights and active participation are interdependent. The Second Vatican Council emphasizes this point: "The protection of personal right is a necessary condition for the active participation of citizens, whether as individuals or collectively, in the life and government of the state".[67] Paul VI, fully aware of the complexity of political choices, spoke out strongly on the "demand made by the man of today" for a greater sharing of responsibility "in the political realm". "This legitimate aspiration becomes more evident as the cultural level rises and the sense of freedom develops, and as man becomes more aware of how, in a world facing an uncertain future, the choices of today already condition the life of tomorrow."[68]

It can be foreseen that this strong option for a participatory society will, of necessity, have its impact also on the structures of the church, just as in past centuries the alliance with the world's monarchies moulded the changeable institutional aspects of the church. A judicious adjustment ought to be made, in careful fidelity to the biblical self-understanding of the church as the people of God, as community gathered and vitalized by the manifold gifts of the Holy Spirit (cf. Acts 2:16-17).

1. Democracy: how and where it works[69]

Church documents see the development towards a democratic style in economic, cultural and especially political communities as a part of the integral development of man and society, but also as a necessary remedy against massive depersonalization. "In order to counterbalance increasing technocracy, modern democracy must be devised, not only making it possible for each person to become informed and to express himself, but also by involving him in a shared responsibility."[70] In Octogesima adveniens by Paul VI, we find an explicit plea for democracy, which at least implies an on-going effort of cultural and political forces to create the conditions that make democracy meaningful and truly possible.

Dictatorship and all forms of totalitarian systems, where one man or a party "club" rule others as mere tools, contradict human dignity and the purpose of public authority. Where, because of historical conditionings, some of the basic rights - for instance, freedom of press and assembly - are temporarily curtailed, everything must be done to restore them to the people as soon as possible.[71]

Public authority finds its own worth and becomes beneficial and effective in a truly human sense if it is recognized by free consent instead of imposing itself and its dictates arbitrarily on the citizens.[72]

Democracy implies a firm option for equality of persons and, as far as possible, equal opportunities for participation, freedom of assembly, alliance, and open expression of one's opinions and convictions. Although we all know that democratic majorities are not at all infallibly right, democracy requires loyalty to majority decisions, but with the minority's right to express dissent and to make honest efforts for a new consent and change. A democratically-elected majority is no longer democratic if it hinders the minorities from publicizing their options and reasons so that new democratic majorities might be formed.

Authentic democracy allows and encourages ethnic and other minorities to cooperate as equals and make their requests openly and clearly. It works with the basic assumption that pluralism, as such, is not so much antagonistic as it is a form of complementarity, of constructive cooperation[73] which, in the long run, guarantees the best possible solutions.

A democracy needs not only appropriate structures but, most of all, its citizens' growth towards moral self-determination and discernment. Structures and all educational efforts should help them to reach that stage of maturity and conscience-development which Lawrence Kohlberg and others call "post-conventional".[74] This means that democracy is never actualized once and forever. It must be constantly improved and renewed by integral development and joint efforts whereby the ruling majority and the opposition are more concerned for the basic principles of democracy than for winning a power struggle.

One of the crucial problems of democracy on the one hand, is the difficult synthesis between a critical mind that opens new horizons for change and, on the other hand, the readiness to cooperate loyally with legislation and government. While a mature citizen will never betray his conscience, he will be ready to work within imperfect structures while working for better ones.

Democracy implies an ethos of tolerance and respectful acceptance of diversity of opinions, convictions and options. But democratic forces can accept neither a libertinism which progressively leads to anarchy, nor an authoritarian, totalitarian system which, by racism or other bigotries, would undermine the very substance of a participatory, democratic society.

Against the terrorism of "extra-parliamentary", anti-democratic groups, firm resistance is a sign of confidence in the meaning and purpose of democracy. This resistance, under the guidance of a good democratic government, will be effective if there is a strong consensus in favour of the basic democratic values and purposes.

In the United States of America the working class as a whole did not join subversive forces because, in spite of all frustrations, the conviction prevailed that democratic forces would at last obtain a minimum and perhaps a maximum of social justice. In France, a consensus in favour of a loyal democracy, although weakened by undemocratic forces of the left and right wings, allowed Charles de Gaulle to preserve a relative freedom. What we can learn from history is that the freedom which a commonwealth can afford is in proportion to the firmness of consensus obtained without any degrading manipulation and thereafter constantly reaffirmed.[75] For the long run, political democracy will work properly if active participation and co-responsibility are distinctive marks in education and in the whole of social, economic and cultural life.

One of the basic rights in democracies is participation in elections at all political levels. Elections ritualize the justification of and accountability for political actors. But no political system and no constitution will be better than the prudence of its representatives; nor does the system automatically guarantee rationality. Efforts in this direction remain always a moral appeal. The criteria by which a citizen fulfils his duty in elections, chooses his candidates, supports their programmes and approves or criticizes their performance are a test of the quality of his political conscience and maturity. It may be better not to participate in an election than to do it without a well-informed and conscientious judgment. One of the main criteria should be the fairness, sense of justice and the peacefulness with which a candidate presents himself or herself.

There is an evident interdependence between a totalitarian system which oppresses people as if they were enemies if they express different ideas, and the tendency to treat simply as enemies those foreign countries that follow different world views, political goals and/or ideologies. If a candidate within a democratic system treats his political opponents as enemies, and fails to appreciate the positive aspects of their programmes and performances, he will probably be no better qualified for the cause of peace than representatives of totalitarian systems.

2. Historic conditioning of political organization

While it is a good thing if a strong consensus for its democratic constitution and tradition reigns in a nation, it is an evil if this goes hand in hand with intolerance of different forms of political organization in other parts of the world. There is not just one form and one stage of a participatory system. The English and North American democracies developed gradually under specific and favourable conditions and, of course, not without crises. The democracies which issued mainly from the French revolution have a different shape and a higher degree of instability.

Any effort of political systems to impose their ideology and organizational principles on other nations or states is not only anti-democratic but also counter-productive. We ought to allow each culture and political community to evolve according to its own traditions and ideals. The best advertisement for democracy is a well-functioning, peace-loving democratic state which abstains not only from supporting dictators but also from any other form of interference in the internal life of foreign nations.

In an era of worldwide communication, there are innumerable opportunities to dialogue about the various historical and actual experiences that may throw some light on the best approaches to participation, freedom and consensus. But it should be clear that there is no such thing under the sun as the absolute and best political organization everywhere and forever. While explicitly expressing an option for the best possible political participation, the Second Vatican Council also insists: "The practical ways in which the political community structures itself and regulates public authority can vary according to the particular character of people and its historical development."[76]

3. Responsible obedience versus civil disobedience[77]

In his encyclical *Pacem in terris*, John XXIII explains what it means that legitimate authority comes from God. He stresses two concerns. The first is that this doctrine, rightly understood, "is fully consonant with any truly democratic régime".[78] The second is that this not only requests obedience but also sets clear limits to it. "Since the right to command is required by the moral order and has its source in God, it follows that if civil authorities legislate for or allow anything that is contrary to that order and therefore contrary to the will of God, neither the laws made nor the authorizations granted can be binding on the consciences of the citizens, since 'we must obey God rather than men' (Acts 5:29). Otherwise, authority breaks down completely and results in shameful abuse."[79]

From the various statements of Thomas Aquinas which authorize civil disobedience, John XXIII chooses here one of the strongest texts: "Human law has the true nature of law only insofar as it corresponds to right reason, and therefore is derived from the eternal law. Insofar as it falls short of right reason, a law is said to be a wicked law; and so, lacking the true nature of law, it is rather a kind of violence."[80]

By discernment, which in normal situations calls the conscience to obedience and in other cases obliges civil disobedience, mature citizens prevent the "breakdown of authority" and avert or resist "shameful abuse". This is what John XXIII sets forth so forcefully. It is also the right interpretation of some biblical texts which frequently were abused by those who wanted absolute and undiscerning obedience. By obeying Caesar only where his laws fit into the moral order willed by God, the citizen gives God what is due to God and to Caesar what is due to him. Thus, loyal citizens who, on given occasions protest against unjust laws and manifest civil disobedience in a non-violent manner, render an indispensable service to the political community and to those in authority. When the apostle Paul insists that obedience should be offered to the rulers, not so much out of fear as because of conscience (Rom 13:5), then it follows that they obey just as far as they can in conscience.

Under given circumstances, a timely political resistance and civil disobedience can be precisely what we owe to the state for its own sake. It is decisive that this be done "timely", before injustice leads to disaster.[81] However, we should not forget that citizens as well as the political actors can come to erroneous convictions that contradict each other. Therefore, just as legislators and administrators must conscientiously clarify and examine their reasons and listen to the reasons of the other side before legislating and enforcing a law, so must the citizen examine his or her reasons and listen to the other side before appealing to conscience in protest and civil disobedience.

Christians should be in the forefront both in favouring just laws and protesting against unjust ones. Their authentic faith in the Redeemer of the world and faithfulness to the mission to be "light to the world" preclude both selfish disobedience and blind loyalties. The Christian can obey without becoming a slave to the state, and he can show reverence and loyalty without divinizing the rulers or the system.

4. Peaceful change, conflict, revolution[82]

Human hopes, and particularly the Christian hope based on divine promises and on the gospel of conversion, cannot accept an unjust and dehumanizing social, economic and political status quo. The prophetic tradition, calling for a profound change in all human relationships, meets a new historical situation in our time, caused by the industrial revolution, the art of invention, the mass media, and historical science which allow us to compare totally different configurations.

In the past, a widespread fatalism was a chief enemy of social, cultural and political progress. Modern man overcomes an age-old intolerance against what is new, against profound changes. Jürgen Moltmann expresses this new consciousness in a distinctively Christian way. "We are construction workers and not only interpreters of the future whose power in hope as well as in fulfilment is God. This means that Christian hope is a creative and militant hope."[83]

The skill to strengthen, deepen and illumine this new

consciousness seems to be the most effective force in preparing a better future.[84] The process of consciousness-raising was developed to engage people in determining their own goals and processes of change. For this, the model of best liberation theology is the "revolution for being".[85] It prepares for a creative change of the decisive structures in a much deeper and more lasting way than the strategy of reformers and revolutionaries who deal first with the revolution of *having* (getting more goods and power). If the "revolution of being" is the "revolution of the saints"[86], a new order will inevitably follow. Just as conversion, in the Christian view, is a never-ending process, so the renewal of economic, cultural, social and political life is never done once and forever.

The difficult task is to grow in critical capacity, to be committed to profound change and, at the same time, to realize that both conversion and socio-political change require enormous patience and the ability to harmonize the indispensable discontinuity with that deep and total continuity which only creative fidelity can discover.

Christian hope and realism call upon us to discern ever anew what, here and now, can be improved and what must be tolerated for the time being, and finally what, by its own value, should be considered unchangeable in the midst of a programme of reform for the long run. On this long journey of exodus from an unjust world, inspired by our faith in the coming and already pressing kingdom of God, there is place for the "absolute utopia" as quintessence of the Christian hope, and the relative utopia of the best possible order obtainable by and with people who are at the same time sinners and redeemed. This relative utopia is only an imperfect symbol, analogous to the kingdom of God proclaimed by the church. It points dynamically in a clear direction;[87] but the hard endeavour follows to find the next viable step and the appropriate means.

Are we, as Christians, making a choice for revolution, or ought we to do so? The answer depends on how we define "revolution". If we understand it generically as a deep, radical, historical process of change, rather than as some minor modifications, then surely, in fidelity to the Creator and Redeemer of the world, we should be or become revolutionaries. Especially in a revolutionary age, it is the church's urgent task to teach us, by word and example, this one great revolution which would make dispensable and meaningless all those violent revolts which remain in the vicious circle of greed, oppression and lust for power. However, it should be made clear that the revolution willed by the gospel has nothing to do with the fanatic who, through anarchy, chaos and violence, wants to produce an imminent "perfect society". This fanatic, with his dangerous dream of a sudden, violent and total change of socio-political life, looks down on the "revisionist".

Orthodox Marxism, before its revolution, resisted all socio-political reforms even if the individual steps pointed towards a profound change, because its faith (ideology) was that only through the dialectic of increasing tension could the way be paved for the thorough-going revolution which promised the classless, perfect society. For a long time, Marxists persecuted revisionists as heretics, just as the most intolerant religionists persecuted those whom they considered heretics. The German Socialist Party has come a long way from the revolutionary belief to a greatly modified revisionism with rather limited reforms. A number of Communist parties in the western world have theoretically and practically chosen revisionism. Through gradual reforms, and within the present democratic institutions, they intend to prepare their society for the hoped-for future of a fully socialist state - the exact character of which they might not, or not yet, agree on among themselves.

The revisionist can be tempted to be satisfied with half-measures and disconnected reforms. But there can be a revisionism which, with the highest ideals and a good proportion of realism, works for a far more profound change in society than the violent revolutionary.

Indeed, the vision of the participatory society, with total commitment to social justice and social love on all levels, means a much more radical change than what orthodox Marxism and other revolutionary ideologies have thus far produced or can ever produce by violent and oppressive means. The sad fact is, however, that Christian groups in political power not infrequently degenerate into the kind of reformers who mask, with many tactical changes, their unreadiness for the "revolution of the gospel". If Christians lose their vision and dynamics, and use means not at all appropriate to Christian hope, they are accountable for the chaos produced by the violent revolutions issuing from dangerous ideologies.

On the problem of violent revolution, Catholic traditional moral theology has been judiciously discerning. Only when a tyrant or political system deprives citizens of basic human rights and/or exploits them in an intolerable way, may - or perhaps must - a violent overthrow be faced by the decisive groups as a last resort. However, they have first to face the questions of the prospective violent revolution: Is there a realistic hope that the evils and sufferings of such a revolution will be less destructive than the present situation? Will the revolution probably lead to a more just order or to greater chaos?

It seems to me that the first question of conscience to be raised today for all of us, and particularly for those who are inclined to choose the way of violent revolution, is this: Have we done and are we doing everything in our power to work for a better world and better political structures by non-violent means? A total lack of creativity in the way of non-violent, solidaric and patient action gives little hope that the violent revolutionaries will be creative in the right sense if they gain power.

One of the most frequent arguments in favour of violent means of revolution is the violence used by the oppressor through police abuse and torture or by violent oppressive, exploitative and alienating structures. It cannot easily be denied that there are in today's world political systems and dictators who sin scandalously by violent abuse of power and totally unjust reinforcements, and that there are structures which do violence to people's dignity and freedom. But the very idea that this calls for nothing more than different forms of violence shows that revolutionaries remain in a vicious circle. We have to call violence, oppression, exploitation and injustice by their names. We have to alarm public opinion and shake the consciences of those who participate in and/or profit from these situations.

Those who raise their voices in protest or discerning criticism and use creative non-violent strategies may have to suffer for quite a while. But the question is whether we believe in the power of conscience to convince and to convert. If we have little trust in these realities, our violence will surely not change the world for the better.

Several democratic countries have huge problems with terrorism organized on national and even international levels, and at least partially promoted by foreign political forces well known for their oppressive practices. The terrorists and their foster-fathers know quite well that they cannot gain a political majority by using democratic means. Therefore, they (a small minority) decide to impose their preferences by violent means. If they were to gain power, they would then, by the very logic of their beginnings, continue to use violence against the majority of citizens. When they accuse modern democracies of oppressive structures and methods, everyone, including the terrorists, should realize that terrorism practised against the democratic majority can lead only to an infinitely more oppressive régime.[88]

The fact that terrorists take innocent people as hostages and kill people indiscriminately proves that they are not concerned for basic human rights. Even a person who might be somehow sympathetic with their declared purposes would have to revise his opinion if their means belie their programmes.

The question about revolution is extremely complicated in today's world. On the one hand, revolutionary groups are organized by foreign political power, using revolutionary ideologies and tools for their own ambitious purposes. On the other hand, competing superpowers tend to develop counter-revolutionary strategies that give all kinds of support to the oppressive rulers who have provoked the revolutionary impetus by their injustices. In addition, the arms industries in various countries take advantage of the situation by selling weapons to oppressors and revolutionaries alike, regardless of the justice or injustice of their cause. The least we can do in this context is consciousness-raising to form a worldwide and strong public opinion against all these abuses.

5. Political education

There is nothing more necessary but also nothing less ambiguous than political education.[89] The educational system of modern society and the mass media make possible a far-reaching, continuing and penetrating political education.[90] We have to inquire into the quality, the opportunity and the risk of the actual political education.

In the past, political education in many nations was triumphal and self-righteous. Frequently it cultivated nationalism rather than a sound patriotism. It neglected a worldwide vision.

Political education is expected to give all citizens a fundamental knowledge of civic rights and duties. They should know the constitution and traditions of their own country in comparison with other political traditions and systems, its international relationships and the prospects of peace. The heart of such education should be to activate the rational citizen through freedom and for responsible freedom. Everyone should know that political indifference and ignorance are nothing less than betrayal of our fellowmen who need our well-informed decisions and participation, just as we need their political expression of solidarity. And as Christians, we all should realize that betrayal of our fellowmen is nothing less than betrayal of Christ.

Man owes it to his own dignity to be and to become ever more a subject (actor) in politics, in solidarity with others. But if he does not acquire the necessary political education, he will be no more than an object of politics. For Aristotle, the man who is not a citizen is not fully man. Today we approach the question differently: Everyone, man and woman, has the right to participate actively in the political community. But how can one do it without competence?

The Second Vatican Council insists strongly on the need for political education. "Civic and political education is today supremely necessary for people, especially young people. Such education should be painstakingly provided so that all citizens can make their contribution to the political community."[91]

A good political education allows the citizens to understand their special vocation and role in the political community. "Thus they can also show in practice how authority is to be harmonized with freedom, personal initiative with consideration for the bonds uniting the whole social body, and necessary unity with beneficial diversity."

If this kind of education is given in the right spirit, then we can hope that there will arise authentic political vocations in sufficient number. The Council says on this point: "Let those who are suited for it, or can become so, prepare themselves for the difficult but most honourable art of politics".[92] The political profession is here called an "art". It needs vision of wholeness, intuition, knowledge and skill. It is called a "most *honourable* art", it needs outstanding honesty and a true sense of honour.

Although political authorities have the duty to guarantee for all the best possible opportunities for civic and political education, and to oblige every citizen to acquire a necessary minimum of knowledge in this field, there should be no state monopoly, just as there should be none in the general field of education. Political education is a public affair, and all parts of society should participate in it in order to guarantee freedom, breadth and wholeness of vision. In this task, Christians should be in the foreground.

A state monopoly of political education, especially if it becomes a monopoly of one party or of the ruling class, degenerates almost unavoidably into brainwashing, with all kinds of manipulation. It will not serve the cause of worldwide justice and peace. A genuinely democratic society cannot exist without a certain pluralism in political education. Of course, the public authorities cannot entrust political education to subversive elements who oppose democracy as such, and try to manipulate people in favour of intolerant ideologies. But political education, as education in general, cannot be neutral to a value system. Christian and other humanistic groups render an invaluable service to the political community by making a sound ethics a part of such education.

IV. TOWARDS A WORLD COMMUNITY

The emphasis of the social doctrine of the church is more and more on planetary society, on planetary social justice.[93] Humanity has reached the point where we can no longer speak meaningfully of the one God, Creator and Redeemer, without a burning zeal for building an authentic world community where everyone's dignity and basic human rights are acknowledged, and where every nation realizes that it cannot think about its own common good without a sincere concern for the common good of all nations.[94] All signs of the times point towards a new worldwide consciousness that humanity is one, and has no future unless it develops a new attitude and new structures that effectively express this solidarity.

1. New dimensions of natural law and the "law of nations"
The Romans studied the law of nations (*jus gentium*) with an

acknowledged objective of colonialism. In order to produce a kind of common law for ruling the subjugated nations, they were seeking what cultures have in common. The law concerning Roman citizens guaranteed a number of rights and privileges for each and all of them, while the law for subjugated nations did not concern individual persons but treated non-Romans only as objects of politics. Nevertheless, the *jus gentium* guaranteed a political order and protected people from arbitrariness on the part of colonial officers.

The classical works on the *jus gentium*, by Francis of Victoria and other sixteenth century Spanish moralists, had an anti-colonial thrust that was intended to protect the rights of groups and individuals. In the last centuries, and particularly after the French revolution, natural law theories had a rather individualistic accent. As far as groups and nations were concerned, the "international law" considered only the nation-states as its subjects.

Since 1919 through the League of Nations, and after the Second World War through the United Nations, there began serious efforts to conceive and promulgate an international law that would protect the basic rights of individuals and groups. But the new concept of a law of nations has not yet an authoritative speaker; it cannot be enforced wherever the government of a nation is unwilling to recognize it or to act in accordance with it. The narrow concept of sovereignty of the nation-states is still an obstacle.

What we need is a worldwide "domestic politics" so that, in the matter of basic rights, no person, no ethnic or religious group, no culture or subculture would be a "foreigner" within the world community. Humanity as a whole has to take up the task of social justice for all peoples, groups and individuals, whereby nobody would be a mere object. All are meant to become subjects, promoting this basic unity and solidarity within all the legitimate diversities.

2. Sovereign states and super-powers

The world which engaged in two world wars, in the "cold war", and has constantly generated new conflicts and wars, has been a society whose members are sovereign states, some of which prevail as super-powers over the others. Individual persons and groups other than states have been "mere objects of it".[95]

Many insightful people feel that the world of today is living the birth pangs of a world community, which will profoundly modify the society of nation-states and free them from their frightful handicaps. The society of nation-states is divided into blocs, where two or three super-powers aggravate the dangerous system of competition - competition in weapons, competition in trade, competition for scarce resources - whereby the security complex of each nation sharpens all the other conflicts. The tension between the super-powers and the blocs is intensified by ideological confrontation which deeply involves even those nations which declare themselves to be "bloc-free", a "third world".

The decisive moral goal for all sensitive people is to work for a general world opinion and attitude that would make the common interest of survival and the necessary bonds of brotherhood among all people prevail over the age-old national security complexes and lust for power. For this, the creativity of millions of people is urgently needed to envision the clear goal and appropriate means, and to discover time and again the next possible step.

As long as national states with absolute sovereignty compete with unbridled selfishness over weapons, production, balance of payments and scarce resources, they will not care first of all for human persons. Declarations and accords on human rights - for instance, the Helsinki Accords - important as they may be, will not change the situation much until there prevails everywhere a new and urgent consciousness that humanity absolutely must find new worldwide organizational principles of solidarity. The conflicting interests can be resolved peacefully and reasonably if the decisive élites in each nation are interested, above all else, in social justice and worldwide brotherhood.

Soviet Communism offers a model of world unification which we find heretical and extremely dangerous.[96] But mere anti-Communism in no way resolves the problem as long as the western world persists stubbornly in the system and ideology of competition among sovereign nation-states. Nor does fear of Soviet Communism help. It seems that aggressive world Communism has lost the attractive power of "faith" and earthly messianism; but there is still a kind of fear among extreme anti-

Communists that becomes almost a faith in Communist power. As a consequence, the principle of hope yields to fear to such an extent that there is not enough imagination and creativity for an infinitely more truthful and effective solidarity of all people than that of the Soviet and other "super-powers".

3. The threat of a super-state

If we have any faith in liberty and in fidelity to God's design, we cannot reject strongly enough the idea of a super-state with absolute power to impose its ideology and dictates on all. If we can see and foresee the necessity of worldwide unification and consequently a world-authority, we should do everything possible to make this a reality by free consent and with all the essential provisions and space for the spirit of liberty in co-responsibility. If it does not happen by free consent and with foresight for the survival of liberty, it will happen by imposition by a super-power driven by an ideology inimical to liberty as we understand it.

The forthcoming world authority should not be structured in the image and likeness of a centralistic nation-state, and especially not in that of a super-power which intends to dominate the economic and political life of other states. One of the most urgent moral responsibilities today, therefore, is to work *creatively* for a world authority by free consent: an authority which should not follow the pattern of a system of powerful states which, for almost six thousand years, have seen their supreme power as the right and capacity to wage wars against other states.[97]

The development of modern weaponry and techniques, as well as the increasing trend towards a one-world economy, force us to speed this process. The most urgent task now is to come to a clear conception of the spirit and structure of such a world authority.

4. The federal principle of a world authority

The last popes have clearly affirmed the need for a supreme world authority, especially in view of peace and a worldwide concept of social justice in the context of the risks and chances of the developing one-world economy.

In his address to the General Assembly of the United Nations

(Oct. 4, 1965), Paul VI expressed this conviction most vigorously: "Your vocation is to make brothers not only of some but of all peoples. A difficult undertaking, indeed; but this is what the task, your most noble task, amounts to. Is there anyone who does not see the necessity of coming thus progressively to the establishment of a world authority, able to act efficaciously on the juridical and political levels?"[98]

On the juridical level as well as on the others, there are embryonic beginnings in a World Court. However, the court's decisions are not binding and cannot be enforced, as became strikingly evident in the case of United States' hostages in Iran. We need a strong universal consent and the appropriate mechanisms to make such juridical decisions efficacious.

But as soon as we call for efficacious structures, we shrink back for fear of the "beast from the abyss", fear of a universal tyranny. The remedy is not to renounce the idea and reality of such a world authority, but rather to implement everywhere, on all levels and in all realms, the federal structure according to the principle of subsidiarity which has insistently recurred in this treatise on moral theology. If this principle becomes reality in the minds, hearts and the will of all people, we can safely entrust to the forthcoming world-authority all the powers it will need for the great task of promoting peace and justice in view of the basic rights of every person, and without encroaching on any of the proper functions of the various cultural, economic and political communities.

NOTES

[1] Cf. F. Mordstein, *Menschenbild und Gesellschaftsidee. Zur Krisis der politischen Ethik im 19. Jahrhundert*, Stuttgart, 1966; F. M. Schmölz, *Chance und Dilemma der politischen Ethik*, Köln, 1966; R. Hauser, *Was des Kaisers ist. Zehn Kapitel christlicher Ethik des politischen*, Frankfurt, 1968; F. E.

Oppenheim, *Moral Principles in Political Philosophy*, New York, 1968; Th. Strohm and H.-D. Wendland (eds.), *Politik und Ethik*, Darmstadt, 1969; J. Sellers, *Public Ethics. American Morals and Manners*, New York, 1970; G. Mattai, *Morale politica*, Bologna, 1971; M. Reding, *Politische Ethik. Eine Einführung*, Freiburg, 1972; P. P. Müller-Schmid, *Der rationale Weg zur politischen Ethik*, Stuttgart, 1972; K. Hertz, *Politics is a Way of Helping People*, Minneapolis, 1974; C. F. von Weizsäcker, *Wege in der Gefahr*, München, 1976; H. Gollwitzer, *Forderungen der Umkehr. Beiträge zur Theologie der Gesellschaft*, München, 1976; Id., *Forderungen der Freiheit*, München, 1962; R. F. Goodin, *The Politics of Rational Man*, London, 1976; D. Sternberger, *Drei Wurzeln der Politik*, Frankfurt, 1978; F. D. Wilhelmson, *Christianity and Political Philosophy*, Athens/Ga., 1978; St. Hampshire (ed.), *Private and Public Morality*, Cambridge, 1978; T. Rendtorff, *Politische Ethik und Christentum*, München, 1978.

2 Cf. J. Hempel, *Politische Absicht und politische Wirkung im biblischen Schrifttum*, Leipzig, 1938; E. F. Scott, *Man and Society in the New Testament*, New York, 1946; P. Lehmann, *Ideology and Incarnation*, Geneva, 1962; Id., *The Transfiguration of Politics*, New York, 1975; R. Hörl (ed.), *Die Politik und das Heil*, Mainz, 1968; R. J. Cassidy, *Jesus, Politics and Society. A Study of Luke's Gospel*, Maryknoll, 1978.

3 Cf. R. J. Cassidy, l.c., 71.

4 Cf. P. C. Hodgson, *New Birth of Freedom*, Philadelphia, 1976, 248.

5 Having read a number of Dorothee Sölle's books I can sympathize with so many of her ideas and her passion for the liberation of the oppressed, but my impression is that her interpretation of "resurrection" as implying above all "insurrection", while constantly denying personal resurrection at all, brings a tone of intolerance and an inclination to violent action into her political theology of liberation. Cf., for example her *Wählt die Wahrheit*, Stuttgart and Berlin, 1980.

6 Cf. R. J. Cassidy, l.c., 37.

7 Cf. W. Pannenberg, "Politische Dimensionen des Evangeliums", in E. Hörl (ed.), l.c., 16-20.

8 Cf. H. Peukert (ed.), *Diskussion zur "politischen Theologie"* (mit einer Bibliographie zum Thema), München and Mainz, 1969; Cl. Geffré and G. Gutiérrez, "The Mystical and Political Dimension of Christian Faith", in *Concilium*, New York, 1974; G. Bauer, *Christliche Hoffnung und politischer Fortschritt. Die politische Theologie von J. B. Metz als theologische Begründung gesellschaftlicher Verantwortung des Christen*, Mainz, 1976; A. Gonzales Montes, *Rázon politica de la fe cristiana. Un estudio historico-teológico de la hermeneutica politica de la fe*, Salamanca, 1976; E. Schillebeeckx, *Christus und die Christen*, Freiburg, 1977, 752-771 (Christlicher Glaube und Politik); A. Dumas, *Théologies politiques et vie de l'Eglise*, Paris, 1977; D. Sölle, *Sympathie. Theologisch-politische Traktate*, Stuttgart, 1979.

9 Cf. J. B. Metz, *Glaube in Geschichte und Gegenwart*, Mainz, 1977, 100ff.

10 Cf. A. Rich, "Theologische Erwägungen zum Integrationsproblem", in Th. Strohm, H.-D. Wendland, *Politik und Ethik*, Darmstadt, 1969, 383-403.

11 Cf. D. Sölle, F. Steffensky (eds.), *Politisches Nachtgebet in Köln. Texte und Analysen*, 2 vols., Stuttgart and Mainz (no publication date).

12 E. McDonagh, "Prayer and Politics" in *The Furrow* 30 (1979), 543-554, quote p. 547.

13 J. Gremillion, *The Gospel of Peace. Catholic Social Teaching since Pope John XXIII*, Maryknoll, 1976, 45.

14 G. Ebeling, "Die Notwendigkeit des christlichen Gottesdienstes", in *Wort und Glaube* III, 1975, 551ff.

[15] E. Jüngel, *Reden für die Stadt*, München, 1979, 32.

[16] Cf. J. Bennett, *Christian Ethics and Social Policy*, New York, 1946; A. Rich, *Glaube in politischer Entscheidung. Beiträge zur Ethik des Politischen*, Zürich and Stuttgart, 1962; K. G. Steck, *Kritik des politischen Katholizismus*, Frankfurt, 1963; A. Schardt, *Integralismus oder Offenheit im politischen Engagement*, Würzburg, 1965; O. von Nell-Breuning, "Sozialer und politischer Katholizismus", in *Stimmen der Zeit* 193 (1975), 147-161; W. Grafl, *Zwischen Rückzug und Aufbruch, Christ und Politik*, Graz, 1976; H. Büchele, *Christsein im gesellschaftlichen System*, Wien, 1976; R. Orfei, *Fede e politica: Il cristiano di fronte al potere*, Milano, 1977; M. Hanna, *Catholics and American Politics*, Cambridge/Mass., 1979.

[17] Cf. *Gaudium et spes*, 43; *Octogesima adveniens*, 50.

[18] T. Rendtorff, *Politische Ethik und Christentum*, München, 1978, 31.

[19] H. Gollwitzer, *Forderungen der Umkehr*, 15.

[20] J. Ellul, *The Ethics of Freedom*, London, 1976, 386.

[21] Cf. A. Rich, l.c., 387.

[22] J. Ellul, l.c., 379.

[23] *Gaudium et spes*, 76; *Octogesima adveniens*, 46.

[24] *Octogesima adveniens*, 4; cf. 48-50.

[25] E. Schillebeeckx, "The Magisterium and the World of Politics", in *Concilium* 4 (1968), 12-21; E. W. Böckenförde, *Kirchlicher Auftrag und politische Entscheidung*, Freiburg, 1973; F. S. Potts, *Kirchen und Politik in Deutschland*, Stuttgart, 1976; F. Furger, "Hilfe zur Freiheit, ethische Verkündigung in einer pluralistischen Gesellschaft", in *Studia moralia* 15 (1977), 713-730; U. Damemann, *Theologie und Politik im Denken Karl Barths*, München, 1977; M. Cordero (ed.), *L'autunno del concordato*, Torino, 1977.

[26] Most significant for this conception is the title of a famous book of Karl Barth, *Christengemeinde und Bügergemeinde*, Zürich, 1970⁴.

[27] *Gaudium et spes*, 76,2.

[28] Ibid., 76,1.

[29] John Paul II quoted in E. W. Böckenförde, "Das neue politische Engagement der Kirche. Zur 'politischen Theologie' Johannes-Pauls II", in *Stimmen der Zeit* 198 (1980), 219-234, quote p. 228.

[30] *Gaudium et spes*, 76,6

[31] Cf. K. Rahner, "Kirche und säkulare Welt", in Id., *Über die bleibende Bedeutung des Zweiten Vatikanischen Konzils*, München, 1979, 6-7.

[32] Cf. H. Maier, "Der Katholik als Bürger" in *Evangelische Kommentare* 13 (1980), 29-32.

[33] Cf. V. Kubálková, "Moral Precepts and Contemporary Soviet Politics", in R. Pitmann, *Moral Claims in World Affairs*, London, 1979, 170-193; Z. Brezinski, *Soviet Marxism: A Critical Analysis*, Cambridge/Mass., 1967; *The Road to Communism: Documents of the 22nd Congress of CPSU*, Moscow, 1961.

[34] Cf. H. O. Vetter, "Die dritte industrielle Revolution", in *Evangelische Kommentare* 13 (1980), 193-195.

[35] Cf. G. Leclercq, *Morale ou moralisme?*, Paris, 1979, 198; J. Habermas, "Über das Verhältnis von Politik und Moral", in Th. Strohm, H.-D. Wendland (eds.), *Politik und Ethik*, Darmstadt, 1969, 61-90.

[36] Cf. E. Kamenka, *Marxism and Ethics*, New York, 1969; Id., *The Ethical Foundations of Marxism*, London, 1971; R. T. de George, *Soviet Ethics and Morality*, Ann Arbor, 1969.

[37] W. Dirks, "Hat der Marxismus Raum für eine Moral?", in Id., *Das schmutzige Geschäft. Die Politik und die Verantwortung der Christen*, Freiburg, 1964, 135.

[38] Ibid., 154.

[39] N. Machiavelli, *Il principe*, written in 1513 and first published in 1531; cf. G. Ritter, "Politische Ethik. Der historische Ursprung ihrer Problematik", in Th. Strohm, H.-D. Wendland (eds.), l.c., 12-27.

[40] R. Niebuhr, *An Interpretation of Christian Ethics*, New York, 1935, 105.

[41] R. Niebuhr, *The Children of Light and the Children of Darkness*, New York, 1944, 68.

[42] Ibid., 71.

[43] Cf. G. Ritter, l.c., 25ff.

[44] A. L. Burns, "Injustice and Evil in the Politics of the Powers", in R. Pittman (ed.), l.c., 125.

[45] H. Dietzfelbinger, "Veränderung durch Vergebung. Über eine elementare Lebensfunktion der Gesellschaft", in *Evangelische Kommentare* 12 (1979), 390.

[46] H. Schlier, "Die Beurteilung des Staates im Neuen Testament", in Id., *Die Zeit der Kirche*, Freiburg, 1956, 3; cf. O. Cullmann, *The State in the New Testament*, New York, 1956; R. Notzik, *Anarchy, State and Utopia*, New York 1974; R. Stone, *Realism and Hope*, Washington, D.C., 1977.

[47] S. Th., I/II, 21, 4 ad 3: "Homo non ordinatur ad communitatem politicam secundum se totum et secundum omnia sua."

[48] *Octogesima adveniens*, 46.

[49] S. Th., II/II, 105, 1.

[50] *Mater et magistra*, 3.

[51] Ibid., 61, 79, 105, 127.

[52] Cf. J. Gremillion, l.c., 5-7.

[53] O. von Nell-Breuning, "Steuermoral", in *Sacramentum Mundi* IV, 733-737 (with bibliography); B. Tretter, *Die Steuermentalität. Ein internationaler Vergleich*, Berlin, 1974; G. H. Udias, "Implicaciones eticas del fraude tributario", in *Pentecostes* 17 (1978), 111-132; K.-H. Mönch, *Steuerkriminalität und Sanktionswahrscheinlichkeit*, Frankfurt, 1978.

[54] Cf. R. Hauser, *Was des Kaisers ist*, Frankfurt, 1968, 19ff.

[55] P. Tillich, *Love, Power and Justice*, London, 1954; H. Schlier, *Mächte und Gewalten im Neuen Testament*, Freiburg, 1958; A. A. Berle, *Power*, New York, 1969; F. Böckle and J. Pohier (eds.), "Power and the Word of God", in *Concilium* 90 (1973), New York; W. Weber (ed.), *Macht, Dienst, Herrschaft in Kirche und Gesellschaft*, Freiburg i.Br., 1974; St. Clegg, *Power, Rule and Domination. A Critical and Empirical Understanding of Power in Sociological Theory and Organizational Life*, London and Boston, 1975; P. Tournier, *Violence et puissance*, Paris, 1977; M. Parenti, *Power and the Powerless*, New York, 1978; H. B. Streithofer, *Macht und Moral. Die Grundwerte in der Politik*, Stuttgart, 1979; F. Hammer, *Macht. Wesen, Formen, Grenzen*, Königstein, 1979.

[56] R. Guardini, *Die Macht. Versuch einer Wegweisung*, Würzburg, 1965[6]; Id., *Der unvollendete Mensch und die Macht*, Würzburg, 1956.

[57] Cf. R. Hauser, l.c., 79.

[58] D. Sölle, *Wählt die Wahrheit*, Stuttgart and Berlin, 1980, 134.

[59] C. F. von Weizsäcker, *Wege in der Gefahr*, München, 1976, 252.

[60] T. R. Armstrong and K. M. Cinnamon, *Power and Authority in Law Enforcement*, Springfield/Ill., 1976; St. S. Nagel, *The Criminal Justice System*, London, 1977; H. Foucauld, *Discipline and Punish: The Birth of the Prison*, New York, 1977; G. Newman, *The Punishment Response*, Philadelphia, 1978; W. Molinski (ed.), *Versöhnen oder Bestrafen. Perspektiven für die Straffällingen Hilfe*, Freiburg and Göttingen, 1979.

[61] Cf. H. H. Punke, *Education, Lawlessness and Political Corruption in America*, North Quincy/Mass., 1978, 120.

[62] Cf. L. L. Berg, H. Hahn, J. R. Schmidhauser, *Corruption in the American Political System*, Morristown, N.J., 1976; A. S. Rose, *Corruption. A Study in Political Economy*, New York, 1978; G. S. Benson, *Political Corruption in America*, Lexington/Mass., 1978.

[63] R. E. Goodin, *The Politics of Rational Man*, New York, 1976, 16 and 18.

[64] Cf. A. Kneier, "Ethics in Government Service: A Critical Look at Federal Conflict of Interest Regulations", in I. Hill (ed.), *The Ethical Basis of Economic Freedom*, Chapel Hill/N.C., 1976, 215-232. quote p. 218.

[65] Ibid., 229.

[66] M.-D. Chenu, "Vox populi - vox Dei. Die öffentliche Meinung in dem Volke Gottes", in R. Hörl (ed.), *Politik und das Heil*, Mainz, 1968, 66; cf. G. Gorschenk (ed.), *Grundwerte in Staat und Gesellschaft*, München, 1977.

[67] *Gaudium et spes*, 73,2; cf. ibid., 75.

[68] *Octogesima adveniens*, 47; the sexist language is not in the original text but only in the English translation.

[69] Cf. M. Imboden, *Die politischen Systeme*, Basel, 1962; R. S. Downie, *Government Action and Morality. Some Principles and Concepts of Liberal Democracy*, London and New York, 1964; R. H. Horwitz, *The Moral Foundations of the American Republic*, Charlottesville, 1977.

[70] *Octogesima adveniens*, 47.

[71] *Gaudium et spes*, 75,5.

[72] Cf. *Pacem in terris*, 138.

[73] Cf. what has been said in *Free and Faithful in Christ* II, 159-165 on the dynamics of democratic pluralism.

[74] Cf. H. Schelsky, *Der selbständige und der betreute Mensch*, Stuttgart, 1976, 34ff; C. F. von Weizsäcker, *Wege in der Gefahr*, 246.

[75] Cf. R. Niebuhr, "Consensus in einer demokratischen Gesellschaft", in Th. Strohm, H.-D. Wendland (eds.), l.c., 201 and 208.

[76] *Gaudium et spes*, 74,7.

[77] Cf. E. Weisband and Th. Frank, *Resignation in Protest. Political and Ethical Choices between Loyalty to Team and Loyalty to Conscience in American Political Life*, New York, 1975; D. Hollenbach, SJ, *Claims in Conflict. Retrieving and Renewing the Catholic Human Rights Tradition*, Paramus, N.J., 1979.

[78] *Pacem in terris*, 52.

[79] Ibid., 51.

[80] S. Th., I/II, q. 93, a 3 ad 2; cf. S. Th., II/II, q. 104, a 6 ad 3: "Man has to obey civil authorities only insofar as the order of justice requires."

[81] E. Jüngel, *Reden für die Stadt*, München, 1979, 36.

[82] On revolution and violence see: T. Rendtorff, *Christentum zwischen Revolution und Restauration. Politische Wirkung neuzeitlicher Theologie*, München, 1970; H. Camara, *Revolution through Peace*, New York, 1971; M. Hengel, *Victory over Violence*, Philadelphia, 1973; Id., *Was Jesus a Revolutionary?*, Philadelphia, 1971; W. Becker, H. Maier, M. Spicker, *Revolution, Demokratie, Kirche*, Paderborn, 1975; J. G. Davies, *Christian Politics and Violent Revolutions*, Maryknoll, 1976; R. Salert, *Revolutions and Revolutionaries. Four Theories*, New York, 1976; C. Audry, *Les militants et leurs morales*, Paris, 1976; J. P. Gunneman, *The Moral Meaning of Revolution*, New Haven, 1979.

[83] J. Moltmann, *Religion, Revolution and the Future*, New York, 1969, 217.

[84] Cf. P. Freire, *Pedagogy of the Oppressed*, New York, 1970; Id., *Education for Critical Consciousness*, New York, 1973.

[85] Cf. G. Lagos, *Revolution for Being*, New York, 1977.

[86] Cf. M. Walzer, *The Revolution of the Saints*, New York, 1969.
[87] Cf. K. Barth, *Christengemeinde und Bürgergemeinde*, Zürich, 1946, 23; H. Gollwitzer, *Forderungen der Umkehr*, München, 1976, 35ff.
[88] Cf. H. Dichgans, *Die Welt verändern. Reform oder Revolution*, Düsseldorf, 1974, 225ff.
[89] Cf. W. Dirks, *Das schmutzige Geschäft. Politik und Verantwortung der Christen*, Olten, 1964; H. H. Punke, *Education, Lawlessness and Political Corruption in America*, North Quincy/Mass., 1978.
[90] Cf. Ch. Zimmer, *Cinéma et politique*, Paris, 1974; M. Tracey, *The Production of Political Television*, London, 1977; P. Nau, *Zur Kritik des politischen Films*, Köln, 1978.
[91] *Gaudium et spes*, 75.
[92] Ibid.
[93] G. and P. Mische, *Toward a Human World Order: Beyond the National Security Straitjacket*, New York, 1977; R. Pittman (ed.), *Moral Claims in World Affairs*, London, 1979.
[94] *Pacem in terris*, 98.
[95] H. Boll, "Human Rights and World Politics", in R. Pittman (ed.), l.c., 82.
[96] V. Kubálková, "Moral Precepts of Contemporary Soviet Politics", in R. Pittman (ed.), l.c., 170-193.
[97] C. F. von Weizsäcker, *Der Garten des Menschlichen*, München, 1978⁴, 103.
[98] N. 16, text in J. Gremillion, l.c., 382.

Chapter Nine

Peace on Earth

Throughout all the chapters of these three volumes, the word "peace", together with "love", "justice", "liberty" and "fidelity" has constantly recurred. Peace is our world's most needed gift of God and the most urgent task of all people. It seems appropriate, therefore, to sum up now the vision of peace, its dynamics and perspectives.

Shalom-peace is a key concept of the Bible (I). War is the most inhumane fact of history and the most striking contradiction to the gift and task of peace (II). The signs of the times tell us how urgent it is for humanity to rid itself of the age-old slavery of war (III). Peace research and peace policy are a response to the signs of the times (IV). The survival and the freedom of humanity depend on peace education (V).

I. THE PROMISE, GIFT AND TASK OF PEACE[1]

Peace is the all-inclusive promise of God to his people, the unique gift of Christ whom the Father has given us as the effective sign of reconciliation and peace. To be peacemakers is the most noble mission of the sons and daughters of God. "Peace is the most inclusive of Christian virtues. . . Peace is love transposed into social or global terms, - a gathering together of many virtues, and their global transmutation onto a level of complexity."[2] It should be a distinctive sign of redemption and covenant fidelity in the midst of strife and conflict.

391

1. The promise of peace

In all cultures of antiquity known to us, peace is a highly religious concept. In ancient Israel it was absolutely central for its religion, its hope and faith.[3]

The noun *shalom* (peace) is derived from the verbal form *shalem* which can mean: to be complete or to make complete, to bring to harmony and fulfilment. Where there is *shalom*, "both the whole and the constituent parts have reached their maximum and optimum of being".[4] *Shalom* is the harmony of a caring community informed at every point by its awareness of God's gift and call.[5] The Creator's design for humankind and for the earth is *shalom*. God, the Creator and Redeemer, is the guarantor of the final fulfilment of history in peace.

"Peace is, in biblical teaching, both eschatological and primordial. It is eschatological in the sense that its full realization belongs to the end of history".[6] It is primordial in the sense that, from the very beginning, God gave humankind the potentiality for peace and the task of peace (cf. Gen 1-2). The foundation of the world is in the Creator's design and promise of peace. He protects the world against chaos and leads his people from the self-chosen phase of dissension and self-annihilation into his *shalom*. God's covenant with Adam, Noah, Abraham and Moses is a covenant for peace. The people can be sure of this covenant for peace if only they keep covenant fidelity.

Shalom flows into salvation. It is wholly God's gift. Whoever receives this gift gratefully is at peace with God, bears peace in himself or herself, radiates peace, and is committed to the task of peace. That *shalom* is God's own initiative is a distinctive teaching of the Old and New Testament. Gideon, building an altar to the Lord, "named it Jehovah-shalom" (Judg 6:24), *"The Lord is peace"*. The faithful know that they have to honour God as the source of peace by humble prayer of petition and thanksgiving. He alone can create peace (cf. Is 45:5-8). Through the prophets he denounces all deceptions and falsehoods about peace in order to pave the way to righteousness and fidelity to peace.

Although the transcendental dimension - peace coming from God and peace with God - receives the greatest emphasis, this does not minimize the horizontal dimension of social and political peace. On the contrary, it gives urgency and a firm foundation to all perspectives and dimensions.

The Israelites, greeting each other with the word *Shalom*, praise the God of Shalom, and thus are committed to honour God by seeking the ways of true peace with each other and the rest of humanity. The truth of the divine promises about the final peace sets them, here and now, on the road of peace (cf. Hos 2:20; Amos 9:13; Is 9:5; Zach 9:9ff; Mic 5:4). The fact that the hoped-for reunification of the two separated parts of Israel is a symbol of the promised messianic peace is a constant call to work for reconciliation and justice. Only thus can they wait confidently for the time "when righteousness shall yield peace" (Is 32:17).

After 597 and 587 B.C., the message of peace becomes the very heart of the prophetic promises, especially in Deutero-Isaiah. Salvation, deliverance, glory and righteousness are the marks of the expectation of peace, of the final "covenant of peace" (Is 54:10; 62:1-2). But at the centre is the forecasting of the coming suffering Messiah, "the prince of peace" (Is 9:6; 61:2) who, in person, will pay the price of peace (Is 53:5). "He shall be a man of peace" (Mic 5:4).

2. The Peace of Christ

From the Christmas song of the angels, "peace on earth" (Lk 2:14) to Christ's solemn entrance to Jerusalem (19:38), Luke presents Christ as the promised "king of peace". With the greeting, *Shalom*, Jesus heals the sick (8:48) and forgives sins (7:50). The gospel of John tells of Christ sharing his own peace with his disciples: "Peace is my parting gift to you, my own peace" (14:27). This is said in the context of the coming of the Holy Spirit who is the supreme gift of the Father (14:26). *Shalom* is the greeting and gift of the risen Lord who breathed on his disciples and said, "Receive the Holy Spirit" (Jn 20:19-25).

This vision is emphatically expressed by Paul. Twelve times he speaks of peace, together with *cháris*, the grace of the Spirit. Like love and graciousness, peace is a fruit of the Holy Spirit (Gal 5:22; Rom 14:17). For Paul, the peace of Christ is a sharing in Christ's own life and peace: "The peace of God which surpasses all understanding will keep guard over your hearts and your thoughts, in Christ Jesus" (Phil 4:7).

Here we are reminded again of the leitmotif of this moral theology "in Christ". Peace is not only a parting gift, it is a sharing, a sign of our "life in Christ Jesus". "He himself is our peace" (Eph 2:14). This central message is given in the context of the reconciliation of Jews and Gentiles in Christ, through the covenant in his blood. This is now much more than the reunification of the two divided parts of Israel[7]; it is the real sacramental symbol of the dawning messianic peace (cf. Col 3:15). In all this, Jesus makes visible for us "the God of love and peace" (2 Cor 13:11).[8]

3. Messengers of peace

Sharing his own peace with his disciples, Christ makes them messengers and builders of peace, ambassadors of reconciliation. By this mission he tells humankind that peace is possible if his message and gift are received. The rule of his kingdom is a rule for peacemakers. "Blest are the peacemakers; God shall call them his sons and daughters" (Mt 5:9).

The Roman emperor was called "son of God - peacemaker", but he made peace by dominating people with a strong arm.[9] Christ gives a peace "such as the world cannot give" (Jn 14:27). His messengers can win the world over to Christ's peace only through their "gentle spirit" (Mt 5:5). He, who reconciled sinners through his long-suffering and non-violent love, shares his peace with his messengers and tells them: "As the Father has sent me, so I send you" (Jn 20:21).

The ministry and message entrusted to the disciples of Christ can be summed up simply as "gospel of peace" (Eph 6:15; cf. Eph 2:17; Acts 10:36). This peace characterizes both the messenger and his work: "Peace is in the subject. It is his work".[10]

Not only is justice the way to peace; it is also its fruit. "True justice is the harvest reaped by peacemakers from seeds sown in a spirit of peace" (Jas 3:18). They shall offer everywhere, with words and their whole attitude, the greeting and gift of peace (Lk 10:5-6). In Christ, the true disciple can be a co-creator of peace. "A creator of peace, he will follow his path, lighting the lamps of joy and playing their brilliance and loveliness on the hearts of men across the surface of the globe, leading them to recognize, across all frontiers, the faces of their brothers, the faces of their friends."[11]

The world is absolutely in need of men and women who, filled with the peace of Christ, act as peacemakers.[12] The work of peace is entrusted to all of Christ's disciples, women no less than men. The ever-wider participation of women in the life of society brings "a specific contribution of great value, thanks to the qualities that God has given them. These qualities of intuition, creativity, sensibility, a sense of piety and compassion, a profound capacity for understanding and love, enable women to be, in a very particular way, the creators of reconciliation in families and in society."[13]

With Jacques Ellul, we insist that "one of the most important functions of Christians is to be a cooling and peacemaking factor among men".[14] The sermon on the Mount was meant for all people of all times. Its gospel of peace can change the world. Indeed, it could not have been written if there were not then - as now - people thoroughly seized by the reality and message of peace. Christians owe it to Christ and to the world to be witnesses to this saving power.[15]

4. Peace in the midst of conflict

Renewed by the peace of Christ, we are sent as peacemakers, yet we are still at war with our own sinfulness. Thus there is a dual battle to be fought in a world redeemed but still obstinate in its antagonisms.

In his very peace mission, Christ found the most violent conflict and rejection. In his passion and death, inflicted by the violent and powerful, God's non-violent love entered into the conflicts of the fallen world. As the Father sent him, so he sends us into a world where the gospel of peace is a two-edged sword. He who is our peace warns us: "You must not think that I have come to bring peace; I have not come to bring peace but a sword" (Mt 10:34). "I have come to bring division. For from now on, five members of a family will be divided, three against two" (Lk 12:51-52). The hidden conflicts and dissensions come into the open. Only through a painful crisis can peace be won. The opposition which we find when we live and proclaim "the gospel of peace" is a challenge for us to root out in ourselves whatever causes discord. Through Christ, the prince of Peace, and his messengers, "the secret thoughts of many will be laid bare" (Lk 2:35).

The disaster of Jerusalem, which chose violent solutions rather than Christ's peace, is more deplorable and shocking than if Christ had not come. But Jerusalem was offered a real chance of peace (cf. Lk 19:42-46). Driving the traders from the temple, Jesus makes a drastic prophetic effort to stop the abuse of religion (Lk 19:45-46) in order to pave the road for truth and peace.

Those who intend to justify violent solutions to conflicts argue with Jesus' words about the "sword" (cf. Mt 10:34; Lk 22:35-38). Luke (12:51) uses the word "division" instead of "sword", and this is what Jesus meant. He surely did not advocate the use of swords by his disciples to whom he entrusted the gospel of peace. The apostles seem to have misunderstood, at first, the symbolic words by which he predicted the imminent outbreak of the final conflict: "whoever has a purse had better take it with him, and his pack too; and if he has no sword, let him sell his cloak to buy one". When they responded, "Look, Lord, we have two swords here", he answered: "Enough, enough" (Lk 22:37-38)! In the context, and also in view of Lk 22:49-51, this probably meant, "Enough of this! No more of this!"[16] The words recorded by Matthew (26:52) give further evidence that Jesus was disturbed about the misunderstanding: "Put up your sword! All who take the sword die by the sword".

While Jesus' death on a cross and many texts in the New Testament will never allow us to minimize the conflict, the resurrection event and the total biblical message of peace leave no doubt that the final word is not conflict, but peace promised by God, in Christ, and to be proclaimed and fostered by peaceable disciples of Christ.

In all this we should see how the biblical message contrasts with that human tradition which, since the times of Heraclites, considers war as "the father of everything" or sees man, with Thomas Hobbes, as "wolf to man".

According to Mao Tse Tung and many others, "Marxist philosophy holds that the law of the unity of opposites is the fundamental law of the universe".[17] We might be able to agree thus far, understanding it with Nikolaus Cusanus as the "complexity of opposites". But Mao tells us clearly: "In any given phenomenon or thing, the unity of opposites is conditional, temporary and transitional, and hence relative, whereas the sruggle of opposites is absolute".[18]

Friedrich Nietzsche tells us bluntly: "You shall love peace as a means to new wars - and short peace rather than long! Let your peace be victory".[19] In the same vein, Niccolo Machiavelli teaches that "A ruler should have no other aim or thought, nor take up anything for his study, but war and its organization and discipline";[20] and he wanted his princes to use religion shrewdly for this prime purpose.

Serving the gospel of peace, we must be fully aware of these ideologies and make a clear and well-grounded decision. One thing is awareness of conflict and violence; another is when "it is thought about, analyzed and consciously desired. Many people interpret it as a law of history. Society is presented as essentially connected with conflict. The struggle of cultures, classes or ideologies is often relied upon to ensure the tansformation of social life".[21]

At this juncture of history it becomes evident that a humanity which follows the classical scheme of power politics and believes explicitly that violence in conflicts is the absolute, is preparing doomsday. Therefore, every Christian who believes in the gospel of peace must make a fundamental option which will permeate his or her whole life, especially in the way of confronting conflicts. And we should never indulge in the illusion that those who have received their psychological training in power politics and ruthless violence, based on an ideology like that of Hobbes, Machiavelli, Nietzsche and Mao Tse Tung will - after their victory - produce an era of peace.[22]

A fundamental option for the truth that peace is possible, and that all of creation yearns and cries for it, obliges us to examine carefully the mind-set of our culture, economics and politics. Do they or do they not contradict this truth and follow the great heresy that wants war to be the procreator of everything? E. F. Schumacher applies this scrutiny to science and technology: "Peace, it has often been said, is indivisible - how, then, could peace be built on a foundation of reckless science and violent technology?"[23]

II. THE CURSE OF WAR[24]

1. War and peace in the New Testament

Concerning the time after Constantine, I think that Roland Bainton is right in asserting that "the Christian ethic of war was not specifically Christian but either Hebrew or Greek with Christian accommodations".[25] A search in the New Testament for detailed precepts - for instance, on the subject of a "just war" - will be disappointing. What is needed is the appropriate approach to the hermeneutics and use of the Bible. Then we get clear perspectives, a most relevant vision and basic principles.

In the history of Israel and in the Old Testament scriptures, we see the conflicts between the mentality of the warrior tribes and peace prophecy. There is the ruthlessness of so-called "holy wars" but also - and this is the line of revelation - the growing awareness that the spirals of killing and war are a striking sign and consequence of sinfulness, and that God wants to stop them (cf. Gen 4:8-16: the Cain story, and Gen 4:19-24: the Lamech story). The prophets awaken a great desire for peace, showing that it is "an enterprise of justice" (Is 32:17), and proclaiming that the Lord's design is peace. "They shall beat their swords into ploughshares and their spears into pruning hooks; one nation shall not raise the sword against another, nor shall they train for war again" (Is 2:4).

The temptation of a nationalistic and perverted messianism is everywhere present in the gospel stories. Jesus does all in his power, by example and word, in life and in death, to show that he is the Servant Messiah. He leaves no place for nationalism, greed or lust for power. The rule of the reign proclaimed by him is gentleness and peacefulness. There is no ambiguity in his teaching. His disciples are those who love their enemies, live at peace with all people insofar as it lies in their power, and use good to defeat evil. Only thus will they not be conquered by evil (Rom 12:18-21).

These positive and forceful directives are more relevant than an incidental and indirect remark about political realism in the parable which takes for granted that only a fool will start war without first considering his chances (Lk 14:31-32). The "realism" will not be effective in view of the utter insanity of modern war and the clear insight into its inevitability, unless we adopt the vision and spirit of the gospel and are willing to free ourselves from anything that might hinder our discipleship (Lk 14:33).

2. On the history of pacifism

In a carefully documented study, Roland Bainton comes to the conclusion that "the early church was pacifist to the time of Constantine".[26] Its pacifism was not derived from a legalistic use of New Testament texts "but from an effort to apply what was taken to be the mind of Christ. Christianity brought to social problems, not a detailed code of ethics or a new political theory, but a new scale of values."[27]

In our military age, Catholic writers tend to explain the pacifism of the first three centuries by non-pacifist considerations.[28] Military service brought dangers of the cult of the emperor, and other occasions of sin. It seems that the church, especially in those borders endangered by invasions, was somehow tolerant of military service. Bainton sees an almost continuous tradition of Christians in military service at the eastern frontier. But on principle, "all the outstanding writers of the east and the west repudiated participation in warfare".[29] Military service was tolerated, at least partially, because it could be considered as a kind of police service. Warfare was seen as a different thing.

During the first century of the constantinian era, the church Fathers, while making some adjustment to the "just war" theories, kept pacifism as an absolute rule for monks and clergy, and drew up rigid directives for non-violent conduct in private life. Ambrose and Augustine did not condone killing for self-defence outside of military or public service.[30] St Basil still expressed the early church's aversion to bloodshed, although he abandoned the general objection to warfare: "Killing in war was differentiated by our fathers from murder. . . nevertheless perhaps it would be well that those whose hands are unclean abstain from communion for three years".[31]

In opposition to a rather militant church, the late medieval sects were generally votaries of the pacifism which had marked early Christianity. Within Protestantism, the Anabaptists (Mennonites) and later the Quakers were and are firmly committed to this tradition, but with a notable difference. Whereas the Anabaptists withdraw from politics, the Quakers combine a strong sense of political responsibility and activity with their pacifism. By their loyalty and tolerance towards those who think differently, they convinced the English government of the rights of conscience, and for the first time were accorded exemption from military service on this ground in 1802. "The English state agreed at last to accord a civil status to an internal conviction deemed wrong by the state."[32]

Although there were always many lovers of peace and peacemakers in the mainstream of the churches, not all had the optimism of the Quaker William Smith, who envisioned the spiritual army marching under the banner of love, which would reach such strength that "wars would cease, cruelty end, and love abound".[33]

3. The "just war" theory and its history

Although the outspoken intention of the Second Vatican Council is liberation from the age-old slavery of war, it takes up the traditional theory of "just war" in a carefully restricted formulation. "As long as the danger of war remains and there is no competent and sufficiently powerful authority at the international level, governments cannot be denied the right to legitimate defence, once every means of peaceful settlement have been exhausted."[34]

It seems to me that in order to be more discerning, we can learn a great deal from the long history of the "just war" theory.

As a result of the close association of church and state since Constantine, and partially because of the threat of barbarian invasions, Christians of the fourth and fifth centuries took over from the classical world the theory of the just war, the object of which should be "to vindicate justice and restore peace".[35]

Aristotle, who first coined the expression "just war", considered its main purpose to be peace among the hellenistic states. Even in the midst of conflict, the over-arching solidarity within this culture should be conserved. But for people outside the hellenistic pale, the picture was different. Populations, designed by nature for servitude, could be forced by war if they resisted their proper assignment in the social state.[36] Cicero made a constructive contribution to the just war theory by insisting on peace as the primary aim of a just war. Of course, he meant the "Roman peace". His greatest concern was for humane treatment of the vanquished tribes and nations, "because only a liberal peace was a sound basis for the building up of an empire. Reviewing the history of Rome until his own time, he gave the verdict that Rome had conquered the world by means of just war and generous peace".[37]

Cicero influenced St Ambrose, who first formulated a Christian ethic of just war. By insisting that priests and monks ought to abstain from war, Ambrose underlined the evil of war, which should never be undertaken without proportionate reasons; and its conduct should be just. "Not eagles and birds must lead the army but thy name and religion, O Jesus."[38] The wars he had in mind were defensive wars against barbarians who were mostly Arians.

Augustine lays down the basic conditions for a just war: (1) the intent must always be to restore peace; (2) the object is to vindicate justice with moderation; (3) war cannot be just without the inner disposition of christian love; love does not exclude wars of mercy waged by the good;[38] (4) war must be just; it is to be waged only under the authority of a legitimate ruler; (5) the conduct of war must be just. Faith must be kept with the enemy. Vengeance, atrocities and reprisals are absolutely excluded.[39] Thomas Aquinas took up this vision and granted it his authority.[40]

The greatest influence on just war theories in modern times came from Francis of Vittoria.[41] He prepared two works on the subject of war: *On the Indians (De Indis)* and *On the Law of War (De jure belli)*. For him, no war that would inflict great damage on the world at large and on its Christian population could be called a "just war". But even Vittoria, who rejected numerous religious grounds for war, accepted the defence of Christian missionaries and their converts as cause for war.[42] The just war tradition absolutely excludes wars of extermination and wars unto unconditional surrender.[43]

The primary intention of the great theologians in their just war theories was to limit war. Erasmus, who subscribed to the traditional ethic of just war, reviewed the wars of Europe and condemned them all as "incompatible with the stipulations of a just war".[44] But unfortunately, churchmen and second-rate moralists often lacked discernment. LeRoy Walter concludes his case study with the shocking statement that "all of the theorists used just war categories to argue that their own countries had a just cause for war in the cases under discussion".[45]

Roland Bainton comes to a similar conclusion. During the first world war "the churches in every land gave support to their governments. . . The Catholic Mausbach and the Protestant Holl looked upon Germany as begirt by foes bent on her strangulation. . . In England the mood fluctuated between the just war and the crusade. . . American churchmen of all faiths were never so united with each other and with the mind of the country that 'this was a holy war' "[46]. We can only wonder at the lack of prophetic spirit. There were all too many "king's priests", bereft of knowledge of salvation.

4. Justice in warfare

The classical just war tradition, including the Second Vatican Council treatment, gives special attention to the just conduct in war (*jus in bello*). There must be only a limited will to war, and everything should be directed to peace and reconciliation. Love of enemy will allow only the minimum of killing, and only with sorrow. Noncombatants must not be damaged; even indirect and non-intentional killing must be avoided as far as possible. There must be no reprisals, as such. The attempt to seduce people to hatred, for example by calumnies, is an abominable sin leading to the most horrifying crimes committed with a dormant or corrupt conscience.

During the second world war, "Hitler first bombed Warsaw and Rotterdam, where civilian populations were destroyed. . . In May, 1940, Britain, by an extension of her old naval policy gave to aerial warfare a new turn in the bombing of cities - no longer in order to facilitate the movement of troops but to wreck the will of the enemy population to resist. Germany, in September, retaliated with attacks on Coventry and Birmingham. Churchill declared, 'there will be no lengths of violence to which we will not go' ".[47]

The apex of this war against civilians was the atom bombs on Nagasaki and Hiroshima, whereby the so-called free world killed, along with hundreds of thousands of children, women and elderly people, its own credibility. I do not say that President Truman did it; there was a shocking proportion of people who made it possible and approved it. All those, including churchmen and moralists, who did not raise their voices against obliteration bombing, have their share of responsibility. "Even after the war ended, a questionnaire conducted by *Fortune* revealed that half of the respondents felt that the decision to use the atom bomb on Hiroshima and Nagasaki had been right. And nearly a quarter of them regretted that more atomic bombs had not been used on other Japanese cities."[48] If all moralists and churchmen had clearly come out against obliteration bombing, as did *Christian Century* and the Catholic theologian, John C. Ford,[49] atomic warfare might never have started.

The supreme authority of the Catholic church, in council, issued one of the strongest statements against the savagery of modern warfare, and especially against the bombing of cities. "Any war aimed indiscriminately at the destruction of entire cities or of extensive areas, along with their populations, is a crime against God and man himself. It merits unequivocal and unhesitating condemnation."[50] While it was a shocking experience to see that a number of churchmen from powerful countries rallied to resist this text, it was consoling to see the firm resolution of Pope Paul VI and the large majority of the Council fathers. The declaration is fully in line with the whole doctrinal tradition which, tragically, was all too often transgressed during wars under the eyes of the "king's priests".

5. The "holy wars" and crusades

The biblical faith of some people is seriously tempted when they read for the first time the stories in the Books of Numbers and Judges about the "holy" wars of extirpation waged in the name of God. How can the all-holy God, who has revealed himself in Jesus Christ, be the same God who commanded the Israelites to kill whole populations, including even children and women?

Biblical scholars tell us today that these wars probably never took place: that the Deuteronomists dated back their own views, and the stories were those of "romancing reformers whose program was never attained".[51] These pages do reveal, however,

the imperfect perceptions of religious men and should inspire the
deepest gratitude for God's full and final revelation in his Son,
Jesus Christ, who gave us a quite different direction. The pity is
that in the historical development of the rise, fall and revival of
the crusading ideal - and, indeed, until the development of biblical
criticism - the church did not realize that these wars of
extermination had never occurred. Yet, if the theologians and the
powerful rulers of the church had conformed with the mind of
Christ, as St Francis of Assisi did, the crusades could have been
avoided, or at least would not have been so scandalously
degenerate. The mood of the crusades was a strange mixture of
barbarian lust for combat and zeal for the holy places.

The heretical ideas on crusading and the connected justification
of the most abominable cruelties were revived in the wars of
religion after the Reformation of the sixteenth century and
partially in the extermination wars against the aborigines in the
Americas. In modern wars waged mainly for the sake of power
and wealth the enemy had to be made to look so bedeviled that
extermination war and/or the insistence on "unconditional
surrender" could be rationalized, with or without "religious"
ideologies.

One of the greatest threats to the survival of humankind and of
co-humanity in our time is the secularized forms of the "holy
war" tradition. The Second Vatican Council rightly speaks of
"unbending ideologies".[52] In this context we should think not
only of extreme Communism but also of those no less fanatical
anti-Communists who in a kind of "holy-war" rage would be
willing to use the whole arsenal of weapons which can
exterminate humankind many times over.

One thing should be particularly clear to us: to make its
genuine contribution to peace on earth Christianity must be
thoroughly purged of the crusading tradition. And we would do
well to listen to men like Roland Bainton who loudly warn against
"Victor's justice" which is least of all capable of administering
justice and working for an enduring peace when the mood and the
old arguments of the crusade tradition prevail.[53]

6. The wars against the aborigines

In the wars against the Indians of the Americas, the Spaniards adapted and grossly falsified the "just war" theory. The real motives were greed and an egoistic superiority complex. The most ruthless conquistadores hypocritically tended to wear the mask of religious motives. "Evangelization" became an excuse for enslavement of populations.

Francisco de Vittoria insisted that the natives were not to be converted by force nor to be killed because of their rejection of the gospel. But his assessment of the real situation was faulty when he allowed the just war theory to apply against them when they hindered travel through their territories or refused to permit the preaching of the gospel. Indeed, the natives had good reasons to refuse both, since practically, these activities were connected with the intention to subject them. The influential Spanish Sepulveda responded to the situation by renewing Aristotle's teaching that there was good ground for just war in enslaving those who were destined by nature to this inferior status.[54] Las Casas did his best to unmask the real motives, and so impressed Emperor Charles V that the emperor ordered a temporary halt to further expansion and asked theologians to study the question.

In North America, the Puritans revived the crusade idea in their wars of extermination against the Indians, while the Quakers in Pennsylvania adhered firmly to the Sermon on the Mount. The New Englanders considered themselves commissioned by God, like Moses, to eradicate the "God-damned" aborigines.[55]

The least that Christians should learn is to leave the name of God out of their wars.

7. False messianism and armament for holy wars

True "chosenness", as fulfilled in Christ, means to be chosen for others. The heretical idea of chosenness over and above others leads to enslavement of others and temptations to impose on others one's own concept of truth and shape of society. This is one of the main causes of wars, especially of the abominable "holy" wars. False messianism disturbed the life and peace-mission of the church. The Puritan idea of a materialistic chosenness was a source of economic success but to the detriment of a peaceful, just and balanced society and socio-economic life.

Wars are normally decided by small élites, who do not fulfil the role of social élites to be and to work for others. They create the myth of wars, as if it were the will of the whole nation. This myth must be unmasked if we want a stable peace.

The church has frequently served the cause of peace, but she has taken part in a war-mentality through coalescence with cultures marked by false elitism. The deeper source of the evil is a partial abandonment of the gospel of peace brought by the Servant Messiah.

III. LIBERATION FROM THE SLAVERY OF WAR

In the second world war, savagery reached its peak. Since 1945 there have been nearly 150 armed conflicts throughout the world. More than 25 million men are in active army service, and at least 12 million reservists can be called overnight to arms. More than 60 percent of them belong to the developing countries. More than six percent of the world's gross income is wasted in arms races.[56]

Looking at this shocking picture, we might well be tempted to agree with Reinhold Niebuhr (1892-1970), the most valiant North American ethicist of this century. He thought that individuals can be converted to peace but the "immoral society" will never rid itself from the curse of war.[57] However, in view of the superabundant redemption in Christ, I believe and intend to proclaim, with John XXIII, Paul VI and his successors, that "peace is possible", and therefore, humanity can be exhorted to decide, "No more war! Never again! It is peace that must guide the destinies of peoples and of all mankind".[58]

Realizing the enormous difficulties, all should join in this decisive hope and endeavour.[59]

1. The time has come

After a sober assessment of the new situation and experiences, the Second Vatican Council entreats humanity to use the interlude, granted by divine providence, to do everything in our power to "free ourselves from the age-old slavery of war. But if we refuse to make this effort, we do not know where the evil road we have ventured upon will lead us".[60] Everyone who has not lost his right mind should agree with Cardinal Roy that "war no longer seems only a crime but an absurdity as well".[61]

After all the experiences through which history teaches us, and in view of the deadly arsenal of weapons that can destroy humankind and poison the whole ecological system, it should be clear, that even on its own reasoning, the traditional "just war" theory can no longer be applied. Kenneth E. Boulding, a leading peace researcher, insists that modern war will affect the total-earth system which is now a reality. As long as the earth was divided into a large number of isolated subsystems, as it was before the modern era, a catastrophe - as, for example, the destruction of the Maya empire - could happen without the rest of the world knowing about it. Now, if anything goes wrong on our small planet, everything may go wrong.[62]

The history of humankind, sad as it is, does not preclude hope. We can find subsystems in which movements towards stable peace have taken place and are now taking place. Another noted peace researcher, Carl Friedrich von Weizsäcker, thinks that there is growing in our generation a new consciousness which, unlike past eras, no longer accepts war as a fate or necessity or as a source of glory.[63]

The experience and history of the unity of humankind appear to an ever-growing number of people as a new truth. This truth is still in its birthpangs, seeking its "body" in a worldwide peace-service which has absolute priority.[64] Should we not be able to orchestrate the appeal of peace apostles like Erasmus of Rotterdam? "I appeal to all who call themselves Christians to unite all their strength and efforts in the combat against war. Everybody may contribute with his advice. Abiding concord must unite all who, by nature and through Christ, are united by so many bonds."[65]

If Christians would be drawn together by the gospel of peace, many people would open themselves to this appeal.

2. Conscientious objection and prophetic protest

We have seen earlier that Christians of the first centuries distinguished carefully between military service considered as service for order and peace, and on the other hand, participation in warfare. In our own day, the United Nations Peace Corps is establishing a new approach. Its presence is marked by non-violence. These men and women from many nations are, indeed, an army for peace. They abstain from supporting any side, and call sides to the observance of truce and non-violent solutions of conflicts.

Military service in a modest army of peace-loving nations does not normally raise problems of conscience. But service in the modern armies of nations involved in power struggles and in military blocs cause more and more serious problems for many men, and can easily lead to conscientious objection.[66]

We distinguish between refusal of military service and refusal of obedience when, in wartime or during bloody revolution, a man is convinced in conscience that an order is unjust and commands a crime. On this point, tradition and the present teaching of the church are very clear. Man's conscience itself gives ever more emphatic voice to the traditional principles about warfare. "Therefore, actions which deliberately conflict with these same principles, as well as orders commanding such actions, are criminal. Blind obedience cannot excuse those who yield to them."[67]

Traditional moral theology taught that no one can enrol in military service or participate in warfare unless he is convinced in conscience about the justice of the cause. But moralists usually emphasized that the presumption of justice is in favour of the legitimate government. Reviewing past wars, one cannot but disagree. A more critical attitude is needed for the formation of mature consciences and for serving the cause of peace by putting greater pressure on governments.

A growing critical consciousness and more severe judgment of past wars, and of war crimes committed under military orders, lead many people to consider general conscription for military service irreconcilable with their sincere conscience. This is not just the pacifism of a religious group (like the Mennonites) but a personal conviction after reflection on the absurdity of modern war and the irrationality of modern armament. The firmness with which many of the objectors accept imprisonment and other disadvantages, and others offer themselves for peace service, makes their objection a prophetic protest, a loud appeal to society for disarmament and international reconciliation.

The Second Vatican Council acknowledges at least the sincerity of conscience, and appeals to the modern state to respect it. "It seems right that laws make humane provisions for the case of those who, for reasons of conscience, refuse to bear arms, provided however, that they accept some other form of service to the human community."[68] If humanity in the future reaches a new peace-mentality, large-scale disarmament and new structures for the protection and promotion of peace, there will be a grateful memory of the peace movements and their martyrs, and of the conscientious objectors who are now helping to prepare this event.

Peace movements call for individual and collective repentance, not just for past wars but for all the present attitudes which are seeds of war.

3. Spirituality and relevance of non-violent action

In Chapter Eight I have written about active non-violence as an alternative to violent revolution. Action-oriented non-violence is, to my mind, not only the alternative to war but the most fearless and forceful weapon against war and for the truth of liberating love and justice.[69]

St Francis and his most creative followers were not just pacifists but aggressive opponents of war and active reconciliators who were willing to take the risk involved in such actions. The pacifist who is content simply not to offer resistance may be actually betraying truth and justice by not taking them seriously enough.

Quite the opposite is the *Satyagraha* of Mahatma Gandhi and Vinoba, which is total dedication to the truth of love, justice and brotherhood. It is aggressively at war against war and its causes, using as weapons the only fitting spirituality and means. "A life of non-violence means not merely occasional sacrifice but perpetual sacrifice, joy in the sacrifice."[70] For a Christian, creative, unbending dedication to non-violent action is the most valiant expression of faith in the Redeemer of the world, the Prince of peace who revealed the power of truth and love unto death on the cross.

Satyagraha liberates the world from the friend-enemy mentality, and thus from the vicious circle of fear and threat. People who live the liberating truth in non-violent, creative action and communication do not wish to crush those on the other side, but to change their hearts. They let the others know that all can become friends, that nobody is a loser. In the realm of non-violence, one side's victory is also the other side's victory. So forceful is the way of non-violence! It is "subversive" in the best sense, changing the whole system of antagonism. It is a transfiguration of politics in and through the story of Christ.[71]

Effective non-violence is both challenging and demanding. It does not work unless we liberate ourselves, and gradually our culture, from enslaving greed and all that greed entails. Those who follow the non-violent way refuse psychic and physical violence, fraud or deception, cowardly silence or manipulation of the mind of others, even in cases of hard conflicts. They have no lust for power. Like Jesus, they confront evil unarmed and without hatred or resentment, and bless those who misunderstand and persecute them. With the power of love and in absolute frankness, they resist evil forcefully, thoughtfully and concretely, but on a new level.[72]

The official church has begun to discover the hope-inspiring value of this non-violent combat against unpeacefulness, injustice and war. The Second Vatican Council has this cautious text: "All Christians are urgently summoned to 'practise truth in love' (Eph 4:15) and to join with all true peacemakers in pleading for peace and bringing it about. Motivated by this same spirit, we cannot fail to praise those who renounce the use of violence in the vindication of their rights, and who resort to methods of defence which are otherwise available to weaker parties too, provided that this can be done without injury to the rights and duties of others or of the community itself."[73] The last phrase, "provided", was a concession to those who had not yet a clear idea of *satyagraha*, the most dedicated and complete service to justice and peace. But how can such a strategy, inspired and filled with non-violent, truthful love, do injury to anyone?

What is needed is a systematic teaching of this spirit and strategy by all churches to all their believers, followed by a concerted effort in union with all peaceable people to convince public opinion, legislators and civil authorities how urgent it is to build up this truly holy action against war and for peace and justice. It is not just a matter of defence of one's own rights. We need a purposeful and comprehensive education and exercise to uproot mutual fear. There also has to be included, however, a strategy of non-violent but most forceful resistance to a military aggressor, in such a way that those engaged in the aggressive actions can experience the power of truth and love.

The non-violent resistance of the people of Czechoslovakia against the Soviet invasion in 1968 was one of the finest testimonies to humanness, freedom and fearlessness. Unfortunately, an occasional outburst of violence gave the invaders an excuse to crush all forms of protest ruthlessly.[74] All peaceful nations should prepare for such events. The very preparation would be of great benefit to the whole culture. This alone is the realistic alternative to the senseless arms race, to war and to cowardly surrender.

4. Disarmament[75]

a) The terror of armament

Violence and terrorism have become the parallels in a "balance of terror" accepted almost as normal and unavoidable among nations and power blocs. Although the existing arsenal of nuclear weapons is sufficient to destroy all of humanity and to devastate the human ecology completely, the USSR was spending in 1979 about 165 billion dollars (17 percent of the gross national income) for weapons still more dangerous.[76] The countries of the Atlantic alliance spent as much for "defence".

The "balance of power" implies a threat of total destruction of the enemy and, at the same time, the risk of almost total self-annihilation of the nation that seeks the advantage of the first strike. Meanwhile, the so-called "traditional" weapons are becoming ever more destructive. If an eventual war waged with these were to give a threatening superiority to one side, then almost inevitably the other side would strike with nuclear weapons.

This abnormal situation seems to be a good reason not to start an outright war, but it is a strange protection for peace. It surely does not deserve the name "peace". There is constant risk that fear and suspicion, together with an error in the alarm system, will lead to more than just "local" wars. If the present situation continues, it must almost inevitably worsen. And even a low risk becomes a high risk in the long run - indeed, the most absurd risk humankind has ever ventured.[77]

b) Urgent call for radical disarmament

The present situation is a monstrous pathology, a collective madness, and an enormous "injustice and theft".[78] "The arms race hurts the poor in an intolerable way."[79] The Second Vatican Council, the Roman pontiffs, the World Council of Churches, and almost all churches cry out to the ears of political leaders.[80] It is absolutely necessary that nuclear and bacterial weapons be banned totally and all nuclear material be put under regional and international control. The so-called strategic nuclear weapons with circumscribed radii should be absolutely tabooed, for if once transgressed, there will be no effective and clear borderline. But disarmament must apply also to traditional weapons. Trading in weapons should be blocked by a strong international public opinion and by an international authority.

c) The main obstacles

The major obstacles to a radical disarmament are the super-powers' desire for hegemony, the national security complexes, disputes over unjust boundaries, the military industrial complex and, last but not least, an aggressive and acquisitive society that has lost the spirit of moderation. Nationalist movements, the political hawks, the lobbies of the war industries have been, up to now, more influential than the peace movements. "It is not surprising that the military tries to create a sense of insecurity, for they benefit from this. Estimates of Russian armaments by the American military and the CIA, for example, are far larger than the estimates by the Stockholm International Research Center."[81]

The concept of the "abominable enemy", is so fundamental to the traditional military ethos, legitimacy and "morale" that a new vision of reconciliation and mutual trust would be perceived as a "threat to the existing military subculture".[82] The presence of ever-growing armaments strengthens fear and suspicion, and these in turn seem to justify resistance to radical disarmament. Self-encapsulation leads to an ever more threatening image of the enemy and blinds people to the absurdity of the present deterrence systems.[83]

Carl von Weizsäcker feels that the main obstacle is not the diversity of the social structures of the USA (the West) and of Russia, but rather the polarization of the hawks and the doves common to both blocs.[84]

d) A "utopia"

Utopias can be signs of a new spirit and a result of creative imagination which may point out the right direction. Such a utopia has gained strength in France, in a movement against nuclear weapons (MCAA). Its adherents urge the French government to renounce, unilaterally and unconditionally, its arsenal of nuclear weapons in the hope that such an initiative may induce other countries to follow.[85]

Such a sober historian as Roland Bainton (USA) dares also to invite the authorities to give serious reflection to this utopia which could become the most realistic approach, if people were imbued with a thoroughly new - and redeemed - thinking. "Let us suppose that our nation should disarm unilaterally. What would happen? We do not know. Such an unparalleled renunciation might have an amazing effect. Weakness, as such, has no power . . . If a nation possessed of strength should voluntarily renounce its advantage, however, the enemy might respond with alacrity and relief. No proof of this can be offered because no nation has ever tried. But there are cases on a more personal level which point to hope."[86]

Just let us imagine the less probable case: that Communist governments would not respond "with alacrity", and furthermore, that the free countries would decide instead for well-prepared and deeply motivated non-violent defence. . . Would this not be the complete end of militant Communism? It would die in the hearts of all its adherents who have preserved their humanity. Would soldiers fight against countries that have made such a generous move?

And yet I know that this proposal is, for the time being, no more than a utopia, since in many people the new spirit has not yet taken root. But it should be shouted from the rooftops everywhere. It should be a dream of hope in every home and should remind everyone of the kind of individual and collective conversion that is the way of salvation.

e) Mutually-agreed and controlled disarmament

Humankind must liberate itself from the arms race which, in the words of the Second Vatican Council, is an utterly treacherous trap for humanity. "New approaches initiated by reformed attitudes must be adopted to remove this trap."[87] The first step proposed is to "put aside national selfishness and ambition to dominate other nations" and to uproot all "feelings of hostility, contempt, distrust, as well as racial hatred and unbending ideologies".[88]

Realists everywhere propose mutually-agreed and controlled disarmament. Until now, not much progress has been made because of a horrifying mixture of distrust and, on the part of the influential hawks on both sides, the unwillingness to renounce superiority in weaponry.

f) Graduated reciprocation: a relative utopia

Charles Osgood, a leading peace researcher, has proposed a graduated reciprocation in reduction of tensions.[89] One part has to begin with a generous first step, a realistic offer and actual initiative, while at the same time doing all in its power to diminish distrust. The late Thomas Merton considered "a radical and sweeping policy of unilateral disarmament" as naïve, but he firmly proposed "unilateral initiatives in gradual steps" as imperative.[90] Roland Bainton makes a helpful suggestion for such initiatives: "We should say that it is to our advantage, and leave them then to see whether it is also theirs. . . but we should act as much in their interest as in our own".[91]

IV. PEACE RESEARCH AND PEACE POLICY[92]

If our history textbooks really reflect past history, then we must confess that our ancestors have done more for war than for peace. Indeed, the textbooks themselves give evidence that our school systems have spoken more about the history of war than anything else, and not with the purpose of making clear the absurdity of war. A new discipline called "peace research" or absurdity of war. A new discipline called "peace research" or "Irenology" is a sign of hope. A statistic of the United Nations in 1973 indicates 297 scholars, 78 institutes, and 483 publications and several journals dedicated to peace and conflict research. At the present time, more than five hundred colleges offer courses in peace education based on peace research.[93] Will modern culture ever reach the state of normality where more intelligence, endeavour and time are dedicated to peace research and peace education than to armament and war?

1. Meaning and purpose of peace research

The purpose of peace research is to fight effectively against war, not only with concern but also with competence, not only with rhetoric but with knowledge, and thus turn the world away from war and onto the road of peace. The purpose is a stable peace, true peace. Therefore, peace research can in no way be a value-free science.

The first thing necessary is to clarify values and priorities. The kind of peace we want determines the approach to peacemaking and its methods. Hence, peace research everywhere necessarily asks: What is truthful peace, and what are the favourable conditions for permanent peace?

Not satisfied with abstract ideas of peace, peace research works inductively towards "a phenomenology of peace".[94] It looks for peaceable people and peaceful relationships, and reviews the history and art of peacemaking. Inquiring into the various forms of unpeacefulness and conflict, it studies the difference between awareness of conflict and its causes and, on the other hand, the hidden conflicts - the efforts of the "top dogs" to convince the underdogs that the situation is normal, and the underdogs' own repression of consciousness.

Since peace research finds that these unbalanced and unjust relationships create explosive situations, it searches for ways to create the kind of awakening and awareness that has the best chance to lead to genuine reconciliation in justice.

For a time, some peace researchers were one-sidedly concerned with Konrad Lorenz's theory on innate aggression; but even from a psychological point of view, the sources of violence are of greater variety.[95]

Peace research, as an interdisciplinary endeavour, studies intensively the objective causes of tension and conflict but gives equal attention to the modes of perception of one's own image and that of the enemy.[96] The perceptual determinants of conflict behaviour must constantly be related to the real situation as objective observers describe it. It is simply not possible to attack the objective causes of conflict without discovering the subjective and psychological sources. This is especially clear in the writings of those peace researchers who speak chiefly in terms of human relationships. The capacity or lack of capacity to cope with conflicts in a reasonable way depends not only on the tensions but also on the characteristics of those involved.

2. From peace research to peace policy

Although drawing from various fields of science, peace research is not a speculative but a prudential discipline. Its practical purpose is to prepare vision and knowledge for general peace education and for peace policy. Peace policy is an approach to political activity which gives conscious priority to social and international peace. It scrutinizes each decision for whether or not it will have a positive influence on the cause of peace, and it includes every political action that makes a constructive contribution to creating, maintaining or strengthening the conditions which make peace possible.

Peace research explores ways to convince decisive groups in the various populations that only a peace policy is a real contribution to the common good. To the leaders who intend to dedicate themselves to that policy, it offers help in the crucial problems: how to ease tensions in dangerous situations while, at the same time, envisioning the affirmative goals; how to bring to public consciousness hidden conflicts and conflict-situations before they explode in such a way that they can no longer be managed; how to change images for greater compatibility and stimulate a readiness to change one's own conduct and one's perception of the other side's cause. The arts of dialogue, conciliation, arbitration and patient development of healthier relationships also are studied in peace research.

Kenneth Boulding deplores the fact that governments, instead of turning to solid peace research, rely more on spies and diplomats for their information, "in spite of the fact that this system is notoriously corrupt and is much more likely to produce misinformation than truth".[97]

3. New structures for peace

A new spirit and new attitudes of peace need their embodiment in new structures. Peace policy and structures for peace should facilitate a new consciousness, and this in its turn should promote a new order and structures favourable to enduring peace. What has been said in these three volumes about space for freedom and embodiment of creative liberty and fidelity applies equally to peace. Our concern is for freedom for all and covenant fidelity in view of peace for all.

Kenneth Boulding suggests that within each government there should be a "peace department" with a number of missions, such as peace research and its application. It could monitor peace policy, foster peace education, collaborate with international institutes for peace, and find ever new relevant tasks. Cultural exchange could be not only expanded but also better coordinated with peace research and peace education.[98]

There are modest beginnings of cooperation among great world religions, for instance, the "World Conferences on Religion and Peace" in Kyoto (1970) and Louvain (1974).[99] More can be done in this direction. Various groups and institutes for peace research are probing models of a just and peaceful world order.[100] The options are generally not for a centralist world government but rather for functional peace agencies that would transfer some important functions from a national to a planetary level. One of their main purposes should be to turn down the national-security motor and limit dangerous concentrations of power structures.

There is a place for utopias in a new world order which can give inspiration to more realistic proposals.[101] The modellers of world order can combine a prophetic vision and normative postulates with realism. Most of the proposals see opportunities to enlarge and strengthen the functions of the United Nations Organization, step by step, while at the same time awakening a worldwide public conviction that peace is the task and responsibility of everyone and every nation.

One of the most urgent beginnings would be a "United Nations Disarmament Organization" and a permanent "Peace Mediating

Agency" with more effective competence than the present US Security Council. These things are possible if world opinion is aroused to their urgency, and that it is a final question of to be or not to be.

V. PEACE EDUCATION[102]

Those who think that new structures alone, and particularly structures resulting from hateful violence, will bring the synthesis of peace are blind guides for blind men. We know that wholesome peace structures will not come into existence and cannot function without a new spirit and new attitudes. It is up to all people - individuals, communities, nations - to be bearers and creators of peace. Hence the outstanding role of peace education is a systematic and solidly-united endeavour to form peaceful persons and communities.

1. Spirit and purpose of peace education

Peace education is based on the conviction that peace is possible, war must and can be vanquished. For Christians, dedication to peace education arises from faith in redemption. "The Christian knows that there are radically sound possibilities in every man. . . Therefore, if he has hope that God will grant peace to the world, it is because he also trusts that man, God's creature, is not basically evil: that there is in man a potentiality for peace."[103] Christians cannot be faithful to God, the Creator and Redeemer, without carefully cultivating this potentiality.

As a scientist and educator, Abraham Maslow has untiringly shared his finding that in every person there are deep sources of creative liberty, generosity, peacefulness. If people are schooled for the discovery and cultivation of these potentialities, they can create the good society. "There is a feedback between Good Society and Good Person. They need each other. I wave aside the problem of which comes first. It is quite clear that they develop simultaneously and in tandem. It would in any case be impossible to achieve either one without the other. By Good Society I mean ultimately *one species, one world.*"[104].

Today's widespread escalation of despair, violence, mental

illness, mutual contempt, is symptomatic of the failure of existing institutions to provide a holistic vision, a sense of purpose and mission to create the peaceful person and the peaceful society.

No doubt, we need thoughtful research and discussion on the theories of Sigmund Freud, Konrad Lorenz and others about inborn aggressiveness; but what is needed, after all, is an education that helps people to channel their psychic energies of aggression into justice and peace.[105] However, mankind's heavy burden of aggressiveness needs redemption and an education based on faith in the Redeemer. The experience of the peace of Christ includes faith in the cross as a part of discipleship and faith in the victory of those who, animated by the Spirit of Christ, put to death their ingrained selfishness.

An education in which peace receives priority can create a new consciousness and lead to a deeply rooted fundamental option for the goal of peace and for the attitudes needed by peacemakers.

Education for freedom and faithfulness in Christ foster liberation from anguish. C. F. von Weizsäcker tells us that anguish is the most urgent theme in a psychology tuned to peace.[106]

Modern men and women need critical minds to defend themselves against deception and manipulation. But critique without the virtue of discernment is running wild. Peace education, therefore, should not only offer criteria but must also foster an attitude of discernment in order to form the discerning person.

This is not possible without *wisdom*. The economist E. F. Schumacher, who is interested also in peace education, tells us that "man is far too clever to be able to survive without wisdom. No one is really working for peace unless he is working primarily for the restoration of wisdom." And he warns us that "the cultivation and expansion of needs is the antithesis to wisdom. It is also the antithesis to freedom and peace".[107]

Genuine peace education allows no escapism into dreams of peace of mind through withdrawal from responsibility. However, it makes equally clear that the peace of the world depends on the peace we achieve within ourselves. And here it is evident to believers that "the psychological method must be accompanied by a spiritual transformation".[108]

2. *Learning the art of peace in the midst of conflict*

Douglas Steere expresses well the purpose of a realistic and yet hope-filled peace education. "The Christian is three things: he is absolutely fearless, always in trouble, and immensely happy."[109] Peace education follows the pattern of the biblical vision: peace in the midst of a world of conflicts, and even in the midst of conflict with the selfishness and peacelessness in ourselves. Not infrequently it is the self-righteous ones who, claiming a monopoly on truth and virtue, commit crimes against peace like those of the past "holy" wars. C. F. von Weizsäcker feels that the awareness that we, all together, are sinners and in need of redemption belongs to the very substance of Christian love and of our peace mission.[110] Redemption, the effort for peace, and this awareness of solidarity-in-sin can build many bridges.

Peace education allows no foul peace with injustice, oppression and manipulation. "There is no doubt that Christ came to bring peace to men, but not the peace of stagnant swamps, not peace based on injustice, not peace that is the opposite of development. In such cases, Christ himself proclaimed that he had come to bring strife and a sword."[111] Yet it must be understood that we mean the resoluteness of peacemakers to use only the two-edged sword of non-violent action, the aggressive truth of love that helps the others to discover their better potentialities for justice and peace.

Peace education wants to foster endurance, peace needs a constant striving. Those who advocate peace in a society in which there is so much restlessness, deprivation and mutual distrust can only hope for success if they patiently expound and exemplify a peace "that will be seen as a growing edge into a changing and better world".[112]

VI. THE CHURCH, A SACRAMENT OF PEACE

Thanks be to God that the era of the "Church-State" and "the churches of the state" has passed, wherein churchmen and an uncritical crowd of Christians tried to justify their wars even on religious grounds! The Christianity of today is regaining its catholicity in a new awareness of the dimensions of its mission to be and to become ever more an effective sacrament of reconciliation for all of humankind.

The process of ecumenical reconciliation and a worldwide opening of the church brings unavoidable new tensions. We still have to learn better how to face them in full awareness of our peace mission on which our right to call ourselves sons and daughters of God depends. The way we radiate and mediate peace in the midst of tensions within our native church and in the ecumenical movement is of immense importance for peace and the unity of humankind. Our very mission as peacemakers for the world "requires in the first place that we foster within the Church herself mututal esteem, reverence and harmony, through the full recognition of lawful diversity". The further the ecumenical reconciliation "advances toward truth and love under the powerful impulse of the Holy Spirit, the more this unity will be a harbinger of unity and peace for the world at large".[113]

On the occasion of the tenth anniversary of the encyclical *Peace on Earth* of Pope John XXIII, Cardinal Maurice Roy, president of the Pontifical Commission on Peace and Justice, expressed pertinent reflections on how the church can fulfil "her vocation to be the sign and 'sacrament' of peace in the world and for the world". The first condition is "to restore peace within herself" and to "exercise the 'discernment of spirits' to which the approach using the signs of the times invites us." "The same ardour with which Christians struggle against all racial, ethnic, national or ideological discrimination must inspire their own relationships within the people of God". By word and witness, the church ought to manifest "love as the driving force of history". In this context we are also reminded that the priority of love in history draws a number of Christians "to prefer the way of non-violent action".[114]

It is understandable that sometimes church leaders cannot come out with a clear "yes" or "no"; but then significant pronouncements of Christian lay men or women should find wide attention, especially if they combine particular competence with profound dedication to the cause of Christ. The German physicist and peace researcher, C. F. von Weizsäcker has this to say: "If I ask myself whether, after reading the New Testament, I can throw a hydrogen bomb, then I know that the answer is 'No'. And if I may not throw it, then I cannot make it for another to throw. And if I cannot make it in order that it may be thrown, can I then make it in order that it may be used to threaten? . . . I cannot believe that the church can say 'Yes' to use the H-bomb. If she is not able to say 'No' she will have to acknowledge her perplexity either openly or else by complete silence. Yet I believe that members of the church can do themselves and the whole world service if, on quite definite presuppositions, they openly say 'No'."[115]

What St Nikolaus von Flüe, the great peacemaker of Switzerland, wrote in his time to the city government of Basel must be said to political authorities of our times in a concrete way. "Peace is thoroughly in God, for God is the Peace, and therefore peace may not be destroyed. Unpeacefulness, however, will perish. Therefore, pay attention to resolve for peace."[116]

What a great "sign and sacrament" of peace the church would be in the world and for the world if the life of all Christians were to reflect the spirit and prayer of St Francis! "Lord, make me an instrument of thy peace. Where there is hatred, let me sow love; where there is injury, pardon; where there is doubt, faith; where there is despair, hope; where there is sadness, joy; where there is darkness, light."

Thanks be to God!

NOTES

[1] R. Schneider, *der Friede der Welt*, Wiesbaden, 1956; E. Biser, *Der Sinn des Friedens*, München, 1960; J. Comblin, *Théologie de la paix*, Paris, 1960; A. Sustar (ed.), *Papst Paul VI: Friede als Auftrag*, Luzern and München, 1968; H. H. Schmid, *Frieden ohne Illusionen. Die Bedeutung des Begriffs "Schalom" als Grundlage für eine Theologie des Friedens*, Zürich, 1971; G. Liedke (ed.), *Frieden, Bibel, Kirche*, Stuttgart and München, 1972; J. Macquarrie, *The Concept of Peace*, New York, 1973; K. Forster (ed.), *Vergebung, Versöhnung, Friede*, Donauwörth, 1976.

[2] J. Macquarrie, l.c., 1f.

[3] Cf. R.H. Bainton, *Christian Attitudes Toward War and Peace. A Historical Survey and Critical Evaluation*, New York, 1960, 18.

[4] J. Macquarrie, l.c., 15.

[5] J.V. Taylor, *Enough is Enough*, London, 1976[7], 41.

[6] J. Macquarrie, l.c., 19.

[7] Could we not perhaps look at the hoped-for reconciliation between Israelis and Palestinians as a partial symbol of the fulfilment of messianic prophecies?

8 The Second Vatican Council frequently refers to these biblical texts on Christ, the peace and bringer of peace; e.g., *Lumen gentium*, 9; *Gaudium et spes*, 38, 77, 78.

9 Cf. H. Beck, "eirene-Friede", in L. Coenen (ed.), *Begriffslexikon zum Neuen Testament* I, Wuppertal, 1967, 388.

10 Cardinal Maurice Roy, *Reflections on Pacem in terris* (April 11, 1973), n. 120, in J. Gremillion, l.c., 555.

11 Paul VI, *Populorum progressio*, 75 (quoting John XXIII's address upon receiving the Balzan Prize for Peace, May 10, 1963, AAS 55 [1963], 455).

12 *Lumen gentium*, 38.

13 Paul VI, *Reconciliation - the Way of Peace: Message for the Celebration of the World Day of Peace* (January 1, 1975), n. 13, text in J. Gremillion, l.c., 611.

14 J. Ellul, *The Ethic of Freedom*, London/Oxford, 1976, 383.

15 C.F. von Weizsäcker, *Der Garten des Menschlichen*, München, 1978⁴, 544f.

16 R.J. Cassidy, *Jesus, Politics, and Society. A study of Luke's Gospel*, Maryknoll, 1978, 45.

17 J. Macquarrie, l.c., 16.

18 *Quotations from Chairman Mao Tse-Tung*, Foreign Language Press, Peking, 1966, 214.

19 F. Nietzsche, *Thus Spake Zarathustra*, (tr. A. Till and M.M. Boznan), Dent, 1933, 39 and 258.

20 N. Machiavelli, *The Prince*, (tr. L. Ricci), Oxford, 1903, 65.

21 Card. M. Roy, l.c., 93, in J. Gremillion, l.c., 548.

22 Cf. C.F. von Weizsäcker, *Wege in der Gefahr*, München, 1976, 115.

23 E.F. Schumacher, *Small is Beautiful*, 34.

24 For this section see: R.H. Bainton, *Christian Attitudes Toward War and Peace. A Historical and Critical Survey and Evaluation*, New York, 1960; H. Asmussen, *Krieg und Frieden*, Osnabruck, 1961; K. Hammer, *Christen, Krieg und Frieden*, Olten/Freiburg, 1972; W. Huber (ed.), *Kirche zwischen Krieg und Frieden*, Stuttgart, 1976; Id., *Christentum und Militarismus*, München and Stuttgart, 1974; M.A. Bressler and L.A. Bressler, *Peace and War. Can Humanity Make the Choice?*, Englewood Cliffs/N.J., 1977; L.L. Farrar, Jr. (ed.), *War. A Historical, Political and Social Study*, Santa Barbara and Oxford, 1978.

25 R.H. Bainton, l.c., 14.

26 Ibid., 14.

27 Ibid., 53-54.

28 Cf. E.E. Ryan, "The Rejection of Military Service by the Early Christians", in *Theological Studies* 13 (1952), 1-32.

29 R.H. Bainton, l.c., 70 and 73.

30 Ambrose, *De Officiis ministrorum*, PL 16, 74-78; 81-86; Augustine, *Epist.*, 47, 5 PL 33, 186-187.

31 Basil, *Epist.*, 101, PG 32, 682.

32 R.H. Bainton, l.c., 161.

33 M.E. Hirst, *The Quakers in Peace and War*, London, 1923, 130.

34 *Gaudium et spes*, 79,5.

35 R.H. Bainton, l.c., 14.

36 Aristotle, *Politics* I, 1256; cf. R.H. Bainton, l.c., 23-26.

37 Cicero, *De Republica* III, 35.

38 Ambrose, *De fide christiana* II, PL 16, 587-590.

39 R.H. Bainton, l.c., 95-99; cf. G. Combès, *La doctrine politique de Saint Augustin*, Paris, 1927.

40 S.Th., II/II q 40.

/

[41] Cf. J.T. Johnson, "Morality and Force in Statecraft: Paul Ramsey and the Just War Tradition", in J.T. Johnson and D. Smith (eds.), *Love and Society: Essays in the Ethics of Paul Ramsey*, Missoula, 1976, 93-114; L. Walter, "Historical Applications of the Just War Theory. Four Case Studies in Normative Ethics", l.c., 115-138; M. Walzer, *Just and Unjust War: A Moral Argument with Historical Illustrations*, New York, 1977; J.F. Childress, "Just War Theories: The Bases, Interrelations, Priorities, and Foundations of their Criteria", in *Theological Studies* 39 (1978), 427-445.

[42] L. Walter, l.c., 133.

[43] Cf. J.T. Johnson, l.c., 107; T. Merton, *On Peace*, London/Oxford, 1976, 22.

[44] R.H. Bainton, l.c., 131.

[45] L. Walter, l.c., 135.

[46] R.H. Bainton, l.c., 207-209; cf. J. Mausbach, *Vom gerechten Krieg*, Münster, 1914; K. Holl, *Gesammelte Werke* III (1928), 147-170 (an address delivered in 1917).

[47] R.H. Bainton, l.c., 225; cf. Vera Brittain, *Seeds of Chaos*, London, 1944, 15.

[48] T. Merton, l.c., 31.

[49] Christian Century (March 22, 1944), 361; J.C. Ford, SJ, "The Morality of Obliteration Bombing", in *Theological Studies* (Sept 1944), 261-309.

[50] *Gaudium et spes*, 80; cf. ibid., 79.

[51] R.H. Bainton, l.c., 51 (on "holy wars" and crusades, l.c., 44-52 and 101-121 with bibliography); G. von Rad, *Der heilige Krieg im Alten Israel*, Göttingen, 1965.

[52] *Gaudium et spes*, 82,6.

[53] R.H. Bainton, l.c., 243.

[54] Ibid., 166.

[55] Ibid., 168.

[56] Cf. U. Albrecht, "Militärhilfe und Rüstungsimporte in Entwicklungsländer", in H. Kunst and H. Tenhumberg (eds.), *Internationale Wirtschaftsordnung*, München and Mainz, 1976, 114f.

[57] Cf. Ph. Schmitz, "Pazifismus mit neuen Akzenten? Zu den Friedensbewegungen in den USA", in *Herderkorrespondenz* 34 (1980), 330-333.

[58] Address of Paul VI to the UN General Assembly, October 4, 1965, n. 19, in J. Gremillion, l.c., 383.

[59] For this section see: F. Böckle and C.A.J. van Ouwerkerk (eds.), "War, Poverty, Freedom", in *Concilium* 15, New York, 1966; K. Fischer, "Erlösung zum Frieden", in *Orientierung* 37 (1973), 80-84; B. Häring, "Gerechtigkeit und Friede", in *Mysterium Salutis* V, Einsiedeln, 1976, 270-284; C.F. von Weizsäcker and U. Scheuner, *Die Christenheit und der Weltfriede*, Bonn and Bad Godesberg, 1976; W.J. Weilgart, *Peace through People. A Human Philosophy of Survival for the Panatomic Age*, Decorah, 1977; R. Schneider, *Einberufung zum Frieden*, Gütersloh, 1978; John Paul II, Message for the Celebration of the World Day of Peace, December 22, 1978, and his address to the UN General Assembly in *Herderkorrespondenz* 33 (1979), 83-88; 554-561.

[60] *Gaudium et spes*, 81,5.

[61] Card. M. Roy, l.c., n. 81.

[62] K.E. Boulding, *Stable Peace*, Austin and London, 1978, 94-95.

[63] C.F. von Weizsäcker, *Wege in der Gefahr*, München, 1976, 111.

[64] C.F. von Weizsäcker, *Der Garten der Menschlichkeit*, München, 1978⁴, 44-45.

[65] Erasmus, *Querela Pacis* (Complaint of Peace), LXXIV.

[66] Cf. D. Prasad and T. Smythe (eds.), *Conscription. A World Survey. Compulsory Military Service and Resistance to it*, London, 1968; U. Duchrow and G. Scharffenorth (eds.), *Konflikte zwischen Wehrdienst und Friedens-*

dienst. Ein Strukturproblem der Kirche, Stuttgart and München, 1970; B. Montanari, *Obiezione di coscienza. Un analisi dei suoi fondamenti etici e politici,* Milano, 1976; F. Rauhaut, *Kriegsdienstverweigerung heute.* Gewissens- und Rechtsfragen, München, 1977[6].

[67] *Gaudium et spes,* 79,2.

[68] *Gaudium et spes,* 79,4. The Roman Synod of Bishops (November 30, 1971), in its document on justice, n. 65, issued a stronger text both on conscientious objection and on a strategy of non-violence, in J. Gremillion, l.c., 526f.

[69] On non-violent action as alternative to pacifism and war, see: Mahadev Desai, *Non-violence in Peace and War* (texts of M. Gandhi), Ahmedabad, 1948-1949; L. Fischer, *The Life of Mahatma Gandhi,* London, 1951; M.K. Gandhi, *An Autobiography: The Story of my Experience with Truth,* (tr. M. Desai), Boston, 1957; J. Bondurant, *Conquest of Violence: the Gandhian Philosophy of Conflict,* Berkeley, 1967; R. Régamey, *Non-violence et conscience chrétienne,* Paris, 1958; A. Roberts (ed.), *Civilian Resistance as a National Defense,* Baltimore, 1969; G. Sharp, *The Politics of Non-Violent Action,* Boston 1973; Id., *Exploring Non-violent Alternatives,* Boston, 1973; A. Montagu, *The Nature of Aggression,* Oxford, 1976; R. Schutz, *Die Gewalt der Friedfertigen. Auf der Suche nach dem dritten Weg,* Freiburg, 1977[6].

[70] L. del Vasto, *Gandhi to Vinoba,* New York, 1974, 215.

[71] Cf. P. Lehman, *The Transfiguration of Politics,* New York, 1975, 79-102; 264-274.

[72] H. Goss-Mayr, "Die Wahreit und Kraft des Friedens", in *Diakonia* 11 (1980), 48-51.

[73] *Gaudium et spes,* 78,4; cf. Card. M. Roy, l.c., nn. 96-98, in J. Gremillion, l.c., 549; Medellin document on Peace, n. 15, in J. Gremillion, l.c., 459.

[74] Cf. A. Roberts, "Czechoslovakia, A Battle Won, a War Lost", in T. Dunn (ed.), *Foundations of Peace and Freedom,* Swansea, 1975, 255-269.

[75] On disarmament, see: W. Dirks, *Friede im Atomzeitalter,* Mainz, 1967; E. von Weizsäcker (ed.), *BC-Waffen und Friedenspolitik,* Stuttgart and München, 1970; D. Senghaas, *Abschreckung und Frieden. Studien zur Kritik organisierter Friedlosigkeit,* Frankfurt, 1969; Id., *Rüstung und Militarismus,* Frankfurt, 1972; L. Knorr, *Vom Wettrüsten zur Abrüstung,* Köln, 1978.

[76] *Wirtschaftswoche,* May 13, 1980, 41.

[77] Cf. K.E. Boulding, l.c., 95ff.

[78] Card. M. Roy, l.c., n. 106.

[79] *Gaudium et spes,* 8.

[80] *Pacem in terris,* n. 112ff; *Gaudium et spes,* 81 and 82; cf. H. Trettner, "Der hl. Stuhl und die Abrüstung", in *Katholische Intern. Zeitschrift* 7 (1978), 151-165.

[81] K.E. Boulding, l.c., 103.

[82] Ibid, 116.

[83] J. Dedring, *Recent Advances in Peace and Conflict Research. A Critical Survey,* London, 1976, 81f.

[84] C.F. von Weizsäcker, *Wege in der Gefahr,* 132.

[85] Cf. R. Coste, Commentary to Gaudium et spes 78ff., in *Lexikon für Theologie und Kirche Ergänzungsband* III, 529.

[86] R.H. Bainton, l.c., 265-266.

[87] *Gaudium et spes,* 81,3.

[88] *Gaudium et spes,* 82,4-6.

[89] Ch. E. Osgood, *An Alternative to War or Surrender,* Urbana/Ill., 1962, cf. J. Dedring, l.c., 173ff.

[90] T. Merton, l.c., 21.

[91] R.H. Bainton, l.c., 259.

[92] On Peace Research, besides the works already referred to, see: C.F. von Weizsäcker, *Der ungesicherte Friede*, Göttingen, 1969; Id. (ed.), *Kriegsfolgen und Kriegsverhütung*, München, 1971; G. Scharffenorth and W. Huber (eds.), *Bibliographie zur Friedensforschung*, Stuttgart and München, 1970; Id., *Neue Bibliographie zur Friedensforschung*, Stuttgart and München, 1973; A. Kuhn, *Theorie und Praxis historischer Friedensforschung*, Stuttgart, 1971; A. Curle, *Making Peace*, London, 1971; E.O. Czempiel, *Schwerpunkte der Friedensforschung*, München and Mainz, 1972; D.W. Wainhouse, *International Peacekeeping at Crossroads*, Baltimore, 1973; D. Senghaas, *Gewalt, Konflikt, Frieden. Essays zur Friedensforschung*, Hamburg, 1974; R.A. Falk, *This Endangered Planet: Prospects and Proposals for Human Survival*, New York, 1971; Id., *A Study for Future World*, New York, 1975; R.J. Rummel, *Understanding Conflict and War*, London, 1975; P. Wehr and M. Washburn, *Peace and World Order Systems. Teaching and Research*, London, 1976; J. Galtung, *The True World*, New York, 1977; M. Funke (ed.), *Friedensforschung. Entscheidungshilfe gegen Gewalt*, Bonn, 1978². Among the dozen or so journals on peace research I mention *Journal of Peace Research. An International Journal of the Scientific Study of Conflict and Conflict Management* (ed.) W. Isard, University of Pennsylvania, 1973 onwards.

[93] Cf. K.E. Boulding, l.c., 127-131; G. and P. Mische, *Toward a Human World Order: Beyond the National Security Straitjacket*, New York, 1977, 321.

[94] Card. M. Roy in his reflections on *Pacem in terris* of John XXIII, n. 56, appraises this encyclical as a "phenomenology of peace".

[95] Cf. R. May, *Power and Innocence. A Search for the Sources of Violence*, New York, 1972.

[96] Cf. C.F. von Weizsäcker, *Wege in der Gefahr*, 145ff.; J. Dedring, l.c., 141-159.

[97] K.E. Boulding, l.c., 142.

[98] Ibid., 114-115.

[99] Cf. G. and P. Mische, l.c., 315ff.

[100] Cf. S.A. Mendlovitz (ed.), *On the Creation of a Just World Order. Preferred Worlds for the 1990's*, New York, 1975.

[101] Cf. R.A. Falk, l.c., J. Dedring, l.c., 64ff.

[102] On peace education see: D. Emeis, *Zum Frieden erziehen. Ein Arbeitsbuch*, München, 1968; M. Montessori, *Frieden und Erziehung*, Freiburg, 1973; Ch. Wulf (ed.), *Handbook for Peace Education*, Frankfurt, 1974; H.L. Elvin, "Education and Peace" in T. Dunn (ed.), *Foundations of Peace and Freedom*, Swansea, 1975, 125-136.

[103] T. Merton, l.c., 115.

[104] A. Maslow, *Farther Reaches of Human Nature*, New York, 1971, 19.

[105] Cf. A. Plack, *Der Mythos vom Aggressionstrieb*, Köln, 1973.

[106] C.F. von Weizsäcker, *Der Garten des Menschlichen*, 39ff.

[107] E.F. Schumacher, "The Economics of Permanence", in T. Dunn (ed.), l.c., 93-106, quotes 101, 102.

[108] Card. M. Roy, l.c., n. 123, in J. Gremillion, l.c., 555.

[109] Quoted by C.F. von Weizsäcker, l.c., 572.

[110] C.F. von Weizsäcker, l.c., 546.

[111] H. Camara, *Revolution through Peace*, New York, 1971, 130.

[112] J. Macquarrie, l.c., 34.

[113] *Gaudium et spes*, 92.

[114] Card. M. Roy, l.c., 159-166 in J. Gremillion, l.c., 564-565.

[115] C.F. von Weizsäcker, *Ethical and Political Questions of the Atomic Age*, London, 1959, quoted by R.H. Bainton, l.c., 260.

[116] Quoted by W. Nigg, *Bruder Klaus. Eine Begegnung mit Nikolaus von Flüe*, Luzern, 1977, 57.

Index

428

429

Language, beauty of, 210-211
"Latin superculture", 221
Law enforcement, 211, 363-364
"Law of nations", 382
Laws
— limitation of, 356
Leadership, political, 354-356,
368-369
Lefebvre, Bishop, 265
Leo XIII, Pope, 217, 262, 270, 299,
308
Lercaro, Giacomo, Cardinal, 221
Lesbianism, 68
Liberalism, 270, 287, 346
Liberation theology, 309, 331, 376
Liberty
— and fidelity, 124, 141, 161,
202-204, 213, 331
— and subsidiarity, 279, 334
Liedke, Gerhard, 175
Life, human
— genetic aspects, 12-14
— meaning and value of, 4, 5
— origin of, 5-11
— rights, 10
— transmission of, 11-12, 23-24
Life, humanized, 10-11
Life prolongation, 82-83, 90-91, 95,
98-100, 102-103
— and retarded, 100
— beneficial vs non-beneficial,
100-102, 104
— ordinary vs extraordinary means,
98-99
Life, quality of, 102
Life-support systems, 103-104
Liturgy, 238-239
"Living will", 104
Loans
— on capital, 303
Lobo, George, 24
Lock-outs, 302
Logotherapy, 59-61
Lord of history, 263
Lorenz, Konrad, 171, 190, 415, 419
Louis XIV, 129
Love
— and peace, 421
— and power, 337, 360
— call to, 126
Luther, Martin, 125, 133-136, 150,
152-153, 155

Machiavelli, Niccolo, 348, 397
Man
— and environment, 168-172
— and nature, 173-175, 178, 181
— and politics, 355, 370
— and technology, 196-197
— as co-creator, 181
— dimensions of, 134-135
— dominion of earth, 175-176
— the maker-manipulator, 169-170,
175, 181
Management
— role of, 304-305
Manipulation, 63, 118, 235
Maple wine disease, 31
Marriage
— and family, 153-154, 344, 369
Martyrdom, 355
Marx, Karl, 88, 123-124, 158-159,
239-240, 248-251, 261-262,
264-265, 287, 295, 296, 346, 348,
352, 377, 396
Maslow, Abraham, 418
Masochism, 67
Masters, William H., 66-67
"Mater et Magistra", 187
Materialism
— dialectic, 263-267
— historical, 261-264
Matter
— and life, 5
Mead, Margaret, 169, 174
Medellín Document
— on family, 249
— on justice, 245
Medical ethics, 51-52
Medical laws
— and legislation, 51-52
Medical lawsuits, 53
Medical practice, 83-84
Megalopolis, 189-190, 312
Marton, Thomas, 414
Messianic promise, 328-329, 351
Messner, Josef, 212, 261, 267
Metabolic death, 90
Meta-ethics, 222-223
Metz, John Baptist, 127, 143, 145,
147, 159, 246, 333
Migrant workers, 311
Military service, 399-400, 407-408
Mische, Gerald, 121
Mische, Patricia, 121
Mises, Ludwig von, 270
Missions, 219

433

435

436